Christian and Critical English Language Educators in Dialogue

Christian and Critical English Language Educators in Dialogue

Pedagogical and Ethical Dilemmas

Edited by

Mary Shepard Wong
Azusa Pacific University
and
Suresh Canagarajah
Pennsylvania State University

NEW YORK AND LONDON

First published 2009
by Routledge
270 Madison Ave, New York, NY 10016

Simultaneously published in the UK
by Routledge
2 Park Square, Milton Park, Abingdon, Oxon OX14 4RN

Routledge is an imprint of the Taylor & Francis Group, an informa business

Typeset in Minion by Wearset Ltd, Boldon, Tyne and Wear
Printed and bound in the United States of America on acid-free paper by
Edwards Brothers Digital Book Center

Library of Congress Cataloging in Publication Data
Christian and critical English language educators in dialogue : pedagogical and ethical dilemmas / edited by Mary Shepard Wong and Suresh Canagarajah.
p. cm.
1. English language–Study and teaching–Foreign speakers. 2. English language–Religious aspects. 3. Language in missionary work. 4. English teachers–Religious life. I. Wong, Mary Shepard. II. Canagarajah, A. Suresh.

PE1128.A2C478 2009
428.2'4–dc22 2008051477

ISBN10: 0-415-99953-7 (hbk)
ISBN10: 0-203-88780-2 (ebk)

ISBN13: 978-0-415-99953-3 (hbk)
ISBN13: 978-0-203-87780-7 (ebk)

This book is dedicated to the Karen, a Hilltribe people of Burma, who strive for positive change in the midst of five decades of war and oppression; and to the teachers and students of Kawthoolei Karen Baptist Bible School and College in Mae La Refugee camp, Mae Sot, Thailand who have taught us the value of human dignity, freedom, justice, and peace. See online, available at: www.freeburmarangers.org.

Contents

Contributors' Spiritual Identification Statements

I am a Christian in the sense that I greatly respect and try to follow the teachings of Jesus Christ. However, I don't feel a need to adhere exclusively to one path. I also consider myself to be a Muslim, in the original Arabic sense of "one who submits" to the will of God, though I prefer not to attempt to know the nature of this being, or even whether or not such a being exists. For me, then, there are many paths to spiritual fulfillment. However, I also have great esteem for those who have chosen to follow one spiritual road, for the Dalai Lama teaches that it is not necessary for people to change their chosen spiritual paths in favor of others, unless they have compelling reasons to do so.

Christopher A. Bradley, Siebold University of Nagasaki, Japan

I consider myself on some days a "progressive Christian," on other days (in the words of Leslie Weatherhead) a "Christian agnostic" (agnostic meaning "not knowing" or certainly "willing to accept my human inability not to know everything about God and Spirit"), and on yet other days (with Bertrand Russell), not a Christian at all (in the media's view of what it means to be a Christian). Maybe the acronym "WOW" describes me (or at least my goals): Warm heart, Open mind, Willing spirit. As for the "O" part of that, I like to think that minds are like parachutes, they only work when they're open.

H. Douglas Brown, San Francisco State University

My personal faith reflects the Anabaptist tradition in which I was born and nurtured. I am part of a Mennonite church body, and my beliefs reflect the influence of this historic peace church and its focus on community life.

Myrrl Byler, Mennonite Partners in China

I believe in the fundamentally spiritual nature of life, which inspires me to struggle for a better world, meaningful teaching, and ethical and caring relationships.

Suresh Canagarajah, Pennsylvania State University

I believe the cumulative arguments for God's existence (moral, design, and cosmological) coupled with the historical reliability of the biblical documents and Jesus' resurrection make the Christian worldview the most reasonable and probable explanation for reality. That said, the hardest step in finding truth in Christ is not intellectual; the hardest step is bending the knee to a God that deserves our worship.

Michael Chamberlain, Azusa Pacific University

Being born and raised in England by Indo-South American parents, my religious upbringing was naturally varied. Initially, my siblings and I were sent to the local Methodist church every Sunday, but later my father introduced us to his religion, Hinduism. My years in Asia in the 1990s gave me the opportunity to learn about Buddhism, Taoism, and other related religious and spiritual belief and practices. My spiritual identity, then, is a function of where I am. So, when in India, I am a Hindu, when in China a Buddhist, and when in England a Christian.

Andy Curtis, Chinese University of Hong Kong

I have been searching for some real meaning in life ever since I remember but coming from a non-believing intellectual family in a Communist country, Hungary, it took me 40 years to finally find the answer in the Christian faith. Nominally christened as a Catholic, then having spent many years in two Baptist churches (in Hungary and the UK) and now attending a Pentecostal church, I don't feel I am tied very closely to any particular denomination—I am a Christian trying to do my best to follow Jesus' Great Commission.

Zoltán Dörnyei, University of Nottingham, UK

We exist briefly as identifiable, self-aware organisms in a continuing dance of cosmic energy/matter. Joy.

Julian Edge, University of Manchester, UK

I am a born-and-bred Episcopalian who as an adult has identified most strongly with the Protestant evangelical tradition. I have identified myself as a follower of Jesus Christ since my early teens and am striving to become a more fully devoted follower. I like the sentiment of the philosopher Kierkegaard who said (to paraphrase): I'm not a Christian yet—I'm becoming a Christian (meaning he hadn't arrived yet). While identification with the Christian community is not always the most comfortable thing for me (because of the church's shortcomings and my own), I am passionate about my love for Jesus and believe that my relationship with him has transformed my life.

Dana R. Ferris, University of California, Davis

No comment.

Bill Johnston, Indiana University

I am a Christian. I have been enriched by participation in interdenominational associations and have spent extended periods of time involved in movements of Pentecostal origin in Canada, Brazil, and Iceland.

Carolyn Kristjánsson, Trinity Western University, Canada

Multiple religious faiths and customs have shaped my background. Attending a Christian kindergarten and Sunday school as a child gave me some sense of being Christian. In my mid thirties, Buddhist teachings influenced my thinking significantly, although Buddhism along with Shinto have constituted the sociocultural aspect of my everyday life since I was born. I value all religious faiths that promote social justice and peace achieved without violence.

Ryuko Kubota, University of North Carolina at Chapel Hill

I am a believer in Jesus Christ. Many years ago I came to the US searching for a successful career, but I found Jesus instead, and my life has changed ever since. Over the past so many years, I have learned that being a follower of Jesus does not mean life is not without unexpected challenges, and yet everyday His grace is sufficient for me. I have also learned that to live is not to merely keep the Grace that God has given me, but to also share the Grace with others, who He also cherishes and values as a unique creation.

John Liang, Biola University

I am a Christian, a sinner, a woman, a daughter, a sister, a bicultural wife, a Caucasian Lithuanian-Irish, Catholic Charismatic Evangelical, an American, a scientist, an artist, a teacher, an observer, a listener, a student, an advocate, a servant, a leader, a colleague, a boss, an Ivy-League employee, an entrepreneur, an English Language teacher, and global educator who spent 12 years in the Middle East with the call to prayer in my heart. I am a complex identity intricately shaped by God who has seen fit to preserve me against all odds in this life and forever more because He sent his Son, Jesus, to die on a cross, shed his blood and die for me.

Karen Asenavage Loptes, University of Pennsylvania

No comment.

Ahmar Mahboob, University of Sydney

I am deeply spiritual and believe strongly in a god, which can be accessed through people endowed with special powers to see into the future. I seriously hope one day to be one of those with such spiritual powers. I don't draw distinctions between spiritual insight and intellectual work.

Busi Makoni, Pennsylvania State University

The distinction between spirituality and life is unnecessary to me, therefore I cannot say where I stand on spirituality, but can say confidently where I stand on life. I believe in a capacity to live and to forge ahead in peace, and war, wellness and disease, poverty and wealth. Death in such a universe is simply an extension of life under different conditions, and nothing to be frightened of while at the same time not necessary to hasten it unduly.

Sinfree Makoni, Pennsylvania State University

As a young boy I attended Synagogue and Hebrew School with some regularity until my Bar Mitzvah. Since then, my sense of being Jewish has become more cultural than religious as I no longer observe the primary faith of my youth in a formal way. I value all religions equally and view them as cultural creations that reflect a common human yearning to explain the complexity, beauty, and horror of our current existence. I also maintain an optimistic belief in a spiritual afterlife and the possibility of a powerful and creative force in the universe.

Brian Morgan, York University, Canada

I am a Christian. I believe that humanity is separated from God because of sin. I believe that Jesus lived a sinless life, died, and rose again so that we must no longer be separated from God. I also believe that much of what goes on "in" His name is neither inspired nor endorsed by Him. I am concerned that Christians in the United States have lost sight of the spiritual nature of Christianity and have instead chosen surrogates that are political, materialistic, intellectual, emotional, and/or condescending in nature. In my view, these counterfeits are a result of the sinful nature of humanity—a nature that continues to plague those who are Christians as part of the human experience.

Terry A. Osborn, Fordham University

From a point of view that cannot accept that any one philosophy, culture, worldview, or religion can have exclusive claims to truth, knowledge or value (which does not mean that some may not have better claims than others in some domains), I am committed to opposing those who wish to promote their vision of the world to the exclusion of others, and to try to understand how it is that different understandings of the world are constructed.

Alastair Pennycook, University of Technology, Sydney

My home and school background were strongly Church of England, and underpinned by a deep-rooted, society-wide British belief that our culture had the right to impose its values worldwide. My youthful but intense integration into institutionalized Christianity gave way to the skepticism, intellectual and spiritual, which was characteristic of the university world in the 1960s. My nomadic life is guided by intercultural tolerance, an agnostic appreciation of diversity, and a wish to combat injustice that is man-made and therefore can be counteracted by ethically impelled humans.

Robert Phillipson, Copenhagen Business School

I am a follower of Jesus. My spiritual identity has been shaped by my childhood in India as the daughter of a Presbyterian medical missionary, by my college experiences with Intervarsity Christian Fellowship, by 25 years at Pasadena Covenant Church ("in essentials, unity; in non-essentials, liberty; in all things, charity"), by my Quaker husband, and by the many people—Christians and others—from around the world I have had the privilege of knowing.

Kitty B. Purgason, Biola University

I proceed from the assumption that all notions of "God" are heterogeneous and uncontainable, and that religious ideals are human creations that need ceaseless probing and critical engagement.

Vaidehi Ramanathan, University of California, Davis

I am a Christian in the sense that I seek with God's grace to follow Jesus Christ and obey his commands, which he summarized as follows: first, love God; second, love people. Thus, my primary goal in life is to know God, and to make people a priority. I believe that God exists and rewards those who seek him; and that he has revealed himself in the person of Jesus Christ, who was conclusively shown to be his only Son based on the evidence of his resurrection from the dead.

Richard E. Robison, Azusa Pacific University

I am a Christian of Reformed persuasion and a member of the Christian Reformed Church. I teach at Calvin College, a liberal arts college rooted in the Reformed tradition.

David I. Smith, Calvin College

I am a Christian of the Protestant variety whose spiritual growth has been nurtured by both mainline and evangelical faith communities. At present I am a Mission Co-Worker for the Presbyterian Church (USA), serving as a teacher in a Chinese university, which originated in part from a Christian university founded in the late 1800s by western missionaries. I thus see myself as a successor to a western mission tradition of promoting education. There are some aspects of the western mission tradition I am quite critical of, and others I am proud of and strive to live up to. With regard to outward expression of my faith, I tend to be most comfortable expressing God's love through service, but am also quite willing to talk about my faith when others express an interest.

Don Snow, University of Nanjing

I am an Anabaptist Christian, and a member of the Mennonite Church, USA.

James Stabler-Havener, Sichuan Normal University

I am a lifelong Christian, who has spent 12 years or more in each of four very different denominations.

Earl Stevick

I believe that it is quite possible to live a moral, ethical, spiritual, contributing life without being religious, and I strive to do so. I was raised in a politically progressive Christian Protestant missionary family; my parents helped many people in India through their medical and educational work. I considered myself Christian until I was 19. My husband is a somewhat observant Bahá'í. Although I believe that much damage has been done by religion, I respect sincere, ethical practitioners of most religions, people who have used their religions to do good.

Stephanie Vandrick, University of San Francisco

I would describe myself as atheist at this point in time although I grew up in a household with a Roman Catholic mother and a Marxist atheist father. I was baptized and went to a Roman Catholic church as a child for a number of years, also receiving my First Communion.

Manka M. Varghese, University of Washington

I believe that one cannot teach people language without touching the spiritual, as humans are spiritual beings, and the ability to create languages is a marvelous gift of God to be explored, enjoyed, and valued. Although I believe that God is truth, I realize that my perception of truth is tainted by my human condition and sin, and so I am open to learning how my understanding of God is incomplete or incorrect. I acknowledge and am deeply saddened by the way institutional religion has used its power to oppress those whom God created and for whom Christ died. I claim both titles, *Christian* and *critical* English language educator, and find it hard to be the former without the latter.

Mary Shepard Wong, Azusa Pacific University

Preface

Within the last several years there have been a number of publications discussing the influence of a teacher's values, faith, and spiritual identity on their language teaching (Baurain, 2007; Buzzelli & Johnston, 2002; Johnston, 2003; Palmer, 2007; Smith & Carvill, 2000; Smith & Osborn, 2007; Snow, 2001). Articles directed toward Christian English teachers about the negative effects of Christianity and language teaching have also surfaced (Edge 2003, 2004; Johnston & Varghese, 2006; Pennycook & Coutand-Marin, 2003; Vandrick, 2002; Varghese & Johnston, 2007). These publications have provided the opportunity for teachers to think deeply about the ways in which their spiritual identities affect their ELT pedagogy both positively and negatively and to consider how to maintain their values and beliefs while respecting the interests of host cultures, nations, students, and the profession of ELT.

This book is a critical examination of how Christian English language teachers integrate their spiritual identities and their pedagogy and grapple with the dilemmas created when their faith agendas conflict with their professional ethic of respect for host countries and students. Although a book seeking to investigate the influence of teachers' religious identities from a wider spectrum of faith backgrounds (Muslim, Jewish, Buddhist, etc.) would be valuable, this volume focuses on the Christian identity because of the recent debate and criticism directed toward Christian teachers and the legacy of English teaching and Christian missionaries.

This volume is unique in that it presents voices from 31 TESOL professionals who come from a wide range of religious and spiritual perspectives. About half of the authors in this volume identify themselves as "Christian" while the other authors identify themselves as Buddhist, atheist, spiritualist, and variations of these and other faiths. What is common for all the authors is that they believe that values have an important place in the classroom. What they disagree on is whether and how spiritual values should find expression in learning and teaching. The book dramatizes some leading scholars in the profession wrestling with ideological, pedagogical, and spiritual dilemmas as they seek to understand the place of faith in education.

To sustain this conversation, the book is itself structured dialogically. The themes addressed by the authors group themselves into four parts in the book: (1) Setting the Tone: Dialogue and Discourse; (2) Ideological and Political

Dilemmas; (3) Pedagogical and Professional Dilemmas; and (4) Spiritual and Ethical Dilemmas. Each part is divided into three. In the first, a set of authors provides position chapters on their views of faith/pedagogy integration. In the second, another set of authors responds to these positions, while articulating their own views on the subject. In the third, the editors list a set of questions that enable the researchers to compare the positions of all the authors, reflect on their own experiences and values, and advance the dialogue in fresh and personal directions. We decided on the option of formulating questions rather than writing a preface or conclusion for each part as the latter might impose a premature closure on the dialogue. Besides, the positions of the authors are so varied and personal that generalizations do violence on this rich diversity. For the reader to adopt one more alternative position on the issues discussed serves better our objective of drawing attention to the important subject addressed in this book.

This book is of interest to several groups of people including education administrators, language policy makers, scholars and researchers in the fields of TESOL and foreign language teaching and learning, second language (ESL and EFL) teacher educators, TESOL or second language graduate students, and ESL/EFL classroom teachers. It could be used as a course textbook in several courses, including Sociolinguistics, Values and Ethics in Education, Professional Issues and Ethics, Issues and Trends in Teacher Education, Cultural Issues in the ESL/EFL Classroom, Current Issues in TESOL, Field Experience in Teaching, and Intercultural Studies.

ESL and EFL teachers-in-training and TESOL graduate students will find the book helpful in developing their teaching philosophies and exploring the ways in which their personal values intersect with and influence their professional practices. Classroom ESL/EFL teachers who seek to integrate their spiritual identities and professional lives while maintaining respect for the host culture and nation, their students, and the profession of English teaching will want to read this book. Christian language teachers teaching overseas, Mission organizations, and NGOs and other agencies that recruit, train, and send teachers would all benefit from perspectives in this book. Finally, those within the TESOL community concerned with critical pedagogy and the implications of the global spread of English will also have an interest in this volume. Thus it has an international audience, suitable as a classroom text and scholarly reference.

We solicited authors who held a wide range of religious and spiritual beliefs in order to hear a variety of perspectives. Since the 31 authors in the volume come from a variety of religious perspectives, we thought it would be helpful to ask each author to write a brief spiritual identity statement in which they comment on their religious background and current religious beliefs (or lack thereof). The spiritual beliefs and religious identities of the contributors do not place the authors in two camps or even along points on a continuum with "spiritual" on one end and "non-spiritual" on the other.

For some of the contributors, the task of writing a spiritual identity statement was difficult, perhaps because this part of their identity was not salient or because revealing it left them feeling vulnerable. Several feared they might be pigeonholed by using a particular term, whether it was "atheist" or "evangelical," so they hesitated and asked probing questions. Wasn't that the very point of this volume to get beyond the labels? How would this help readers understand the rich diversity we represent and how our spiritual identities are complex and unique? And how does one put this ever-changing notion of spiritual identity into words or separate it from who we are? One person asked if we wanted a statement of faith, a description of how we practice spirituality, or a brief explanation of what we mean by our self-designated label. Another person feared retribution if their religious identity were revealed. These concerns suggest the discomfort scholars and teachers feel about spirituality in education today.

However, a volume that focuses on faith beliefs should try to make them explicit so that they can be examined and discussed, and thus we have asked each author to disclose where they are coming from in this discussion of spiritual identities. Some discuss what has shaped their religious beliefs, whether it was growing up as an "MK" (missionary kid) or an altar boy. For some, encounters with insensitive religious zealots dissuaded them for all things spiritual, while for others, such encounters solidified their faith, and yet others are still seeking. In all, the personal statements and chapters help to bring spirituality into the open. We hope that our readers feel inspired to wrestle with their own values and beliefs as they read the pages of this book.

Most of the contributors in the volume have strong opinions about religion and faith yet they are committed to what Varghese and Johnston state was their intention when researching Christian English teachers—to "seek not to condemn but to understand" (Johnston & Varghese, 2006, p. 195). We hope the contributors and readers will continue this dialogue in future publications, conferences, coffee shops, pubs, and discussion lists. Many of the authors submitted their chapters with comments like, "I ended up getting very much into it, exploring and re-examining my own faith in ways I have not done for a while. So, thank you again for that opportunity," and "I found the task quite challenging and stimulating." We hope readers similarly find this volume thought provoking, provocative, and even transformative.

References

Baurain, B. (2007). Christian witness and respect for persons. *Journal of Language, Identity, and Education, 6*(3), 201–219.

Buzzelli, C., & Johnston, B. (2002). *The moral dimension of teaching: Language, power, and culture in classroom interaction.* New York: RoutledgeFalmer.

Edge, J. (2003). Imperial troopers and servants of the Lord: A vision of TESOL for the 21st century. *TESOL Quarterly, 37*(4), 701–709.

Edge, J. (2004). Of displacive and augmentative discourse, new enemies, and old doubts. *TESOL Quarterly, 38*(4), 717–721.

Johnston, B. (2003). *Values in English language teaching.* Mahwah, NJ: Lawrence Erlbaum.

Johnston, B., & Varghese, M. (2006). Neo-imperialism, evangelism, and ELT: Modernist missions and a postmodern profession. In J. Edge (Ed.), *(Re-)locating TESOL in an age of empire* (pp. 195–207). Basingstoke, UK: Palgrave Macmillan.

Palmer, P. (2007). *The courage to teach: Exploring the inner landscape of a teacher's life.* New York: Jossey-Bass.

Pennycook, A., & Coutand-Marin, S. (2003). Teaching English as a missionary language (TEML). *Discourse: Studies in the Cultural Politics of Education, 24*(3), 337–353.

Smith, D. I., & Carvill, B. (2000). *The gift of the stranger: Faith, hospitality, and foreign language learning.* Grand Rapids, MI: Eerdmans.

Smith, D. I., & Osborn, T. A. (Eds.). (2007). *Spirituality, social justice and language learning.* Greenwich, CT: Information Age.

Snow, D. (2001). *English teaching as Christian mission: An applied theology.* Scottdale, PA: Herald Press.

Vandrick, S. (2002). ESL and the colonial legacy: A teacher faces her "missionary kid" past. In V. Zamel, & R. Spack (Eds.), *Enriching ESOL pedagogy* (pp. 411–422). Mahwah, NJ: Lawrence Erlbaum.

Varghese, M., & Johnston, B. (2007). Evangelical Christians and English language teaching. *TESOL Quarterly, 41*(1), 5–31.

Varghese, M., Morgan, B., Johnston, B., & Johnson, K. A. (2005). Theorizing language teacher identity: Three perspectives and beyond. *Journal of Language, Identity, and Education, 4*(1), 22–44.

Acknowledgments

We would like to thank the following people who supported us in compiling this volume. I (Mary) wish to thank Michael Whyte, David Weeks, and Rich Robison for encouraging me and providing release time; Richard Slimbach, Don Dorr, Don Snow, and Tom Scovel for numerous references and encouragement. Thanks also go to the many readers who helped inform the text in its final stages, Michael Lessard-Clouston, Carolyn Kristjánsson, Eleanor Peace, Rita Stahl, Tasha Bleistein, Beth Thompson, and Tom Scovel. Finally, to my family, Sam, Laura, and Justin, thank you for allowing me to follow my heart.

Suresh thanks Nanthini, Lavannya, Nivedhana, and Wiroshan for their forgiving attitude whenever he lets slip the fine balance between faith, scholarship, and family in his life. He is also grateful to his colleagues and administrators in the universities he has taught—University of Jaffna, City University of New York, and Penn State University—for accommodating his very expressive faith and politics.

Special thanks go to Carolyn Kristjánsson who made several cross-country trips to work with Earl Stevick to record his thoughts on this volume. Most of all, we would like to thank Naomi Silverman who was brave enough to take on such a controversial and complex project. Both of us had worked with Naomi individually on other projects and were delighted that she agreed to work with us together on this one. Naomi's insight and judgment helped to bring the book balance, and her patience and perseverance helped to see it through to completion.

Abbreviations

AAAL	American Association for Applied Linguistics
ACR	American Civil Religion
AERA	American Educational Research Association
CELT	Christian English Language Teachers (grass roots conference)
CET	Christian English Teachers
CETC	Christian Educators in TESOL Caucus (dissolved July 2008)
CETHEG	Christian English Teachers with Hidden Evangelistic Goals
CLL	Community Language Learning
CLT	Communicative Language Teaching
CP	Critical Practitioners
EFL	English as a Foreign Language
ELT	English Language Teaching
ESL	English as a Second Language
ESP	English for Special Purposes
GILLBT	Ghana Institute of Linguistics, Literacy, and Bible Translation
IATEFL	International Association of Teachers of English as a Foreign Language
IEP	Intensive English Program
LCEA	A fictitious organization: Loving Christian Evangelistic Association or Linguistic Capital for Economic Advancement
MK	Missionary Kid
NNEST	Nonnative English Speakers of TESOL
NNS	Nonnative Speaker
NGO	Non-Governmental Organization
PPE	Post-Positivist Educators
SARS	Severe Acute Respiratory Syndrome
SIL	Summer Institute of Linguistics
TEFL	Teaching English as a Foreign Language
TEML	Teaching English as a Missionary Language
TESL	Teaching English as a Second Language
TESOL	Teaching English to Speakers of Other Languages
TESOL	The professional organization of TESOL, sometimes indicated as TESOL, Inc.

1 Introduction

New Possibilities for the Spiritual and the Critical in Pedagogy

Suresh Canagarajah

> No set of issues is as explosive, controversial, emotional, and threatening as moral and religious disputes. None is more vital.
>
> (Purpel, 1989, p. 68)

> While acknowledging the important contributions of postmodern social theory, it is also crucial to recognize its serious limitations. For instance, it has not sufficiently addressed the central issue of how identities and subjectivities are constructed within different moral experiences and relations … it has failed to develop a substantive ethical discourse and public morality that is necessary for overcoming existing forms of exploitation and subjugation.
>
> (Giroux & Freire, 1989, p. xiv)

It is indeed curious that the popularity of postmodern discourses in academic disciplines hasn't facilitated a fruitful dialogue among professionals whose teaching and scholarship are motivated by deeply held values. Though the departure from positivistic assumptions has created a space for the expression of one's values and identities, we are still unsure how to personally relate to the diverse values and identities others bring to the classroom. Even more curiously, though values are acknowledged now in education, we are still unsure how to deal with moral and spiritual values. The academy seems to be uncomfortable with spirituality.

It is good to remind ourselves of the road we have traveled so far to understand the new bases for teaching and scholarship, and to map the territory we still have to cover in order to grapple with the new challenges raised for all of us. The positivistic tradition, which accompanied modernity, imposed a values-neutral and somewhat controlled orientation to learning and knowledge. This tradition was founded on the idea that we live in a closed universe whose mysteries are open to the mind and senses of those who could separate themselves from their predisposition, feelings, and values. The questioning of that tradition has ushered a new outlook into the educational domain. In a post-positivist education (see Scheurich, 1995), there are spaces for a broadened scholarly discourse, inclusive professional orientation, and expansive pedagogical resources. Scholars from different cultural traditions and geographical regions find more spaces for practicing their knowledge. Diverse identities find expression in scholarly discourses. Scholars from different philosophical traditions are compelled to negotiate their differences. The aim of this book is to facilitate a more fruitful dialogue among two specific groups of TESOL professionals who occupy some of the most divergent discourses and intransigent positions on the place of moral/spiritual values in the profession—i.e., critical practitioners (CP), who bring a keen sensitivity to the pedagogical negotiation of power, and Christian English Teachers (CET) who bring a keen sensitivity to spirituality in learning and scholarship. If we meet with the appropriate attitude, religion doesn't have to be a "conversation stopper" (Rorty, 1994, p. 1) anymore, whether in TESOL or in the academy generally!

There is already a dialogue—of sorts—in TESOL circles relating to the expression of spirituality in English language teaching. The problem is that it has produced more heat than light. Scholars of both spiritually based and politically based perspectives feel that their discourses are too disparate for a dialogue to be possible. The point is expressed loud and clear even by some contributors to this book. If modernist assumptions still influence one's thinking, the discourses of CP and CET will certainly seem incommensurate. On the other hand, if the developments of post-positivistic inquiry are taken to their logical conclusion, the differences in discourses of any school shouldn't keep one away from dialogue. Incommensurate discourses are the norm in the post-positivist academy. Perhaps, as Morgan points out in his contribution to this book, there is a "blind spot" relating to spirituality in TESOL (p. 193).

The confusion in TESOL circles regarding moral/spiritual values reflects the uncertainty more broadly in popular discourse and academic discussions as to the framework guiding such a dialogue. As the platform for discussion is shifting, making space for a constructive dialogue, there is a search for footing by all parties in this discussion. Signs of the renewed epistemological search are evident in the popular debates on spirituality unleashed by a wave of new books.[1] In the confusion, the volume against spirituality has been turned up in some quarters. Paradoxically, this vitriol is itself spawned by the renewed interest in spirituality in many circles. The recent books by Richard Dawkins (2006) and Christopher Hitchens (2007) show a continuation of stereotypes relating to the connections between spirituality, politics, and rationality. Though this attitude is not surprising, what is remarkable is that these books have been roundly criticized by even non-religious reviewers for being so clichéd. The *Chronicle of Higher Education* has culled some of the reviews on Dawkins in the scholarly community. No other than the Marxist theorist, Terry Eagleton, argues:

> Card-carrying rationalists like Dawkins, who is the nearest thing to a professional atheist we have had since Bertrand Russell, are in one sense the least well-equipped to understand what they castigate, since they don't believe there is anything there to be understood, or at least anything worth understanding. This is why they invariably come up with vulgar caricatures of religious faith that would make a first-year theology student wince. The more they detest religion, the more ill-informed their criticisms of it tend to be.
> (Critical Mass, 2006, p. B4)

Similarly, in a review of Hitchens, Berlinerblau (2007) argues:

> Crude polemic, I would be the first to admit, has its charms. But if Hitchens truly believes his warning that "as I write these words ... people of faith are in their different ways planning your and my destruction," then sobriety and informed discussion would seem more suitable. *God Is Not Great* fails in precisely the same way that a spate of recent, ear-piercing works written by militant nonbelievers fails. The author so simplifies and underestimates his "adversary" as to obviate useful analysis. His misconceptions about religion, however, do reveal some of the questionable assumptions that secular elites make about their fellow citizens. With American secularism about to enter one of the most challenging periods in its short history, those assumptions will need to be re-examined.
>
> (p. B6)

Thoughtful post-positivist scholars are becoming tired of the stereotypes relating to religion. They see a need for a fresh discussion in the context of the epistemological shifts taking place both inside and outside the academy.[2]

In this introduction, I will consider how the terms of the dialogue in TESOL can be broadened or redefined for practitioners to engage with each other's position more constructively. We need a new platform built on the recent epistemological realizations to facilitate a richer discussion. Before I articulate the attitudes and values that can facilitate a productive dialogue, let me first take stock of the changes in the philosophical mood that enable the construction of a more solid and constructive platform.

Revisiting the Old Platform

With the split of the spiritual and the scientific during modernity, human inquiry has been shaped by the following values:

- the belief in the possibility of final answers in a closed world where all enigmas could be accounted for in terms of the here and now (positivism);
- the faith in reason to unravel mysteries and provide solutions (rationalism);
- the assumption that a dispassionate orientation, devoid of values, is the appropriate stance for scholarly inquiry (objectivity);
- the primacy of physically available evidence to establish truth (empiricism);
- the professionalization and self-definition of academic disciplines, leading also to the removal of scholarly inquiry from ecological, moral, and social considerations (autonomy);
- a disinterested and pragmatic approach to knowledge and pedagogy, removing larger questions of ends, means, and values from consideration, and engaging in knowledge for its own sake (pragmatism).

Such tendencies created a suspicion of religion and spirituality among teachers and scholars. Spirituality was treated as irrelevant at best, distorting and distracting at worst, for human inquiry. If they countenanced spirituality at all, scholars and teachers adopted an attitude of compartmentalization, keeping it separate from their professional life.

The reaction against the narrowness of modernist assumptions has created openness for moral and spiritual considerations. The philosophical changes that augur well for dialogue between scholars and teachers of diverse values can be termed broadly post-positivist (Scheurich, 1995).[3] The changes in thinking in the post-positivist age make a space not only for spirituality but also politics, morality, and identity in education. Here are the counter-values that inform post-positivist educators (hereafter PPE):

- The realization that everything is value laden. PPE in fact go further to acknowledge the shaping role of values in learning and inquiry.
- A place for the personal in learning and knowing. PPE realize that our own experience, background, and identity, in addition to values, have implications for how we conduct inquiry. We are not shy of acknowledging our interests, investments, and predisposition in inquiry. PPE in fact appreciate how the personal opens up unique insights that a dispassionate stance cannot.
- More importance to consciousness and agency in explanations. We are treating the learning subject as a complex, situated, multifaceted being, not amenable to reduction, control, or stereotyping. Scholars are reacting against the overdetermined nature of the human subject in models in which people are perceived as inflexibly conditioned by environmental, social, linguistic, and even psychological structures to behave in predictable ways. More scholars are now giving agency to the subject who can shape these structures to suit his/her interests. We are beginning to give more importance to such intangible and "virtual" factors as imagined communities (Anderson, 1984), structures of feeling (Appadurai, 1996), and performed identities (Rampton, 1995; Pennycook, 2003) in explaining communicative and learning outcomes.
- Acknowledgment of indeterminacy in knowledge. Even at the material level, PPE are now open to the possibility that multiple factors, some personal and situational, go into explaining social and natural phenomena. PPE are also open to the possibility that our models of explanation can't be closed and final, as changing knowledge and contexts generate additional problems for explanation. For example, dynamic systems perspective, aka chaos theory, explains how the smallest components of a system can affect other parts and continually reshape the whole (see Larsen-Freeman, 2002). It adopts just the opposite approach to structuralism, which explained the parts as composing the whole in a tightly knit and stable system. It was difficult to consider features like beliefs, morals, and attitudes in a system that was defined in highly abstract terms. Chaos theory allows for constant reshaping of the system, with patterns emerging out of idiosyncratic factors.
- A desire to accommodate difference in learning, diversity in social life, and pluralism in inquiry. The values of modernity were after all cultural, belong-

ing to the dominant communities of Western European civilization, even though they presented themselves as universal. With the decline of modernity, education is now more open to intellectual traditions and educational orientations from elsewhere. Furthermore, whereas there was a quest to pin down the most rational, logical, or correct orientation in modernity, PPE are now open to the possibility that multiple orientations of inquiry can co-exist. There are increasingly more spaces for diverse ways of knowing in research and inquiry. Negotiating these different intellectual traditions and community orientations is itself an important point of education.

- Openness to the metaphysical, complexity, and unpredictability in explanations. An important consequence of the challenge to positivism is that not all factors are visible or tangible. PPE are able to look beyond the physical and natural manifestation of things for explanations. Some are even accommodating such factors as hope, faith, and belief to explain human behavior in current interdisciplinary research.[4]
- The return of tradition (see Appadurai, 1996). If modernity represented a move away from values and identities associated with tradition, origin, or roots, encouraging a more urban and cosmopolitan identity (that was also somewhat homogeneous), we are seeing the resurgence of unique ethnic, racial, and religious identities and claims today (Appadurai, 1996). In some ways, this turn is a resistance to the colorless world of technological efficiency and uniformity of modernity. In another sense, the more pressure there is toward connectedness in thinking and values in globalization, we also see a parallel pull toward what is distinctive, personal, and idiosyncratic (Barber, 1995). Some might even consider this a desirable strategic essentialism (see Spivak, 1995, p. 214). Part of this resurgence of primordialism is the very vocal and visible expression of religion in life today, whether in the East or in the West. Of course, not all expression of religion is harmonious or beneficial. However, what globalization scholars like Appadurai and Barber point out is that there is a need to recognize the reality of religion for a vast majority of people in the world today. Wishing spirituality would die away is not helpful.

Despite these developments, some colleagues in our field still feel that one's spiritual identity is irrelevant, or even dangerous, in the language classroom. Though a values-based teaching is considered acceptable, even PPE are suspicious of spiritual values in teaching. In my opinion, such a bias simply shows the lingering influences of positivism in our field. Some scholars are unable or unwilling to take to their logical conclusion the epistemological shifts underway. Despite questioning the values of modernity, some still prefer to inhabit a closed natural world that is easy to predict, explain, and control. The discourses of modernity have been internalized so deeply that it is difficult for many to see the possibility of a universe that confounds human and physical determinants. Rationalism is so strong that discussions of faith or spirituality are discomforting. In calling this limitation a "blind spot" in the TESOL profession, Brian Morgan observes that "the sociolinguistic and cognitive variability that might arise from religiosity has yet to insert itself alongside gendered, racialized, and ethno-linguistic factors as a publishable debating point" (this book, p. 193). It is certainly intriguing that while many previously suppressed subject positions have won a space in learning and scholarship, religious identities haven't.[5]

There is also the curious assumption among some PPE that not all values-based professionals can engage in an equal dialogue. They apparently feel that dialogue is possible only when the values relate to a common secular framework. They doubt the possibility that there could be dialogue between faith-based and secular scholars. Considering the chapters in this volume, Pennycook despairs at the "sheer incommensurability of the worldviews on display here. The arguments pass each other by, and this lapses into an impossible incommensurability" (Chapter 6, this volume). Johnston raises "doubts about whether dialogue between evangelicals and non-evangelicals is in fact possible … the underlying assumptions of both sides are so radically different and mutually incompatible that it's extremely hard to envision how dialogue can take place" (Chapter 3, this volume). However, this assumption also goes against the spirit of postmodernism. The starting point of many contemporary theoretical frameworks, such as the contact zones model and communities of practice perspective, is the possibility of inhabiting a pluralistic world where nothing is shared between members of a "community." The concern of these models is to explain how people can collaborate on mutual interests even when nothing is shared. For example, the communities of practice perspective (see Wenger, 1998) accommodates the idea of overlapping community memberships and identities that members bring to a social domain, with differently held values and beliefs. It then posits how shared practices (rather than shared beliefs and values) can help accomplish mutually shared goals. The model allows for a unity with diversity. It thus helps explain how contact zones (Pratt, 1991) where people from diverse backgrounds meet don't have to be dysfunctional or destructive. We have to formulate new classroom pedagogies and discourse conventions that would make a space for disparate identities and values in education.

It is important for scholars to re-examine their assumptions and consider the full implications of a post-positivist and pluralistic worldview. While one has every right to hold an atheistic position in a post-positivist environment, it is unnecessary to rule that spiritually inclined practitioners cannot share the same space. While it is possible, and even necessary, to be committed to one's own values, it is unnecessary to assume that one's commitments preclude working together with or even enjoying community with those who come from a different worldview. The most important test case for values-based professionals is the possibility of dialogue between CET and CP and their ability to share the same educational space. To work toward the full extent of the possibilities afforded by post-positivism in TESOL, a good starting point is this volume.

The Fractured Platform in TESOL

We have read some critical essays on the deceptive and coercive uses of religion of some ELT missionary institutions in recent TESOL publications (Edge, 2003,

2004, 2006; Johnston, 2003; Johnston & Varghese, 2006; Pennycook & Coutand-Marin, 2003; Pennycook & Makoni, 2005; Vandrick, 2002; Varghese & Johnston, 2007). These publications serve an important purpose in developing more ethical pedagogical practices. However, there is the danger that the spotlight on certain problematic historical episodes, personalities, and agencies might get exaggerated to the point that accommodating any religious values in language teaching will be rejected. We have to be careful, therefore, not to use a justifiable critique of excesses to condemn all representations of religious values in our profession or stereotype all spiritually minded language teachers as driven by ulterior motivations. Also, we mustn't stop with critique, but move on to facilitate an ethical and enriching accommodation of spiritual values in the classroom. We must begin by acknowledging the biases, stereotypes, and exaggerations on all sides that might prevent dialogue.

For understandable reasons, the dialogue on spirituality in pedagogy has been conducted mostly between CP and CET. Christians, specifically evangelicals, are the religious group that has featured most often in values-based teaching in the current debates in TESOL. There are certainly a lot of implications from this discussion for other religions on the appropriate ways of representing their values in teaching. However, TESOL professionals are justified in feeling that Christianity has a special connection to our field. For many, Christianity has had a problematic association with English, English language teaching, and modern education since colonial times. Therefore Christianity merits special attention. Within Christianity, evangelicals draw attention as they are perceived as closely aligned with the US political establishment and enjoy significant national status. While critical practitioners have been most articulate about the dangers posed by evangelical mission in TESOL, they enjoy a special connection with values-based professionals because of their shared post-positivist epistemological orientation. In order to clear the air, first we have to discuss the misunderstandings and stereotypes on both sides of the debate.

Here are some of the charges against CET that prevent dialogue:

a. *Historical baggage.* The collaboration of missionaries with colonizers is always evoked to show CETs' imperialistic motivations in teaching. Some see a continuation of those interests in present-day language teaching, with missionary ELT organizations serving as the arm of US imperialism and Western hegemony (see Pennycook & Coutand-Marin, 2003).
b. *Tainted institutions.* The extreme statements and activities of certain missionary organizations or churches have been used to cast aspersions on all evangelical teachers (as we can see in the articles by Pennycook & Coutand-Marin, 2003).
c. *Fundamentalism.* CET have been characterized as fundamentalist and, therefore, irrational, narrow-minded, and backward. Their fundamentalism then makes CET unsuitable for dialogue with academics who claim to be reasonable, broad-minded, and progressive (see Varghese & Johnston, 2007). Related to the above charge is the notion that evangelicals are *absolutists* because of their literalist orientation to texts and essentialist attitude to

language (see Pennycook & Makoni, 2005; Pennycook, this volume). That makes them unsuitable for dialogue with those who consider themselves relativists or constructionists.

d. *Strange bedfellows.* While some scholars accept the fine ideological distinctions within the evangelical camp, they argue that it is the duty of socially conscious CET to denounce the bigoted approaches of their fellow Christians (see Johnston, this volume). CP scholars argue that until such denunciation takes place, socially conscious CET are guilty of the same sins by association (see also Vandrick in this book).
e. *Commitment = Closed-mindedness.* Some scholars argue that CET come with certainties, while non-evangelical professionals come with skepticism (Varghese & Johnston, 2007). The implication is that non-CET professionals go relentlessly after facts, while CET are blinded by their beliefs that give them ready-made certainties.
f. *Solidarity = Clannishness = Stealth.* CET are accused of "furtiveness" (Johnston, p. 37; this book) because they have their own specialist publishers for their books, their own journals, their own university training programs, and their own strand of presentations in the TESOL convention (in addition to the pre-convention CELT conference and the caucus itself). Other critics charge that evangelicals take to English language teaching only to convert students under the professional cover, and that they keep their identity hidden in classrooms and schools in order to manipulate the curriculum and discussions for conversion purposes. They have labeled this modus operandi "stealth evangelism" (see Pennycook & Coutand-Marin, 2003).

To consider these charges point by point would take us too far afield. However, some of these accusations are commonly encountered by all PPE (see Canagarajah, forthcoming). For example, positivist educators accuse critical practitioners of dogmatism, tainted association with radical regimes, and practices of imposition (as I have discussed in Canagarajah, 1999). The chapters in this volume will help readers understand the response of CET to these issues much better. There are many evangelicals who will readily criticize the past and present association of Christians with military force and conquest (see Byler, Chamberlain, Osborn, Stabler-Havener, Snow, Ferris, Wong, this volume). They are inspired by how Christianity has motivated resistance against unfair exertions of power in many non-Western communities during colonialism and at present (see Osborn, Smith, Ferris, this volume). They condemn "stealth evangelism" and articulate more complex forms of spiritual representation and stances of rational openness that can be coupled with commitment to values (see Snow, Wong, this volume).

We have to also become familiar with a broader range of theologians in the evangelical camp to consider the charges of literalism and fundamentalism. For example, "postmodern evangelicals" (see Brueggemann, 2005; Middleton & Walsh, 1995), adopt a situated, even deconstructionist, orientation to the scripture.[6] They argue for a time- and space-sensitive revelation from God. They hold that revelation is still unfolding and that scripture is not a closed book. Furthermore, they are open to the possibility that the interpretation of the Word is based considerably on the location of the hearer. They argue that this humility toward God's teachings and purposes is precisely the attitude that is encouraged in the scripture. They urge Christians to not close their mind with simple certainties, but be open to constantly revisiting and questioning their theological assumptions.

What is more important here is to clarify the imprecise use of terms like *fundamentalist* and *evangelical.* We must note that fundamentalist applications of a theology or philosophy have a particular character, and they are not the only ways in which any religious group understands its mission. To define the terms carefully, *fundamentalism* is a literal reading of scriptures/teachings without an interpretive role for the changing social conditions and contexts. It is a direct application of values and principles of a different historical context from contemporary conditions without consideration for relevance or creative adaptation. While some circles in all religions adopt this approach, there are others who adopt a more contextual, creative, and critical interpretation and application. Religions are not fundamentalist per se, just as there could be fundamentalists in all value systems and schools of thought, including critical practitioners.

We should also re-examine our use of the term *evangelical.* The word derives from the Greek *euangelion,* "good news," which is proclaimed by the *gospel* (the Old English translation of the Greek root), which for many Christians is the point of the whole scripture. In other words, the term is made up of the following notions: evangel = good news = gospel = scripture. For many, *evangelical* simply means the worldview and value system that derive from the scripture. Evangelical and fundamentalist are not synonymous, as I demonstrated in the previous paragraph that the interpretation of the scripture is contextual and revelation is progressive. Even for those for whom being evangelical is limited to proclaiming the gospel (i.e., evangelizing), Christ's good news has a social, political, and cosmic as well as a personal dimension. In other words, the gospel implies the regeneration of all of life. Of course, there are some for whom the good news means only personal salvation and, therefore, calls for conversion. In this regard, we have to distinguish evangelize from evangelical. To *evangelize* (i.e., to proclaim the good news, and thus preach and convert people) is not the same as holding an evangelical worldview (which includes personal conversion, but not limited to it). Furthermore, even to evangelize is not always to preach verbally and ask people to change their religion. For many evangelicals, to evangelize is to proclaim through representation—i.e., to represent the good news in all forms, not discounting one's everyday life and social interactions. It is therefore unfair to conflate evangelical with evangelize, and make it stand for the following partial connotations: evangelical = evangelize = preach = win souls. To be an evangelical is to extend the regenerative vision of the scripture to all domains of life through all forms of representation.

Consider also that the attitudes and practices of evangelicalism (note: not "evangelism") vary around the world. They are cultural. Evangelicalism has connotations of being asocial, pietistic, and conservative in the United States (see, however, Wallis, 2005). However, it holds different identities and implications elsewhere. In many third world communities (including my native

Sri Lanka), evangelicalism is countercultural and anti-establishment (as the early church was before it became the Roman Empire's state religion). Evangelicals adopt critical positions against the status quo—whether of the church hierarchy or the political establishment (see Ramachandra, 1996). In the volatile local political climate, compounded by ethnic conflict, poverty, and human rights violations, Sri Lankan evangelicals consider an engagement in justice and peace part of their calling. And this is the case in many South American and African communities.[7]

While exploding such stereotypes, it is also important to focus on the concerns CET and CP share about the direction of contemporary education. As Morgan (this volume) and Purpel (1989) observe, PPE share a critical perspective on the functionalist, commercialized, and dehumanizing tendencies in present-day education. Critical and spiritual practitioners resist a utilitarian and narrowly pragmatic orientation to learning. This shared vision should enable both camps to work toward constructing a common platform for conversation, one that takes into account the newly afforded philosophical advantages.

A Personal Resolution

My professional history proves that I have earned the right to be treated as an insider to both the CET and the CP camps, and that I can confidently claim community with each. It might sound ironic that I consider evangelicalism and radical social activism compatible. Can this be? I must be schizophrenic—or aware of a deeper connection between both camps that others don't see. To make matters more complicated for everyone, I am a South Asian who calls himself Christian. I am from a community that has lived through what scholars might consider the evils of the colonizing and missionary experience. Even worse, among all the denominations and theological movements in Christianity, I identify myself as an evangelical—a movement associated with right-wing ideologies and war-mongering in contemporary US politics.

Since my CP credentials are well known in TESOL circles (interestingly enough, the only citations by others in this volume are to my work on linguistic and pedagogical resistance), let me explain the evangelical side of my identity. Most colleagues in TESOL know me only as a critical practitioner from the periphery—and, for that reason, an uncompromising ideologue or a radical activist. Few colleagues realize that my politics and social activism derive from my faith. And both inform my pedagogical practice.

My childhood and upbringing in Sri Lanka shaped my faith. In a multi-religious country, where Buddhists, Hindus, Muslims, and Christians live side by side, I grew up in an environment where spirituality was everyday reality. I had to struggle to develop my own spiritual position, even though I came from a family of Hindus who converted to Christianity during colonization and then slumped into a life of nominal middle-class Christianity that didn't even involve attending church. Spirituality (and politics) gained urgency when my idyllic childhood of easygoing rural, tropical living descended into an ever-escalating (and still unresolved) ethnic conflict. As a member of the minority ethnic community of Tamils, I felt vulnerable. I saw the human rights violations of the Sinhala state and the Tamil resistance groups, and the deaths of innocent civilians (80,000 in the last three decades). Christianity gave me a coherent social vision that inspired me to commit myself to work for justice. I found inspiration in the scripture to struggle for fundamental changes in the social order. Evangelicalism also made me value the life of the individual. In a context where the dead were just statistics, I valued each person. In a context where life was cheap, I found a place for the dignity of human life. Most of all, I found a message of personal regeneration and spirituality that integrated my social and political vision consistently. Politics wasn't an impersonal struggle for abstract principles like justice and equality. My spiritual convictions prevented me from adopting a Machiavellian attitude to politics, treating life as expendable for a worthy cause. Most of all, I realized that structural changes in society have to be sustained by lifestyle and moral changes in individuals. This outlook gave me the dual missions of working for personal regeneration and social transformation.

This background makes me a different critical practitioner. Though I have always made a strong case for taking material life seriously in pedagogical practice (Canagarajah, 1999) and discourse analysis (Canagarajah, 2002a), I am not a materialist. I can't be. My worldview makes me give importance to spirituality and consciousness in communication and education. Similarly, though I am concerned about locating knowledge and discourses in their specific contexts (which I call *location of enunciation* in Canagarajah, 2002b) and localizing our pedagogy and scholarship, I am not a relativist. I can't be. My clear spiritual and political commitments help me make a distinction between relativism and pluralism. While the former might encourage an anything goes approach, the latter holds the possibility of being committed to important principles and values with an understanding of other orientations to life and knowledge (Canagarajah, 2005). These positions, deriving from my Christianity, make me a different kind of CP.

My political sensibility and postcolonial background also make me a different evangelical. I cannot identify with what passes for evangelicalism in some quarters in the West. I am critical of the xenophobia, war mongering, prosperity theology, and smug self-righteousness that find expression in some quarters of Christianity. I am critical of the extremes to which missionaries have gone during the colonial period, and still do in some regions, in imposing their values on others. I might go further in my social activism and political commitments than many other evangelicals, refusing the dichotomy of spirituality and politics that gives the latter only secondary importance. However, I also look at the history of Christianity with balance. I have resisted the tendency of my nationalistic colleagues in Sri Lanka to look at missionaries in stereotypical terms. In my publications, I have argued for a more complex view of the missionary experience in Sri Lanka (even though I also critique the colonial experience for its impositions)—see Canagarajah, 1999; see also Makoni and Makoni, this book, for a balanced approach to the missionary experience. There are many complicating factors that postcolonial nationalists ignore. For example, the state and church didn't always see eye to eye on their agenda in the colonies. They had different interests: for example, the colonial regime didn't want to invest in vernacular education, while the clergy saw the implications of the vernacular for encouraging a wider group of people to read the Bible and for preaching the gospel. Often, missionaries resisted the unsound economic and educational policies of the colonial regime. For example, missionaries joined local leaders in critiquing English education for the damage it did to the intellectual and social development of children. Therefore, missionaries emphasized vernacular or bilingual education, sometimes disappointing local people who desired English education. Though missionary education denigrated local culture in some quarters, it also made long-standing contributions to it in other ways. For example, because of missionary efforts in translating the Bible, Tamil developed a prose tradition. Editing a book on *Missions and Empire* in the influential Oxford History of the British Empire, Norman Etherington bemoans the lack of objective scholarly research on this connection and goes on to say: "In this volume the most striking feature of missions is *diversity*. Not only did a variety of approaches to mission coexist at any one point, the missionary enterprise as a whole went through remarkable changes over time" (2007, p. 15). He concludes: "It seems likely that future scholars, like the scholars of this volume, will shy away from mono-causal explanations of the modern missionary movement" (2007, p. 18).

The ways in which my politics and faith combine make me a different evangelical among CET and a different critical theorist among CP. There are of course tensions in my faith and politics (generated by my membership in both camps) that help me conduct a dialogue within myself at times. This tension is creative and constructive. It is this tension that keeps me growing both in my spirituality and in my politics. For example, my familiarity with political discourse enabled me to progress from social action based on charity to consider fundamental structural changes and alliance with resistance groups against the human rights violations of authorities in Sri Lanka. I realized that the salvation Christ offers goes beyond change of heart to active social and ecological regeneration. My Christianity enabled me to move beyond social action as a project to treating it as lifestyle. I have to constantly struggle with developing an ethic of selfless giving of oneself that demands modeling my personal life and relationships around the values I want to inculcate in society. I have to find creative ways of embodying the values rather than just preaching them, infusing all of social and material life with the desired values rather than merely presenting them for everyone's contemplation.

Both politics and spirituality influence the type of pedagogical practice I bring to my classroom. I have to always wrestle with questions like the following, many of which go beyond the immediate concerns of the classroom and curriculum but are nevertheless fundamentally influential in pedagogy:

- *Attitude*: Do I treat my work as duty, personal advancement, a means of living, or also as caring engagement with lives and service to others?
- *Policy*: Whose interest does my teaching serve—i.e., state, educational institution, teachers, textbook publishers, students, local communities?

- *Objective*: Does learning help students transform personal, social, and educational conditions?
- *Classroom relations*: Are there spaces for students for collaboration, individuality, and resistance to negotiate their interests fairly in the classroom?
- *Identity*: Do students achieve positive identities and values in English? Does my pedagogy go beyond imparting just the knowledge or skills and hold the possibility of transforming lives?
- *Pedagogy*: Do my instructional practices encourage learning in a holistic and critical manner, rather than accepting unchallenged truths and skills?
- *Curriculum*: What is the hidden curriculum of the teaching materials and activities in the classroom? Do I take the curriculum for granted, or do I accommodate the possibility for students to critique their underlying values, and reconstruct knowledge creatively?
- *Assessment*: Are the assessment procedures fair in reflecting the proficiency of students and the interests they would like education to serve?

In other words, I have to always ask myself whether my approach is a pedagogy of possibility or closure. Thus, my faith finds an expression that is larger than one of merely preaching in the classroom or converting students. My pedagogical mission is the regeneration of everything in life—not just individuals, but social structures, environment, and knowledge paradigms. Furthermore, the way to do this is not only by word but also by representing the regenerative values in my everyday classroom life. Of course, there are direct representations of my faith in the classroom. Students won't see me making clichéd jokes about religion in the classroom. Though I am critical of unjust practices and unethical policies of the people and institutions that have claimed to represent religions through history, students will see me treating diverse religions, theologies, and philosophies with great respect. They'll find me engaging in these discussions, to the extent permitted by the topics or students' questions, with enthusiasm. Needless to say, the underlying values that inform my teaching would be evangelical. And, of course, there are occasions when I have talked about my faith directly, both inside and outside the classroom, at poignant moments in classroom life when the topic or discussion warranted it.

Just as in the case of faith and politics, my spirituality and scholarship are in creative tension in my professional life, making me develop further as a scholar and Christian. Notable among my struggles has been the one on the place of modernist assumptions in my teaching and thinking. I became a Christian at a point when my mentors were influenced by modernism. I was made to value reason and objectivity in the interpretation of the scripture. I grew up with what was called *inductive Bible studies* as the appropriate way to understand God's word. As the term implies, this reading involved an objective reading within the textual context, treating the scripture as a finished product to retrieve timeless truths. This interpretive approach was consonant with the dominant orientations to literary interpretation (i.e., New Criticism in the UK or Practical Criticism in the USA) and the scientific trend in general academic culture. When I came to the USA for graduate studies in the late 1980s, I faced conflicts from the emerging postmodern approaches. It appears as if I might have lived a split life for some time. I understood the limitations of an overly rationalist and objective approach to truth, but I adopted the view that Christianity was the most rational religion, that the scripture had one meaning for all people, and that one can adopt an objective approach to theology and systematize one's faith. I thought I could make a scientific apology for my faith and reason out the limitations of other worldviews. I soon realized the limits of rational arguments for countering beliefs. On the other hand, I found the postmodern turn empowering for my spiritual life. If values are accepted as influential in all domains of my life, I found it liberating to acknowledge the values that motivated my thinking and faith. I could understand how people from diverse backgrounds understood the scripture differently in different historic periods. I could accept the limitations of reason in either explaining to others or to myself the full scope of my faith. I saw a legitimate place for beliefs in everyone's life. I therefore sought out evangelical thinkers who wrestled with postmodern epistemological shifts, and considered ways of integrating my academic and spiritual pursuits in line with my new realization.

I now see the validity of an influential group of thinkers in the evangelical camp who hold that Christians have confused a specific discourse of a specific time and place (i.e., European notion of modernity) with the whole of their faith. As Mark Noll observes: "The evangelical embrace of the Enlightenment at the turn of the eighteenth century still remains extraordinarily important nearly two centuries later because habits of mind that the evangelical Enlightenment encouraged have continued to influence contemporary evangelical life" (1994, p. 83). Others point out that the modernist influence has made evangelicals reduce the complexity of what it means to understand life and faith: "By adopting rationalism so completely, Western Christianity virtually abandoned half of what it means to be human. The creative, artistic, emotional, experiential, personal, relational…" (Poe, 2001, p. 133). Eventually, the evangelical commitment to modernism has resulted in a mental laziness (the inability to discern the relevance of the gospel for changing conditions), pride (developing ways of understanding God that affirms our own preferred approaches), and diffidence (lacking the courage to live with critical thinking, intellectual openness, and spiritual questioning).

I am now growing in a faith that is more consistent with my academic orientation and political commitment. For example, my orientation to the scripture constitutes the following assumptions:

- Truth has a temporal dimension and is, therefore, progressive. God's revelation takes place gradually over time. It is ongoing. The scripture is not a closed book.
- Truth has to be constantly reinterpreted. God speaks to our own local contexts and experiences, for our own time and place. To this extent, the gospel is socially constructed.
- Reason is not capable of accounting for everything in faith. I am open to living with some amount of tension and unresolved questions—in fact,

taking things with faith. My theology has some loose ends, but not to the extent that they affect my faith in its core principles and values.

Though I accommodate a place for the personal, plural, situated, constructed, and local in faith, I also see the need to constantly negotiate the complete text of the Bible and the whole historical Christian tradition for my spiritual life. Tradition and scripture provide a framework for engagement and serve as valuable checks and balances against an "anything goes" approach. In this sense, I am a postmodernist only in a qualified sense. Also, postmodernism has only limited uses for me as a philosophical paradigm. I am prepared to abandon postmodernist discourses when my spiritual walk reveals richer orientations that illuminate faith and life better. This attitude enables me to discourse across differences as I constantly seek to enlarge my paradigms and also be sensitive to progressive revelation.

This Book

This chapter is the most personally challenging and vulnerable writing I have ever done. I have had to loudly invoke the labels that I would rather quietly live by. Still, making my positions and identities explicit is warranted in the present moment of our professional history. As I mentioned at the beginning of this chapter, social and philosophical trends have led to a point when (once again in history) the spiritual cannot be kept out of the mainstream. Also, we live in a time when the personal finds a legitimate place in the academy. Furthermore, part of my objective is to reclaim a tradition of evangelicalism that is lost in Western society and in academia. The Christian tradition that has combined social radicalism, intellectual vibrancy, and moral integrity has been overshadowed by an alternate strand that represents conservatism, anti-intellectualism, and chauvinism. It has also been my purpose to move this dialogue away from an arid academic polemic. I want to represent my faith as action. I want to explain how my faith informs my teaching and scholarship, accounting for both the struggles and passions in my professional life.

I hope my testimony will explain the complex profile of the evangelical camp, and explode some of the stereotypes associated with the CET label. However, I must acknowledge that my positions on education and politics are not shared by all Christians, or even evangelicals for that matter. Even in Christianity, our different backgrounds and life stories make us understand and practice our faith and teaching differently. Some of my positions on politics and society would sound unchristian to my evangelical colleagues. The same applies for my ideologies and politics among critical practitioners. CP colleagues would consider the spiritual motivations of my social activism suspicious. *My* dialogue with my CET and CP colleagues will continue—both in this book and elsewhere.

The chapters in this book are meant to challenge the main parties in the post-positivist debate in TESOL. While CP are challenged to address the role of faith and spirituality in pedagogy, CET are challenged to address the complex ideological and political implications of their work. This book emerges from the hope that all TESOL professionals, of whatever ideological camp, are always open to self-reflection, self-criticism, and self-improvement. We hope that this book presents challenges that make all of us re-envision our pedagogical priorities and professional expertise. The arguments made in this book about spirituality or politics are not the only ones that matter in the PPE encounter. The book serves as an invitation to bring out all values and beliefs of the diverse interest groups in our profession to the dialogue. It represents the promise that we can collectively enrich ourselves by making our positions (and complaints) heard in a supportive environment. It is indeed a good sign that we can engage in a discussion on spirituality, morality, and politics in mainstream journals and publications in our profession. We don't have to keep our beliefs hidden or unintegrated anymore. It is hoped that TESOL professionals of other religious and ideological camps will join the dialogue in search of an appropriate post-positivist teaching practice. We should prod each other on in the direction of discovering richer pedagogies of possibility by practicing a transformative dialogue.

Has this book succeeded in constructing the new platform for dialogue among values-based professionals as we originally envisioned? Maybe not. As many authors point out in the collection (Johnston, Pennycook, and Phillipson among others), the chapters sometimes work at cross-purposes from each other. They operate at different wavelengths. Perhaps we have only managed to achieve a *conciliatory dialogue* of clarifying the misunderstandings—as Johnston and Pennycook point out. We are still far from the stage when a Freire or a Giroux in TESOL can express solidarity with a spiritual perspective on critical education by writing a Foreword to such a book—as they did to Purpel (1989). But it is important to clear the air of misconceptions. Christians move toward broadened political and pedagogical orientations (though not without suspicion from CP that they still show traces of bias). Critical practitioners move toward acknowledging some of their stereotypes of CET, and clarifying the rationale behind some of their assumptions (though not without doubts about providing a legitimate place for spirituality in the profession). For both parties to dialogue within the covers of the same book and encounter each other's positions, rather than fight their wars in different camps, is an important achievement in its own right. Our mutual presence in the same book, engaged in a discussion on issues of common concern, makes us critically reflect on our own assumptions. We qualify our claims, we modify our tone, and we decrease the pitch of our charges against each other. We are at least aware of being heard by the other side. Our awareness of our mutual presence in the conversations in the field is already part of change.

Notes

1. For a list of at least 11 semi-scholarly books that have appeared in the past five years, see the review article by Barash (2007) in the *Chronicle of Higher Education.*
2. This is not to ignore the fruitful debates that have taken place from a rationalist tradition in the past. Matching those like Bertrand Russell were Christian academics like C. S. Lewis. While some might wish to continue that dialogue from a rationalist tradition, I like to move the conversation to the post-positivist framework.

3. We need to realize that all these philosophical movements are under contestation and conflicting interpretations. For example, in some quarters, spirituality made a happy compromise with modernity. The valuation of a rational orientation to religion and an objective interpretation of scripture are forms in which modernity still influences spiritual life for some.
4. Some universities, including Harvard, are sponsoring research on the efficacy of prayer and meditation in healing and psychosomatic well-being (see Monastersky, 2006).
5. Some may argue that the spiritual enjoys some cachet in the academy, especially as it encompasses New Age spiritualities among others. However, it is the religious that is typically associated with institutions and organizations and considered tainted with evil.
6. Other theologians include: Brian McLaren, Nicholas Wolterstorff, John Atherton, Sally McFague, and Jurgen Moltman.
7. I am not saying that such an evangelical strand is not present in the West. It is simply more prominent in the East.

References

Anderson, B. (1984). *Imagined communities: Reflections on the origins and spread of nationalism.* London: Verso.

Appadurai, A. (1996). *Modernity at large: Cultural dimensions of globalization.* Minneapolis: University of Minnesota Press.

Barash, D. P. (April 20, 2007). The DNA of religious faith. In the Chronicle Review. *Chronicle of Higher Education, 53*(33), B6.

Barber, B. (1995). *Jihad vs McWorld: How the planet is both falling apart and coming together—and what this means for democracy.* New York: Times Books.

Berlinerblau, J. (June 1, 2007). Secularism in the elimination round. In the Chronicle Review. *Chronicle of Higher Education, 53*(39), B6.

Brueggemann, W. (2005). *The book that breathes new life: Scriptural authority and biblical theology.* Minneapolis, MN: Fortress Press.

Canagarajah, A. S. (1999). *Resisting linguistic imperialism in English teaching.* Oxford, UK: Oxford University Press.

Canagarajah, A. S. (2002a). *A geopolitics of academic writing.* Pittsburgh, PA: University of Pittsburgh Press.

Canagarajah, A. S. (2002b). Editorial introduction: Rediscovering local knowledge. *Journal of Language, Identity, and Education, 1*(4), 243–260.

Canagarajah, A. S. (2005). Reconstructing local knowledge, reconfiguring language studies. In A. S. Canagarajah (Ed.), *Reclaiming the local in language policy and practice* (pp. 3–24). Mahwah, NJ: Lawrence Erlbaum.

Canagarajah, A. S. (forthcoming). Shared criticism and common responses: Christian and critical practitioners.

Critical mass (November 10, 2006). In the Chronicle Review. *Chronicle of Higher Education, 53*(12), B4.

Dawkins, R. (2006). *The god delusion.* New York: Houghton Mifflin Company.

Edge, J. (2003). Imperial troopers and servants of the Lord: A vision of TESOL for the 21st century. *TESOL Quarterly, 37*(4), 701–709.

Edge, J. (2004). Of displacive and augmentative discourse, new enemies, and old doubts. *TESOL Quarterly, 38*(4), 717–721.

Edge, J. (2006). Background and overview. In J. Edge (Ed.), *(Re-)locating TESOL in an age of empire* (pp. xii–xix.). Basingstoke, UK: Palgrave Macmillan.

Etherington, N. (2007). Introduction. In N. Etherington (Ed.), *Missions and empire.* Oxford, UK: Oxford University Press.

Giroux, H., & Freire, P. (1989). Introduction. In D. E. Purpel (Ed.), *The moral and spiritual crisis in education* (pp. xiii–xviii). Granby, MA: Bergin and Garvey.

Hitchens, C. (2007). *God is not great: How religion poisons everything.* New York: Warner.

Johnston, B. (2003). *Values in English language teaching.* Mahwah, NJ: Lawrence Erlbaum.

Johnston, B., & Varghese, M. (2006). Neo-imperialism, evangelism, and ELT: Modernist missions and a postmodern profession. In J. Edge (Ed.), *(Re-)locating TESOL in an age of empire* (pp. 195–207). Basingstoke, UK: Palgrave Macmillan.

Larsen-Freeman, D. (2002). Language acquisition and language use from a chaos/complexity theory perspective. In C. Kramsch (Ed.), *Language acquisition and language socialization: Ecological perspectives* (pp. 33–46). London & New York: Continuum.

Middleton, R., & Walsh, B. (1995). *Truth is stranger than it used to be: Biblical faith in a postmodern age.* Downer's Grove, IL: IVCF.

Monastersky, R. (May 26, 2006). Religion on the brain: The hard science of neurobiology is taking a closer look at the ethereal world of the spirit. *Chronicle of Higher Education, 52*(38), A14.

Noll, M. A. (1994). *The scandal of the evangelical mind.* Grand Rapids, MI: Eerdmans.

Pennycook, A. (2003). Global Englishes, rip slyme, and performativity. *Journal of Sociolinguistics, 7*(4), 513–533.

Pennycook, A., & Coutand-Marin, S. (2003). Teaching English as a missionary language (TEML). *Discourse: Studies in the Cultural Politics of Education, 24*(3), 337–353.

Pennycook, A., & Makoni, S. (2005). The modern mission: The language effects of Christianity. *Journal of Language, Identity, and Education, 4*(2), 137–155.

Poe, H. L. (2001). *Christian witness in a postmodern world.* Nashville, TN: Abingdon.

Pratt, M. L. (1991). Arts of the contact zone. *Profession, 91*, 33–40.

Purpel, D. E. (1989). *The moral and spiritual crisis in education.* Granby, MA: Bergin and Garvey.

Ramachandra, V. (1996). *The recovery of mission: Beyond the pluralist paradigm.* Grand Rapids, MI: Eerdmans.

Rampton, B. (1995). *Crossing: Language and ethnicity among adolescents.* London: Longman.

Rorty, R. (1994). Religion as conversation stopper. *Common Knowledge, 3*(1), 1–6.

Scheurich, J. (1995). *Research method in the postmodern.* London: Falmer.

Spivak, G. (1995). *The Spivak reader: Selected works of Gayatri Chakravorty Spivak.* New York: Routledge.

Vandrick, S. (2002). ESL and the colonial legacy: A teacher faces her "missionary kid" past. In V. Zamel, & R. Spack (Eds.), *Enriching ESOL pedagogy* (pp. 411–422). Mahwah, NJ: Lawrence Erlbaum.

Varghese, M., & Johnston, B. (2007). Evangelical Christians and English language teaching. *TESOL Quarterly, 41*(1), 5–32.

Wallis, J. (2005). *God's politics: Why the right gets it wrong and the left doesn't get it.* New York: HarperCollins.

Wenger, E. (1998). *Communities of practice: Learning, meaning, and identity.* Cambridge, UK: Cambridge University Press.

Part I

Setting the Tone

Dialogue and Discourse

2 Non-judgmental Steps on a Road to Understanding

Julian Edge

I have no inkling why some people believe (I almost wrote, "choose to believe," but that would be to beg the question I am trying to address and to engage in the type of rhetorical trickery I am trying to avoid) in the existence of a supernatural creator of the world in which we live. At the same time, I have no glimmer of a response to the implicit counter-question as to what exactly preceded, or caused, or provided a context for the "big bang" with which our universe is thought (by those of an evolutionary mind-set) to have begun. I acknowledge immediately that these two perspectives are by no means necessarily incompatible with each other.

I acknowledge, too, that my everyday concepts of "before" and "cause" and "context" are inadequate to this discussion in ways that I am not able to comprehend. I find some respite in the notion that it is the very nature of the universe, outside a concept of time, to be in a constant state of inflation and retraction (Steinhardt, 2003). I find affirmations of such a view in the fragmentary writings of Heraclitus "Everything flows and nothing abides; everything gives way and nothing stays fixed.... It is in changing that things find repose" (as cited in Wheelwright, 1959, pp. 70–71).

I acknowledge that there are many ways of knowing and learning, all of them bound up with some form of communication. A frequent difficulty is found in communication between and among these different ways of knowing and learning, and that is the issue to which I wish to attempt some small contribution. While the specifics of this collection concern Christian belief, I want to make a more general beginning with regard to communication in the "Western" culture with which I am most familiar.

Arguments and Challenges

Two relatively recent books by well-respected sociolinguists (Tannen, 1998 and Cameron, 2000) have delivered startlingly opposed visions of a major discourse challenge facing British and American society. To summarize in the briefest of terms, Tannen's thesis is that there exists a deep-seated cultural overcommitment to argument that is unhealthy. It has led, to take an institutional example, to a legal system in which truth is sacrificed to rhetoric. That is to say, lawyers are not educated to discover and reveal what has happened in any particular case, they are educated to put forward the best possible representation of their client's position. This, and not a commitment to truth, is the ethical core of the lawyer's commitment and issues of guilt and innocence are decided according to which side is seen to have been more persuasive. In this light, one may also note the prevalence of lawyers among British and American political representatives and reflect on the influence of their presence on the governance of those societies.

In domestic terms, communications and relationships are too often dominated by a desire to have the last word and to come out the winner. Tannen presents us with an "argument culture" that, at individual, social, and international levels, is internally corrosive and externally aggressive. Tannen (1998) writes, in conclusion:

> We need to use our imaginations and ingenuity to find different ways to seek truth and gain knowledge.... It will take creativity to find ways to blunt the most dangerous blades of the argument culture. It's a challenge we must undertake, because our public and private lives are at stake.
>
> (p. 298)

Equally briefly, Cameron's thesis is that through such widespread phenomena as workplace training, particularly in the service industries, confessional television chat shows, and communication skills courses throughout the education system, we are producing classes and generations of people all too ready to confess, compromise, and concede, but unable to sustain an argument and stand up for their rights. She presents us with a "communication culture," rife with manipulative "discourse technologies" (Fairclough, 1992) with which people are trained to fit into patterns of phony communication that serve the purposes of others. As an outcome, Cameron (2000) writes:

> The general devaluation of argument as a communication skill has some potentially worrying implications.... A society which conducts its discourse on the principle that "everyone has a right to their opinion but no one's opinion is preferable to anyone else's" is in one sense "democratic", but how can it move towards any collective notion of what might constitute the common good?
>
> (p. 163)

Both writers make serious points and both, I believe, put forward partial (in both senses of the word) arguments in order to serve their own immediate purposes. Tannen selects her examples well in order to highlight instances in which an overreliance on agonistic discourse alone limits our human potential to communicate with each other. One intuits, however, that such an academically socialized writer and skilled rhetorician would be unlikely to be in favor of a situation in which the power of lucid, rational argument were to be devalued, or in which the ability of some sections of the populace to stand up for their rights (and clarify their responsibilities) were to be lost. Cameron, in complementary fashion, looks out examples of non-argumentative discourse, which she finds inappropriate. With reference to Phillips (1998), for instance, Cameron (2000) writes in these terms:

> Consider the following description of "Circle Time", an approach to teaching interpersonal and communicational skills that is used in some British Schools:
>
> The object is to provide a safe environment in which everyone has an equal opportunity to speak and to be listened to.... Within the circles children are encouraged to talk about their feelings and about problems that may have arisen at school (or elsewhere). However, no child may use the circle as a means of shaming others. The emphasis is on expressing feelings rather than accusations.... [I]f a child talks about having sweets stolen or being pushed around by another child, the circle may ... offer support and talk about their own experience of being victimized.... [The circles] encourage the very complex social skill of mirroring (reflecting mood in a way which displays empathy).
>
> The norms of Circle Time talk as described or implied in this passage are evidently designed to promote discourse which is egalitarian, emotionally "literate", non-judgmental, supportive and empathetic. Conversely, they are intended to discourage more confrontational or adversarial forms of discourse. Thus a child who has been the victim of stealing or bullying may seek support from others in the circle, but s/he is specifically prohibited from confronting the thief or bully.
>
> Whatever one thinks of the discoursal (and moral) preferences embodied in the practice of Circle Time, it clearly operates with a selective notion of what constitutes "skill" in interactive spoken discourse. ("Mirroring" is encouraged; arguing, accusing and name-calling are not.)
>
> (pp. 147–148)

In this instance, however, I doubt that a compelling argument has actually been made. Neither in the excerpt quoted, nor in the work from which Cameron takes it, is it suggested that non-judgmental interaction encompasses the whole of "skill" in interactive discourse. My own interpretation is rather that "arguing, accusing and name-calling" are forms of interaction widely available to us and widely practiced. They have not, however, always proved successful as strategies for resolving conflict. It might be that, by setting up an interaction situation outside the prevailing rules of social discourse, different understandings might be made available, allowing the resolution of difficulties that had previously proved intractable. This does not take away the need to put a stop to theft and bullying at school. It does not deny the need, when appropriate, to accuse, to confront, and to punish thieves and bullies. It states that the Circle Time is not the appropriate arena for these acts. The Circle Time offers an alternative in the sense of an additional possibility. To appropriate in advance the argument that I wish to develop below, it offers a chance to augment (rather than displace) our current discoursal potential as the basis for shaping our actions.

Academic and Professional Discourse

In professional and academic domains, the default position on the generation of knowledge is that it is produced by argument, by disagreement, and by debate. This position is asserted in the generally accepted Popperian stance that science progresses not so much by proof as by disproof and by the displacement of earlier theories by more powerful ones; it is noted as fundamental in move-based genre analyses (e.g., Swales, 1990) that demonstrate that writers find a niche for the presentation of their own work by first identifying a lack or weakness in work that has gone before; it is the underlying assumption that leads writers to allow themselves quite extravagant tropes of attack on, and dismissal of, ideas other than their own, such as Widdowson (2003) on an argument of Cook's: "The learner, it would seem, is conceived of not as a human being but as a digestive system" (p. 132).

Finally, it is the attitudinal set that can boil over into something between exasperation and personal antipathy, even as expressed in the measured terms of academic journals (Lightbown, 2002): "Perhaps, in future, Sheen will devote less time to criticizing the work of others and more to publishing the kind of work that will answer the questions that are important to him" (p. 534).

In short, the academic community has a long-term investment in the proposition that a good idea will find a worthy champion and that one's thinking is sharpened in challenge and response. This investment pays a perfectly satisfactory dividend, as Brumfit (2001), for example, warmly acknowledges "The debt I owe to past and present students and colleagues is immeasurable, both for their willingness to argue and force me to clarify, and for their persistently motivating insistence on the central role of language in the education process" (p. xv).

However (a signal that this argument now turns in order to establish its own niche), accepting the centrality of rational debate and disagreement to our discourse of inquiry is not the same thing as committing ourselves to it in an exclusive way, at all times, for all purposes. Let us admit that, at least in principle, rationality can take other rhetorical forms. Rigor in thought and discipline in speech are not confined to disputation. The experience that drives the work referred to in this chapter is that truth can be sought, and knowledge created, in interaction without disagreement. In this sense, the work is a domain-specific response to Tannen's call. We can invest our language awareness and our creativity in the enhancement of our discourse of inquiry emphatically not by replacing argument, but by extending our repertoire of interactive ability. I hope, therefore, *not* to be understood as attempting to argue against the importance of robust discussion and critique. I *do* want to argue that restricting ourselves to such styles is an unnecessary limitation of our potential.

Non-judgmental Approaches

The key source from which the ideas and argumentation of this chapter arise is the work of Carl Rogers, emerging in response to the hypothesis that he first proposed for consideration in 1951: "that the major barrier to mutual interpersonal communication is our very natural tendency to judge, to evaluate, to approve or disapprove, the statement of the other person, or the other group" (as cited in Teich, 1992, p. 28).

As well as being a barrier to communication, Rogers (1969; Rogers & Freiburg, 1994) argued that such evaluation was also a barrier to education and learning in general. In the field of TESOL, we have become familiar with adaptations of Rogers' thinking through Curran's Community Language Learning (Curran, 1972, 1976; Rardin, Tranel, Tirone, & Green, 1988). This work was also memorably brought into the TESOL mainstream by Stevick (1976, 1980, 1982) in ways that helped bring out a broader, non-judgmental attitude that asserted, for example, the importance of deeper human values in being a teacher, without stipulating what those values should be:

> Teaching language is only one kind of teaching, and teaching and learning are only two limited aspects of being human. I therefore hope, first of all, that you will take time to sit down and read again whatever philosophical or religious writings you have found most nourishing to you.
>
> (Stevick, 1982, p. 201)

Non-judgmental attitudes and interaction styles have also proved effective in teacher education (e.g., Korthagen, 2001), particularly in the area of giving feedback after teaching observations (e.g., Freeman, 1982; Oprandy, 1999).

Axiomatic to all this work is the proposition that the person speaking has the potential to engage in their own self-development, and that this development can be facilitated by skillful and sensitive understanding. This understanding is based on a set of attitudes, drawn from Rogers, that I shall briefly gloss as:

respect: an unqualified acceptance (involving neither agreement nor disagreement) of the speaker and of what the speaker has to say;

empathy: a non-evaluative attempt to see things from the speaker's point of view, without oneself committing to that point of view;

sincerity: a commitment to place the above respect and empathy at the service of the speaker, toward the speaker's purposes, with no attempt to influence the outcomes in directions favored by the understander.

Unsurprisingly, non-judgmental discourse has proven particularly effective in the area of teacher self-development (e.g., Bailey, Curtis, & Nunan, 2001). In this field, it has provided the wellspring of the work that has proved the most stimulating in my own professional life, and which I have called *Cooperative Development*. This has been documented from early schematic attempts at devising a developmental discourse framework (Edge, 1992), to more detailed, data-based reports and analyses (Edge, 2002), and on into more sociopolitical arenas (Edge, 2006a) and online environments (Edge, 2006b). Other case studies involving this same approach can be read in Boshell (2002), Mann (2002), Stewart (2003), Boon (2003, 2005), and De Sonneville (2005, 2007). I expand on this approach briefly below in order to give an insider's view of some of the experiences involved.

In this interactive framework, Understanders organize their verbal interaction around a set of agreed moves that can also be simply characterized as follows, where no specific sequence is suggested by the listing:

Reflecting: where Understanders mirror back to Speakers what they have Understood, both in cognitive and affective terms.

Relating: where Understanders draw attention to possible relationships between elements of that they have Understood, whether these elements appear to be complementary (Thematizing) or contradictory (Challenging).

Focusing: where Understanders invite Speakers to go into more depth with regard to some element of what they have Understood.

Based on this support, Speakers commit themselves to a style of non-defensive speaking that leads them to explore their ideas and practice, to make individual discoveries, and to plan future action.

In addition to breakthroughs on individual agendas, the group reported on in Edge (2002) also experienced an increase in collegiality. This is a difficult claim to substantiate, but the following factors seem important. First, Understanders were regularly impressed and intrigued by the ideas, associations, and plans that Speakers produced when working in this way. Second, Understanders took pride and pleasure in seeing Speakers reach conclusions, make discoveries, and plan future actions that were their own, but which they may well not have found without the group's assistance. We referred to this process as a creative co-construction, in which involvement in the process is shared, but ownership of what is produced by the Speaker belongs to the Speaker. Third, by putting aside their own opinions and preferences in order better to focus on the individual Speaker, the group came to appreciate more fully individual differences that were previously only dimly perceived. With this increased understanding over time came an ability to recognize what was meant and intended beyond its idiosyncratic presentation. One person's liking for analogy, another's for extended metaphor, and yet another's taste for hyperbole might be simply annoying, but in this deliberately caring context (Noddings, 1992; Katz, Noddings, & Strike, 1999) these preferences came to be seen not as weaknesses to be condoned, but as individual strengths to be nurtured.

For those who find the work compatible, there is a unique satisfaction to be found in discovering one's next best step forward on the basis of an exploration of one's own resources that is supported by the work of colleagues who have decided to commit the time and the care required. Similarly, there is a unique satisfaction to be gained from being that kind of colleague. One of the group (of six people, who met for one hour each week) provided the following feedback on the experience:

> For me, whatever else this may be, it's a weekly demonstration that as colleagues we really do have time for each other and respect for one another. To know that at some point my colleagues are going to give five hours a week of their combined time to something I think is important enough to tell them about fills me with a sense of wonder, surprise, gratitude and, most of all, faith in what we can all do together. It's a weekly affirmation of our sense of shared responsibility and commitment.

We in the group saw the deliberate acquisition and use of this style of discourse as an important element of our general development as teacher-researchers. We felt that we had enriched our own small community and we heard echoes of Lave and Wenger's (1991) proposition that, "learning to become a legitimate participant in a community involves learning how to talk (and be silent) in the manner of full participants" (p. 105). We certainly experienced the truth of Wenger's (1998) statement that a discourse stands in a negotiable and reflexively constitutive relationship to its community of practice, and we did so in creative, pro-active terms.

This is not the place for me to expand further on this scheme and its uses. I refer interested readers to the data-based studies cited above and to my contact details.

Discourse and Community

If one accepts the point made in the previous part of this chapter regarding a reflexively constitutive relationship between discourse and community, it becomes important to articulate more precisely than I have thus far attempted what one understands the nature and function of the discourse presented here to be. Although I have grown accustomed to this work being referred to as an application of counseling, or therapeutic, discourse (see Cameron, 2002, pp. 67–82), I am by no means resigned to accepting this designation, which I find unhelpful in its associations and anyway inaccurate.

First of all, one needs to distinguish this work from those educational, medical, and managerial situations (e.g., Farr, 2003; Handal & Lauvas, 1987; Kerry & Shelton-Mayes, 1995; Sarangi & Roberts, 1999), which feature an asymmetrical counseling relationship in which the counselor is in the more powerful position (as teacher educator, mentor, manager, doctor, consultant) and may well carry ultimate responsibility for guiding or evaluating the other's progress. In Cooperative Development, the Speaker takes full and self-motivated responsibility for directions and outcomes in a way that is completely free of ends, means, or standards to be evaluated by Understanders, who function by definition as members of a peer group.

More interestingly, once guidance and evaluation have been put to one side, one must initially concede demonstrable common ground between non-directive forms of counseling (see Nelson-Jones, 2000) and our Cooperative Development work in terms of the attitudes required and the discourse moves made. Furthermore, debts to Rogers (e.g., 1980, 1992; Rogers & Freiberg, 1994) and to Egan (1986) are enthusiastically acknowledged. There is much common ground, therefore, but our professional development work operates far removed from a domain of analysts and analysands, clients and patients, counselors and therapy, deviance and recovery. There, at the risk of some oversimplification, we may assume a desire on the part of the client to conform to norms that will offer a greater possibility of happiness, norms that are to a great extent represented, and not only facilitated, by the therapist. Our professional development work seeks to facilitate individual development with no implication of the Speaker being a person with behavioral or psychological problems to solve. The work is based in Rogerian thinking along the lines that one does not have to be sick in order to get better, and we can all get better (see Teich, 1992; Barrett-Lennard, 1998), but this is not, I would submit, what is most usually understood by the idea of someone being "in counseling."

At fundamental levels of principle and philosophy, Cooperative Development is also distinct from Counseling-Learning (e.g., Curran 1972, 1976; Rardin et al., 1988), which maintains learner dependence on the role and status of the Understander/Knower, until the learner progresses to a state of independence from the Knower. Our work depends on an already independent Speaker/Knower being keen to establish some measure of interdependence among a supportive peer group.

One hopes that, to a readership of language professionals, it is not too difficult to make the argument that if, in a speech situation, one changes the setting, the attitudinal key, the participants, their relationships, and, above all, their purposes, then one is dealing with a different event. This is, therefore, not counseling.

To broaden the picture further, non-judgmental discourse of the type that we employ can be seen to play a significant role in the domains of conflict resolution (e.g., Isenhart & Spangle, 2000; Katz & Lawyer, 1993; Stewart, 1998, also the example of "Circle Time" discussed above) and of intercultural communication (e.g., Alred, Byram, & Fleming, 2003; Byram, 1997).

To pursue the point, Bredella (2003) suggests that to be intercultural is to be open to difference in ways that might seem uncomfortable, or even threatening. It is to suspend evaluation of those differences in order better to empathize with others. It is to realize that one's own taken-for-granted assumptions are as much the product of circumstance as anyone else's. It is to use this experience in order to further one's own growth in the sense of an increased ability to interact with others on the basis of an understanding of their own motivations, rather than an evaluation of them in terms of one's own norms and expectations. Having understood, having grown, in this sense, one then has to go on to make evaluative judgments to a greater or lesser extent in order to maintain a sense of identity or, if one prefers, a manageable sense of coherence among one's identities. If negative evaluation of others' ideas or actions proves unavoidable, one hopes at least for an ability to disagree with increased understanding and respect.

In the domain of professional development, our mutual agreement to employ non-judgmental discourse in specifically designated sessions allows for the development of individual ideas and plans along lines that the give-and-take of argument do not, as well as the development of mutually respectful collegiality. Outside those sessions, we return to the dominant discourses of our profession, where we may disagree with views that we have helped to facilitate, and still take pride in having supported a colleague's articulation of those views.

What we are seeking to do, therefore, is to distinguish between the specifics of counseling and the general qualities of non-judgmental discourse. Here, the work of the nineteenth-century German philosopher, Wilhelm Dilthey, is also relevant, pre-dating, as it does, modern psychology. Dilthey not only differentiated between experiential and intellectual knowing and learning (*erfahren* and *verstehen*), but also wrote on the power of articulation (*ausdrücken*) to unite these forms of knowledge and to "lift mental content from unconscious depth" (as cited in Rickman, 1988, p. 75). The contemporary Canadian philosopher, Charles Taylor (1985), has also foregrounded the importance of articulation as a process that develops what is being said in and through the saying:

> Articulations are not simply descriptions. On the contrary, articulations are attempts to formulate what is initially inchoate, or confused, or badly formulated. But this kind of formulation, or reformulation does not leave its object unchanged. To give a certain articulation is to shape our sense of what we desire or what we hold important in a certain way.
>
> (p. 36)

In our professional development work, we release this power of articulation by replacing the pressure of argument with the pressure of acceptance. In a related way, we also imply that our general professional predilection for what we might call *displacive* discourse—it is not enough for me to be right, others must also be wrong—could usefully be tempered by what we might equally well call *augmentative* discourse—a use of language that allows for the differing authentic perspectives that we all, multiply, have on the world. Our fundamental interactive response in this work is not, "Yes, but..."; it is "Yes. And?" In this way, we extend our interactive repertoire and make available more possibilities for creative thinking and action.

What one *is* dealing with, therefore, in the various uses of non-judgmental discourse that we have considered, is the facilitation of human creativity through the temporary suspension of evaluation. Steiner's (2001) work on the creative act, on making the move from nothing to something, highlights the importance of self-observation through language, along with the contemporary loss of a social habitat in which this is possible: "We are less and less trained to hear ourselves be, where such hearing may be the key condition to the creative" (p. 261).

Non-judgmental discourse can facilitate this creative process, and through it the recognition of previously unperceived coherence, the accessing of hitherto only tacit knowledge, and the drawing out of a discovery from one's explorations. It is for these reasons that non-judgmental discourse can, of course, work so powerfully in a counseling situation. To refer to this style of language use generically as "counseling discourse," however, is to confuse the superordinate term, non-judgmental discourse, with a hyponym, and thereby to muddy the waters of further discussion and exploration of our discourse possibilities by obscuring the existence of important co-hyponyms defined at the level of particular purpose, such as conflict resolution, intercultural understanding, and professional development.

Evaluation Endures

I have gone into some depth regarding different possible understandings of the term, non-judgmental discourse, because I see a certain level of specificity as essential to its appropriate use in different circumstances. One question that frequently arises in this context, and which might be seen as relating in particular to the theme of this collection is, "What happens if I try to Understand someone, but I simply cannot respect their views? What if they are racist, or sexist, for example?"

Exactly because we are not in a counseling relationship of client and therapist, the question provides its own answer. If you really cannot respect my views, as the term is defined above, then you cannot Understand me and we should break the relationship off. If I cannot, or do not wish to, empathize with your viewpoint and purposes, it would be insincere of me to pretend that I can. I may well wish to use such techniques as Reflecting in order to establish that I have indeed properly understood your position, but then if that which divides us is greater than a collegial wish to support each other in the variety of our endeavors, then we should acknowledge this and move into a more appropriate form of discourse.

Here the need for clarity, argumentation, and standing up for what one believes to be important, takes over. I remain committed to dialogue with all and anyone, but I do not attempt to deny the fact that with some people I expect to remain in fundamental disagreement and, as I have no wish to help them further their purposes, I could not offer them the support of non-judgmental discourse.

In my final analysis, I must take responsibility for my actions, and that will necessarily include an act of judgment. Let us take two examples that are already in the public domain and that might be thought relevant to the theme of this collection. If there are teacher educators in the world who approved of the killing of Professor Hitoshi Igarashi for translating the novel, *The Satanic Verses*, into Japanese, I would not expect to be able to assemble sufficient respect for their values, principles, or beliefs to wish to support them in their thinking (Edge, 1996). The same would apply to anyone committed to the use of English language teaching as a manipulative front for covert Christian evangelism (Edge, 2002, 2004; Griffith, 2004; Purgason, 2004).

And yet, even as I write those words, another voice tells me that this repugnance is a weakness that gets in my way. I know that as an Understander, I am at my best when I am most open to being changed myself. And as a good Understander, I am best equipped to help people articulate themselves clearly to themselves, as well as to me, and thus come to their best decisions. Even here, there is the prospect of what Edwards and Mauthner (2002) refer to as:

> "asymmetrical reciprocity," which means accepting that there are aspects of another person's position that we do not understand, yet are open to asking about and listening to. Asymmetrical reciprocity involves dialogue that enables each subject to understand each other across differences without reversing perspectives or identifying with each other.
>
> (p. 26f.)

It is at this point of clarity that one needs to accept that some disagreements are not misunderstandings, and that some disputes need to be faced up to and seen through. We all, I think, have a bedrock of values and beliefs, even if we call our own a foundation, and accuse those of whom we disapprove of being fundamentalists.

There is, however, a broad swathe of professional activity between such extreme cases and everyday matters of opinion and practice where I could suspend my powers of evaluation but usually do not. It is in this area that non-judgmental work of the kind I have presented operates. The extent to which it is liberating, or useful, or perhaps individually constraining, or culturally inappropriate is not, of course, a matter for argument alone, but can be judged effectively only by those who choose to take up the invitation to experience this mode of work.

In Conclusion

I am convinced, both intellectually and experientially, that the disciplined use of non-judgmental discourse offers my own community of professional practice a real opportunity to enrich our investigations by extending our discoursal repertoire. This is not an attack on the importance of debate and argument. How could it be? The persuasive effect of this piece of writing itself depends on my ability to present three mutually supporting arguments: first, an argument against the monolithic position that only an agonistic discourse of argument, debate, disagreement, and criticism can help us move our ideas forward; second, an argument against the categorization of the type of developmental practice presented here negatively as a "discourse technology," or inaccurately as "an application of counseling"; and, third, an argument *for* the creative operationalization of the discoursal awareness that we do have available to us, and according to the use of which we ossify, vegetate, or develop.

When I return, with this conviction, to the broader social themes that I raised earlier in this chapter, it seems clear to me that we should heed both Cameron's warning about manipulative pseudo-communication and Tannen's warning about the limitations of argument. Unsurprisingly, our preferred response should not be to side with one or the other in blanket fashion, but rather, more subtly, to look closely at which forms of discourse can be beneficial to us under which circumstances. My own position is that it would be unnecessarily wasteful to ignore the positive potential contribution of sincerely non-judgmental discourse to the facilitation of human creativity, across a range of activities, merely because we can identify examples of the fraudulent misuse of insincere imitations, or because we must sometimes accept the reality of sincere dispute. In this sense, I accept the legitimacy of the challenge of Tannen's with which I began this chapter, and find in the aware use of non-judgmental discourse one way to meet that challenge.

With regard to communication concerning the role of religious belief as motivation for, content of, or agenda in language teaching, the disciplined adoption of non-judgmental discourse could help us to understand each other better, to learn from each other, and to know where disagreement is sincerely necessary, beyond the rhetorical devices of clever argument.

References

Alred, G., Byram, M., & Fleming, M. (Eds.). (2003). *Intercultural experience and education.* Clevedon, UK: Multicultural Matters.

Bailey, K., Curtis, A., & Nunan, D. (2001). *Pursuing professional development: The self as source.* Boston: Heinle & Heinle.

Barrett-Lennard, G. (1998). *Carl Roger's helping system: Journey and substance.* London: Sage.

Boon, A. (2003). On the road to teacher development: Awareness, discovery and action. *Language Teacher, 27*(12), 3–7.

Boon, A. (2005). Is there anybody out there? Instant messenger cooperative development. *Essential Teacher, 2*(2), 38–41.

Boshell, M. (2002). What I learned from giving quiet children space. In K. Johnson, & P. Golombek (Eds.), *Teachers' narrative inquiry as professional development* (pp. 180–194). Cambridge, UK: Cambridge University Press.

Bredella, L. (2003). What does it mean to be intercultural? In G. Alred, M. Byram, & M. Fleming (Eds.), *Intercultural experience and education* (pp. 225–239). Clevedon, UK: Multicultural Matters.

Brumfit, C. (2001). *Individual freedom in language teaching.* Oxford, UK: Oxford University Press.

Byram, M. (1997). *Teaching and assessing intercultural communicative competence.* Clevedon: Multilingual Matters.

Cameron, D. (2000). *Good to talk? Living and working in a communication culture.* London: Sage.

Cameron, D. (2002). Globalisation and the teaching of "communication skills." In D. Block, & D. Cameron (Eds.), *Globalisation and language teaching* (pp. 67–82). London: Routledge.

Curran, C. (1972). *Counselling-learning: A whole-person model for education.* Apple River, IL: Apple River Press.

Curran, C. (1976). *Counselling-Learning in second languages.* Apple River, IL: Apple River Press.

De Sonneville, J. (2005). Do I understand you? Cooperative development. *English Teaching Matters, 6*(1), 28–30.

De Sonneville, J. (2007). "Acknowledgement" as a key in teacher learning. *ELT Journal, 61*(1), 55–62.

Edge, J. (1992). *Cooperative development.* Harlow, UK: Longman.

Edge, J. (1996). Cross-cultural paradoxes in a profession of values. *TESOL Quarterly, 30*(1), 9–30.

Edge, J. (2002). *Continuing cooperative development: A discourse framework for individuals as colleagues.* Ann Arbor: University of Michigan Press.

Edge, J. (2004). Of displacive and augmentative discourse, new enemies and old doubts. *TESOL Quarterly, 38*(4), 717–721.

Edge, J. (2006a). Non-judgmental discourse: A role and roles. In J. Edge (Ed.), *(Re-) locating TESOL in an age of empire* (pp. 104–118). London: Palgrave Macmillan.

Edge, J. (2006b). Computer-mediated cooperative development: Non-judgmental discourse in online environments. *Language Teaching Research, 10*(2), 205–227.

Edwards, R., & Mauthner, M. (2002). Ethics and feminist research: Theory and practice. In M. Mauthner, M. Birch, J. Jessop, & T. Miller (Eds.), *Ethics in qualitative research* (pp. 14–31). London: Sage.

Egan, R. (1986). *The skilled helper* (3rd ed.). Belmont, CA: Wadsworth.

Fairclough, N. (1992). *Discourse and social change.* Cambridge, UK: Polity Press.

Farr, F. (2003). Engaged listenership in spoken academic discourse: The case of student–tutor meetings. *Journal of English for Academic Purposes, 2*(1), 67–85.

Freeman, D. (1982). Observing teachers: Three approaches to in-service training and development. *TESOL Quarterly, 16*(1), 21–28.

Griffith, T. (2004). Unless a grain of wheat.... *TESOL Quarterly, 38*(4), 714–716.

Handal, G., & Lauvas, P. (1987). *Promoting reflective teaching: Supervision in action.* Milton Keynes, UK: Open University Press.

Isenhart, M., & Spangle, M. (2000). *Collaborative approaches to resolving conflict.* London: Sage.

Katz, N., & Lawyer, J. (1993). *Conflict resolution: Building bridges.* London: Sage.

Katz, M., Noddings, N., & Strike, K. (Eds.) (1999). *Justice and caring: The search for common ground in education.* New York: Teachers College Press.

Kerry, T., & Shelton-Mayes, A. (Eds.) (1995). *Issues in mentoring.* London: Routledge.

Korthagen, F. (2001). *Linking practice and theory: The pedagogy of realistic teacher education.* Mahwah, NJ: Erlbaum.

Lave, J., & Wenger, E. (1991). *Situated learning: Legitimate peripheral participation.* Cambridge, UK: Cambridge University Press.

Lightbown, P. (2002). The role of SLA research in L2 teaching: Reply to Sheen. *Applied Linguistics, 23*(4), 529–535.

Mann, S. (2002). Talking ourselves into understanding. In K. Johnson, & P. Golombek (Eds.), *Teachers' narrative inquiry as professional development* (pp. 195–209). Cambridge, UK: Cambridge University Press.

Nelson-Jones, R. (2000). *Introduction to counseling skills.* London: Sage.

Noddings, N. (1992). *The challenge to care in schools: An alternative approach to education.* New York: Teachers College Press.

Oprandy, R. (1999). Making personal connections to teaching. In J. Gebhard, & R. Oprandy (Eds.), *Language teaching awareness: A guide to exploring beliefs and practices* (pp. 122–145). Cambridge, UK: Cambridge University Press.

Phillips, A. (1998). *Communication: A key skill for education.* London: BT Forum.

Purgason, K. (2004). A clearer picture of the "Servants of the Lord." *TESOL Quarterly, 38*(4), 711–713.

Rardin, J., Tranel, D., Tirone, P., & Green, B. (1988). *Education in a new dimension: The counselling-learning approach to community language learning.* East Dubuque, IL: Counselling-Learning Publications.

Rickman, H. (1988). *Dilthey today: A critical appraisal of the contemporary relevance of his work.* London: Greenwood.

Rogers, C. (1969). *Freedom to learn.* Columbus, OH: Merrill.

Rogers, C. (1980). *A way of being.* Boston: Houghton Mifflin.

Rogers, C. (1992). On communication: Its blocking and its facilitation. In N. Teich (Ed.), *Rogerian perspectives: Collaborative rhetoric for oral and written communication.* Norwood, NJ: Ablex.

Rogers, C., & Freiberg, H. (1994). *Freedom to learn* (3rd ed.). New York: Macmillan College Publishing.

Sarangi, S., & Roberts, C. (Eds.) (1999). *Talk, work and institutional order: Discourse in medical, mediation and management settings.* Berlin, Germany: Mouton de Gruyter.

Steiner, G. (2001). *Grammars of creation.* London: Faber & Faber.

Steinhardt, P. (2003). The cyclic universe. In J. Brockman (Ed.), *The new humanists* (pp. 298–311). New York: Barnes and Noble.

Stevick, E. (1976). *Memory, meaning and method.* Rowley, MA: Newbury House.

Stevick, E. (1980). *Teaching languages: A way and ways.* Rowley, MA: Newbury House.

Stevick, E. (1982). *Teaching and learning languages.* Cambridge, UK: Cambridge University Press.

Stewart, S. (1998). *Conflict resolution: A foundation guide.* Winchester, UK: Waterside.

Stewart, T. (2003). Insights into the interplay of learner autonomy and teacher development. In A. Barfield, & M. Nix (Eds.), *Autonomy you ask!* (pp. 41–52). Tokyo: JALT Learner Development SIG.

Swales, J. (1990). *Genre analysis.* Oxford, UK: Oxford University Press.

Tannen, D. (1998). *The argument culture.* London: Virago.

Taylor, C. (1985). *Human agency and language.* Cambridge: Cambridge University Press.

Teich, N. (Ed.) (1992). *Rogerian perspectives: Collaborative rhetoric for oral and written communication.* Norwood, NJ: Ablex.

Wenger, E. (1998). *Communities of practice: Learning, meaning and identity.* Cambridge, UK: Cambridge University Press.

Wheelwright, P. (1959). *Heraclitus.* Princeton, NJ: Princeton University Press.

Widdowson, H. (2003). *Defining issues in language teaching.* Oxford, UK: Oxford University Press.

3 Is Dialogue Possible?

Challenges to Evangelicals and Non-Evangelicals in English Language Teaching

Bill Johnston

For six years now, both alone and with my colleague Manka Varghese of the University of Washington, I have been conducting research on evangelical Christians working in English language teaching. This research has led to Christian-affiliated colleges training English teachers; to an evangelical Christian literature largely unfamiliar to those outside the evangelical community; to the past, and the history of both evangelical and non-evangelical Christian mission work worldwide; and, perhaps most enlightening of all, to innumerable, fascinating conversations with evangelicals and non-evangelicals alike around the subject of religious beliefs and their place in the lives and work of English teachers around the world.

The non-evangelicals I have spoken to tend to be fascinated when the extent and nature of evangelical Christian involvement in TESOL is revealed. The evangelicals, in turn, have frequently expressed their approval of inquiry into the intersection between their religious beliefs and their work. Conference presentations I have given, usually with Manka Varghese, have always provoked lively discussion and debate involving both groups.

Yet if I am to be honest, I am still skeptical of the extent to which these discussions constitute genuine dialogue. In the most extensive published report on our work (Varghese & Johnston, 2007), Varghese and I raise doubts about whether dialogue between evangelicals and non-evangelicals is in fact possible. We argue that the underlying assumptions of both sides are so radically different and mutually incompatible that it's extremely hard to envision how dialogue can take place. Nevertheless, as the preceding paragraphs indicate, in a great number of cases individuals on both sides of the divide have in fact proved willing to talk with one another, and this is a very hopeful sign. The present book is the perfect illustration of this goodwill.

In my chapter I'd like to pursue this line of thought and to consider what it would take to make proper dialogue possible. It seems to me that if dialogue is indeed to be enabled, both sides must take certain steps. I present these steps in the form of challenges to both evangelicals and non-evangelicals. I must warn you that at times my tone in addressing both sides will be harsh; I feel I have earned the right to speak in this way. The purpose of my harshness is not to alienate or offend, but to stimulate and invigorate thinking. It seems to me that both sides have lapsed into certain set patterns of thinking and speaking, and that a rude awakening from this state is necessary if we are to be able to talk to one another.

This chapter will take the form of three challenges presented to evangelical Christians, and three challenges presented to non-evangelicals. These challenges concern changes of thinking and of acting that I believe to be essential if we are truly to be able to enter into dialogue. Before this, however, I'd like to spend a few moments considering what I mean by dialogue and why dialogue is necessary in a case such as this one.

The Nature and Uses of Dialogue

Dialogue is one of those notions that everyone intuitively understands. But in the present context, its meaning is not entirely obvious, and needs to be made clear and explicit. The word "dialogue" has at least two distinct and separate realms of meaning. In many educational contexts, it refers to what takes place when students and teachers have a forum—spoken or written—in which to express their own views, tell their own stories, and raise their own questions, and to encounter and listen to those of others (see e.g., Burbules, 1993). In this context, true dialogue serves the dual function of giving participants voice and allowing exposure to the voices of others, leading to the mutual shaping of ideas and views. This sort of exchange might be called *exploratory dialogue.*

Yet in the case of the divide between evangelicals and non-evangelicals, this is not exactly what we have in mind when we talk about dialogue. In this context, the notion of dialogue rather recalls the kind of dialogue between separate ethnic communities, for example, or between opposing political parties in a parliament. In this dialogue, the intention is not primarily to change the beliefs of the other side—in terms of their public faces, both sides are often too entrenched in their positions to be truly open to change—but to try to make the other side understand how things look from a different perspective. Such dialogue often initially concerns itself with overcoming misconceptions and prejudices on either side. This kind of dialogue might be called *conciliatory dialogue.* This is the kind of dialogue I am envisioning in this chapter.

It occurred to me as I was thinking about this chapter that some might question not only whether dialogue is possible, but also whether it is necessary. After all, evangelical Christians have been around in TESOL for a long time without this fact precipitating a crisis. Could the two groups not simply continue to exist alongside one another, one largely ignorant of the other? Why should we need to talk to one another?

In my view, dialogue really is needed. I have several reasons for saying this. First, the research I have conducted over the last few years has uncovered an extraordinary level of ignorance and mistrust on either side. We surely cannot be indifferent to this antagonism at the heart of our professional world. Second, developments in the outside world have placed the intersection of English teaching and evangelical mission work at center stage; in the present day, it is no longer possible to ignore the fact of our field's involvement in politics, and evangelical Christianity forms a major part of that involvement. Last, for me personally the question of the relationship between one's religious beliefs and one's work as a teacher lies at the very heart of the moral dimension of teaching; though the matter has been ignored for a very long time, now that moral perspectives on education have finally been acknowledged it is crucial to address this issue, with a particular emphasis on the need for teachers and teacher educators to know and understand the various beliefs of their students and colleagues.

For these three reasons, then, it seems to me that is it indeed vital to attempt dialogue. Yet as mentioned above, in order to do so both sides must take certain steps. It is these steps that I lay out in the rest of the present chapter. I have formulated my suggestions in the form of three challenges presented to the evangelical Christian community in TESOL, and three challenges to "non-evangelicals," a term intended to include a wide range of identities including members of other non-evangelical Christian denominations, those of other faiths, and atheists.

Challenges to Evangelical Christians

Here, I will address evangelical Christians in TESOL. I have three challenges to them, as follows.

Stop Hiding

From a non-evangelical perspective, there is something furtive about the behavior of evangelicals in TESOL. I'm not suggesting that this is deliberate; but I do think that evangelicals must acknowledge this perception and realize that it is not groundless.

What do I mean by "furtive?" I mean that evangelical life in TESOL takes place off the radar screen of non-evangelical TESOL. Its books are put out by specialist publishers that do not exhibit at our conventions—Don Snow's *English teaching as Christian mission: An applied theology* (2001), for example, was published by Herald Press, a Mennonite publishing house, while Smith and Carvill's (2000) *The gift of the stranger: Faith, hospitality, and foreign language learning* was brought out by Eerdmans, another religious publisher. The evangelical language teaching world has its own journal publications, such as the *Journal of Christianity and Foreign Languages*, issued by the North American Christian Foreign Language Association. It has its own university training programs. Even at the TESOL Convention, there exists a separate evangelical program within the regular program, whose identity, though it is not a secret, is de facto known only to other evangelicals (Varghese & Johnston, 2007).

Of course, part of the fault lies with non-evangelicals for not taking the trouble to look at, or for, the kind of literature and professional activity referred to here. Nevertheless, the above-mentioned factors make this a literature search unlike those we normally engage in; this literature does not come up on ERIC, nor can it be found by perusing the catalogs of our usual publishers, or browsing through the book exhibits at professional conferences. All this produces a sense that there is something systematic about the concealment of an alternative discourse. I used the word "furtive" above because it seems to me further that an element of hesitancy or even embarrassment can be detected in the way the evangelical world imagines its own discourses potentially entering the professional discourse of TESOL. This sense is compounded by the fact that the few times this has happened, in each case it has been in response to critical articles by non-evangelicals—I'm thinking of Edge's (1996) piece in *TESOL Matters*, to which Stevick (1996) responded, and Edge's more recent (2003) article on the relationship of evangelical Christianity to U.S. neo-imperialism, which also prompted responses from evangelicals (Griffith, 2004; Purgason, 2004). To the best of my knowledge, the present book represents the first proactive attempt by the evangelical world to engage with the field as a whole on the latter's turf.

I acknowledge too that fear of ridicule and of not being taken seriously may partially motivate evangelicals' unwillingness to show their face publicly to non-evangelicals. Such reactions are certainly a common feature of non-evangelical responses to evangelical discourse (see below for more on this subject).

Nevertheless, the net result cannot be denied. The factors outlined above together produce an abiding impression that evangelicals are at best reluctant to appear in public, at worst actually hiding. I believe that evangelicals must acknowledge that this perception is real even if it is mistaken. And they must recognize that dialogue is not possible if they will not participate in it.

Acknowledge Who You Are in Bed With

It is an undeniable fact that in the public imagination, in the realm of politics the evangelical movement is primarily associated with the so-called Christian Right. In the 1970s, evangelical Christian activists took a leaf from the book of the Civil Rights movement and entered the political arena as a conservative force. Since then, through lobbying organizations such as Jerry Falwell's Moral Majority they have remained a major influence on the American political scene—and thus on world politics. Mamdani (2004), for example, describes Falwell's backing of the apartheid regime in South Africa (p. 93) and Pat Robertson's support for the brutal Contra counter-revolution in Nicaragua (p. 110), both in the early 1980s. The influence of political evangelism (to adapt a phrase from Mamdani) continues to gather strength, not least because George W. Bush, US president at the time this chapter was written, is himself a born-again Christian.

Documentation of conservative evangelical involvement in national and world politics is certainly not news; nor is this the place to detail it. It is in fact an ever more prominent feature of American politics, and interested readers will have no problem finding extensive resources on the topic (see, for example, some of the references in Edge, 2004).

I will emphasize only one more aspect of the work of the Christian Right—that, as well as being conservative, it is also frequently racist (as in Falwell's support of apartheid), anti-Semitic, profoundly xenophobic, and hostile to women's rights.

The point I wish to make here is this: regrettably, all evangelicals are tarred with the brush of the Christian Right, just as any American traveling abroad these days is tarred with the brush of U.S. neo-imperialism. I am well aware that not all evangelicals have conservative beliefs or support the Bush administration; I imagine that very few if any evangelicals in TESOL would consider themselves xenophobic, anti-Semitic, or misogynistic. Nevertheless, these are the associations that membership in evangelical churches carries in the minds of non-evangelicals.

I believe that if dialogue is to be rendered possible, it is vital that evangelicals who are not aligned with the Christian Right make a concerted, sustained, and public effort to distance themselves from this lobby. In my travels in the Middle East, Central Asia, and Europe since 9/11 and especially since the invasion of Iraq, I have had repeatedly to explain to non-Americans both publicly and privately that I do not support the neo-imperialist ambitions of the Bush administration, and that furthermore a significant portion of the American public shares my views. In parallel fashion, if evangelicals in TESOL wish to dissociate themselves from their conservative fellow-worshipers, they must do so openly and unambiguously. This is not a simple matter of guilt by association, nor of collective responsibility: A great many of the evangelical churches (in the sense both of individual churches and of national organizations) are right-leaning in nature, and, even setting aside the excesses of the Pat Robertsons and Jerry Falwells, the connection between conservatism and evangelical Christianity is a powerful one that operates at many levels. Furthermore, there is no doubt about the involvement of many evangelical organizations in the neo-imperialist agenda (see Edge, 2003). If you do not wish to be seen as concurring with this worldview, you must say so clearly and publicly.

Admit That the Other Side May Sometimes be Right

In reflecting on his own discursive skirmishes with evangelicals, Edge (2004) has pointed out the dangers of what he calls "displacive discourse" (p. 717)—the confrontational, thrust-and-parry style of discussion that tends to dominate in academic exchanges. Under such conditions it's extremely hard to be able to pause for a moment, look at one's interlocutor and say: "You know what, you have a good point there." But this is the very essence of conciliatory dialogue—to see things from the other's perspective and occasionally, occasionally, acknowledge that she or he is right. And this is what is needed for dialogue between evangelicals and non-evangelicals.

Much of what we're talking about boils down to belief, and it's impossible to establish for sure which side if either is in the right. But some matters are not really debatable; and it seems to me that it would help the dialogue if evangelicals would recognize some of these facts. (Later on I will make a similar appeal to non-evangelicals.)

I can think of at least three examples of "issues" between evangelicals and non-evangelicals about which there is not a lot of doubt. The first is the association of the evangelical movement with ominous right-wing ideologies, as discussed in the previous part of the chapter. The second is the fact that at bottom, evangelical Christianity aims at conversion; the Great Commission represents a goal shared explicitly or implicitly by the vast majority of evangelicals. Some evangelicals believe in pursuing this goal aggressively and overtly; others prefer the approach of "planting seeds" and allowing potential converts to reach their own conclusions. But, ultimately, evangelical Christianity does not allow for the possibility that members of other faiths would be better off retaining their own religious beliefs and rejecting Christianity. I believe that this fact has significant repercussions for the extent to which evangelical Christianity can claim to embrace other cultures and values.

Third, it is undeniable that the practice of much evangelical Christianity is bound up with politics and business at least as much as it is with religious beliefs. Certainly, the unending stream of solicitation from televangelists bespeaks a decidedly materialistic approach to religious activity. *The Economist* (Onward Christian shoppers, 2005) recently reported that the market in "religious products" was worth $8.6 billion in 2003. Someone is benefiting from this trade, and in many cases the beneficiaries are churches, organizations, and individuals within the evangelical community.

As for the politics, a case in point is the so-called "debate" over intelligent design, which has made the United States the mockery of the civilized world. It seems to me blindingly obvious that whatever one's religious affiliation, any intelligent person (if you pardon the choice of words) can see that in fact there is absolutely no debate here, and that the whole matter is a discursive fabrication of political evangelism to further its political interests.

One of the fundamental prerequisites for dialogue is for both sides to agree on at least certain points. It seems to me that in any reasonable discussion the issues brought up here are not debatable. In the following part of the chapter, as you will see, I will suggest parallel points that I believe non-evangelicals in turn must accept in the same spirit.

Challenges to Non-Evangelicals

Here I will be talking, as it were, to myself, and to others like me who are not evangelical Christians—for that reason I shall occasionally use the first person.

Do Not Essentialize

One of the most important things that has been learned from discussions about identity and discourse in recent years is that the practice of essentializing groups of people is fundamentally wrong. In the field of TESOL this has emerged, for example, in discussions of "Asian learners," who are said to be passive, unwilling to talk, overly obedient, and so on (e.g., Kubota, 2001, 2002; Littlewood, 2000). Such generalizations are worse than mistaken—they are dehumanizing, in the sense that they reduce individual human beings to small collections of stereotypical traits. Essentializing practices of this kind deny both the personhood and the agency of those they categorize. Thanks to the work of scholars and writers such as those mentioned, we have learned to question these kinds of generalization, and to be constantly on our guard when such "explanations" of behavior and psychology are invoked—one thinks, for example, of the essentializing practices of many politicians and political writers (not all of whom are conservative) in discussing the so-called link between terrorism and Islam. (For a devastating refutation of this link, see Mamdani, 2004.)

Yet for all our willingness to challenge and discard prejudicial and previously unquestioned generalizations about Asians, women, Muslims, and so on, we continue to essentialize evangelical Christians. And when I say "we," that's exactly what I mean. This was brought home to me in the reviews of the first version of Varghese and Johnston (2007) when it was submitted to *TESOL Quarterly*. Though Varghese and I had tried our best to keep the discussion at the level of recognizable human beings, the reviewers pointed out in a number of places that we fell back into essentializing ways of thinking, making statements about "evangelicals" that were supposed to apply to all evangelicals regardless.

Part of the problem lies in a profound ignorance amongst non-evangelicals of the wide spectrum of evangelical beliefs and doctrines. Perhaps most egregiously, non-evangelicals have an abiding tendency to think of all evangelicals as fundamentalists; in fact, fundamentalist Christians form only a small minority of the evangelical community, and they are not strongly represented in TESOL. Along the same lines, as discussed above, non-evangelicals associate evangelical Christians with the right-wing politics of Pat Robertson, the Moral Majority, and so on; this is equally misinformed, and has the effect of denying the existence of powerful liberal lobbies in various evangelical organizations.

Beyond doctrinal and political differences, though, essentializing evangelicals closes the minds of non-evangelicals to two crucial things. First, it fails to acknowledge that any given evangelical is a unique and uniquely thinking individual who is quite capable of doubt, of weighing evidence, and of forming her or his own opinions and views that may differ in any number of ways from doctrinal positions. Second, it ignores the very vigorous debate raging within evangelical circles (see e.g., Marsden, 1997; Noll, 1994; Wallis, 2005), which in fact addresses many of the concerns that non-evangelicals have concerning evangelical Christianity. In this regard, the parallel with Islam is striking—here too, the essentializing practices of many Western political discourses are only able to exist by denying the personhood of individual Muslims and by ignoring the extensive debates going on in Muslim circles concerning what Mamdani (2004) calls "political Islam."

If non-evangelicals are to commit to dialogue, they must recognize their persistent and prejudicial tendency to essentialize the evangelical Christian Other, and to acknowledge the rich and complex face of the actual evangelical community.

Do Not Dismiss

Each academic year, at the beginning of the fall semester my department holds an informal orientation session for incoming students. At some point, we ask each new student to briefly introduce herself or himself. A couple of years ago, one Korean student took the opportunity to inform us that a few years earlier he had met Jesus Christ, and that Jesus had guided him to come to the United States and pursue a graduate degree in English teaching.

The reaction of my colleagues, and of many people to whom I have mentioned this incident, was dismissive. They discounted this student's pronouncement with a tut, a sigh, an ironic smile. I confess that I shared this response.

I mention this story because it is representative of most non-evangelical reactions to encounters with evangelical utterances of this kind. At one level, such responses are understandable. The fact is that pronouncements such as that uttered by the Korean student are profoundly alien to us non-evangelicals. They represent a way of speaking and of thinking that is the absolute opposite of our own preferred speech and thought, in which, for example, one keeps one's religious convictions to oneself.

Yet it seems to me that such an explanation does not justify dismissing what the student said. Such a dismissal extends not just to his words on that occasion, but by implication to the student himself as a person. It was certainly true that as a result of this incident, the student acquired a certain reputation, or perhaps identity, in the department; we all remembered him. In an advising session with me he repeated his explanation of why he had joined the program, though I never personally heard him go beyond this. Yet by this point he had been effectively stigmatized in the department.

At one level, I would argue that little actual harm was done. The student gave no indication that he was hesitant to tell his story; quite the contrary, he continued to do so openly and confidently. Nor did his declarations affect the way he was treated in the program.

At another level, though, we do ourselves a profound disservice by our dismissal of evangelicals. Our entire training in linguistics, anthropology, ethnography, and cross-cultural relations has taught us that "ordinary" people find such encounters disturbing because they cannot understand the Other and thus stigmatize or essentialize them; but that the response of thinking academics and intellectuals should be instead to try and understand the Other and to be able to present her or his worldview to members of our own communities. This is the essence of the kind of ethnographic work proposed by Geertz (1973) and many others. The watchword has always been: make the familiar strange, and the strange familiar. Beneath a certain technical exhortation, there is a moral message here—that other belief systems, while strange, deserve respect and sustained inquiry, and that this is the job of the scholar.

It seems to me that in dismissing evangelicals, we non-evangelicals are neglecting our duties as thinking people. Our reactions to evangelicals remind me of the eye-rolling that used to (and sometimes still does) greet comments by feminists about women's issues, and that still plague White reactions to Black claims of racism. I'm not suggesting that evangelicals can be considered an oppressed or underprivileged group. My focus is the stance that non-evangelicals take in respect to them. This dismissive response is unworthy of us. Do we respond in the same way when one of our students mentions Allah or Buddha? Are we afraid that we might accidentally be converted? In any case, for dialogue to be possible, it behooves us to approach evangelicals with the same respect and openness that mark our encounters with people from other cultures and faiths. No dialogue is possible if one side refuses to take the other seriously.

Admit That the Other Side May Sometimes be Right

In the preceding part of this chapter, I called on evangelicals to set aside for a moment the antagonistic style of discourse to which we academics have become accustomed, and to open up a possibility for occasionally acknowledging that the other side may be right. Here, I make the same appeal to non-evangelicals. As with the previous appeal, recognizing that the evangelicals sometimes have a good point is not tantamount to handing the world over to them or, heaven forbid, opening oneself to conversion. It is, however, a necessary precondition to the possibility of dialogue.

Admitting that evangelicals may sometimes be right will stick in the craw of many non-evangelicals. Many of us find evangelical discourse so profoundly alienating (see the example of the Korean student cited above) that it is hard to see where we might agree. Yet there do seem to be a few areas at least where, as was the case above, the facts are really beyond discussion.

For example, it's simply a fact that evangelical faith is being embraced by unprecedented numbers all around the world. The number of Christians in the world has increased from 1.2 billion in 1970 to two billion in 2000, and it is primarily the evangelical churches that have seen growth in members, while the congregations of traditional denominations are shrinking (see references in Varghese & Johnston, 2007). What are we non-evangelicals to think about these figures? Perhaps we could simply dismiss the fact by saying that all these millions of thinking adult human beings are deluded, or are simply out for a better life, or to make friends, or whatever. But this would seem to be a colossal and trivial generalization of the kind that, as mentioned above, in other contexts we have rightly learned to be wary of. It seems to me a more reasonable and open-minded approach to think that maybe there is something in this.

Second, while one might be skeptical of the business aspects of the megachurches that have emerged in the last few years in the United States, it is also undeniable that they, and many smaller churches, frequently provide a sense of community, and actual social services such as child care, that their members would not otherwise have. The same is true of many of the evangelical churches in developing countries (Cox, 1993). Once again, such phenomena cannot be dismissed lightly. We non-evangelicals must acknowledge such positive aspects of the work of evangelical churches.

For some reason, the idea of conversion is particularly distasteful to many non-evangelicals. Yet the fact is that across the world, millions of people do convert, and many appear to be the better for it. I find it indefensible to dismiss people in such large numbers. We must take them, their beliefs, their agency, and their actions seriously if we truly wish to engage in dialogue.

Conclusion

The more I investigate the world of evangelical Christianity in the United States, the more I'm struck by the impression that there are two different countries living side by side, one largely unaware of the other. Evangelical Christians partake of the life of the rest of their country; yet at the same time they have their own schools, universities, literature, bookstores, popular music, television—in a word, an entirely separate culture. To a significant extent, this situation is replicated within the field of TESOL. Under such conditions, dialogue is certainly not easy.

Nevertheless, for the reasons stated above I believe that dialogue is essential. Otherwise, we run the risks outlined in this chapter—risks of hostility and dismissal based largely on ignorance, stereotyping, and distrust. I believe that such a failure would be unworthy of a profession founded on principles of openness, acceptance, and willingness to learn and to strive to understand alternative worldviews.

I wish to make it clear that I personally remain very skeptical toward the evangelical project in TESOL. However, I think the only way to address this issue is through open and respectful dialogue. Silence, avoidance, essentializing, and dismissiveness will get us nowhere. I applaud the intent of this volume, and I call on both sides to continue to engage with one another in the ways I have laid down in the present chapter.

References

Burbules, N. (1993). *Dialogue in teaching: Theory and practice.* New York: Teachers College Press.

Cox, H. (1993). *Fire from Heaven: The rise of pentecostal spirituality and the reshaping of religion in the twenty-first century.* Cambridge, MA: Di Capo Press.

Edge, J. (1996). Keeping the faith. *TESOL Matters, 6*(4), 1.

Edge, J. (2003). Imperial troopers and servants of the lord: A vision of TESOL for the 21st century. *TESOL Quarterly, 37*(4), 701–708.

Edge, J. (2004). Of displacive and augmentative discourse, new enemies and old doubts. *TESOL Quarterly, 38*(4), 717–721.

Geertz, C. (1973). *The interpretation of cultures.* New York: Basic Books.

Griffith, T. (2004). Unless a grain of wheat ... *TESOL Quarterly, 38*(4), 714–716.

Kubota, R. (2001). Discursive construction of the images of U.S. classrooms. *TESOL Quarterly, 35*(1), 9–38.

Kubota, R. (2002). The author responds: (Un)raveling racism in a nice field like TESOL. *TESOL Quarterly, 36*(1), 84–92.

Littlewood, W. (2000). Do Asian students really want to listen and obey? *English Language Teaching Journal, 54*(1), 31–36.

Mamdani, M. (2004). *Good Muslim, bad Muslim. America, the cold war, and the roots of terror.* New York: Pantheon Books.

Marsden, G. M. (1997). *The outrageous idea of Christian scholarship.* New York, Oxford: Oxford University Press.

Noll, M. (1994). *The scandal of the evangelical mind.* Grand Rapids, MI: Eerdmans.

Onward, Christian shoppers (December 3–9, 2005). *The Economist*, pp. 60, 63.

Purgason, K. B. (2004). A clearer picture of the "Servants of the Lord." *TESOL Quarterly, 38*(4), 711–713.

Smith, D. I., & Carvill, B. (2000). *The gift of the stranger: Faith, hospitality, and foreign language learning.* Grand Rapids, MI: Eerdmans.

Snow, D. B. (2001). *English teaching as Christian mission: An applied theology.* Scottsdale, PA: Herald Press.

Stevick, E. (1996). Response to Julian Edge's "Keeping the faith." *TESOL Matters, 6*(6), 1.

Varghese, M., & Johnston, B. (2007). Evangelical Christians and English language teaching. *TESOL Quarterly, 41*(1), 5–31.

Wallis, J. (2005). *God's politics: Why the right gets it wrong and the left doesn't get it.* New York: Harper San Francisco.

4 First, the Log in Our Own Eye

Missionaries and their Critics

Michael Chamberlain

> And why worry about a speck in your friend's eye when you have a log in your own? How can you think of saying, "Friend, let me help you get rid of that speck in your eye," when you can't see past the log in your own eye? Hypocrite! First get rid of the log in your own eye; then you will see well enough to deal with the speck in your friend's eye.
>
> (Luke 6:41–42, Holy Bible, New Living Translation)

I was part of the problem. That seems like the best place to start. I've participated in overseas short-term Christian missions for over a decade—as a "language tutor" in the Middle East, ESL director for a large Christian missionary organization, and trainer/supervisor of missionary teachers in Southeast Asia and Central Europe. Although I now teach in a Christian university, I studied and taught in secular environments where I was on the receiving end of religious intolerance and stereotyping against Christians. In this chapter I first examine the negative consequences of the market-driven church and its resulting pedagogical dilemmas. I then ask secular critics to consider their own ignorance of religious belief as well as their undervaluing the agency of students in making decisions regarding faith. It is my hope that by looking at our own respective faults (i.e., "removing the log from our own eye" to paraphrase Jesus), we can facilitate discussion between missionary agencies and their secular critics to encourage more professionalism and healthier pedagogy in our field.

Addressing the Christian

Leaders of missionary organizations must internalize James' warning, "Let not many of you become teachers … knowing that as such we shall incur a stricter judgment" (James 3:1). How much more strict, then, will God hold trainers of teachers? Undoubtedly, we will be held accountable for how we recruit and train as well as the conduct we encourage at home and abroad.

How We Recruit and Train—The Market-Driven Machine

One of the most scathing, yet accurate criticisms of evangelical Christianity comes not from the secularist, but from a Christian—David Wells (1993), who argues against market-driven approaches to ministry:

> Now, there is nothing wrong with entrepreneurship or organizational wizardry or public relations or television images and glossy magazines per se. The problem lies in the current evangelical inability to see how these things carry with them values that are hostile to Christian faith.... What is plainly missing, then, is *discernment*, and this has much to do with the dislocation of biblical truth from the life of the church today and much to do with the dying of its theological soul.
>
> (p. 55)

Perhaps mission agencies' frenetic speed in "filling teams" to "serve abroad" amidst competition drowns out quiet reflection necessary to hear the heart of God pertaining to our calling to be teachers. Discernment and speed seldom go hand in hand. Compare this to God's training pace:

- Moses spent 40 years tending sheep before God appointed him Deliverer.
- Joseph received his vision as a boy, but it took years of slavery and prison before God elevated him to prime minister.
- After his Damascus-road conversion, the apostle Paul studied for 3 years before public ministry.
- Even Jesus had only 3 years of public ministry out of his 33 years on earth.

This overview isn't meant to preclude youth from ministry. After all, it's to young Timothy that Paul imparts character qualifications for leadership (2 Tim. 3). The point is if we use teaching authority to establish spiritual authority, then spiritual maturity must trump arbitrary hiring timelines or set quotas. Those recruiting and sending teachers would do well to invest more resources screening recruits for character and qualifications than developing marketing campaigns recruiting adventurers at the expense of those being "served" and "saved."

An advertisement at a mission fair recruiting Christian English Teachers (CET) depicts Uncle Sam pointing straight to his reader, exclaiming: "I WANT YOU TO SAVE SOMALIA!" (The country's name is a pseudonym.) Even though the ad is a decade old, it still makes one cringe to think it was created by a major North American mission agency that should have known better. It continues:

> Currently we are teaching English as a *second* language through our educational center. We have found this to be effective because:
>
> - English is the international trade language and a world market requirement.
> - *Friendships come naturally through the English classes.*

- Our professional approach and high-profile location attract our target group.
- It establishes our credibility as an organization and provides our visas.

> ... We also seek to develop a sense of community in the classroom and treat all of our students equally and with respect—an uncommon approach according to *every* Somali's previous educational experience.
>
> (emphasis mine)

Did it occur to the mission agency that a jingoist wartime recruiter Uncle Sam, looking for "a few good men" to "save" the people of Somalia, a war-torn country with a history of US military involvement, may come off as grossly insensitive at best or imperialistic at worse? Note that the brochure unintentionally screens out the "culturally sensitive" Christians who would question the discernment of its creators.

The use of Uncle Sam also validates the assumption that the organization is recruiting Americans who, the *National Geographic-Roper 2002 Global Geographic Literacy Survey* confirms, are geographically illiterate with nearly 11% of Americans polled unable to locate the USA on a world map and 15% unable to locate either Israel or Iraq. To compound the problem, philosopher William Lane Craig (1996) notes evangelical anti-intellectualism, quoting from formal Lebanese ambassador to the US, Charles Malik, in his inaugural address to the Billy Graham Center in Wheaton, IL:

> I must be frank with you: the greatest danger confronting American evangelical Christianity is the danger of anti-intellectualism. The mind in its greatest and deepest reaches is not cared for enough ... Who among evangelicals can stand up to the great secular or naturalistic or atheistic scholars on their own terms of scholarship? Who among evangelical scholars is quoted as a normative source by the greatest secular authorities on history or philosophy or sociology or politics? Does the evangelical mode of thinking have the slightest chance of becoming the dominant mode in the great universities of Europe and America that stamp our entire civilization with their spirit and ideas?

This anti-intellectualism is a by-product of the church's adoption of market-driven values. Slimbach (2000) summarizes the logical outworking of this flaw as it relates to missions—the great gulf between the goers and the receivers in the short-term missionary enterprise:

> The majority of those occupying the least-evangelized world are characteristically poor, nonwhite, non-English-speaking women and men who live marginalized lives within multiethnic urban centers and hold collectivist cultural values and oftentimes nativist political views. Their Western counterparts, by contrast, are typically affluent, white, monolingual (in English) persons raised in homogeneous suburban communities with individualist cultural values and conservative (if not reactionary) political views. Just how

will such a gap even begin to be bridged during even a two-year mission venture? And if we can't hope to bridge it, how will short-term workers hope to genuinely encounter the host people in something other than a paternal and intrusive mode?

(p. 432)

While eighteenth-to-nineteenth-century missionary societies were fueled by career missionaries investing the best years of their lives learning other languages and cultures, many current short-term "teachers" invest comparatively little. What did it cost me on my short-term trip to Eastern Europe? Two thousand dollars, two weeks' vacation, and a weekend "training" retreat. Take away the retreat, and it costs less than a Disney cruise.

Violation of Teacher–Student Boundaries in the Classroom

Perhaps most disconcerting in the aforementioned brochure is the suggestion that "Friendships come naturally through the English classes." While I was on a mission stint in my college years, one of my "students" and I became "friends." Months later, he disclosed through a letter that he had "faked conversion" so that he could spend time with me. In his mind, "free" classes came at a cost—conversion.

Let me further explain these boundary violations. Most would concede that teacher–student dating is wrong. Teaching is not wrong in itself. Romance is not wrong in itself. However, mixing the two compromises academic integrity. Likewise: teaching is not wrong in itself. Sharing one's faith is not wrong in itself. Friendship is not wrong in itself. However, a missionary mandate to mix the three invites ramifications that amateur teachers cannot imagine.

Certainly in academia TESOL trainers may allow a certain level of "collateral damage" when sending teachers-in-training to ESL learners. We, however, try to minimize the damage by ensuring the student teacher has a mentor to guide them, lesson plans to follow, and some previous practice in implementing the actual lesson. Some agencies, however, display no qualms whatsoever—throwing 21-year olds into classrooms in war-torn Muslim countries, mandating teacher–student friendship with instruction to evangelize ... naturally ... of course ... all within (let's say) 60 days. That thought should bring us pause. If not, we may suffer from market-machine mentality.

Addressing the Secularist

While secular critics have valid criticisms of our ELT missionary enterprise, they might consider what "logs" may be blinding their perspective of reality. Their default posture that the naturalist worldview is devoid of question-begging philosophical presuppositions is highly dubious. The scope of this chapter will allow me to discuss only a few misunderstandings.

Pennycook and Coutand-Marin (2003) critique Christians of "targeting the weak" and condemn the Adult Migrant Educational Service because they target migrant Muslim women who are needy. To suggest that the migrant women who are needy are unable to "evaluate ideas in the free market" as Stevick has stated, by virtue of the fact that they are female, lonely, undereducated, and migrant, is deplorable. This is the point of Canagarajah's (1999) book, *Resisting Linguistic Imperialism in English Teaching*, in which local students successfully resist the attempts in missionary schools to impose English according to Western expectations. To suggest such students have no agency disenfranchises those who they are trying to protect. After all, as Johnston (2003) contends, "Students are agents in their own right and are not mechanistically manipulated by the teacher" (p. 65). While the article offers helpful criticism to the Christian, it is undermined by its acrimonious tone and unfounded assertions, such as its quip that one mission organization seeks to "wipe out Islam." What burden of proof should we require to make such a serious allegation against a religious group? Such a tone must be suspended to further future discussion.

Religious Reductionism

Many TESOL educators teaching in the West assume that all religions are *fundamentally* the same but *superficially* different when, in fact, Zacharias (1997) accurately asserts that "All religions are *superficially* the same but *fundamentally* different." This categorical reduction is conveniently asserted in secular societies, particularly those that are pluralistic. However, Zacharias (2000) reminds us that "to deem all beliefs equally true is sheer nonsense for the simple reason that to deny that statement would also, then, be true. But if the denial of the statement is also true, then all religions are not true." Other popular, yet indefensible, dictums uttered by cross-cultural educators include "All beliefs are products of culture." The rejoinder then is: is the statement "All beliefs are a product of culture" also then a product of culture? The point here is to simply point out that every scholar (religious and secular) has a worldview. Our worldviews contradict each other at various points, opening up the uncomfortable possibility of a disparity of validity. This logically promotes discussion and leads us to the question: should certain worldviews be silenced, promoted over others, or sterilized through reductionism in the academy?

Silencing the Discussion

My Alma Mater, a premiere cross-cultural training institute and pioneer in the field of language training, employed a different strategy in addressing religion in its required MA TESOL intercultural communications class—total avoidance. As is typical within many cross-cultural training institutes in the West, not once did we talk about, much less research, the role of religion in culture. How can one say they understand Arabic without understanding the fundamentals of Islam? The avoidance of meaningful academic discussion involving religious truth claims creates a culture of ignorance amongst those whose job it is to foster understanding. If not in the classrooms, where then can one safely explore these all-important issues? Allow me to share an example of the consequence of silencing this discussion.

Sociological Bullying—the Consequence of Silence

During closing ceremonies of a prestigious North American training event in the 1990s, world-class scholars in our field (in attempts at humor) said the following over microphones to a crowd of 100 TESOL trainees from various countries:

- "G-d damn" and "Jesus Christ"—blasphemed numerous times;
- "I'm born again!" uttered in mocking gestures;
- biblical scripture read as set-up for joke with Jesus Christ in a punchline.

Would these scholars dare read from the Koran or tell jokes involving Mohammed? Would Buddhist nirvana experiences ever be treated with as much disdain as the evangelical salvation experience? After my complaint, the event chair acknowledged wrongdoing on letterhead:

> You have reminded me that it is too easy and thoughtless to make fun of the dominant religion in one's own culture. It accomplishes nothing and it conveys a form of intolerance … Every person's cultural ethnic and religious background must be accepted as valid … [You have reminded] all of us that diversity is everywhere in all forms and behaviors.

A faculty member from the School for International Training (now SIT Graduate Institute) who witnessed the event invited me to speak of my experience at SIT's Diversity Day 1997. Why would SIT invite an evangelical to discuss the "religious oppression" of Christians in our TESOL field if it didn't legitimately exist? Are other institutions as honest about the issue?

Conclusion

I would like to conclude with reflection on the ultimate ringleader of this controversy—Christ Himself. Jesus was apolitical, absolutely pure in His motivations and sacrificial love and yet always found Himself at the center of controversy. Volf (1996) noted that "During [his] trial [before Pilate] Jesus [was] caught in the field of social forces with religious, ethnic, and political bases, all interested in maintaining and bolstering their power" (p. 264). Amidst the debate, discussion, and controversy in this book, let us not forget to investigate with clarity the teachings, claims, and person of Christ Himself. Regardless of our worldview, we can all learn from the manner in which Christ faced those opposing Him. Our frank engagement and candid disagreement does not preclude us from demonstrating respect for one another. Nor does it preclude us from removing the logs from our own eyes.

References

Canagarajah, S. (1999). *Resisting linguistic imperialism in English teaching.* Oxford, UK: Oxford University Press.

Craig, W. L. (1994). *Reasonable faith: Christian truth and apologetics.* Wheaton, IL: Crossway Books.

Johnston, B. (2003). *Values in English language teaching.* Mahwah, NJ: Lawrence Erlbaum.

Pennycook, A., & Coutand-Marin, S. (2003). Teaching as a missionary language. *Discourse: Studies in the cultural politics of education, 24*(3), 338–353.

Slimbach, R. (2000). First do no harm. *Evangelical Missions Quarterly, 36*(1), 428–441.

Volf, M. (1996). *Exclusion and embrace: A theological exploration of identity, Otherness and reconciliation.* Nashville, TN: Abingdon Press.

Wells, D. F. (1993). *No place for truth, or, whatever happened to evangelical theology.* Grand Rapids, MI: Eerdmans.

Zacharias, R. (1997). *The Harvard Veritas Forum* (Audio Series). Atlanta, GA: RZIM Ministries.

Zacharias, R. (2000). *Jesus among other Gods.* Nashville, TN: Thomas Nelson.

5 A Preliminary Survey of Christian English Language Teachers in Countries that Restrict Missionary Activity

Karen Asenavage Loptes

Discussion surrounding the issue of English teaching and missionary agendas percolates among ELT educators, but it boils over when it involves Christian English teachers (CET) in a limited access country.[1] There are many opinions about what CET do and don't do; however, empirical data is lacking and would help inform this discussion. This chapter summarizes the results of a preliminary survey I conducted among 44 CET working in countries that restrict missionary activity.

Yeoman (2002) and Pennycook and Coutand-Marin (2003) have commented on the "undercover" nature of CET who teach abroad, yet in my years of living in the Middle East, I found that most CET openly acknowledged their Christian beliefs. So the question arises, where does this portrayal of "ulterior motives" among CET come from and how prevalent is it?

The stereotype that many CET work in a "stealth" or "undercover" capacity may be due in part to how CET are constructed in discourse (Bearak, 2001; Dixon, 2005; Sachs, 2000; Yeoman, 2002). In TESOL-related publications this stereotype portrays CET as Western missionaries with an ethnocentric agenda who lack TESOL training and experience and do not respect host cultures (Edge, 2003, 2004; Johnston, 2003; Karmani & Pennycook, 2005; Pennycook & Coutand-Marin, 2003; Pennycook & Makoni, 2005; Syed, 2003; Vandrick, 2002). In my experience, this "missionary zealot" profile is true of only a small portion of CET, not the vast majority.

A few Christian TESOL educators (Griffith, 2004; Purgason, 2004a, 2004b; Snow, 2001; Stevick, 1997) have responded to this stereotype, but actual studies of CET are needed to better understand the scope and nature of CET working abroad. In June 2005, of the 882 members listed with the Christian Educators in TESOL Caucus (CETC), 137 (16%) worked overseas, with 20 (2%) in countries that restrict missionary activity. Welliver and Northcutt (2004) and Dickerson and Dow (1997) list estimates of CET who go abroad through North American churches and organizations that provide some preparation with overseas teaching opportunities. But neither account for the large and growing number of CET who are not from Western countries (Scanlon, 2004). At a Christian English Language Teachers (CELT) Conference held in Chiang Mai in January 2006, CET represented more than 10 nations. These numbers also do not account for the many CET not affiliated with mission organizations or who do not consider themselves missionaries.

The Preliminary Survey

Given the fact that this population is not easily identified or accessible, non-probability and snowball sampling were utilized (Trochim & Donnelly, 2006). I invited several CET I knew to complete a survey including members of TESOL CETC and individuals from organizations that had CET in countries that restrict missionary activity. I also asked them to forward the survey to qualified candidates. Survey-takers were restricted to those working in countries that restrict missionary activity because if CET were "undercover," they would most likely be in regions where religious activity, especially of missionaries, was monitored. Snow (2001) states that it is often possible for CET to get jobs and a work visa where Western missionaries are generally not welcome and "that this is especially true in Communist, recently ex-Communist or Muslim nations" (p. 25).

This survey has several limitations. A non-randomized sample of convenience was used, as I sought out CET I knew and teachers they knew who were teaching in countries that restricted missionary activity. The survey is in no way exhaustive or meant to provide a representative sample of the CET population. It is simply information from 44 CET, which provides some insight into how they view their role and work.

Respondents

A majority of the 44 respondents were native English speakers from Western countries (predominantly the United States). Three (7%) were nonnative English speakers (NNS), 33 (71%) were married, and 28 (64%) were women. The average age was 44.4. Of the respondents, 34 (77%) held Master's degrees in TESOL/TEFL or Linguistics, and several held doctoral degrees. Only five of the respondents held degrees that were not related to English or education. Twenty were affiliated with mission organizations and the remaining 24 respondents were not.

Where They Teach

The respondents taught in 12 countries representing eight regions: Middle East, North Africa, Africa, South Asia, Southeast Asia, the Pacific, North Asia, and Europe. Twenty-seven (61%) taught in the Middle East and North Africa. Of those surveyed, 36 (82%) indicated that the government of their host country was aware of their religious beliefs and 42 (96%) indicated that colleagues, friends, and acquaintances were aware of their religious beliefs. Respondents who worked in mostly government-run tertiary institutions totaled 28 (64%), while 14 (32%) worked in private schools, and two (4%) worked specifically in government (military) institutions. The majority taught pre-intermediate to advanced students in integrated language skills classes, some taught a variety of English for Specific Purposes (ESP) courses, and 11 were administrators.

Their Purpose

Twelve Likert-scale questions addressed the CET rationale for choosing the country in which they obtained a work visa. Thirty-nine (89%) of CET identified God's leading as a compelling reason for choosing their country of employment. The next most frequent choice of the host country was for employment opportunities. Overwhelmingly, missionary or not, 42 (95%) CET indicated that their purpose was to serve the local population. When asked if they were engaged in the actual position indicated on their visa, 40 (90%) said "yes." The same number indicated that they did not use their visa as a cover for other religious activities. The remaining 10% were not doing what their visa stated and they used teaching as a cover.

The following themes emerged in open-ended questions and will be discussed briefly below: respecting the culture, getting training and teaching well, reflecting on missionary activity, and religion in the classroom. I will discuss several of these themes below and provide teachers' comments.

Respecting the Culture

Thirty respondents (68%) described the necessity of respect for the religious beliefs of the country. A missionary CET in Indonesia stated, "The gospel should be interpreted appropriately and uniquely in each culture." A teacher from China stressed it was important to "understand the Confucian idea of relationships." Another teacher emphasized it this way: "Bend toward them and their culture, rather than waiting for them to bend to yours. This is often unconscious as we are teaching them our culture in our language."

A Pakistani nonnative English-speaking teacher cautioned about evangelism: "I am careful not to discuss my faith publicly; not to evangelize." In Afghanistan, CET stressed that, "Cultural guidelines equal Muslim guidelines." "No proselytizing. Don't insult Islam. No literature distribution." They reported, "Christian expatriates are given some freedom; proselytizing is illegal, yet sharing [one's] own belief or opinions [is] not illegal."

Getting ELT Training and Teaching Well

Many wrote about the importance of being trained to teach English. A Pakistani NNS CET stated, "A Christian's work is worship." From Egypt, a teacher stated, "Be linguistically and professionally prepared." From Iraq, a teacher said, "Be so good that they can't have complaints. Always think of things that haven't been thought of before program-wise." From the UAE a teacher noted, "If you teach you should be qualified to do so otherwise your witness is impaired."

Critical (and Noncritical) Reflection of Missionary Activity

Five (11%) missionary CET remarked specifically that their mission organizations were culturally insensitive in the way they promoted Christianity. One commented, "More research needs to be done on how the Christian church/mission is manipulating ELT." He suggested that CET should "seriously consider the ethical implications of being a member of a mission organization."

Although not directly stated, a few CET revealed that they did not think it was wrong to influence others in nations that prohibit proselytizing. One teacher stated, "Understanding how things work in that place is a critical first step before making suggestions or *pressing our own understandings*" (emphasis mine). One person stated, "Don't believe your students who tell you that you can ignore the rules, since you are an outsider. Respecting them wins you much more influence." This seems to indicate that being culturally sensitive is done to "win you much more influence."

One teacher mentioned that CET should not be "undercover" or "caught up in the hype" of being "a secret agent for Jesus," thus indicating that some CET may be doing this. She stated:

> Teach with excellence, don't compromise your teaching by overemphasizing "reaching the lost" (especially if you have signed a contract), and don't get caught up in the hype of being an undercover missionary or secret agent for Jesus, be transparent and authentic with who you are.

Another teacher scolded overly evangelically minded CET in this way:

> Don't have a scalp counting mentality; these are real people, not notches on your evangelical belt. I don't want to make learning English conditional to learning about God. I will teach and treat all of my students with equality and respect regardless of their interest in God.

This "scolding" may imply this behavior is what she has found among some CET she has encountered.

Religion in the Classroom

Respondents explained how their cultural contexts impacted teaching, learning, and the teacher–student relationship. Their students frequently inquired about their Christian identity asking honest questions about Western culture and their teacher's beliefs. However, some questions were not so innocuous and CET admitted they were unsure how to respond. They wanted to respect the culture and rules of the country, but they also wanted to talk about their lives and identities and develop honest relationships with students. A Christian teacher in Turkey indicated her understanding of power issues she had with students and stated: "Your most important relationships, as far as discussing matters of belief, should probably be colleagues, neighbors, and former students, not current students because of issues of teacher–student power differential."

A teacher in China stated, "A tension is when it is appropriate to bring up matters of faith in class." A male teacher in Egypt said, "Sometimes awkward questions arise about religion in the classroom." Another male teacher in Oman reported, "Students ask about my faith in class and I have to tell them I can't talk about such things. Sometimes I say, I'd like to answer that but I am not free in this country to talk about my religion."

A teacher in Saudi Arabia stated that he felt that he was able to discuss his faith with students but then he was subjected to students proselytizing him:

> When students ask questions about Christian beliefs and practices, I do not feel [that I am] able to talk with them for fear of possible retribution. This is not proselytizing on my part just their own curiosity, which I deflect by saying that the government of their country through the leadership of my university has instructed me not to discuss religious matters with them. On the other hand, I am subjected to open unhindered proselytizing activity by students.

Respondents also cited dilemmas involving religious topics in the curriculum. Several teachers gave examples of explaining items in student textbooks like Christian holidays or themes in literature that were counter to the majority culture or religion. An NNS South African, teaching in the Middle East, found that, "the cultural content of the English language (literature) is mostly based on the Christian background." In China, one teacher reported that she was criticized for explaining Christianity even when it related specifically to literature they were reading. One teacher spoke of purposely using holiday materials to encourage discussion of religious issues.

Conclusions

The CET in this preliminary survey expressed a sense of God's calling to work in their locations and were struggling with various religious, cultural, and ethical issues both inside and outside the classroom. These issues were inextricably related to their identities and roles as educators, Christians, and, for some, missionaries. Most of their responses revealed a sense of professionalism, integrity, and respect for the host culture, though in some cases there was an uncritical acceptance of asserting their influence on the people in the host culture.

Contrary to stereotypes, the CET in this survey were not all missionaries, nor were they all American, Western, or native English speakers. The vast majority of the CET in countries that restrict missionary activity in this survey was not working "undercover." However, it seems that some were working illegally, were not professionally trained, and used English teaching to proselytize. Two other key issues emerged as teachers' cultural understanding and assimilation increased with time spent in the host country, and in some cases teachers did not make learning the host language a priority in spite of being language educators. Also significant is the CET acknowledgment of a missionary identity separate from a Christian or English teacher identity. And finally, several CET question the ethics of some mission organizations working in countries that restrict missionary activity.

The challenge of providing information about CET working in countries that restrict religious activity and allowing them to speak has been encouraging and sobering. This preliminary survey provides some data to help clarify how CET view their identity. But the picture is by no means complete. More investigation needs to be done to explore this complex group of English language teachers. It is hoped that this study will encourage others to ask more questions, conduct research, and think deeply about CET and their impact.

Note

1. "Limited access" or "creative access" countries are terms used in missionary discourse for countries where missionaries are restricted. The less tendentious phrase "countries that restrict missionary activity" will be used from here on.

References

Bearak, B. (August 23, 2001). Religious arrests cast a pall over Afghanistan aid efforts. *New York Times*, A1.

Dickerson, L., & Dow, D. (1997). *Handbook for EFL teachers.* Wheaton, IL: Billy Graham Center, Wheaton College.

Dixon, D. N. (2005). Aid workers or evangelists, charity or conspiracy: Framing of missionary activity as a function of international political alliances. *Journal of Media and Religion, 4*(1), 13–25.

Edge, J. (2003). Imperial troopers and servants of the Lord: A vision of TESOL for the 21st century. *TESOL Quarterly, 37*(4), 701–709.

Edge, J. (2004). Of displacive and augmentative discourse, new enemies, and old doubts. *TESOL Quarterly, 38*(4), 717–721.

Griffith, T. (2004). Unless a grain of wheat. *TESOL Quarterly, 38*(4), 714–716.

Johnston, W. (2003). *Values in English language teaching.* Mahwah, NJ: Lawrence Erlbaum.

Karmani, S., & Pennycook, A. (2005). English and 9/11. *Journal of Language, Identity and Education, 4*(2), 157–172.

Pennycook, A., & Coutand-Marin, S. (2003). Teaching English as a missionary language. *Discourse: Studies in the cultural politics of education, 24*(3), 337–353.

Pennycook, A., & Makoni, S. (2005). The modern mission: The language effects of Christianity. *Journal of Language, Identity and Education, 4*(2), 137–155.

Purgason, K. (2004a). A clearer picture of "Servants of the Lord." *TESOL Quarterly, 38*(4), 711–713.

Purgason, K. (2004b). The last word. *CETC-Newsletter, 7*(1). Retrieved March 12, 2004, from www.cetesol.org.

Sachs, S. (December 31, 2000). Threats and responses: Religion: With missionaries spreading Muslims' anger is following. *New York Times*, A11.

Scanlon, C. (2004). South Korea's zealous mid-east missionaries. *BBC News.* Retrieved June 20, 2008, from http://news.bbc.co.uk/go/pr/fr/-/2/hi/asia-pacific/3690259.stm.

Snow, D. (2001). *English teaching as Christian mission: An applied theology.* Scottdale, PA: Herald Press.

Stevick, E. (1997). Response to Julian Edge's "Keeping the Faith." *TESOL Matters, 6*(6), 1.

Syed, Z. (2003). TESOL in the Gulf: the sociocultural context of English language teaching in the Gulf. *TESOL Quarterly, 37*(2), 337–341.

Trochim, W., & Donnelly, J. (2006). *The research methods knowledge base* (3rd ed.). New York: Atomic Dog/Cengage Learning.

Vandrick, S. (2002). ESL and the colonial legacy: A teacher faces her "missionary kid" past. In V. Zamel, & R. Spack (Eds.), *Enriching ESOL pedagogy* (pp. 411–422). Mahwah, NJ: Lawrence Erlbaum.

Welliver, D., & Northcutt, M. (2004). *Mission handbook: U.S. and Canadian protestant ministries.* Wheaton, IL: EMIS.

Yeoman, B. (May/June, 2002). The stealth crusade. Retrieved June 16, 2005, from www.motherjones.com/news/feature/2002/05/stealth.html.

Response

6 Is Dialogue Possible?

Anti-intellectualism, Relativism, Politics, and Linguistic Ideologies

Alastair Pennycook

The most significant theme that emerges from these chapters is a will to dialogue. And while Edge's "non-judgmental dialogue" is perhaps chimerical, we can at least see here an attempt to understand, to unpick the stereotypes, to ask "both sides" of these debates to avoid reductionist accusations. And yet I have several misgivings here: the first is that we have to have this discussion at all. As Ashis Nandy (2006) notes, after the secularity of the twentieth century, nobody expected religion to emerge from the shadows to occupy center stage at the beginning of the twenty-first century. And for many of us this is not a welcome return. Now, in the twenty-first century we are still arguing about religion? It is not that I follow Dawkin's (2006) scientific rationalist dismissal of religion (though he reveals much that is deeply foolish in religious belief), nor Hitchens' (2007) attempt to show that, as he puts it, religion poisons everything (though he does mount a strong case about the culpability of religion for so much that is distressing in human history); nor that I do not welcome discussion of spirituality, belief, philosophy, and ethics. But to have to engage with ancient organized religions in their new incarnations, with claims to the existence of an almighty being still, after so much, seems a desperate regression.

In the same way that evolutionary scientists have recently been obliged to return to old and hapless arguments invoked under the name of Intelligent Design, so I wonder why in ELT or the social sciences more broadly, we are obliged to return now to issues that surely should not have much space in current intellectual debate. For those of us who have ourselves been critics of humanism and the arrogant assumptions of European Enlightenment, it has been a sadly regressive step to have to return to much earlier debates about belief. If these can be raised to the level of discussion of values, ethics, responsibilities, cultural difference, and politics that Johnston (2003) achieves in his thoughtful book, we can move forward; but while this sinks back into the mud of faith, we are lost. And this touches on the second misgiving, which is the sheer incommensurability of the worldviews on display here. The arguments pass each other by, misunderstanding and misrepresenting each other, with little common ground to move forward.

What can we salvage from all this? Johnston's injunction for evangelicals to stop hiding, acknowledge their political complicities, and admit others may be right, and for non-evangelicals to avoid essentializations, not to dismiss others' viewpoints, and also to admit that others may be right, is a fair and reasonably balanced starting point. And he is surely right that this can only be conciliatory dialogue rather than exploratory dialogue since we are talking across too great a divide here. Loptes' attempt to balance the discussion by showing the diversity of Christian English language teachers, to "challenge the missionary stereotype of CET" is useful but is marred on several counts. Above all, the study lacks reflexivity, especially with its terminology; the use of phrases such as "limited access countries" and so on surely cannot just be used as if they were self-evident. Where respondents report their position as "Don't have a scalp counting mentality; these are real people, not notches on your evangelical belt," such statements surely speak to the bigger problem that for many CET, students are indeed notches on your evangelical belt. The phrase makes me shiver.

Clearly, however, we get a useful picture from both Loptes' and Chamberlain's studies of the pernicious work of the large missionary organizations and the need, as one respondent put it, for more research "on how the Christian church/mission is manipulating ELT." CET, this respondent continued, should "seriously consider the ethical implications of being a member of a mission organization." Perhaps most interesting is Chamberlain's attempt, like Johnston's, to produce a balanced message to both camps. He is certainly to be commended for his critique of missionary activity. If such work could open the gates to critical, reflexive, work by CET, we might be able to move forward. Yet Chamberlain's chapter falls apart in its second part: while Johnston produces a balanced call to both sides by keeping his feet in a secular camp that allows for a diversity of views, Chamberlain, by contrast, boldly tries to argue from two positions and, in doing so, reveals in the second part many of the weaknesses he critiques in the first. Of course, it might be argued that my reading of this is the result of a closer alignment with Johnston's stance, and that my own position inevitably leads me to an accord with Johnston and the first part of Chamberlain's chapter. Yet to argue along these lines of relative partiality would be to fall into the trap of the relativism Chamberlain decries. I therefore wish to suggest that there are broader reasons for rejecting a number of Chamberlain's later contentions. In the rest of this chapter I will discuss four concerns arising from this and the other chapters: relativism, anti-intellectualism, political accountability, and linguistic ideologies.

The hardest issue here is one of relativism and incommensurability. It is clear that at one level, we cannot avoid this: one side says the other does not believe in an Almighty Being, the other says there is no Almighty Being to believe in. Or one side says they have the right path to access this being while the other claims that theirs is the true way. With such divides based at heart only on belief, there can be no discussion toward reconciliation of views here. Chamberlain takes secular critics to task for the belief that "all religions are fundamentally the same but superficially different when, in fact, all religions are superficially the same but fundamentally different (Zacharias, 1997)." There seems no escape here from the point that from the outside religions look very similar, yet from the inside, they of course look different. Coming from the first position, this is why I wondered at some point if we were to believe the claims to intercultural understanding made by Loptes and Chamberlain, which seem to express a certain multiculturalism, an appreciation of difference, an acknowledgment perhaps that there are other and equal ways of doing things, this could not also be extended to other belief systems: why cling to one set of beliefs and practices when another seems to be trying to get at the same thing in a slightly different way? But no, as Chamberlain asserts, following Zacharias, from an internal religious point of view, the fact that all religions are at their core exclusive (not in fact the case) and do not claim similarity with other religions (also not the case), renders such pluralism impossible. Yet here, Chamberlain falls into two traps that he accuses others of: anti-intellectualism and relativist tautologies.

Unfortunately, by adhering to the views of Ravi Zacharias, President of Ravi Zacharias International Ministries, Chamberlain gets caught in bad philosophy, where atheism is misunderstood as a worldview, and Nietsche's philosophy is misrepresented as a secular precursor to Nazism. One aspect of the "furtive" Christian activity that Johnston critiques is the tendency to publish in little-known presses and journals (well known in Christian communities but little known outside). This is also, I would like to suggest, part of the anti-intellectualism of the movement, an anti-intellectualism that goes deeper than Chamberlain's account: they publish in these presses not only to hide but because other presses would not publish their work (hence in part the struggle to get this book published). And Zacharias is not going to assist us much in working through these issues. The point is this: if one wishes to dismiss a view of the relativity of religions (that is, that they sit in relationship to each other), it is hard to also maintain a vision of respect for non-religious viewpoints, other religions, or even other cultures. If one wishes to adhere to this exclusivist interpretation of religion, then it is not plausible also to claim a position of respect for others. What Chamberlain does here is to conflate a strong epistemological relativism (an absolute relativism, as it were) with other, more inclusive relativistic viewpoints. The fallacious argument that relativism—as a way of thinking that acknowledges the position of the other, rather than a position that suggests inherent incommensurability—is impossible, since if everything is relative, then nothing is, is itself tautological since it only acknowledges an exclusivist and non-relativist position. Loptes' and Chamberlain's chapters constantly reveal this tension between on the one hand a will to acknowledge others' perspectives, to accept the possibilities of pluralism, of difference, that the other may be right, and on the other hand, the need to assert a righteousness about their own beliefs.

Another concern here is that the call by Johnston for some self-disclosure about political agendas is still absent. Again, it is not enough here to follow Zacharias' arguments that conflict and violence are an illogical product of religion but a logical product of atheism (a disgraceful claim). It is surely a profound denial of responsibility to simply dismiss the Christian role in the invasion of Iraq, or in the abuse of children by priests, or in the persecution of non-believers, as an atheist problem. Unless Christians confront the deep connections between their religion and the many atrocities done in its name, between extreme right-wing politics and evangelical Christianity, between subjection and abuse, belief and ignorance, rather than disclaiming any connection, dialogue will remain impossible. In this context, Chamberlain's claim that Jesus "was apolitical, absolutely pure in His motivations and sacrificial love" and yet "always found Himself at the center of controversy" is a strange description of a man who supposedly struggled against religious orthodoxy and political domination. Missing in all this is a sense of power, and an understanding that to operate in the name of Jesus can never be to behave with apolitical purity.

This emerges in Chamberlain's argument against the notion that missionaries prey on the weak. His argument is problematic when he suggests that to describe people as weak is to disenfranchise them. He is right that to talk in terms of "the weak" is to overlook questions of agency, but given that he has already cited Slimbach's (2000) description of the relation between the "characteristically poor, nonwhite, non-English-speaking women and men who live marginalized lives within multiethnic urban centers" and missionaries who "are typically affluent, white, monolingual (in English) persons raised in homogeneous suburban communities with individualist cultural values and conservative (if not reactionary) political views," it seems to me impossible to remove issues of power and politics from this. The Somali women he discusses are of course not individually and universally weak in terms of their possibility for action, but the relations of power by which they are positioned do render them politically weak. And as long as any discussion of power is absent, as long as a belief in apolitical purity of motivation is claimed, we need to continue to demand, as Johnston does, "to acknowledge who you are in bed with."

A related concern is that connections between religion and culture are not explored in any depth. One aspect of this that has received little attention in ELT circles is the relation between religion and language ideologies. At issue here are the ways in which different Christian groups understand the role of language. Most obviously, of course, a fundamentalist orientation to religion often equates to a fundamentalist orientation to language. I recall here a story told to me by a colleague teaching in the American Mid-west who dared to suggest that texts had multiple readings. He did not stay long in the job. As Heath (1983) observed with respect to the literacy practices of the communities she studied, the white working-class (Roadville) religious practices linked to the ways their children dealt with texts:

> The church insists on verbatim performance as a prime way of showing off knowledge; parents demand verbatim performance from their children at home as a way of showing they are learning. The church imposes memorization tasks from simplest to most difficult; parents buy educational toys according to their graded difficulty and introduce these to their preschoolers with demonstration and question-and-answer drills.
>
> (p. 144)

As she goes on to explain:

> The patterns of teaching language in Roadville homes are consistent with those of the church. At both individual and group levels, the belief in and

> practice of using "the right word" help structure the cognitive patterns which children draw of the world, i.e. what they come to know, and their notion of how to show what they know.
>
> (p. 144)

More broadly, we need to understand the linguistic ideologies of all Christian sects. As Robbins (2001) points out, Protestantism, for example, with its rejection of formal ritual "is prone to appear as a religion that is fundamentally, one might say, almost exclusively, constituted through language" (p. 904). Protestant linguistic ideology is closely tied to broader Modernist ideologies in which intention and meaning are closely coupled "in the postulation of a speaker who has both an ability and an inclination to tell the truth" (p. 905). As Robbins goes on to show, for the Urapmin of Papua New Guinea (PNG), this presents an ideological dilemma for:

> while they recognize that as modern, Christian subjects they are supposed to speak truthfully at all times by accurately and openly representing their inner states in speech, their traditional linguistic ideology does not constitute them as subjects capable of performing in this way.
>
> (p. 906)

Other studies of the effects of Christian missionary work in PNG show how the introduction of literacy "challenged and changed Kaluli notions of truth, knowledge, and authority, thereby affecting Kaluli linguistic as well as social structures" (Schieffelin, 2000, p. 294). The point here is that whether teaching first language literacy or English as a second language, CET come with particular linguistic ideologies that make any claims to cultural neutrality impossible to maintain (Pennycook and Makoni, 2005).

To show that Christian ideologies are also linguistic ideologies is to demonstrate that to teach from different Christian perspectives is akin to teaching from different cultural perspectives. Likewise, to teach from a humanist perspective is, as Tolman (2006) argues, to demand very particular language acts of self-disclosure, which for one student seemed like "losing the barrier between private and public that held her persona in place and protected her from the politics of the market. Speaking openly about something private made her an object of surveillance" (p. 193). And yet "as teachers we plod forward oblivious to the consequences of humanist, communicative policy" (p. 193). The point here, then, is that linguistic ideologies are tied not only to ethnic cultures but also to other cultural formations. Neither humanism nor religion is neutral with respect to the linguistic ideologies that underpin their pedagogical practices. This does not, however, render them all equal—a conflation of epistemological and moral relativism—but suggests that what is at stake here is far more than an acknowledgment that culture is never neutral, or a desire to bridge cultural difference, but rather a need to understand the complex array of cultural and ideological beliefs that are put into play even before the proselytizing begins. To follow Jesus (or any other religious figure) is never a path to political neutrality.

To conclude, this attempt at dialogue is at least to be partially welcomed. Whether it can achieve much will have to be seen. My own position is not against Christianity or any other religion; indeed I welcome debate on matters spiritual, ethical, cultural, and political. What I am profoundly against is arrogance, bigotry, self-righteousness, homophobia, misogyny, racism, anti-intellectualism, and hypocrisy. It is perhaps just my misfortune that CET I have had dealings with have had such attitudes in abundance. I have chosen not to list examples here of the shocking bigotries, ignorance, and hypocrisy I have encountered, since it would surely foreclose the possibility of dialogue even further. The writers here are absolutely right that I should not let such experiences fuel stereotypical beliefs about CET; but CET apologists will need to seriously counter such impressions if we are ever going to be able to have anything close to a dialogue. Chamberlain is mistaken when he asks why Christians are criticized for these traits when others are not: All are criticized, but when they are institutionalized through organizations and belief systems in a highly systematic way, they will continue to attract the attention of those of us struggling for a better world. If CET wish to join me in battles against bigotry, homophobia, heteronormativity, racism, sexism, and more, and if they are happy to acknowledge the equality of languages, cultures, people, and beliefs that have to be part of such struggles, they are very welcome. But on the evidence here, I doubt that this can happen.

References

Dawkins, R. (2006). *The God delusion.* London: Bantam Books.

Heath, S. B. (1983). *Ways with words: Language, life, and work on communities and classrooms.* Cambridge, UK: Cambridge University Press.

Hitchens, C. (2007). *God is not great: How religion poisons everything.* Sydney, Australia: Allen & Unwin.

Johnston, B. (2003). *Values in English language teaching.* Mahwah, NJ: Lawrence Erlbaum.

Nandy, A. (September 12, 2006). The return of the sacred, the language of religion and the fear of democracy in a post-secular world. Trans/forming Cultures Annual Lecture, University of Technology Sydney. Retrieved January 23, 2009, from http://hdl.handle.net/2100/44.

Pennycook, A., & Makoni, S. (2005). The modern mission: The language effects of Christianity. *Journal of Language Identity and Education, 4*(2), 137–155.

Robbins, J. (2001). God is nothing but talk: Modernity, language, and prayer in a Papua New Guinea Society. *American Anthropologist, 103*(4), 901–912.

Schieffelin, B. (2000). Introducing Kaluli literacy: A chronology of influences. In P. Kroskrity (Ed.), *Regimes of language: Ideologies, politics and identities* (pp. 293–327). Santa Fe, NM: School of American Research Press.

Slimbach, R. (2000). First, do no harm. *Evangelical Missions Quarterly, 36*(4), 428–441.

Tolman, J. (2006). Learning, unlearning, and the teaching of writing: Educational turns in postcoloniality. *Critical Inquiry in Language Studies: An International Journal, 3*(2/3), 189–200.

Response

7 Dialogue and Discourse

Robert Phillipson

> Nothing has proved harder in the history of civilization than to see God, or good, or human dignity in those whose language is not mine, whose skin is a different colour, whose faith is not my faith and whose truth is not my truth ... A god of your side as well as mine must be a God of justice who stands above us both, teaching us to make space for one another, to hear each other's claims and to resolve them equitably ... Only such a God would teach mankind to make peace other than by conquest and conversion, and as something nobler than practical necessity.
>
> (Sacks, 2002, p. 65)

I assume that the editors have invited me to respond to this set of chapters because my scholarly writings raise issues of ethics and accountability in English Language Teaching (ELT), human rights, and colonial legacies in education. I feel privileged to be invited to comment on this quartet, because however discordant it is—and there is a real clash of civilizations here—all four are impelled by a wish to contribute constructively to professional discourse and dialogue. My own voice may not bring harmony to the quartet, but it attempts to clarify our values as teachers of English. These can, in my view, be spiritual and moral, irrespective of whether they derive from religious faith. But the essential issue is whether attempting to convert others to one's own branch of Christianity is defensible.

I feel I should precede my comments by coming clean about where I stand in relation to Christianity, since the book builds on a confrontation of a range of positions that I have not had cause to reflect on or analyze earlier. I agree with the British chief rabbi, Jonathan Sacks (above), who argues for values that rise above "conquest and conversion." As a European, I was surprised to learn that ELT and missionary activity are (still) so intertwined. I am frankly shocked to learn that people who are avowedly Christian engage in conversion by stealth and covert proselytizing. I had assumed that the openness of missionary bodies like the Summer Institute of Linguistics represented the norm.

I was brought up in a devoutly Christian home in England. From the age of 8 to 14 I attended a cathedral choir school as a boarder. We sang cathedral services 13 times a week, and also had prayers morning and evening seven days a week in the school chapel. I was confirmed by the Bishop of London after lengthy preparation, which included me delivering a confession, since we were "high church." It so happened that the priest I was supposed to confess my 12-year-old peccadilloes to was my headmaster, a situation that did not encourage candor or self-incrimination (I was astute enough to arrange for a direct line to God in my thoughts), or faith in the morality of the institution. The school I attended from age 14 to 19 was only slightly less permeated by institutional Christianity.

My education has thus given me first-hand insight into how the church (of England, Anglican) functions. However, my faith in institutionalized Christianity of any kind and its theology is non-existent, although I respect the right of people to worship in any way they wish, and know that many individual Christians in different parts of the world behave in selfless, admirable ways. My beliefs correspond closely to those articulated in "Why I am not a Christian" (Russell, 1985):

> Where there is evidence, no-one speaks of "faith". [...] We only speak of faith when we wish to substitute emotion for evidence. [...] The whole conception of God is a conception derived from the ancient Oriental despotisms. [...] A good world needs knowledge, kindliness, and courage; it does not need a regretful hankering after the past, or a fettering of the free intelligence by the words uttered long ago by ignorant men. [...] With very few exceptions, the religion which a man accepts is that of the community in which he lives, which makes it obvious that the influence of the environment is what has led him to accept the religion in question.
>
> (pp. 39, 48–49, 53)

Europe as a whole is now deeply secularized, both in states that have historically been strongly Catholic (Italy, Spain) and those that have a state church (Greek Orthodox or Lutheran Denmark). Education aims increasingly at producing consumers rather than creative, critical, or devout citizens. My own school education was one-sided and inadequate. I never heard Darwin's name mentioned, let alone that the three monotheistic Abrahamic religions had the same geographical and historical roots. I left school in 1961, and at no point was it suggested that the British Empire would ever end, let alone that it had had a profoundly disruptive and often evil effect on foreign countries. Gandhi and Nehru, Kenyatta and Mandela were, after all, terrorists and infidels, despite the British education lavished on them.

A historical perspective is needed, since US missionaries have for centuries served to push frontiers forward both at home and abroad. In 1838 the "Board of Foreign Missions of the USA," which then consisted of 13 states, distinct "colonies," propounded "a belief in the manifest destiny of Anglo-Saxon culture to spread around the world" (Spring, 1996). The USA was consolidating early British efforts, those of the Society for Promoting Christian Knowledge (1698), the Society for the Propagation of the Gospel in Foreign Parts (1701), etc. Whereas empire was largely a matter of extraction economies, albeit with massive cultural consequences, the "settling" of continents by Europeans, as though they were in *terra nullius*, had much more devastating and often genocidal consequences, particularly in the Americas and Australasia. Military violence dovetailed with the school and the church, the "civilizing" mission. Interestingly, the term "foreign," as in Foreign Missions, was used for North America's aboriginal inhabitants. Relations between the two parties were enshrined in treaties, which in international law are legal instruments negotiated between sovereign states. The European invaders reneged on their treaty obligations, and Europeanized countries worldwide are thus founded on immoral fraudulent occupation. Canada and New Zealand are beginning to address the issue, whereas the USA and much of Latin America are still in denial. Being aware of the crimes of our ancestors, often in the name of a Christian "mission," would be a first step toward assessing the moral foundations of the churches that have evolved in their wake.

My secular skepticism makes me suspicious of missionizing of any sort, whether cloaked in the gospel of "development," "good governance," or any religious faith. I have worked in Islamic and communist countries, dispatched there both to teach English and to represent British interests, an ambivalent dualism. I am skeptical about most aspects of the "aid" business, which is often doctrinaire, and in the case of education, tends to be culturally, pedagogically, and linguistically inappropriate. What I do believe in is human rights values, provided that these do not assume that we know best. Cultural and linguistic diversity should be respected, since they are at the heart of the biological diversity that humanity has developed (see www.terralingua.org). One universal human rights principle is that no one should be discriminated against on religious grounds. This represents a hurdle that no missionary can ignore, unless they tackle head-on the issue of whether a given faith can claim a monopoly of theological truth. I fear that only the blinkered or naive, rather than the intellectually well informed, can attempt this. The four chapters in this part of the book all confirm that missionizing ELT people tend to be deeply ethnocentric and Western/Americanocentric. To my mind, this disqualifies their efforts, however well intentioned.

Julian Edge's presentation of a range of different styles of argument and pedagogy is clearly impelled by an urge to create conditions for, to use his terms, non-judgmental interaction, so that scholarly discourse can prove augmentative. He stakes out an intellectually honest position in a field where collegial interlocutors are poles apart. But he only exemplifies differences of faith in his conclusions, due to his wish to create a framework for positive rather than displacive argument—and doubtless because he stuck his neck out earlier. However, the attempt to present philosophical reflections that can bring about conflict resolution seems to me to run the risk of endorsing "anything goes" pedagogy (the Circle example) in the scholarly discourse of this edited volume, rather than engaging with the existential issue of whether religious faith, however well motivated, belongs at all in education outside denominational schools. I have difficulty in seeing how an augmentative discourse can be ontologically defensible when there are conflicting views of whether the missionary task is misguided. This is a matter of principle. In addition, in education the teacher is in a position of power vis-à-vis learners. This asymmetrical interaction is compounded if the missionary activities of a hegemonic faith (whether Islamic or Christian), overt or covert, are added. Isn't the underlying assumption the belief in the right of a Converter to proselytize in what is by definition seen as the inferior infidel world of the potentially Convertible? I find it impossible to endorse Christians taking upon themselves the role of delivering a faith worldwide when Christianity itself has a history of division dating back to the territorial and theological share-out between Rome and Constantinople, and with doctrinal fragmentation ever since (Luther, Calvin, Baptists, et al.) and recurrent internecine bloodshed to this day (Catholics and Protestants).

Since missionaries apparently exist in large numbers in ELT, *Bill Johnston* makes a plea for dialogue, preferably of a conciliatory nature, between evangelicals and others, if only for pragmatic reasons that reflect the reality of ongoing professional activities. His practical suggestions are constructive, even if his extensive experience tells him that reciprocal understanding is likely to be elusive. Facilitating a higher level of information about alternative perspectives is laudable, as is his insistence on not essentializing, both about other ELT colleagues and even more importantly about groups of learners. He is also right to connect religious activities to economic and political agendas. It therefore strikes me as surprising that he presents figures for the expansion of believers in Christianity, without a corresponding figure for the expansion of Islam, and more seriously, without suggesting that such trends are due to social and political factors (e.g., modernization ideologies, or a need for reassurance in an increasingly unstable, changing world). Belief can in any case mean active fellowship, going through occasional rituals, or zero activity.

Michael Chamberlain would have liked religion to figure in intercultural studies. But it is not surprising that religion has been totally absent from the language sciences since Europeans "discovered" Sanskrit and the common origins of Indo-European languages two centuries ago. Awareness of the nature of human language evolution saw the take-off of philology as the key humanistic discipline in nineteenth-century scholarship, which then led to modern linguistics. Edward Said (1985, pp. 132ff.) traces how philology triggered the recognition that "the so-called sacred languages (Hebrew, primarily) were neither of primordial antiquity nor of divine provenance": the task of philology was "to continue to see reality and nature clearly, thus driving out supernaturalism [...] philology enables a general view of human life and the system of things." This demolished the view that "God delivered language to man in Eden" (p. 135) and ensured that all linguists from the mid-nineteenth century have been obliged to see the study of language in detachment from religion, a development that parallels the path of Darwinism in the natural sciences.

In *Karen Loptes*' chapter it became clear that what she means by "limited access countries" is countries that are unwelcoming to foreign missionaries. Loptes' esoteric terminology strikes me as singularly inappropriate, since countries like China and the United Arab Emirates recruit vast numbers of teachers from abroad, i.e., foreigners have far from "limited access."

It is clearly useful to have a collection of a set of frank comments on a range of concerns to CET. Unfortunately the data are uneven: in effect this is a pioneering pilot study. One weakness is that the factors supposed to correlate with cultural sensitivity are heterogeneous: most are banal and should go without saying in any context, domestic or foreign. It is also disappointing that the study fails to clarify whether there is any decisive difference between CET who see themselves as missionaries as opposed to those who do not but for whom their Christianity is central to their professional as well as personal identity. Loptes (initially and finally in the chapter) conflates ethical principles and Christianity. To do so is merely a statement of the particularity of her faith.

How far informants go in learning a local language should have been a central component of a study of language teachers. The fact that it was not confirms evidence from other studies that ELT teachers often do not set a good example of language learning. To me this signifies cultural insensitivity and professional insufficiency.

Loptes notes that CET who are living abroad longer seem to be more culturally sensitive. Endorsement of a long-term commitment by ELT makes sense educationally, but when this is considered part of a "global educational endeavor," this represents a continuation of the "manifest destiny" that the USA has arrogated to itself. The imperialist white (wo)man's burden is still being taken up, adjusted to the conditions of the evolving corporate Empire (see Harvey, 2005a, 2005b), a central feature of which is a focus on communicative networks and the creation of subjectivities (see Hardt & Negri, 2000). An analysis of these factors, which determine the context of ELT in the neoimperial world, ought to be central to ELT training.

Michael Chamberlain is refreshingly objective about the shortcomings of mission teachers, their inadequate training, their cultural arrogance and blindness, and fundamental ethnocentricity. It is extremely healthy that such criticism comes from someone who is in sympathy with the notion of Christian evangelizing, since this is potentially a significant way of taking that group forward. Chamberlain also validly challenges the selective denunciations of secularists, and his insistence on addressing the truth value of particular religions is a challenge to evangelist and secularist alike, but not one that can be undertaken lightly. For an individual's role to be condemned as imperialist presupposes a structure of (linguistic) exploitation and an overarching ideology that ELT activities cannot escape from, irrespective of an individual's beliefs. In any given context, whether this is so is empirically verifiable. As my introductory remarks indicated, many aspects of aid and the use of "native speakers" are indefensible, in my view, but these are different issues from ELT professionalism being teamed up with a particular type of religious faith. This raises issues that are not merely ethical or moral but theological.

But what right can anyone have to question and subvert the faith that others subscribe to? Is this a task that any individual can take upon her- or himself? Seen historically and sociologically, have Christians in any state brought about a society of justice and humane living for its entire population, a model that merits being exported? My answer would be clearly no. These pragmatic considerations fit well with the essential theological question of whether any religion can be considered more true than others, where my position was made clear earlier.

Chamberlain's conclusion seems to endorse the notion that treading in

Christ's footsteps can be apolitical. I fear this is self-deception. In multifaith communities such as parts of India, or Bosnia before the disintegration of Yugoslavia, tolerance was widespread, not least because conversion was not attempted. Tragically, the evidence is that inter-group mobilization along lines that may be ethnic, linguistic, or religious can lead to appalling bloodshed. But this has nothing to do with ethnicity, multilingualism, or religious diversity—and everything to do with injustice, oppression, and politics. I suspect that many of Christ's actions when challenging privilege (whether of Roman overlords or local money-changers) were deeply political and consciously so. The same applies, in my view, to all CET activity.

So we need dialogue, which my outspoken but honest discourse hopes to contribute to. Only in this way can we expect to strengthen our professionalism and our ideological awareness. In my own work as a committed (immigrant) teacher of English, I feel that many of the dilemmas that we inevitably face in ELT can be resolved by challenging orthodoxy and dogma of any kind, as a means toward creating learning conditions that result in students with high levels of both English competence and political awareness.

References

Hardt, D. & Negri, A. (2000). *Empire.* Cambridge: Harvard University Press.

Harvey, D. (2005a). *A brief history of neoliberalism.* Oxford, UK: Oxford University Press.

Harvey, D. (2005b). *The new imperialism.* Oxford, UK: Oxford University Press.

Russell, B. (1985). *Bertrand Russell's best.* London: Unwin.

Sacks, J. (2002). *The dignity of difference: How to avoid the clash of civilizations.* London: Continuum.

Said, E. (1985). *Orientalism.* Harmondsworth, UK: Penguin.

Spring, J. (1996). *The cultural transformation of a Native American family and its tribe 1763–1995.* Mahwah, NJ: Lawrence Erlbaum.

Response

8 Questioning Religious "Ideals" and Intentionalities

Staving off Religious Arrogance and Bigotry in ELT

Vaidehi Ramanathan

Let me begin by saying that some of these chapters evoke in me a response that surprises me. I find myself in corners that threaten to position me as a colonized subject once more, a "native" who has to be shown the light, a non-Christian from a "limited access country" (India in my case). While I have no intention of countering some of these (offensive?) strains on their own terms, I do feel that as someone in ELT, as one who would be prime "meat" for CET, and as one having grown up in a postcolonial, multi-religious space[1] where Christianity can only be understood against a most heterogeneous landscape, it is important that I speak to what may be perceived as irrationality and arrogance implicit in some of the "Christianity Only" strains in CET. My aim in this small piece is to nudge this discussion to another plane, one where we are speaking not so much about any particular religious discourse but what it is we ELT people need to be vigilant about when we begin to speak about (our and others') religious affiliations in relation to our profession.

Running thickly through the Loptes and Chamberlain pieces seems to be an unalterable, fixed idea of Truth and God. Such an unmutating understanding—and that, too, of the uncontainability of God—belies the historicity behind religious "ideals" (Christian, Hindu, or any other), something about which we teachers and academics cannot be sensitive enough. Missing from their chapters is a quiet, deliberate reflection on what sense of the ideal—Christian in the present case—is reproduced by CET, and how tugs toward preserving this "ideal" can be seen to convey a sense of regression. The relative intemporality in their positions seems to overlook some crucial issues: the Husserlian corpus of geometry that all religions follow, mandates to carefully pass on "traditions" over generations, a teleological establishment of religious themes that gain credence with repeated enactments over time (as in the case of particular religious rituals), a constant eye to the future that younger generations are being "socialized" into. Religions the world over are predicated on such assumptions, and succeed in creating systematized, "geometrical" horizons in order to circumscribe coherent, "stable" domains. Furthermore, these ideals are presented to us in all their historicities and traditions. It seems to me that it remains up to us teachers, academics, to recognize that these religious geometries are not natural phenomena—like stones and mountains—but our human assemblages that exist in our collective space of humanity.

While it may not be Chamberlain's and Loptes' intentions to engage in critical self-reflection as much as to speak openly about how their religious leanings inform their identities as teachers—a worthy cause in itself—to not also address some dangers in this thinking strikes me as inherently myopic (although Chamberlain at least voices some discomfort). The historicity of religious ideas is not just our being able to slot them into particular temporal spaces and assign them unique temporal locations. The historicity of an idea is the positing by us humans of a task that echoes back to earlier plateaus, of an awareness of how our interjections—through engagements in our professions among other things—simultaneously move us forward, while also pointing back. And to arrive at this sense of history, we need not historical documents but a critical self-awareness that we are each of us points in history that carry reverberations of times past and possibilities for the future.

I emphasize this point about religious idealities and historicities and the need for constant critical scrutiny because it is, among other things, the lack of a historicized sense about our cultivation of our religious ideals, and generalized notions of superiority with which we may have suffused them (the very act and mission of evangelizing by CET is predicated on this assumption) that partially accounts for some of the most unspeakable crimes in the world. Ahmedabad, the city in which I grew up (in Gujarat, India), has been home to some of the worst Hindu–Muslim riots in recent years (see Ramanathan, 2006, for a detailed account), and while at first glance this reference to these riots might seem out of place in a book devoted to Christianity and ELT, the general point I am making about the importance of retaining a constant historicized meta-awareness of how various strains of ourselves inform our engagements in professional realms coupled with thick strains of critical self-reflection is crucial here. Indeed, it has been in Gujarat that Christian missionaries have until recently come under brutal attacks; their attempts to proselytize gets read as arrogance and gall.

So how, then, is one to proceed? One way might be to interrogate *intentionalities*. What is it that we individually or collectively intend when we do or do not speak about religious discourses or speak about them in certain ways? What are Loptes, Chamberlain, Edge, and Johnston intending when they speak about their efforts, discomfort, the need for non-judgmental discourses, and dialogue respectively? Clearly they have read their realities in certain ways, ways in which particular aspects of this topic about Christianity and ELT have stood out, and their consciousness about particular strains has been heightened. However, nothing about probing our own and others' intentions and intentionalities is straightforward; indeed, even a brief pause to consider the complexities around them brings home to us the quicksand into which we step because everything about what we and others *intend* evades our languaging. Our readings of others' intentions may sometimes give voice to what might otherwise remain mute (or at least we may justify them that way), but it falls short even as it does so, since the object of our "intentional" scrutiny is always much more than what appears. While CET may proceed on the assumption that their students in China or Egypt need to hear about Christ and the Truth, and Loptes may proceed on the basis that the views of CET are important to represent, the fact that they emerge as so is because they are bound by what Husserl would call "horizon structures," invisible borders that draw structures around our understanding, while laminating some of our realities. It is these horizon structures that we need to probe and question since they contain our "readings" of the intentions inherent in both our own religious discourses and those of others. Our religious discourses partially make up our horizon structures, limiting our visions, feeding our intentionalities, serving as blinkers disallowing other ways of being, living, thinking. Full and certain knowledge about Truth or God is simply not possible, and to proceed full steam ahead, sure that it is unproblematic to spread "the word" is myopic at best and hopelessly blind at worst. Phillipson comes to the heart of the matter when he asks: "Isn't the underlying assumption the belief in the right of a Converter to proselytize in what is by definition seen as the inferior infidel world of the potentially Convertible?" I ask, "Whence came that right?" An open acknowledgment of this point and an honest wrestling with the discomfort (à la Chamberlain) on the part of CET, as well as a genuine acceptance of the fact that there are other ways of knowing God, that Truths are multiple, provisional, and of our making might move us toward the dialogue that Johnston mentions. Ultimately, it might be the unceasing questioning of our own intentionalities and horizon structures, of religious ideals and their historicities, of our roles and engagements with and about them, that will save us from religious arrogance and bigotry. Indeed, how can we as teachers, researchers, academics not do otherwise?

Note

1. A tiny Jewish community comprising Jews from the first century of the Common Era exists in the southern state of Kerala. The first Christian church there was founded by St Thomas the Apostle in AD 72. A group of Zoroastrians who fled Iran arrived about 900 BC and comprise the Parsi community. Islamic invasion began in the tenth century, with Muslims today constituting the largest minority population. India is where the Buddha was born and Buddhism thrives along with Jainism whose founder Mahavira lived and preached roughly at the same time as the Buddha. Sikhism—the religion that draws from both Hinduism and Islam—began in 1469. With colonial expansion came Protestant and Catholic missionaries—the Salvation Army, Irish Presbyterians, Danish Protestants, the Church of the Brethren, and of course Catholic religious orders, notably the Society of Jesus. How, given such a historical background, is one to view the preoccupations of evangelizing English teachers today in a postcolonial world?

Reference

Ramanathan, V. (2006). Gandhi, non-cooperation, and socio-civic education in Gujarat, India: Harnessing the vernaculars. *Journal of Language, Identity, and Education*, 5(3), 229–250.

Response

9 Can We Talk?

Finding a Platform for Dialogue among Values-based Professionals in Post-positivist Education

Suresh Canagarajah

Though the authors in this volume are all interested in dialogue, their positions present diverse frameworks, conditions, and caveats. It is important, therefore, to consider the possible outcomes of these proposals, and the desirability of the process and product of such dialogue.

Finding a New Platform

Let's start with the proposals offered by critical practitioners and secular professionals in this book to facilitate a more constructive dialogue. Bill Johnston makes a distinction between *exploratory* dialogue and *conciliatory* dialogue. While the latter "concerns itself with overcoming misconceptions and prejudices on either side," *exploratory dialogue* performs "the dual function of giving participants voice and allowing exposure to the voices of others, leading to the mutual shaping of ideas and views" (p. 36). Johnston considers exploratory dialogue irrelevant and even impossible for the parties under consideration in this book, as CET are too entrenched in their positions to dialogue with others.[1] He rather favors conciliatory dialogue, as the best CET and non-CET professionals can hope to achieve is understanding each other's positions in an effort to overcome misconceptions and prejudices on either side.

Though Johnston makes a useful distinction and points to the higher forms of dialogue that all PPE should aspire to, I would question his assumption that some groups are not capable of exploratory dialogue or that they don't qualify for that level of interaction. We have to be careful of either holding out or refusing exploratory dialogue for selected parties. Where do we draw the line? How do we decide that some are open for dialogue with us but not others? Would this distinction be based on our biases for or against certain groups? Isn't there a logical slippage when we say we are open to dialogue with groups that have values different from ours, but some are more preferable than others for higher forms of dialogue? Would this become a self-fulfilling prophecy of having some groups always excluded from dialogue—i.e., when we exclude certain groups because their values are too far from our preferred positions, they will always remain misunderstood and unappreciated and, thus, excluded from dialogue?

Though conciliatory dialogue is always needed as a way of clearing the air between debating parties, it doesn't have to be the end point in any dialogue.

However, I am also of the opinion that even Johnston's exploratory dialogue doesn't go far enough in capturing the type of dialogue we should aspire to. As operationalized, the label "exploratory" puts too much emphasis on the "exposure to the views of others," and less on "leading to the mutual shaping of ideas and views" (p. 36). In the examples Johnston gives, we don't see a mutual shaping of ideas. We should consider dialogue as a collective achievement, enabling both parties to help each other progress further in their thinking and values. Besides, it is not just "ideas and views" that we are concerned about, in a product-oriented sense. The dialogue should enrich participants in a holistic manner, not just contribute to exchanging ideas. We should accommodate changes in one's orientation to self, relationships, feelings, and values. We should therefore consider moving from conciliatory dialogue, and exploratory dialogue, to *transformative* dialogue to accommodate such possibilities. The latter term conveys the need for both parties to contribute to each other's transformation as persons, in a rounded and holistic manner—as I will theorize below.

Julian Edge has made further observations on the dialogical practices and procedures that would facilitate the encounter between Post-positivist Educators (PPE). He points to the limitations of *displacive argument*, which is based on an agonistic framework, bent on demolishing the opponent's position. One party's position is proven completely correct, in a winner-takes-all outcome. In the place of this, Edge proposes the notion of *non-judgmental discourse*, which he considers "the facilitating of human creativity through the temporary suspension of evaluation" (p. 29). He develops this discourse more fully as a process of "cooperative development" (p. 25). This mode of discourse requires one to be "open to difference in ways that might seem uncomfortable, or even threatening.... If negative evaluation of others' ideas or actions proves unavoidable, one hopes at least for an ability to disagree with increased understanding and respect" (pp. 28–29). This is a higher position we should aspire to in our dialogue. Being open to difference in ways that might seem uncomfortable can facilitate conversation with the groups Johnston disqualifies for such engagement.

Edge then moves on to consider the difficult problem of what to do with those whose positions one can't agree with even after dialogue, as they present serious moral differences from one's own. Considering dialogue with racists and sexists, for example, he says,

> If I cannot, or do not wish to, empathize with your viewpoint and purposes, it would be insincere of me to pretend that I can. I may well wish to use such techniques as Reflecting in order to establish that I have indeed properly understood your position, but then if that which divides us is greater than a collegial wish to support each other in the variety of our endeavors, then we should acknowledge this and move into a more appropriate form of discourse. Here the need for clarity, argumentation, and standing up for what one believes to be important, takes over. I remain committed to dialogue with all and anyone, but I do not attempt to deny the fact that with some people I expect to remain in fundamental disagreement and, as I have no

> wish to help them further their purposes, I could not offer them the support of non-judgmental discourse.
>
> (p. 30)

Edge is facing up to an important moral dilemma here: how can we have an open dialogue without erasing significant differences? How do we engage freely, while preserving the ability to critique the immoral and antisocial positions of others?

Though these are important considerations, and it is understandable that Edge sees a need for some space to adopt clear positions of one's own and not be wishy-washy about important moral principles, I don't think Edge resolves the dilemma in a manner consistent with the openness required of non-judgmental discourse. (To his credit, he himself expresses some dissatisfaction with this position in a later paragraph.) Where do we draw the line between an acceptable and unacceptable position for dialogue? At what point does disengagement and standing up for one's own position take over? Edge's "if I cannot or do not wish to" sounds a bit too intransigent and predefined. It doesn't carry the suspension of judgment required for the capacity to disagree with increased understanding. There is a curious logic at play here: we need openness to dialogue with people we disagree with, but if we disagree with some too radically, we don't have to be open for dialogue with them.

Besides, it is not one's own position and integrity of values that is at issue here. There is also a cooperative responsibility on one's part to contribute to the critical reflection and enrichment of the other's position. In fact, we have to facilitate a dialogue that enables mutual enrichment. Dialogue is not just to confirm one's own moral uprightness; it is also to help the other party progress to more humane and richer values, if one sees limitations. Of course we can't "help them further their purposes," but what about helping them reconsider their purposes? For these things to happen, there is a need for vulnerability on the part of both parties and the ability to stretch themselves to consider new possibilities they didn't contemplate before. To help the other party in examining their assumptions, I mustn't adopt a righteous or a holier-than-thou attitude. I am prepared to continue a conversation with even a racist though I disagree with that person's position. I don't mind making myself vulnerable by association with such a person because I feel committed to help this person rethink and revise his/her assumptions, while I try to understand what makes that person adopt such a position. It is my social responsibility to contribute to the other person's moral thinking, even as I broaden my understanding of things.

A dialogue that is committed to positions, yet engaged with others unconditionally and ceaselessly, and sincerely interested in enlarging and enriching everyone's positions and values with social responsibility in a collaborative manner requires a different footing. Brian Morgan's proposal in this book takes us in this direction (see Chapter 20). Morgan makes a useful distinction between interactional and transactional dialogue, in a dialogical or monological form of interaction, respectively. Morgan argues: "Dialogue may purport to be *interactional*, whereby participants allow themselves to be reformed as a consequence, but in effect remain stubbornly *transactional*, where predetermined values are guardedly exchanged without any intention of change" (p. 197; this volume). In moving toward interactional dialogue, Morgan still makes a space for one's own values, as his concern is: "how we might ideally and ethically address such concerns in pedagogy without denying our own identity, humanity, or spirituality—if such a denial were even consciously possible" (p. 195). In saying this, Morgan is going against the position that we can have a non-committal discussion. Note that Edge sees a need for "temporary suspension of evaluation." Is it possible to be aware of the differences in our positions, and yet engage in a mutually enriching dialogue? Similarly, relativism—i.e., holding that what's okay for another person need not be okay for me—is not an outcome that satisfies Morgan. We will see below that some PPE are prepared to raise moral values in the classroom in the safety of the position that we need not make others or ourselves uncomfortable with a critical engagement. This is a cop out. In fact, it is doubtful one can remain non-committal in a dialogue involving morality and values. Morgan, though a non-evangelical practitioner, acknowledges that the mere reading of the positions by evangelicals in this volume draws him into a virtual dialogue with CET and makes him aware of his own values.

Conducting dialogue in such a manner requires *vulnerability*, a key characteristic Morgan expounds upon. He makes a useful distinction with *humility*—a characteristic that would still preserve your identity and positions while engaging with the other. Vulnerability opens one up for self-criticism, reflection, and change. Compared to this, humility (which finds expression in non-judgmental or conciliatory dialogue) sounds condescending. Morgan would go so far as to say that even for teachers to think that they are imparting what is good and true to their students is to stand safe in their certainties and not open themselves up to being changed by the interaction. Morgan connects this dialogical approach to a pedagogy of possibility (Simon, 1992) where "the strangeness of the Other is a source of self-learning and of new possibilities" (p. 198). He contrasts this approach with a "a pedagogy of closure" (Lusted, 1986) that looks for the comfort of final answers, or affirms one's own predisposition and preferences as the only route to answers. The possibility of self-criticism, learning from others, and constant reconstruction of one's own values and self, with a commitment to help others enrich their lives, which Morgan aligns with a pedagogy of possibility, I see as a platform for dialogue that TESOL'ers are yet to achieve.

It is fascinating that even those who are committed to pluralism can invoke what they consider as universal values to trump the need to acknowledge the positions of others. For example, raising skepticism as a universal value can then lead to cutting off conversations with those who come with beliefs. Or treating rationality as a central value that should guide discourse, and then treating the groups that one is against as irrational, we can cut off conversation with those we don't like. There is thus a solipsism and self-serving argument involved in this procedure when we refuse to engage in dialogue with those positions we have already condemned as morally or rationally repugnant. From racists and sexists one can quickly slide to censoring evangelicals or any other group one doesn't like.

In a thought-provoking essay, Ruth Abbey (2006) compares the positions of contemporary philosophers Stuart Hampshire (2000) and Charles Taylor (1998) to clarify the ways in which pluralism can limit its capacity for dialogue. Though both philosophers are committed to pluralism, they differ in the way they go about relating to diversity. Charting what he calls an "aggressively secular and liberal" position (2000, p. 51), Hampshire sees monotheistic religions as inimical to pluralism. He also holds values such as intellect over imagination, procedure over substance, reason over passion, necessity over contingency, absolute over relative, and universal over local as criteria that help resolve the conflict between diverse positions. Abbey points to an inconsistency in this argument. She argues, "as a pluralist who revels in human diversity, Hampshire is surprisingly dogmatic about, and dismissive of, religion … Exempting religious interpretations of life from this wondrous fecundity seems not only historically and culturally insensitive but, from a theoretical standpoint, arbitrary" (2006, p. 218). In fact, this is a fundamental dilemma that PPE who oppose religions have to face up to. It is understandable that values such as intellect, reason, and universals will be eventually used to resolve the moral tensions one faces. If we can do so with the understanding that these values themselves are open to diverse interpretations and application, this should be appropriate. However, what would be missing is the ability to put oneself in a position of vulnerability to be challenged by the diverse discourses one dialogues with.

Taylor, on the other hand, views individuals as faced with moral positions that are not always combinable and therefore not chosen—but still worthy of affirmation. Therefore, he accommodates the possibility of sacrifice and loss as part of the negotiation of plurality. The way to arbitrate these conflicts, he sees as not lying in abstract values such as rationality or universality, but community. He sees the need to negotiate the differences together with others, and work toward collective enrichment. Abbey translates his position as:

> an alternative model of democratic inclusion, one that celebrates the differences among groups and encourages citizens not simply to tolerate but to learn about and engage with one another, understanding that their differences enrich one another and the polity as a whole.
>
> (p. 223)

As I have pointed out earlier, this kind of commitment to collective enrichment is not evident in TESOL'ers who wish to conduct dialogue with set views on the rightness of their own position and or the wrongness of others. On an interesting side note, Taylor's view of relentless engagement in plurality is motivated by spiritual values, especially those of Christianity. It follows from his view of creation as essentially plural and diverse. For him, human diversity is the image of God, going to the roots of God's own triune being (as father, son, and holy spirit). And since this diversity is God-created, nothing is to be discarded outright, even those that conflict with his preferred Christian values. Whatever one might feel about Taylor's understanding of the Bible, we can't discount the fact that there are elements in Christianity and other religions that facilitate open dialogue and affirm plurality. Holding Christians as necessarily absolutist or bigoted sounds unreasonable from this point of view.

This kind of engaged, critical, and creative conversation of what I would label *transformative dialogue* is being undertaken by many other PPE in other disciplines in the academy today. Notable among such conversations is the one organized by the Erasmus Institute in the University of Notre Dame. It is a remarkable experiment of not only scholars from different disciplines, but also those from different religions, attempting to engage more collaboratively on the place of spirituality in their fields. Their project aims for "a pluralism that does not dissolve into universal relativism" (White, 2006, p. 5). The scholars assume the incommensurability of discourses as their starting point, not something to be avoided. The tensions generated call for self-criticism, not self-righteousness. They remember that:

> in talking about the religions of others we should make a constant effort to be conscious of the implications of our own language, and aware of what is possibly misleading and incomplete in it … if you insist on maintaining without change your own worldview—your own sense of the way things are, your own sense of yourself as neutral and objective observer—you may not ever really understand what it is like for other people to imagine the world as they do and to live on those terms.
>
> (White, 2006, p. 4)

Thus they avoid the subjectivism and solipsism involved in using one's own values to decide who is worthy of dialogue. They also realize that for such a conversation to work the orientation has to be communal: "the talk about religion, to be successful, should be both sharply diverse and deeply communal … we were thus engaged in a kind of collective thought, which over time became richer and deeper" (pp. 6–7). For this collective thought to succeed, they realize that they have to learn not just to talk but also to listen—"acceptance of difference, willingness to learn, and trust in each other are crucial to any hope of success" (p. 8). Most of all, they adopt a position of vulnerability and don't resort to the comfort and authority of their disciplines as they realize that they have to stretch themselves and find spaces outside their accepted discourses in order to understand the other: "We were thus forced as it were into a terrain between the language of our discipline, or among them, where none of us claimed to know much and all of us were ready to learn" (p. 8). This precariousness of philosophical footing, willingness to be vulnerable by stepping into spaces which are new and uncomfortable, and a commitment to collaborative thinking, are prerequisites for a constructive engagement with spirituality in our field.

Platform for Teaching

The framework for dialogue outlined above is important because it will guide our approach to values and spirituality in pedagogical practice. It is possible to create a classroom where students and teachers acknowledge their commitment to their own set of spiritual and moral values and even feel comfortable to represent them in their classroom relations and learning, but are yet open to be challenged by dialogue with others. It is such a classroom environment that would facilitate a pedagogy of possibility. Students and teachers should be prepared to collaborate in "educating" each other and developing a richer moral and spiritual orientation, in addition to shaping deeper intellectual perspectives.

Though a teaching practice that ignores moral and spiritual values has been well critiqued in recent TESOL publications, and there is an emerging consensus that values play an important role in language teaching and professional development, we are still some way off from developing appropriate models for accommodating values in the classroom. It is a challenge to fashion alternative teaching practices that would create a space for all diverse values represented by PPE, or even better, reconcile the concerns of values-based and positivistic professionals. Let me take up for closer analysis the positions outlined by Bill Johnston (2003), as he has worked the hardest to articulate a place for values-based teaching in our profession.[2]

Johnston makes a strong case for teachers negotiating their classroom moral tensions in a situation-specific manner. He brings out the complexity of the decisions teachers have to make in their everyday professional life and shows the competing claims that motivate them to resolve them in their own way. Johnston insists, "it is impossible to produce generalized solutions—each individual solution has to be understood in its own terms" (p. 4). For this reason, he states: "In this book I suggest many aspects of language teaching that I believe you ought to think *about*, but I will not tell you *what* to think about them" (p. 5; emphasis in original). He goes on to say, "I am not recommending or arguing for any particular teaching methodology but for a way of *seeing* the classroom" (p. 5). Johnston thus performs the wonderful service of awareness building among teachers. He opens up teachers to the dilemmas inherent in negotiating conflicting moral claims in the classroom.

However, I find it intriguing that there are no guidelines, directions, or end goals for negotiating the moral dilemmas teachers face. Part of the reluctance to provide any framework lies in the fear of imposing one's own agenda on others. So Johnston insists, "I want to state clearly that I do not have an agenda in terms of specific values. I do not write from a particular religious or ethical standpoint. I simply believe that these matters are worth talking about" (p. 5). Such claims bring Johnston close to saying that he can keep his own values and moral positions outside the treatment of this subject in his book. Is it possible not to take a moral position on something you discuss? This noncommittal stance is a curious position for one who believes that everything is moral—i.e., that the moral cannot be separated from teaching or life. Ironically, even Johnston's position of non-imposition implies certain values and morals he prefers to adopt—for example, individualistic, relativistic, and apolitical, as I will explain below.

Johnston's position may lead to a radical individualism—i.e., that each person has a moral position that is unique to him or herself, and cannot be critically discussed by others. Good and bad would take different definitions and implications from person to person. Consider the ironic situation of a teacher who says she likes to avoid the moral issues that arise in the classroom, as they are emotionally charged and divisive. That would go against the basic premise that motivates Johnston's whole book—i.e., the inevitability of moral issues. Certainly, Johnston won't say that the position of this teacher is acceptable. Though I sympathize with Johnston's desire to preserve the "polyvalence" (p. 20) of moral positions and adopt a non-impositional attitude to moral decisions in the classroom, I don't think that this complexity should prevent us from developing frameworks for negotiation. An acknowledgment of polyvalence of values needn't imply suppression of one's own values. It should actually send us looking for more complex models for negotiation.

Johnston's position can lead to a classroom where there is no deeper engagement or learning about adopting moral positions. It can lead to a relativism of saying we all have our own ways of dealing with values—and they are all fine. I understand that Johnston's position is influenced by the concern about teachers imposing their values on students. Therefore, he explains, "In doing so I also wish to try to reclaim the use of the term moral by those of us who think in moral terms yet do not necessarily align with particular religious or political factions" (p. 5). "Factions" is a strategically chosen word. We all know that factions create factionalism, hatred, and intolerance. Should we keep away from adopting specific moral positions, as they would lead to factionalism? Does commitment to a specific set of values make one a factionalist? Is it possible to adopt a moral perspective that doesn't belong to an overarching framework or isn't informed by a coherent deeper rationale? Religious beliefs and political ideologies are simply that—a coherent discourse based on a clear rationale for dealing with moral dilemmas—when one looks beyond their labels.

Consistent with his position, Johnston doesn't insist on any individual or collective outcomes from these moral negotiations in the classroom. He states: "Whether change follows as a result of this different way of seeing is a matter for the individual teacher to know" (p. 8). It is unfortunate that the moral awareness of the teachers or the students are not expected to constructively help develop deeper moral positions, examine their own values, or challenge and critique each other for alternate possibilities. For teachers to know if change follows or not, and to initiate desirable changes, they need some form of heuristic or framework that would help them in the process. Moral growth and outcomes are too important to be left to the whims of individual teachers. Moreover, it is not enough for an individual teacher to be personally satisfied with the outcome. There is a collective dimension to moral negotiations as well, as we discussed in the framework for dialogue. Teachers must have a social consciousness to facilitate moral enlargement in their students and work collaboratively to facilitate their own moral growth.

Johnston does acknowledge in other places that there is a need to collectively negotiate morality: "Rather than worrying about the extent to which morality is individual or social ... I suggest that in fact morality exists precisely in the interplay between the personal and the social" (p. 6). Though Johnston accepts that morals are social, he doesn't include the students in the morality negotiated by the teachers. In the examples and situations Johnston discusses, rarely do teachers find out the moral position of students on a particular issue and attempt to arrive at a reconciliation that is satisfactory to both of them or challenge each other to move on to a suitable compromise. The "context" or the "social" Johnston typically invokes leave out the sense of morality students bring with them. When he says "We have to re-examine our values and how they play out in the given circumstances; the morality of our decision making lies in the encounter between our own values and the complex details of particular contexts and cases" (p. 47), context here means the expectations of the institution, social conditions of the students, and the situational background of the dilemma faced. But what is the place of the morals and values of students, and even their aspirations and desires, in the moral decisions taken by teachers? Though the context includes the morality of our students, they rarely feature in the examples analyzed in Johnston's book. How would the decision change if teachers attempted to inquire, accommodate, and mutually negotiate the moral values influencing their students? Things become complicated when we have to take into account the perspectives of others in moral decisions we make for joint enterprises, such as education. Morality, therefore, is not about being right to oneself, but also developing a position that is consonant with wider social and human well-being.

To give an example, Johnston wrestles with the possible plagiarism of his student Hea-young. He takes into account many diverse issues in the student's social background and educational context to adopt a lenient attitude. However, we know that students from non-Western cultures don't share the same assumptions about the ownership of words and texts in the United States. What is understood as plagiarism for the teacher might be motivated for the student by a higher moral value of sharing and communal ownership (Pennycook, 1996). A teacher has to ask: Why does this student not treat this borrowing as plagiarism? Is her act of borrowing influenced by a set of morals she brings with her? Are there other considerations here about her borrowing that I am not aware of? How can I introduce the student to other ethical principles that impinge on her act of borrowing that she might not be aware of? How can we both challenge each other with our positions, negotiate our morals with sensitivity, and move to a higher moral plane on the ethics of borrowing? Engaging with the morality others bring with them leads us to mutually critique our positions and develop a richer perspective. This is already happening for our understanding of plagiarism in the context of the Internet—even the legal understanding of copyright is being reconsidered in relation to common ownership and open source codes. It is from this line of consideration that we have to consider the benefits of transformative discourse.

It is understandable that in his focus on the context-specific nature of values, Johnston (2003) doesn't want to offer any rules or framework for negotiating morality. He argues, "I believe strongly that morality cannot in any interesting or meaningful sense be reduced to unconditional rules of the type 'always do X' or 'one should never do X or Y' " (p. 7). However, the fear of adopting positions is an unfortunate outcome of the politically correct and relativist climate in academia. Not specific rules perhaps, but general guidelines are possible. If not, we might have to adopt a situational ethics, which might lead to a debilitating relativism. It is not impossible to find exceptions to some of the pedagogical guidelines we might come up with; but Johnston himself is against spurious examples for the sake of argument. Even in the case of exceptions, the need to struggle with our moral priorities shows the importance of negotiation. If we have to choose the "lesser of two evils" sometimes, there should still be no confusion about what we really value in normal circumstances. These are only two evils. The positions Johnston personally espouses, such as "empowerment" or an "ethic of caring," are useful maxims for all of us. One doesn't have to shy away from such broad guidelines. In fact, without some broad moral guidelines, it is difficult to negotiate a satisfactory position on the dilemmas we face.

We have to develop a more sophisticated understanding of the relationship between commitment to an ideal and engagement with those of others in the classroom. In fact, constructive dialogue is possible only under certain conditions of commitment. If one is unsure of one's position, or vacillates periodically, it is difficult to engage with him/her in dialogue. I have been in many fruitless debates with people who conveniently shifted their positions at every move so that the conversation didn't lead to anything productive. Those who are not sure of their bearings are difficult to talk to. They may even be so insecure about their positions that they are unable to have a calm and open dialogue. Similarly, it is those who are committed to a position who can engage in a clear and confident dialogue with those holding divergent positions. One who is insecure of his or her position will find it difficult to engage with others' point of view. The belief that a healthy dialogue is possible only when people keep their values and beliefs in abeyance is a defensive, insecure, and disempowering position. Those who are comfortable with their values and commitments don't have to fear engaging with the positions of others. Paradoxically, the values of some allow for constant self-critique and revision. It is important to acknowledge our morals and engage with others and their divergent moral positions to broaden our point of view. My position is that morals are too important to be kept to ourselves or left pedagogically undefined. We have a moral responsibility for the betterment of all of us as a human community.

There are of course special problems for teachers in classrooms as there is an in-built power difference over their students. They can't claim to negotiate moral dilemmas as equals as they can do with their peers and colleagues in their professional relationships. In their chapters for this book, many authors (i.e., Phillipson, Vandrick, Morgan, and Kubota) are rightly concerned about the unfair advantage teachers hold in their discussion of spirituality in the classroom. Though this issue of power difference is raised mostly against CET in this book, all teachers have to mind their status in the classroom. The unconscious representation of our own values and positions may receive exaggerated significance because of our power and authority. In fact, Johnston (2003) treats the possibility of classroom ideological imposition as a cause of concern in expressing his reservations against CP. However, the answer to how teachers can hold an ideological or moral position and yet negotiate their power differential fairly to engage in an ethical and constructive classroom discussion has been addressed by many critical practitioners in the past (see Canagarajah, 1999, pp. 173–198 for a review). Giroux (1983) has argued that it is important for teachers to have the humility to learn from their students, even as they exercise their intellectual authority to facilitate critical reflection. He uses the metaphor of *organic intellectuals*, borrowed from Gramsci, to describe the symbiotic relationship between the leaders and followers to shape each other's positions in their struggle for social change. Though leaders have to exercise their authority to give guidance and direction to others, they have to still display the openness to learn from their followers and think along their interests and contexts to provide meaningful leadership. This dialectical engagement will help leaders to themselves examine their biases and complicity in power. It is only through such recourse that leaders can negotiate the bind of attempting to represent the interests of the disempowered from their positions of power. The notion of a servant leader, practiced by Christ for example, provides models for teachers—as some of our contributors discuss.

We teachers stand to gain by participating in such classroom moral negotiations with our students. Our own spiritual and moral growth depends on such challenging interactions. Similarly, an ongoing negotiation of positions enables values-based professionals to continue their ideological reflection and development in relation to diverse social groups and changing political equations. Furthermore, if we want our students to learn from our experiences, values, and knowledge, we have to give them the courtesy of listening to *their* wisdom. It's a challenge to suspend our authority on intellectual matters to listen to the spiritualities and moralities our students bring with them. To be a teacher and also a learner is a paradox but not an impossibility. It is possible to be open-minded for correction, but also share one's well-researched and reflected opinion on matters. This is the ethic of vulnerability that was discussed in the preceding part of the chapter.

Julian Edge (2006) reminds us of an added complication in our ability to negotiate morality in the classroom. Whether we like it or not, all TESOL professionals are implicated in the military and imperialist designs of Anglophone regimes. Both CET and non-CET will be perceived in the light of the dominant political context and ideologies represented by the UK and USA when they teach abroad. And this includes TESOL professionals who claim not to have an ideology as well as those who are staunchly committed to critical practice. We are always implicated in a nexus of power relations, whether or not we are committed to democratic ideals. There are many ways to approach this dilemma. I adopt an openness to acknowledging that pedagogy is always implicated in power and wider geopolitical contexts, and then collaborate with students and local communities to make spaces for their values and interests. It is such resistance from within that I have articulated for English teaching in postcolonial contexts (Canagarajah, 1999). Teachers can develop a reflexive awareness of their implication in the wider nexus of power relations, make this an agenda for discussion with students as they teach, reconstruct the discourses and grammars of English to suit democratic and multicultural ends, and thus collectively work to renegotiate power differences. CET adopt a similar strategy of making spaces for spiritual values in classrooms, aware of the way Christianity is and was used for domination in diverse communities (see Byler, Chamberlain, Osborn, Stabler-Havener, Snow, Ferris, Wong, this volume).

Conclusion

The relativistic position that specifies that one should keep one's morality to oneself or work out one's own pedagogical alternatives in a way that sounds appropriate for oneself sounds insecure, defensive, and defeatist. Such a position doubts the capacity students and professionals display for tolerant engagement despite strong moral commitments of their own. It is possible to be proud of one's values, represent what one stands for, and still be engaged in dialogue with those with different value systems. In fact, constructive dialogue is possible only when one brings one's own values to the table, and is also committed to facilitating the moral upliftment of others in the classroom. Those who are worried about alienation, divisions, and domination do not have faith in the post-positivistic project of discoursing across difference. In the spirit of full disclosure, I must acknowledge that the framework I have developed above is consistent with my practice as a CET and a CP. I am committed to sharing my perspectives with others, constantly examining our mutual positions in a respectful manner, challenging ourselves to move to higher moral and spiritual grounds, thus ceaselessly transforming personal lives and social relations. To use the jargon of the insiders in both camps in this dialogue, such a practice is *evangelizing* from the Christian tradition or *conscientization* from the critical tradition.

Notes

1. He makes an exception for the dialogue achieved in this book.
2. I am piggy-backing on Johnston's discussion to develop my own position here. I thank Johnston for his pioneering book in ELT that enables his colleagues to develop their own classroom pedagogies.

References

Abbey, R. (2006). The primary enemy? Monotheism and pluralism. In J. B. White (Ed.), *How should we talk about Religion?* (pp. 211–230). Notre Dame, IN: University of Notre Dame Press.

Canagarajah, A. S. (1999). *Resisting linguistic imperialism in English teaching.* Oxford, UK: Oxford University Press.

Edge, J. (2006). Background and overview. In J. Edge (Ed.), *(Re-)locating TESOL in an age of empire* (pp. xii–xix). Basingstoke, UK: Palgrave Macmillan.

Giroux, H. A. (1983). *Theory and resistance in education: A pedagogy for the opposition.* South Hadley, MA: Bergin.

Hampshire, S. (2000). *Justice is conflict.* Princeton, NJ: Princeton University Press.

Johnston, B. (2003). *Values in English language teaching.* Mahwah, NJ: Lawrence Erlbaum.

Lusted, D. (1986). Why pedagogy? *Screen, 27*(5), 2–14.

Pennycook, A. (1996). Borrowing others' words: Text, ownership, memory, and plagiarism. *TESOL Quarterly, 30*(2), 201–230.

Simon, R. I. (1992). *Teaching against the grain: Texts for a pedagogy of possibility.* Toronto, Canada: OISE Press.

Taylor, C. (1998). The dynamics of democratic exclusion. *Journal of Democracy, 9*(4), 143–156.

White, J. B. (2006). Introduction. In J. B. White (Ed.), *How should we talk about religion?* (pp. 1–10). Notre Dame, IN: University of Notre Dame Press.

Discussion Questions

Part I: Setting the Tone: Dialogue and Discourse

1. The contributors in this volume provide a "spiritual identification statement" (pp. xi–xvi). Discuss the spiritual identification statements and how their authors' beliefs influence their chapters and pedagogy. Write your own spiritual identification statement and discuss how your spirituality or religious faith and beliefs have (or have not) influenced you as a language educator.
2. In his introduction, Canagarajah offers several questions to help teachers explore to what extent they are pursuing a pedagogy of closure or of possibility. Read the list of questions on pages 12–13 and discuss ways in which you have sought either a pedagogy of possibilities or closure. Which of the areas (Attitude, Policy, Objective, Classroom relations, Identity, Pedagogy, Curriculum, Assessment) are you most concerned about and which would you like to explore? How will you follow up on this?
3. In his response, Canagarajah discusses transformative dialogue, which requires vulnerability "which opens one up for criticism, reflection, and change" (p. 78). Read and discuss the example of plagiarism and answer the questions he provides (p. 83). Provide an example in which you engaged with the morality of your students, and an instance in which you sought out, were challenged by, and transformed through negotiation with your students' moral values.
4. Applying the Rogerian attitudes Edge describes (respect, empathy, and sincerity) and the skills in intercultural communication (suspending evaluation and being open to what might seem uncomfortable or threatening), respond as an Understander in a non-defensive style to one of the authors in this book with whom you disagree. If, as Edge describes, "negative evaluation of others' ideas or actions proves unavoidable" (p. 29), then provide evidence that you have "an ability to disagree with increased understanding and respect" (p. 29).
5. Edge quotes Stevick (1998) who states:

   > Teaching language is only one kind of teaching, and teaching and learning are only two limited aspects of being human. I therefore hope, first of all, that you will take time to sit down and read again whatever philosophical or religious writings you have found most nourishing to you.
   >
   > (as cited by Edge, this volume, p. 25)

What philosophical or religious writing has nourished you? Describe in 500 words or fewer how this has impacted your teaching and students.

6. Johnston asks whether dialogue is possible between evangelical Christians and their critics and defines different types of dialogue. What evidence can you find in each of the chapters and responses in this part of the book that demonstrates exploratory dialogue, conciliatory dialogue, and asymmetrical reciprocity? Provide an example of each if you can.
7. What do you think of the three challenges Johnston presents to both evangelicals and non-evangelicals? Which do you feel have the most merit and why? To what extent do the authors in the chapters and responses in this volume demonstrate that they are working toward these challenges?
8. One of the points Johnston makes to evangelicals is that they should stop "hiding." Yet when a student shared that "Jesus had guided him to come to the United States and pursue a graduate degree in English teaching" (p. 42), Johnston states that this was "profoundly alien to us non-evangelicals" and "the absolute opposite of our preferred speech and thought, in which, for example, one keeps one's religious convictions to oneself" (p. 42). What should students of strong religious faith do in such a situation: "keep their convictions to themselves" and avoid the perception of proselytizing, or "stop hiding" and state their faith openly in a transparent way?
9. Pennycook has some rather harsh criticism for two of the authors in this part of the book. Which of his points do you agree or disagree with? How do you respond to the following: "If one wishes to adhere to this exclusivist interpretation of religion, then it is not plausible also to claim a position of respect for others" (p. 62)? To what extent do Byler and Stabler-Havener and others in this volume address Pennycook's and Johnston's concern for self-disclosure about political agendas?
10. Phillipson asks a key question that both Edge and Johnston allude to, "whether attempting to convert others to one's own branch of Christianity is defensible?" (p. 66). Discuss this question and provide and defend an answer and the implications this may have for CET.
11. Ramanathan speaks about the inherent dangers when "religious leanings" are allowed to inform our identities as teachers, and contends that we need "to interrogate *intentionalities*" and ask ourselves, "What is it that we individually or collectively intend when we do or do not speak about religious discourses or speak about them in certain ways?" (p. 73). What questions about your own intentions (religious or otherwise) should you ask of yourself? What actions or attitudes do you exhibit in class that may be perceived as arrogant, superior, and even bigoted? How might you investigate how your religious or other ideological leanings affect your students?
12. Write your own response to this part of the book stating what you feel are the central issues and where you stand on them. What areas of commonality can you find among the authors and which points do you see little hope for mutual understanding?

Part II

Ideological and Political Dilemmas

10 Deconstructing/Reconstructing the Missionary English Teacher Identity[1]

Mary Shepard Wong

In language teaching publications, Christian scholars have explored ways in which their spirituality and faith might positively influence their pedagogy (Baurain, 2007; Palmer, 2007; Scovel, 2004; Smith, 2000; Smith & Osborn, 2007; Smith, Sullivan, & Short, 2006; Snow, 2001), while other scholars have raised concerns about Christianity and ELT and the use of English teaching by Christian missionaries (Edge, 1996, 1997, 2003, 2004, 2006; Johnston, 2003; Johnston & Varghese, 2006; Pennycook & Coutand-Marin, 2003; Pennycook & Makoni, 2005; Vandrick, 2002; Varghese & Johnston, 2007). This has caused Christians to ask some difficult questions about the actual and potential ways in which their spiritual identity impacts their language teaching and the profession of TESOL (Wong, 2005a, 2005b, 2006, 2007). In this chapter, I posit that a reconstructed identity from a "missionary who is teaching to gain access" to a "global Christian professional language teacher" has the potential to redress the concerns raised while enhancing many of the benefits that can occur when teachers align their spiritual and professional identities and live and work with a newfound wholeness and integrity that respects their faith, profession, colleagues, and students.

Teaching as Vocation vs. Teaching as Access

Evangelical Christian mission as defined by Moreau (1994)

> is the human responsibility to serve as ambassadors of Christ in communicating the message he commissioned to the church ... seek[ing] to discover *appropriate* means of entering new cultures, *sensitively* and completely communicating the good news and meeting the needs of the *whole* person.
>
> (p. 783, emphasis mine)

This view of Christian mission reflects a shift to a postmodern paradigm, which is critical of Christian missions' connection with the political and economic powers of the West (Bosch, 1991; Dyrness & Engel, 2000; Escobar, 2003; Kraus, 1998; Moreau, Corwin, & McGee, 2004; Pocock, Van Rheenen, & McConnell, 2005; Sanneh, 2003; Shenk, 2002).

Within the evangelical missions movement, "tentmaking" is a term that refers to the Apostle Paul's work of making tents so as not to burden the church at

Corinth in his work as an itinerant preacher as recorded in the Bible. For a discussion of the various views of "tentmaking" from the evangelical missions perspective, see Clarke, 1997; Hardin, 1998; Purgason, 1998; Siemens, 1996, 1997; Tennant, 2002; and Wilson, 1979, and for biblical references related to Paul's tentmaking see Acts 18:3, 20:34, 28:30; Rom. 15:17–20; I Cor. 4:12, 9:6, 9:15–18; II Cor. 12:14; Eph. 4:11–12; I Thes. 2:9. The biblical concept of self-support for mission is an alternative to the model of someone who is sent out from and supported financially by a church, a model that Paul also used. However, the way in which "tentmaking" is used and understood today among some mission agencies has strayed from this biblical concept. This distorted understanding of Paul's "tentmaking" removes Paul's primary concern of self-support and replaces it with the notion of taking on and using an occupation as a means of gaining access to a country in which missionaries are not permitted to work.

Thus "tentmaking" is used today to describe missionaries who enter "limited access countries" (countries in which traditional missionaries are restricted) after finding legitimate employment in order to perform their *real* missionary work. Barnett (2005) refers to "tentmaking" as a "creative-access platform" that he defines as "the practical means for providing mission workers the opportunity and relational basis for effectively accomplishing their main goal" (p. 211). This main goal, according to Barnett, is "evangelism or church planting" (p. 211).

This type of English teaching-as-access is deceptive. In some cases, the "teachers" may not be who they portray themselves to be. For example, they may not be trained, qualified, or experienced as foreign language teachers. They may have the mistaken notion that being a "native speaker" bestows them with an innate ability to teach English. Those who teach-as-access may be untrained monolingual speakers attempting to teach students a skill that they have not acquired (e.g., becoming bi- or multilingual) and thus may be unable to respond to grammatical queries or lack an insider's understanding of the process of foreign language acquisition. (However, this critique is not confined to only Christian English teachers.)

Furthermore, such people may be engaging in unlawful activities. This is not only deceptive but also potentially dangerous as it may jeopardize the local Christians. When foreigners arouse the government's concern by proselytizing when it is forbidden, the local believers might suffer from more severe restrictions or persecution by the authorities. (See Wong, 2001, for a depiction of the role of Western evangelicals in China.) Thus teaching-as-access violates Moreau's definition of missions methodology stated earlier, and is suspect of being inappropriate, insensitive, and unable to meet the needs of the whole person.

Occasionally the use of deception by women and men of God is found in Scripture. (See Robison's chapter in this volume for a theological look at honesty as applied to missions and TESOL.) Christians are instructed to follow God rather than humans, which in rare instances demands that they act unlawfully. Martin Luther King Jr., for example, broke the law in conscientious resistance to state power, but not out of pragmatism. As Moreau (1994) states, "[Missions] is to be done without surrendering to a pragmatism that only evaluates methodologies in light of their success" (p. 783). Living peacefully, legally, and ethically in a community and performing one's work with excellence is God honoring and is a biblically based concept, which serves as the norm rather than the exception. Viewing teaching as only a "creative access" is treating it as just a means to an end. This distorted view of "tentmaking" is inappropriate because those who *use* teaching and do not *engage* in it devalue the profession, their students, and their primary calling as Christ followers.

Struggle and Resistance, but not Silence and Censor

In order to be sensitive, appropriate, and mindful of meeting the needs of the whole person, we must explore how to *prevent* ourselves from imposing our views on students while *ensuring* our identity informs our teaching. For just as Holliday (2005) *struggles* to teach English as an international language and Canagarajah's students (1999) *resist* linguistic imperialism, teachers must make their values (religious or otherwise) explicit, and *avoid* viewing students as "foreign Others" who we seek to know in order to make like us, which Holliday in a discussion of Nativespeakist views, refers to as "cultural correction."

Holliday uses the term "Nativespeakerist" to describe someone who views "non-native speakers" as linguistically deficient, who need to be taught by "native speakers" how to correct their English and change their "backward" teacher-centered pedagogical practices to more advanced, enlightened ones that are student-centered, communicative, autonomous, and empowering. Teachers with strong views (religious or otherwise) may have a similar tendency, to view students as culturally or spiritually deficient, and regard their religion or ideology as superior to all others. When we do this, we don't respect our students and their cultures and lose the opportunity to see with new eyes that which we hold most dear, whether it be our pedagogy, ideology, or faith. Morgan (2004) warns teachers of the power they have and the constant checks they must make when seeking to use teacher identity as pedagogy. He states "Teacher identity as pedagogy is always potentially 'dangerous.' Teachers have considerable influence and, in some settings, substantial power over students' futures" (Varghese, Morgan, Johnston, & Johnson, 2005, pp. 34–35). Morgan continues, "Therefore … [we need to be] always open to new accents, reinterpretation, and critical readings" (Varghese et al., 2005, pp. 34–35).

One might consider ESL classes offered in a US church the proper place for Bible-based English classes, for surely one can proselytize in a church in the United States. However, considering the vulnerability of immigrants and their children and the power teachers of the dominant majority have, we may want to reconsider this assumption. A colleague who is a consultant for church-based Adult ESL programs in the United States, said (personal communication September 26, 2008):

> During my years of teaching adult immigrants, I know that many immigrant parents do not have the time, English language skills, or knowledge to monitor what their children are learning. When churches of the dominant culture evangelize immigrant children, because it's easier, rather than finding some way to first engage their non-English-speaking parents, they

> are aggravating already fragile relationships between immigrant adults and their children. The adults have lost power through immigration because they cannot speak the dominant language. They acquiesce to neighborhood churches' proselytizing of their children out of necessity or stress. A Hmong Christian told me, "This is what Hmong people think: 'We like to send our children to your Vacation Bible School because we don't know what to do with them during the summer. But don't baptize them.'" Evangelizing children without respecting the parental hierarchy can cause disastrous rifts. We have to put ourselves in those parents' places and ask ourselves how we would feel if well-meaning people from a more powerful culture were bypassing our parental authority to influence our children.

Treating others as we would like to be treated by not imposing our views on them is a basic Christian (but not only Christian) value that we need to keep in mind.

That being said, preventing ourselves from imposing our views does not mean a moratorium on discussing them. A silence and censor of all things spiritual in the classroom is hardly the answer. One might make the claim that we are in fact imposing our Western views on our students by *not* allowing space for classroom discussions of spiritual identity or religion. As Newbigin (1989) states

> The sharp line which modern Western culture has drawn between religious affairs and secular affairs is itself one of the most significant peculiarities of our culture and would be incomprehensible to the vast majority of people who have not been brought into contact with this culture.
>
> (p. 172)

Thus we may be promoting the Western dichotomy of secular and sacred by ignoring the spiritual dimensions of our students and the spiritual practices embedded in their cultures. Since culture is shaped in profound ways by religious beliefs and practices, it seems odd that discussion of things spiritual is absent in TESOL materials and regarded as taboo in ELT classrooms. Two important questions to explore are: how can one redress the spiritual void in ELT materials and how do non-Western teachers avoid the spiritual/secular dualism found in the West and engage in a pedagogy that is holistic? For a discussion of the former, see Smith (this volume and 2000), and Smith and Carvill (2000), and for a discussion on researching teachers' spirituality and ELT pedagogy that goes beyond a discussion of specific religions, see Bradley this volume and 2005.

A Worst-Case, Typical, and Hopeful Scenario

But one might ask, how does a teacher resist imposing strongly held views, struggle to respect their students, and yet ensure that their values inform and guide their work? In the following, Elizabeth, Matilda, and Peter are presented as fictional characters in scenarios to illustrate a worst-case, typical, and hopeful sce-

Table 10.1 Three fictional scenarios of Christian English teachers

	Elizabeth: Teaching as Access (a worst-case scenario)	*Matilda: Striving for Excellence (a more typical scenario)*	*Peter: Open to Possibilities (a hopeful scenario)*
Goal	Her goal is to win as many souls as she can, which she believes is accomplished by active evangelism.	Being a witness of her faith and glorifying God are her aims, which she believes is accomplished through teaching English well and learning the host language.	His goal is to glorify God in his teaching and scholarship. His commitment to be a witness is not reduced to strategies but encompasses all he says, is, and does.
Pedagogy	She believes English is best taught by a native speaker using CLT. She enforces "English only" in class by fining students who speak L1.	Her pedagogy is evolving as she actively reflects on ways to incorporate a missing spiritual dimension without imposing her views.	He regards local teachers as reservoirs of knowledge and explores collaboratively with them in developing appropriate pedagogies.
Interactions with others	Most out of class encounters are with expatriates and are conducted in English.	Out of class she interacts with a few locals in the local languages, although English is used most often.	He interacts both with expatriate and local colleagues in a number of dialects and languages.
Correspondence	Letters home have stories of these "strange" people and their "quirky" ways, requests for funds, and little about her learning.	Letters home at times reveal understanding and respect of the host culture and what she is learning spiritually and professionally.	His correspondence and scholarship honors God. He engages in both Christian and secular conferences and publishing endeavors.
Supporting Or Sending Agency	Her mission sending agency has a concealed evangelistic objective, requires minimal qualifications, hires only "native" English speakers, provides minimal teacher development opportunities, and is unaware of the negative impact of their presence and work.	Her sending agency seeks to be transparent in its aims and practices, requires appropriate experience and academic qualifications for the tasks assigned (but not "nativeness"), promotes professional development, and is aware of some of the negative consequences of their presence and work.	He is financially self-supported; however, his home church communicates with him regarding his work and what he is learning from the local Christians and church. He serves as a cultural mediator connecting the churches, helping Western churches see God through a new lens.

nario of a Christian English teacher who does this to varying degrees of success. They are provided to stimulate reflection upon the extent to which Christians have discovered and engaged in "*appropriate* means of entering new cultures, *sensitively* and completely communicating the good news and meeting the needs of the *whole* person" (Moreau, 1994, p. 783, emphasis mine). Although they are fictional, they are composites of people I have encountered based on my experience of teaching in China (1981–82), my 2-year study of Christian teachers abroad (Wong, 2000), 8 years of directing and teaching in a field-based MA/TESOL program comprised mostly of Christians teaching internationally, and a recent sabbatical trip to several countries in which I interviewed and observed 30 Christian teachers (Wong, forthcoming).

The scenarios in Table 10.1 are not fixed, but fluid. Multiple factors influence a teacher's goals, pedagogy, interactions, and correspondence in countless, complex ways. The scenarios are not meant to reduce the attitudes, aims, and activities of all Christian English teachers into three types. Rather, they are provided to stimulate reflection on the ways in which one's faith and understanding of mission can profoundly affect one's teaching. Peter represents a hopeful scenario of openness and possibilities and is not meant to portray "the" ideal, just as Elizabeth is but one example of a Christian teacher. Fortunately, it is not Elizabeth but Matilda who represents the majority of Christian teachers working internationally.

Teaching as Access: Elizabeth

Elizabeth (a worst-case scenario) regards teaching as a means to an end, a way into a country in order to evangelize. In class, Elizabeth's pedagogy is based on communicative language teaching (CLT), which she believes comprises games and group work. Although her students need to prepare for national exams, she focuses on conversation since she is not able to teach grammar. This doesn't bother her since she feels qualified to teach by virtue of the fact that she is a "native speaker." Her pet peeves include eliminating her students' "Chinglish," plagiarism, and their use of L1 in the classroom. Feeling that locally produced texts are substandard, she insists on texts published in the US. Out of class, she spends time with the students she views as most open to conversion. In letters home, Elizabeth regales her readers with amusing anecdotes of her "exotic" students and their strange habits. A list of "seekers" is provided in code for her supporters to pray for, followed by a plea for funds.

The agency that has recruited Elizabeth (LCEA), has a double name, one ideal for recruiting Christians in the US (**L**oving **C**hristian **E**vangelistic **A**ssociation) and another name used in the host country that conceals their proselytizing agenda while appealing to the global corporate mentality (**L**inguistic **C**apital for **E**conomical **A**dvancement).[2] The agency requires no teaching experience or academic qualifications beyond a college degree and offers little ELT training. The teaser on their website reads "No experience? No problem! As long as you can speak it, you can teach it." It is concerned with placing as many Christians as possible on every campus, and has as its primary mission evangelism rather than teaching. The agency recruits only "native" English speakers and requires their candidates to raise hundreds of dollars of support each month. None of the founders or executives has degrees in education, and they are unaware of or choose to rationalize the negative consequences caused by short-term missions, as discussed in Slimbach (2000) and the Standards of Excellence (downloaded

2006), and they have not considered the dangers of the global spread of English, as discussed by Masters (1998), McKay (2002), Phillipson (1992), and Pennycook and Makoni (2005).

Striving for Excellence: Matilda

Matilda, who is a teacher striving for excellence, views her work differently from Elizabeth. Trying to understand her vocation as a Christian teacher, she is learning how to integrate in all aspects of her life what was once considered a separate, independent call to obey the Great Commission (Mat. 28:18–20). She maintains that teaching English well and learning languages are valid ways to be a witness. Her pedagogy is evolving as she actively reflects on ways she can include a missing spiritual dimension in her class materials and class discussions.

Matilda's sending agency does not conceal its religious identity in its promotional materials. It seeks to recruit qualified, experienced teachers (regardless of first language status) whose main concern is to teach with excellence. Less experienced teachers are trained and mentored by more experienced teachers. Stakeholders are informed in writing if explicit religious materials are used in class. Teachers are given clear guidelines of what is and is not appropriate to discuss in class regarding religious beliefs. (See *A Teacher's Guide to Religion in the Public Schools* for a useful resource in helping teachers in the US expose students to religion without imposing their own views on the topic.) The agency encourages professional development among its teachers (e.g., in-service training and membership in professional organizations) and several board members hold degrees in education and have cross-cultural experience and so are aware of the potential negative impact of their work (e.g., displacement of local teachers and endangerment of local dialects).

Open to Possibilities: Peter

In contrast to Elizabeth, but not too far from Matilda, is Peter, who represents a hopeful scenario, open to possibility (for a discussion of pedagogy of possibility vs. pedagogy of closure see Canagarajah and Morgan, this volume; Lusted, 1986; and Simon, 1992). Peter is a qualified and experienced teacher seeking to learn from the local teachers who he views as reservoirs of cultural knowledge. Being a language learner himself, he is empathetic to the challenges his students face and includes L1 in the classroom, encouraging an exploration of code mixing and switching, which is present in interactions among peoples in multilingual societies. He has adjusted his pedagogy and materials to what he has learned from local colleagues about his students' preferences and situations. He no longer focuses on American culture or American English and discusses the rich variety of Englishes used in the world. His students reflect upon how cultural difference affects communication and how cultural representations are constructed and contested.

Peter finds many Western-produced texts inappropriate and uses the dialogues and situations as springboards for critical reflection in which students are asked to problematize the cultural messages and implicit assumptions. In so doing, he seeks to help students develop a critical understanding of how language, texts, and pedagogy are ideological (see Canagarajah, 1999). He values and is eager to learn about his students' faith traditions and religions and avoids imposing his own religious views on his students. He attends the local church and fellowships with both local and expatriate colleagues, and so he can refer students to local fellowships if they inquire to learn more. He refrains from offering Bible studies in his home with his students as this may pressure or privilege them. However, he has had such studies with his local colleagues. His correspondence home reveals a deeper understanding and appreciation of the culture, the local church, and the people. He engages in writing that impacts his profession and presents at both Christian and secular conferences.

What can be learned from these three CET scenarios? I posit that a reconstructed identity for Christian teachers from one who is teaching for access to one who is working as a global Christian professional language teacher, has the potential to address the concerns of: (1) trust and disclosure in securing positions, (2) the imposition of strongly held views on students, (3) the alleged uncontested support of the global spread of English, (4) the lack of interconnectedness between one's pedagogy and spiritual identities, (5) the spiritual void found within ELT materials, and (6) the spiritual/secular dualism in Western culture. Such a teacher has the potential to teach from a pedagogy of possibility (Morgan, this volume; Simon, 1992) and not a pedagogy of closure (Morgan, this volume; Lusted, 1986). These teachers are open to "the possibility of self-criticism, learning from others, and constant reconstruction of [their] own values and self, with a commitment to help others enrich their lives" (Canagarajah, this volume, p. 78). In the next part of the chapter, I focus on exploring how one's spiritual identity can help to support and sustain teaching by describing each term in the reconstructed identity "global Christian professional language teacher."

Global Christian Professional Language Teacher

I use the term "global Christian professional language teacher" in the following sense:

> *global*: to emphasize an understanding of and need for diverse perspectives,
>
> *Christian*: to marking my spiritual identity,
>
> *professional*: to stress the importance of being qualified, skilled, and knowledgeable,

language: to covey sensitivity to English's domination and the importance of all languages and not just English,

teacher: to note our role, responsibility, and vocation.

I will now discuss each term, starting with the last term, "teacher."

Teacher

Snow (2001) has noted that "English teaching can and should be Christian vocation in its own right and not simply a means to other ends or a secular task only *incidentally* engaged in by Christians" (p. 19). He argues that teaching *is* witness expressed through the quality with which Christians carry out their teaching and posits "Rather than being incidental to witness or even evangelism, the quality of CET' teaching work is the primary vehicle through which they share the love of God with their students" (p. 65). I concur. When Christian teachers diligently prepare for class, listen attentively to students, are genuinely concerned for their students' well-being, cooperate with colleagues (especially when wronged), and make an effort to continually learn and grow professionally, they are a witness. Scovel calls this type of teaching "pedagogical compassion" and quotes Stevick as saying, "It seems to me that doing all this for the sake of the Gospel ... becomes almost a sacramental act, and that every classroom is a holy place where such acts can be performed" (as cited in Scovel, 2004).

The Christian literature on vocation might help inform this discussion (see Guinness, 1998; Hughes, 2005; Placher, 2005; Stevens, 1999; Volf, 1991). In the words of Frederick Buechner (1993), vocation is "the place where your deep gladness and the world's deep hunger meet" (p. 119). Guinness (1998) describes a *primary calling* to God and *secondary callings* to one's profession. Thus our primary call to God might be realized through our secondary calling of teaching.

Language (not English)

As English teachers, we are also language educators and thus we should be familiar with second language acquisition theory and practice and have learned and acquired a second or foreign language ourselves. For how can we teach others the skill of becoming bi- or multilingual if we have not accomplished this ourselves? Knowledge and competency in the specific language one is teaching is also required, but this alone is not sufficient. Having gone through the experience of learning a foreign language as an adult or being engaged in language learning ourselves as we are teaching a language, helps us to have empathy for our students. Snow insists that langauge learning is a form of ministry as it places teachers in the learner's position and demonstrates that they value their students' culture. Although Kubota and Ferris (this volume) believe that learning languages may give students' teachers more power, Snow (personal commication September 30, 2008) views it differently:

> Study of our students' languages is one of the best ways for English teachers to humble ourselves and empty ourselves of power and take on a humble servant role, and also one of the most powerful ways for us to incarnate our commitment to an ideal of multilingualism.

In many cases the teaching of other languages or dialects in addition to or instead of English may be of greater benefit to students than the teaching of English. For example, in the refugee camps along the Thai/Burma border, becoming literate in Burmese or in their native tribal languages such as Karen, or even the language host country, Thai, may be the priority for some refugees if it holds more benefits than learning to speak English. As language educators (and not simply English teachers) our work may be to learn from experienced local teachers how to assist emerging teachers to teach literacy skills in their own languages rather than or in addition to teaching English. Regarding our role as language teacher or educator may help to focus our attention on the benefits of encouraging the acquisition of other languages.

Professional

How does one know if one is a professional? Professionals possess the theoretical background, mentored experience, professional affiliations, and required credentials for meeting the standards of excellence in their field. Nunan (1999) adds that they act as advocates for their field. Thus, professionals have the knowledge, know how, qualifications, connections, and accountability to engage in their professions as advocates. People who are considered "professional" represent what is best in their fields and are endorsed and respected by colleagues. Professional language teachers, therefore, are expected to have the appropriate education, qualifications, and experience for the specific tasks they perform and work in ways that reflect positively upon TESOL. This definition would not apply to those who use English teaching as access and as a means to an end.

Christian

In his address "What is a Christian English Teacher?" Scovel (2004) asserts that a Christian teacher is defined by what one says, does, and who one is. Guinness (1998) affirms this and, in a discussion of vocation and calling, states,

> Calling is the truth that God calls us to himself so decisively that everything we are, everything we do, and everything we have is invested with a special devotion and dynamism lived out as a response to his summons and service.
>
> (p. 29)

Scovel contends a Christian has loving words, pedagogical compassion, and spiritual scholarship. She or he is a coherent, reflective, and faithful teacher. Scovel states,

> our faith gives us confidence … infuses joy into our daily work … allows for the indwelling of the Holy Spirit and gives us the spiritual gifts of building up, encouraging, and consoling. And always, in whatever we say, or do, or are, we know we are not alone.
>
> (p. 6)

Smith and Carvill (2000) emphasize that "loving attention to the other in a context of mutual giving should be at the heart of a Christian approach to foreign language education" (p. 142). They present hospitality and being a stranger and the recipient of other people's hospitality as an overarching metaphor for Christian teaching and quote Susanne Johnson who writes, "Hospitality in its deepest sense is a willingness not only to receive the stranger, but also to be changed and affected by the presence of the other, not only personally, but also institutionally, curricularly, and politically" (as cited in Smith & Carvill, 2000, p. 88).

Global

A final necessary component of the reconstructed identity of the Christian professional language teacher is a deep desire to understand, value, and learn from those who differ from ourselves, which I have expressed in the term "global." Chamberlain, Stabler-Havener, Byler, and many others in this volume have discussed that there are Christian teachers teaching abroad who harbor feelings of national and cultural superiority. History (both ancient and recent) is filled with examples of people who, in the name of Christianity, have acted on a false sense of political, moral, and spiritual superiority and engaged in acts of hostility, dominance, and even war. But there are also Christians (and I am one of them) who believe that God is truth, yet we are aware that our understanding of this truth is imperfect and tainted by sin and our human condition. Thus we seek to be open to learning how our views are limited or inaccurate and how encounters with the other, including the religious other, can enlarge our understanding of others, our faith, and ourselves.

As Hughes (2005) notes, to engage in a disciplined search for truth, truth cannot have already been defined or there can be no serious discussions with people who represent a diversity of perspectives, since we "know" in advance that these people with different perspectives have nothing to contribute to our conversation. The term "global" represents an openness and understanding of our need for a diversity of perspectives in order to see God and ourselves with greater depth.

Conclusion

I will conclude with a quote from a "Peter" (although Jacques is his pseudonym), a Christian teacher who expresses the openness described above in the following story about a Muslim family he got to know. Jacques states:

> He told [me] a little bit about their story during the Cultural Revolution. He suffered terribly and they kept their faith and they were so loving. They

> shattered my preconceptions about what it was to be Muslim. I had these feelings about Muslims and stuff like that, but these people were not like that. They were tender. They cared for me. Welcomed me and they knew we were Christians. And one day the uncle came up to me and said "Christians and Muslims should be friends." And he said to me, "no matter what happens to you, keep and nurture your faith, keep your faith intact." And I left there feeling exhorted, encouraged and blessed in a way that I had not in many churches.
>
> (Wong, 2009, interview conducted with "Jacques" March 17, 2008, central China)

Jacques' preconceptions were "shattered," his understanding enlarged, and someone who may have been perceived as a potential "convert" became a source of wisdom and encouragement, a fellow spiritual traveler.

In this chapter I have tried to demonstrate how a teacher who understands what it means to be a global Christian professional English language teacher has the potential to teach from a connectedness, from an integrity that unites who they are, what they believe, and what they do, while at the same time maintaining a respect for others and a sensitivity to the context in which they live and teach. It is not an easy task to seek to live out one's faith and not impose it on others, and as teachers we must be aware of our power and privilege and be vigilant to not abuse it. Much harm can and has been done by those who use English teaching as means to ends, yet many Christian teachers are mindful of this danger and are living out their faith in ways that respect their students, colleagues, and their profession, seeking to teach from a pedagogy of possibility and not of closure.

Notes

1. A version of part of this chapter appeared in the Newsletter of Christian Educators in TESOL caucus, July 2006, Volume 10, Number 2.
2. LCEA is a fictitious organization.

References

A teacher's guide to religion in the public schools. Published by the First Amendment Center. Retrieved September 15, 2008, from www.freedomforum.org/publications/first/teachersguide/teachersguide.pdf.

Barnett, M. (2005). Innovation in mission operations: Creative access platforms. In M. Pocock, M. G. Van Rheenen, & D. McConnell (Eds.), *The changing face of world missions: Engaging contemporary issues and trends* (pp. 209–244). Grand Rapids, MI: Baker Academic.

Baurain, B. (2007). Christian witness and respect for persons. *Journal of Language, Identity, and Education, 6*(3), 201–219.

Bosch, D. J. (1991). *Transforming mission: Paradigm shifts in theology of mission.* Mary Knoll, NY: Orbis.

Bradley, C. (2005). Spirituality and L2 pedagogy: Toward a research agenda. *Journal of Engaged Pedagogy, 4*(1), 26–38.

Buechner, F. (1993). *Wishful thinking: A seeker's ABC.* San Francisco: Harper San Francisco.

Canagarajah, S. (1999). *Resisting linguistic imperialism in English teaching.* New York: Oxford University Press.

Clarke, C. (1997). Tentmaking: State of the art. *International Journal of Frontier Missions, 14*(3), 103–105.

Dyrness, B., & Engel, J. (2000). *Changing the mind of missions: Where have we gone wrong?* Downers Grove, IL: InterVarsity Press.

Edge, J. (1996). Keeping the faith. *TESOL Matters, 6*(4), 1 & 23.

Edge, J. (1997). Julian Edge responds. *TESOL Matters, 6*(6), 6.

Edge, J. (2003). Imperial troopers and servants of the Lord: A vision of TESOL for the 21st century. *TESOL Quarterly, 37*(4), 701–709.

Edge, J. (2004). Of displacive and augmentative discourse, new enemies, and old doubts. *TESOL Quarterly, 38*(4), 717–721.

Edge, J. (Ed.) (2006). *(Re-)locating TESOL in an age of empire.* Basingstoke, UK: Palgrave Macmillan.

Escobar, S. (2003). *The new global mission: The gospel from everywhere to everyone.* Downers Grove, IL: InterVarsity Press.

Guinness, O. (1998). *The call: Finding and fulfilling the central purpose of your life.* Waco, TX: Word Books.

Hardin, D. (1998). Teaching English as a tool of evangelism: Problems and limitations. *Journal of Applied Missiology*, Retrieved September 21, 2008, from www.ovc.edu/missions/jam/english.htm.

Holliday, A. (2005). *The struggle to teach English as an international language.* Oxford, UK: Oxford University Press.

Hughes, R. T. (2005). *The vocation of a Christian scholar: How Christian faith can sustain the life of the mind.* Grand Rapids, MI: Eerdmans.

Johnston, B. (2003). *Values in English language teaching.* Mahwah, NJ: Lawrence Erlbaum.

Johnston, B., & Varghese, M. (2006). Neo-imperialism, evangelism, and ELT: Modernist missions and a postmodern profession. In J. Edge (Ed.), *(Re-)locating TESOL in an age of empire* (pp. 195–207). Basingstoke, UK: Palgrave Macmillan.

Kraus, C. N. (1998). *An intrusive gospel? Christian mission in the postmodern world.* Downers Grove, IL: InterVarsity Press.

Lusted, D. (1986). Why pedagogy? *Screen, 27*(5), 2–14.

McKay, S. L. (2002). *Teaching English as an international language: Rethinking goals and approaches.* Oxford, UK: Oxford University Press.

Masters, P. (1998). Positive and negative aspects of the dominance of English. *TESOL Quarterly, 32*(4), 716–726.

Moreau, A. S. (1994). Missiology. In W. A. Elwell (Ed.), *Evangelical dictionary of theology* (p. 783). Grand Rapids, MI: Baker Book House.

Moreau, A. S., Corwin, G. R., & McGee, G. B. (2004). *Introducing world missions: A biblical, historical, and practical survey.* Grand Rapids, MI: Baker Academic.

Morgan, B. (2004). Teacher identity as pedagogy: Towards a field-internal conceptualisation in bilingual and second language education. *International Journal of Bilingual Education and Bilingualism, 7*, 172–188.

Newbigin, L. (1989). *The gospel in a pluralist society.* Grand Rapids, MI: Eerdmans.

Nunan, D. (1999). President's message: October/November 1999. *TESOL Matters, 9*(5), 1.

Palmer, P. (2007). *The courage to teach: Exploring the inner landscape of a teacher's life* (10th Anniversary ed.). New York: Jossey-Bass.

Pennycook, A., & Coutand-Marin, S. (2003). Teaching English as a missionary language (TEML). *Discourse: Studies in the Cultural Politics of Education, 24*(3), 337–353.

Pennycook, A., & Makoni, S. (2005). The modern mission: The language effects of Christianity. *Journal of Language, Identity, and Education, 4*(2), 137–155.

Phillipson, R. (1992). *Linguistic imperialism.* Oxford, UK: Oxford University Press.

Placher, W. C. (Ed.) (2005). *Callings: Twenty centuries of Christian wisdom on vocation.* Grand Rapids, MI: Eerdmans.

Pocock, M., Van Rheenen, G., & McConnell, D. (2005). *The changing face of worldmissions: Engaging contemporary issues and trends.* Grand Rapids, MI: Baker Academic.

Purgason, K. (1998). Teaching English to the world: Options and opportunities. *International Journal of Frontier Missions, 15*(1) 33–39.

Sanneh, L. (2003). *Whose religion is Christianity? The gospel beyond the west.* Grand Rapids, MI: Eerdmans.

Scovel, T. (2004). What is a Christian English language teacher? *CETC Newsletter, 8*(1). Retrieved March 1, 2006, from www.tesol.org/NewsletterSite/view.asp?nid=3124.

Shenk, W. R. (Ed.) (2002). *Enlarging the story: Perspectives on writing world Christian history.* Maryknoll, NY: Orbis.

Siemens, R. (1996). Why did Paul make tents? Retrieved March 3, 2006, from www.globalopps.org/papers/whydid.htm.

Siemens, R. (1997). The vital role of tentmaking in Paul's missionary strategy. *International Journal of Frontier Missions, 14*(3), 121–130.

Simon, R. I. (1992). *Teaching against the grain: Texts for a pedagogy of possibility.* Toronto, Canada: OISE Press.

Slimbach, R. (2000). First, do no harm. *Evangelical Missions Quarterly, 36*(4), 428–441.

Smith, D. I. (2000). Faith and methods in foreign language pedagogy. *Journal of Christianity and Foreign Languages, 1*(1), 7–25.

Smith, D. I., & Carvill, B. (2000). *The gift of the stranger: Faith, hospitality, and foreign language learning.* Grand Rapids, MI: Eerdmans.

Smith, D. I., & Osborn, T. A. (Eds.) (2007). *Spirituality, social justice and language learning.* Greenwich, CT: Information Age Publishing.

Smith, D. I., Sullivan, J., & Shortt, J. (Eds.) (2006). *Spirituality, justice and pedagogy.* Nottingham, UK: The Stapleford Centre.

Snow, D. (2001). *English teaching as Christian mission: An applied theology.* Scottdale, PA: Herald Press.

Standards of Excellence in Short-Term Mission. Retrieved March 1, 2006, from www.stmstandards.org/.

Stevens, R. P. (1999). *The other six days: Vocation, work, and ministry in biblical perspective.* Grand Rapids, MI: Eerdmans.

Tennant, A. (2002). The ultimate language lesson. *Christianity Today, 46*(13), 32–36.

Vandrick, S. (2002). ESL and the colonial legacy: A teacher faces her "missionary kid" past. In V. Zamel, & R. Spack (Eds.), *Enriching ESOL pedagogy* (pp. 411–422). Mahwah, NJ: Lawrence Erlbaum.

Varghese, M., & Johnston, B. (2007). Evangelical Christians and English language teaching. *TESOL Quarterly, 41*(1), 5–31.

Varghese, M., Morgan, B., Johnston, B., & Johnson, K. A. (2005). Theorizing language teacher identity: Three perspectives and beyond. *Journal of Language, Identity, and Education, 4*(1), 22–44.

Volf, M. (1991). *Work in the spirit: Toward a theology of work.* New York: Oxford University Press.

Wilson, J. C. Jr. (1979). *Today's tentmakers.* Wheaton, IL: Tyndale House.

Wong, M. S. (2000). The influence of gender and culture on the pedagogy of five Western

English teachers in China. Unpublished doctoral dissertation, University of Southern California, Los Angles.

Wong, M. S. (2001). Reflections on the role of the western evangelicals in China. *Evangelical Missions Quarterly, 37*(3), 290–291.

Wong, M. S. (April, 2005a). Christian identity and the TESOL profession. Paper presented at the TESOL International Convention, San Antonio, TX.

Wong, M. S. (April, 2005b). Respecting religious differences in ESL classrooms. Symposium conducted at the 39th Annual TESOL Convention, San Antonio, TX.

Wong, M. S. (January, 2006). Forming an open academic response to concerned colleagues. In L. McAllister (Chair) Responding to the Critics. Symposium conducted at the Christian English Language Teachers Conference, Chiang Mai, Thailand.

Wong, M. S. (March, 2007). Spiritual dimensions and dilemmas of English teaching. Symposium conducted at the 41st Annual TESOL Convention, Seattle, WA.

Wong, M. S., & Robison, R. (2009). The relevance of teacher religious beliefs on identity formation among EFL teachers in Thailand, China, Vietnam, South Korea, and Taiwan. Paper presented at AAAL, Denver, CO.

11 English and Education in Anglophone Africa

Historical and Current Realities

Sinfree Makoni and Busi Makoni

In this chapter, we focus on the historical and contemporary role of English in "anglophone" Africa.[1] We use this term circumspectly because it emphasizes the connection between language and place—what Canut (2002) refers to as *territorialization.* The connections between language and place implicit in terms such as *anglophone, lusophone, francophone* are rendered difficult to maintain because of people's constant movement across different geographical regions. The complexity of using local categories arises not only because of the inconsistencies in the ways the terms are used within the same local communities. In addition, even when the same community uses the term consistently, it may be interpreted radically differently by educated and non-educated speakers.

The place of English in Africa, particularly in what is known as anglophone Africa, has been shaped over centuries by historical, social, and political forces. Unlike other parts of the world in which English usage and English-language teaching are relatively recent linguistic phenomena, Africa has a long history of contact with and usage of the English language. Unquestionably, Christian institutions played a significant role in establishing English as a language of prestige in British colonial Africa. Today, however, attitudes and uses of English are mediated by far more influential institutional forces of state, society, and economics.

In this chapter, we analyze the role that institutions such as Christianity and colonial governments have played in shaping and determining the prestige of English in anglophone Africa. The role of these institutions was also in part shaped by African demands for education in English, which continues to partially determine the status of English in popular imagination in Africa. We also comment on the ethical and moral dilemmas of language planning research, which advocates an expanded use of African languages in contexts in which there is a strong pro-English educational orientation both from parents and students (Ferguson, 2003).

English in Colonial Africa: Mission Perspectives

The historical role of Christianity in establishing English as the language of prestige and formal employment in anglophone Africa is undeniable. As the founders of formal education systems in the British colonies, Christian missionaries were integral to the formation of early colonial policy on language in education. However, debates on language choice were vehement and frequent among mission educators and among mission-educated Africans as well. These debates centered on questions of cultural integrity, the communicability of the Christian gospel, the new meanings that African words and speech acts assumed under the impact of Christianity, and "appropriate" knowledge for the Africans being educated, especially according to the Africans themselves. Africans literate in Western formal education did not regard their cultural identities as compromised through learning English. Even if Africans may have associated Western formal education with English, it is not self-evident that they readily accepted nonnative teachers of English because in African popular imagination English was construed as White.

The debates among African intellectuals did not focus on whether it was appropriate to use English as a medium of instruction; that was taken for granted. Instead, the debate focused on the standardization of African languages because missionaries could only incorporate a relatively restricted range of Africans' stylistic repertoire, thus excluding associative discourses characteristic of oral cultures (Makoni & Meinhof, 2003). African languages that were a product of this standardization were received with mixed feelings by educated Africans. It is, therefore, instructive to note that, at least in Zimbabwean social linguistic history, the term *colonial language* was first used by African intellectuals to refer *not* to English but to standardized African languages because of the limited input and serious involvement by Africans in the standardization process and the perceptible shifts in the meaning and forms of African languages due to standardization.

In fact, the English language did not arrive on the African continent through the mission's medium. Adegbija (1994) argues that it was first mercantile contact and then the conquering colonizing powers that brought English and other European languages into the linguistic picture for Africans. At the moment of African encounters with Europe, it's unlikely that Africans maintained any firm distinctions between the various European languages. However, the early association of these languages with military and economic gain might set the stage for their subsequent high regard in the minds of the conquered. Adegbija notes that:

> The basis for the European languages as languages of the masters, of power, of high position of prestige and of status were solidly created in these early days. Many Africans began to look up to the European languages as the master's language and yearned to learn them.
>
> (p. 31)

Although Adegbija's argument is well made that Africans might have expressed strong interest in European languages, this was not necessarily accompanied by a desire to acquire European cultural habits. This strong interest in learning European languages has to be situated within a context in which Europeans, in order to facilitate their control of colonized Africans, learnt African languages, albeit their own written versions, as part of an unfolding European colonial project.

Although Christian missionaries in the early colonial period tended to be highly sympathetic to the use of local African languages for education and communication, and inimical to the use and promotion of European languages in terms of policy, some missions clearly favored the use of local languages. The crucial issue, however, is not so much that the missionaries promoted the use of local languages but rather what they understood by the concept of "local language" and the impact of their linguistic perspective on local African linguistic ecologies. These perspectives facilitated the emergence of new relationships between languages and dialects and, in some cases, even led to a breakdown of precolonial social structures. An example of the latter can be found in the development of a missionary-based *lingua franca* (Tsonga) in colonial southern Africa, which facilitated the breakdown of some traditional systems of chieftainship and kinship (Spolsky, 2003).

The activities of missionaries in some contexts led to the emergence of new language varieties, as well as a new social and political hierarchy between particular local languages. The work of Protestant and Catholic missionaries in Zimbabwe led to the emergence of five different dialects, namely Karanga, chiManyika, Zezuru, Korekore, and Ndau, which were associated with different religious denominations (Errington, 2001). Karanga was subsequently associated with the Dutch Reformed Church, chiManyika with the Anglican Church, and Zezuru with the Roman Catholic Church (Chimhundu, 1992). Furthermore, in Botswana, Nyati-Ramahobo (2004) links the development of the Setswana language to the influence of eighteenth-century missionaries with the London Missionary Society.

Furthermore, there was considerable latitude in how the missionaries understood African multilingualism and the use of African languages. For example, in southern Africa, the American Mission Board continued to use isiZulu for their everyday work (e.g., medical advice and farming) in a region in which the Africans actually spoke chiNdau (Jeater, 2007). Similarly, the Basel missionaries operating in what was then the British Cameroons used the Mungaka language (spoken by the Bali people) extensively, even in regions where the dominance of the Bali was strongly resented by the local non-Bali populations (Trudell, 2005b, p. 74).[2]

In this environment, mission-educated Africans entered into the language debate as well, not just regarding whether to use English but also regarding which of the local languages should be used in schools. In colonial Rhodesia of the 1930s, fierce debate raged between mission-educated Africans who supported the continued use of Zulu in Ndebele schools as part of a pan-African nationalist project and Ndebele nationalists who supported the introduction of Ndebele as part of a cultural nationalist project. The London Missionary Society, which had played a key role in systematizing Ndebele, was also in favor of the introduction of Ndebele (Ranger, 1995; Samkange, 1936). However, the pan-African nationalists argued for the continued use of Zulu because they felt that introducing Ndebele would divide the Ndebele in Rhodesia from those in South Africa. They used English as a model to support their argument, contending that just as in England where there are still counties that have the main language as the King's English but speak their own dialects, so maintaining Zulu as the language of education would be preferable to the introduction of Ndebele in schools. Pan-African nationalists also disparaged Ndebele, describing it as a mixture of Zulu words and Kalanga (a dialect of chiShona).

Thus, questions of language in education fueled extended and fervent debate. The missionaries' enthusiasm for developing and teaching local languages was rooted largely in their belief that, in order that their evangelistic endeavors be effective, Christian texts such as the Bible needed to be available in "the language of the soul." For the missionaries, competence in local languages included but was not restricted to an ability to translate from English into local languages in order to facilitate the translation of Christian texts. By using local languages instead of European languages, the missionaries created opportunities for Christianity to be understood through African languages, since the religious concepts that they used were embedded in African languages. Notions of God, sin, and prayer were not introduced as new concepts but were derived from existing concepts for new evangelistic purposes. In southern Africa the term *God* was translated in a number of different ways, one of them being *wedenga*, derived from *kudenga* (meaning "in the sky"), a word that, although already existing, excluded the possibility of a god of the caves (Pennycook & Makoni, 2005).

In addition to the Bible, the texts most frequently produced by missionaries were lists of words or vocabularies. The preponderance of vocabularies over grammars reflects an orientation toward "using words" rather than speaking (Fabian, 1986; Jeater, 2007). The missionaries' production of local-language texts established a connection between Christianity and literacy and situated Christianity within a specific literate tradition. Since the church provided opportunities for becoming literate, those who became literate in the colonial days were also perforce exposed to Christianity. This is not to say that there were no literacy practices that predated Christianity or were developed independently of Christianity in Africa; Ṣwahili was previously written in an Arabic script, and the Vai language in Liberia had an orthographic system that predated Christianity and colonialism in that region. Nevertheless, the connection between Christianity and local-language literacy practices in Africa was strong.

Christian missions thus involved two types of conversion (Errington, 2001): the conversion of local people to Christianity and the conversion of African languages from unwritten into written forms. The development of orthographies for indigenous languages, carried out in many cases with a great degree of linguistic naïveté, affected the way indigenous languages were codified and distinguished. In some cases, distinctions were made between varieties of the same language, as the case of Runyakitara in Uganda and Nguni languages in South Africa illustrates (Bernstein, 1996). In addition, phonological characteristics not commonly found in European languages (such as tone or vowel quality) were often either ignored or underrepresented in early orthographies of African languages, rendering reading in these languages extremely difficult. The constant changes made to African orthographies and the limited literature available also made reading in these languages extremely difficult.

Stylistically, the missionaries tended to use a very restricted range of the African language stylistic continuum. They were also frequently not well disposed to the associative rhetorical styles typical of African cultures, favoring instead linear reasoning styles. The reduction of African languages to writing, therefore, contributed to the emergence of new rhetorical styles, some of which were distant from traditional African rhetorical patterns. The impact of the conversion of African languages into written forms was also evident at a lexical level. For example, Willan (1984) describes the efforts of early African novelist Sol Plaatje to extend the range of Tswana words to include words that were not included in early dictionaries (Makoni & Meinhof, 2003).

The determination to use local African languages in mission contexts caused Christian missionaries to campaign energetically in favor of language policies that favored African language development and use in education. Adejunmobi (2004) observes that: "European advocates of vernacular literature in Africa during the colonial period made their views known in books, journal articles, and at international conferences linked to specific interest groups, namely missionaries, education officials, linguists and anthropologists" (p. 5). Missionaries' energies on this question were directed toward the persuasion of expatriate authorities, and their arguments often contributed to debates about the status of Africans that were taking place in Europe. For example, the argument that African languages were as complex as European languages was used to demonstrate that Africans were not racially inferior to Europeans (Irvine, 1989).

Missionary protest against the use of English in education was linked to larger beliefs about the integrity of African cultures, as well as a significant degree of distrust of the European-educated African, the so-called "trousered African" (Mamdani, 1996). Many missionaries and educationists involved in this debate expressed both respect for African cultures and regret for the negative impact of European colonialism on those cultures.

At the 1926 Le Zoute Conference, a gathering of the leaders of Christian missions to Africa, the value of "the African as a man [*sic*]" was affirmed, and doubt was expressed as to "the desirability of imposing European institutions on Africans instead of developing their own" (Smith, 1926, pp. 13–14). However, neither opposition to English instruction nor support for English instruction was unanimous. For example, de Vries (2004) reports on an acute division in the Kom community's reaction to mission schools. While Catholic education was warmly received by the religiously converted, the non-Catholics were deeply wary of surrendering their children to the white men, seeing education as deeply ideological. Arguing on behalf of the demonstrated desire of African parents for education in the language spoken by the colonial powers, Smith (1926) describes the pro-English sentiment of many educators at the time:

> The African wants to learn English—indeed this is clearly why he clamours for education … any attempt to adopt the vernacular as the medium of instruction would meet with the strong opposition of certain classes of literate Africans who would feel that the door of opportunity was slammed in the face of their children.
>
> (p. 68)

Indeed, this was a highly accurate reading of the reality for African parents. Keen to advance in the colonial African context, parents looked to European language education as a primary means to this end. According to Adejunmobi (2004), "[P]arents wanted an education that would enable their children to compete for the best paying jobs in the colonial administration or set up business independently of European control" (pp. 9–10). Missionary education was, therefore, not always imposed on unwilling locals. Certain segments of the local community were even empowered by English education. However, African parents were also aware of the potentially socially adverse effects of English education, such as the production of an African elite that was ill-suited to its local communities and alienated from it. Roy-Campbell (2001) describes a similar situation in colonial Tanganyika, in which English was valued over Kiswahili: "By the end of the colonial period, Kiswahili remained in the minds of many Africans a second class language, while English was the prestigious language of modernization, the conveyor of knowledge" (p. 57). The source of this attitude lay in the political, economic, and social realities of the colonial state, regardless of the opinions of the English-speaking missionaries.

Along with the desire for an education that would provide real opportunities for their children, African parents had more political motivations for demanding education as well. Inviting missionaries to set up schools in their areas was a way to protect their land from possible takeover by the colonial government, since it now fell under the jurisdiction of the missionaries. The Africans thus used schooling as a strategy for protecting and advancing their interests within the constraints of colonial rule (Summers, 2002).

However, in analyzing the development of African education, Summers (2002) observes that even though African parents might have been unanimous in their demands for education in English, their sons and daughters were not always in agreement with them. That the sons and daughters were not as enthusiastic about schooling as parents is understandable, given the significant expectations on them for carrying out physical work at schools and the threat of corporal punishment.

Still, formal education in English was in Africa to stay. In this environment of parental demand for English-language education, Christian missions in Africa eventually came to recognize that communities would tolerate Christian presence and influence only if the missionaries offered a Western-type education that featured English as well as other concepts such as "time discipline, literacy, arithmetic, and other essentials of European culture, ranging from the new forms of cleanliness to the complex codes of manners, and dignity inherent in furniture and clothes" (Summers, 2002, p. 87). Mission schools thus had little choice but to oblige African parents and communities, as well as government, in this regard. The missionaries lost their campaign for local languages at this point, a fact that is often missed in historical analysis of language policy. Adejunmobi (2004) remarks that:

> In hindsight, one cannot but be struck by the irony of the fact that subsequent generations of Africans have tended to attribute sole responsibility

> for the prominence of English in the school system to the missionaries, in much the same way as they have held missionaries responsible for privileging the humanities over instruction in vocational skills in colonial schools.
>
> (p. 11)

This loss of local-language instruction may not have been recognized at the time, but it was nevertheless significant to the quality of learning that took place in schools. Most of the reading material used in the teaching and reading of English was foreign to Africans' cultural traditions and ways of thinking, and reading in English came to be treated as a technical exercise rather than an intentional effort to produce meaning. Nor was the shift to English purely linguistic in nature; it was also characterized by replacing African construal of learning and teaching with Western norms. Western education also introduced an emphasis on individualism, undermining the communal practices of African societies. The individualizing practices of this form of education are evident today:

> Teachers call on students to perform both privately and publicly without assistance from their peers: they are required to write exams, do assignments, and speak out in front of others. Teachers may take steps to prevent collective or collaborative efforts to ensure that any information supplied within such interactions can be attributed exclusively to the demonstrator. School personnel diligently supervise tests and exams. They penalize students during testing situations for such things as talking or soliciting information.
>
> (Ryan, 1992, p. 105)

Parental demands for English-language education during the colonial period can be situated within a broader context of the general orientation of Africans toward Western education. Africans were laying claim not only to a particular type of education but also to being treated in a manner that they thought was commensurate with their social status as educated Africans, reinforced by education in English (Summers, 2002).

The subsequent development of formal education in anglophone Africa was characterized by the establishment of English as the standard. English fluency became the key characteristic behind the formation of a small, educated elite who could successfully negotiate the language and content of formal education and whose resulting economic and social successes stood (and still stand) in stark contrast to those of the majority of the population (Trudell, 2005b, p. 121). English was frequently used to stratify educational provision; in colonial Zimbabwe and Tanganyika, for example, highly discriminatory parallel education systems for Africans and for Whites were put in place, with language of instruction acting as a key differentiating marker (Roy-Campbell, 2001).

With independence, this trend continued. Postcolonial governments maintained and nominally extended the position of English in national education systems in terms of policy, not necessarily in terms of practice. Adegbija (1994) analyzes the postcolonial place of European languages in this way:

> Post-colonial policy makers in Africa have largely rubber-stamped or toed the line of language and educational policies bequeathed to them by the colonial masters.... Educational systems, which have widened and extended beyond what they were in colonial days, have been further used to entrench and perpetuate the feeling of the inviolable worth of colonial languages.
> (pp. 33–34)

The language policies instituted in newly independent Ghana and Malawi exemplified this trend. In 1957, the independent Ghanaian government established an English-medium policy for primary education across the country. Despite subsequent recommendations from a committee of educators who were concerned that there were not enough competent primary school teachers of English to carry out the policy, the Ghanaian minister of education decided in 1963 to confirm the 1957 pro-English policy (Bamgbose, 1991, p. 114). In Malawi, the postcolonial language policy established in 1969 upheld earlier government decisions to prioritize Chichewa and English as the languages of education over the Christian missions' choices of Tumbuka and Chinyanja (Kayambazinthu, 2004, p. 110).

Professional educators and linguists have had a very limited impact on the way African governments formulate their policies and implement them, and the situation is unlikely to change. It is, therefore, more reasonable for professional educators and language educators to expend their energies on seeking to alter changes at the micro-level rather than at a macro-level (Ferguson, 2003), thus establishing a mode of operating maximally even under policies that they might not fully endorse and that may raise ethical problems for some applied linguists.

Current Policies on English and Education in Anglophone Africa

The fact that debates regarding the appropriateness of English in education are virtually nonexistent in anglophone Africa is ironic. Even more ironic is the fact that some present-day Christian teachers insist on English-only teaching. Contemporary missionaries can learn from the early sponsorship of the vernacular by early missionaries, while at the same time becoming aware that the teaching of the vernacular among early missionaries consisted largely of a transference of modes of teaching and assessment from English.

English remains embedded in the community understanding of proper education. The policy to use English in schools is reinforced by the interests of foreign donors in spreading the teaching of English, which they support through the donation of teaching materials, training of teachers, and supply of expatriate teachers and consultants (Bamgbose, 1991, p. 77). While local languages have gained entry into schools, it is with the clear understanding that English fluency is still the ultimate goal. In such situations, African languages are seen as the building blocks of transition toward English. In other words, even when African languages are used as media of instruction, a hierarchy between the languages is introduced in which English has a higher status than local languages. Psycholinguistic models of language learning, such as additive bilingualism are based on the idea that learning a second language is facilitated after consolidating the learning of one's mother tongue. Pushing aside the inherent sociolinguistic complexities of determining what constitutes one's mother tongue in heteroglossic situations in Africa and sociologically inferring from the additive bilingual model, there seems to be a subtle assertion that learning African languages is useful only as a basis for learning English.

This assumption is evident not only among government decision makers but within the research community as well. Questions being addressed have more to do with the best means of increasing access and improving English ability than with whether English is the appropriate language to use in schools. For example, Kyeyune (2004) decries the low level of English ability among Ugandan students who have studied it and used it as medium of instruction for years and recommends more intentional English instructional strategies in school (pp. 78–79). Ferguson (2003) argues that since it is unlikely that African governments will radically shift away from English, applied linguists might use their time and resources more productively by exploring ways of mitigating the effects of shifting from local languages toward English, rather than trying to convince African governments to change their pro-English policies. This perspective on English is highly pragmatic, based on awareness of the realities of globalization and the dominant position of European academic education in anglophone Africa.

Where local language use in education is promoted, it is generally based on beliefs regarding the greater effectiveness of mother tongue-medium instruction in attaining educational outcomes, such as school-leaving examinations (Benson, 2002; Trudell, 2005a). Sympathy exists in certain quarters for the use of local languages, as Kembo-Sure (2004) demonstrates in his argument for making room for bilingual education in developing an English syllabus for Kenyan schools (p. 114). Such sympathy is rooted in the ongoing vitality and dynamism of African languages, especially in popular culture and the media. Despite the relatively long history of English use in Africa, relatively few Africans (outside South Africa) speak English as their first language. The "dystopic vision of linguistic catastrophe" within which studies of the spread of English have been framed thus might be misplaced (Jacquemet, 2005).

However, what seems clear is that in anglophone Africa today the debate regarding English is by no means the purview of Christian missions or the Christian church. Powerful forces of state, community, and international agencies keep English in its dominant position in African education systems. This situation underlines the fact that language policy analysts in Africa lack an in-depth understanding of how the state makes its decisions in Africa. Researchers may complain that policy makers do not take into account their recommendations about the effects on children of learning in a language they do not fully understand, e.g., English or French. But the reality is that policy makers inhabit a world in which popular opinion is key and research evidence is of secondary importance. Levin (2005) explains:

> From a political perspective, however, evidence is only one factor that shapes decisions, and it will often be one of the less important factors. I have had

> politicians tell me on various occasions that while evidence I was presenting for a particular policy might be correct, the policy was not what people believed, wanted or would accept. As Bernard Shapiro, whose experience includes a stint as Ontario Deputy Minister of Education, put it, "All policy decisions are made by leaping over the data. For politicians, what people believe to be true is much more important than what may actually be true."
>
> (p. 619)

Current Christian Institutional Perspectives on Language

In the current pro-English environment, the stances of Christian institutions regarding language vary. The Christian church, which in the vast majority of cases has become truly African owned, tends to accept use of local languages, particularly in rural areas. Regarding South Africa, for example, Kamwangamalu (2004) notes, "In general, every church [denomination] has (on a national level) a sizable representation of 10 or more languages. At the local level, especially in the rural areas, there are however many monolingual congregations" (p. 221). Urban or multilingual congregations, however, require use of a language of wider communication, whether African (such as kiSwahili in Kenya or Pidgin in anglophone Cameroon) or European. Nyati-Ramahobo (2004) notes that in Botswana, the Christian church has helped to increase the use of Setswana and English over local languages (pp. 33–35). The two are used alternately in church services and events, although Setswana is dominant in rural churches. The orientation of the African Christian church seems largely pragmatic: one uses the language(s) that can communicate best to a given congregation in a given place. It is also true that, like government leaders, denominational leaders in anglophone Africa tend to be members of the educated elite who would naturally choose English as the language of prestige.

Denominational providers of formal education in Africa today are controlled by government language policy regarding education and, therefore, take their cues from that policy. For example, Kayambazinthu (2004) notes that mission schools in Malawi are controlled by government language policy, which stipulates vernacular language use in early grades, transitioning to the use of the English and Chichewa languages (p. 99).

Non-African Christian institutions are involved to a certain extent in English-language teaching in anglophone Africa today. This activity is primarily found in denominational seminaries and Bible schools, which may still utilize non-African staff and use English as the medium of instruction. One of the major international, faith-based institutions involved in language development and language teaching in Africa is SIL International, formerly known as the Summer Institute of Linguistics. SIL's focus in Africa is almost entirely on the development of African languages, particularly the smaller and less developed languages of the continent. Given the lasting damage done to the vitality and use of African languages through the dominance of English in educational and national life, it is not surprising that SIL's language development focus does not include English at all. It seems that by its exclusion of English, SIL is trying to avoid some of the mistakes of the colonial past.

On the other hand, the enthusiasm that African populations, even those in rural areas, show for English-language fluency and literacy is not lost on SIL or its national partner organizations in anglophone Africa. In response, local-language literacy programs may include instruction in English as a foreign or second language. One such adult literacy program, offered by a Ghanaian NGO called the Ghana Institute of Linguistics, Literacy, and Bible Translation (GILLBT), consists of two terms of local-language literacy learning and two further terms of ESL and English literacy instruction (Aggor & Kofi, 2003). In other anglophone nations such as Kenya (Schroeder, 2004) and anglophone Cameroon (Gfeller, 2000), SIL supports multilingual primary education initiatives in specific rural areas. This focus on local languages draws criticism from two very different sources: those who see English as the future and consider local-language development initiatives to be detrimental to national progress and those who object to the involvement of non-Africans in language and culture change among minority African populations.

The impact of Christian institutions on English-language use and teaching in anglophone Africa today is thus neither consistent nor extensive. Compared to the impact of government language policy, community opinion, and the globalizing influences of media and education, the contribution of specifically Christian institutions adds little to the prestigious position of the English language.

Conclusion

In this chapter, we examined the historical and contemporary roles of Christian institutions in shaping the nature of English-language policy and practices in Africa. While African parents demanded education in English, missionaries were more likely to emphasize local languages. The tension between these groups regarding the use of English in educational contexts continues to be played out in contemporary anglophone Africa, where Africans engaged in language planning research are likely to continue to argue for the beneficial role of using local languages in school, while policy makers are reluctant to implement such language policies. An historical view of education and language policy in anglophone Africa is thus very helpful to understanding the place of English in African societies today.

As for the desires of African communities and parents in particular, Pennycook (2001) may well be correct in his concerns about the deleterious effects of English on local-language speaking societies. Nevertheless, it is difficult to dismiss Africans' experience and understanding of their own socioeconomic and linguistic realities and to ignore the primacy they give to English-language fluency. In addition, the continued use of local languages, combined with the continued interest in English, should lead us to question whether the "dystopic vision" of English swamping out local African languages does not require reconsideration (Jacquemet, 2005). The future of effective education in anglophone

Africa may depend on the ability of researchers, communities, and policy makers to find common ground in which linguistically contextualized learning and mastery of English are part of every child's schooling experience.

Notes

1. We are using the term *anglophone Africa* advisedly because "anglophone," "lusophone," and "francophone" African nations have a great deal in common in terms of language, social practices, and ethnocultural histories. These commonalities are easily overlooked when Africa is viewed through colonial categories. We are, therefore, using the term *anglophone Africa* for stylistic convenience, not because we necessarily subscribe to the ideology that it represents (Makoni, Smitherman, Ball & Spears, 2003).
2. Debates about what constitutes a local language are still pertinent even in contemporary Africa. For example, the general scholarly tendency has been to construe English as alien and "indigenous" languages as local, overlooking Africanized varieties of English.

References

Adegbija, E. (1994). *Language attitudes in Sub-Saharan Africa: A sociolinguistic overview.* Clevedon, UK: Multilingual Matters.

Adejunmobi, M. (2004). *Vernacular palaver: Imaginations of the local and non-native languages in West Africa.* Clevedon, UK: Multilingual Matters.

Aggor, R. A., & Kofi, S. (2003). *Literacy: A key to development—the GILLBT Literacy Programme in Ghana.* Accra: Ghana Universities Press.

Bamgbose, A. (1991). *Language and the nation.* Edinburgh, UK: Edinburgh University Press.

Benson, C. (2002). Real and potential benefits of bilingual programmes in developing countries. *International Journal of Bilingual Education and Bilingualism, 5*(6), 303–317.

Bernstein, J. (1996). Runyakitara: Uganda's "New" Language. *Journal of Multilingual and Multicultural Development, 19*(2), 93–108.

Canut, C. (2002). Perceptions of languages in the Mandigo region of Mali. In D. Long, & D. Preston (Eds.), *Handbook of perceptual dialectology* (pp. 33–39). Amsterdam: John Benjamins.

Chimhundu, H. (1992). Early missionaries, and the ethno-linguistic factor during the invention of tribalism in Zimbabwe. *Journal of African History, 33*(1), 87–101.

De Vries, W. H. (2004). The interface between prophecy as narrative and prophecy as proclamation: A study of three prophetic legends. In J. H. Ellens, D. L. Ellens, R. P. Knierim, & I. Kalimi (Eds.), *God's word for our world: Volume I, biblical studies in honor of Simon John De Vries* (pp. 211–246). London, New York: Clark/Continuum.

Errington, J. (2001). Colonial linguistics. *Annual Review of Anthropology, 30,* 19–39.

Fabian, J. (1986). *Language and colonial power.* New York: Cambridge University Press.

Ferguson, G. (2003). Classroom code-switching in post-colonial contexts: Functions, attitudes and policies. *AILA Review, 16*(1), 38–51.

Gfeller, E. (2000). *La Société et l'Ecole face au Multilinguisme.* Paris: KARTHALA.

Irvine, J. (1989). When talk isn't cheap: Language and political economy. *American Ethnologist, 16*(2), 248–267.

Jacquemet, M. (2005). Transidiomatic practices: Language and power in the age of globalization. *Language and Communication, 25*(3), 257–277.

Jeater, D. (2007). *Law, language, and science: The invention of the "native mind" in southern Rhodesia, 1890–1930.* Portsmouth, NH: Heinemann.

Kamwangamalu, N. (2004). The language planning situation in South Africa. In R. B. Baldauf, Jr., & R. B. Kaplan (Eds.), *Language planning and policy in Africa, Volume 1: Botswana, Malawi, Mozambique and South Africa* (pp. 197–281). Clevedon, UK: Multilingual Matters.

Kayambazinthu, E. (2004). The language planning situation in Malawi. In R. B. Baldauf, Jr., & R. B. Kaplan (Eds.), *Language planning and policy in Africa, Volume 1: Botswana, Malawi, Mozambique and South Africa* (pp. 79–149). Clevedon, UK: Multilingual Matters.

Kembo-Sure. (2004). Establishing a national standard and English language curriculum change in Kenya. In M. J. Muthwii, & A. N. Kioko (Eds.), *New language bearings in Africa: A fresh quest* (pp. 101–115). Clevedon, UK: Multilingual Matters.

Kyeyune, R. (2004). Challenges of using English as a medium of instruction in the multilingual contexts: A view from Ugandan classrooms. In M. J. Muthwii, & A. N. Kioko (Eds.), *New language bearings in Africa: A fresh quest* (pp. 77–88). Clevedon, UK: Multilingual Matters.

Levin, B. (2005). Improving research policy relationships: The case of literacy. In N. Bascia, A. Cummig, A. Datnow, K. Leithjwood, & D. Livingstone (Eds.), *International handbook of educational policy* (pp. 31–62). New York: Springer.

Makoni, S., & Meinhof, U. H. (2003). Introducing applied linguistics in Africa. In S. Makoni & U. H. Meinhof (Eds.), *Africa and applied linguistics* (pp. 1–12). Amsterdam: John Benjamins Publishing.

Makoni, S., Smitherman, G., Ball, A. F., & Spears, A. K. (Eds.) (2003). *Black linguistics: Language, society, and politics in Africa and the Americas.* London: Routledge.

Mamdani, M. (1996). *Citizen and subject: Contemporary Africa and the legacy of late colonialism.* Princeton, NJ: Princeton University Press.

Nyati-Ramahobo, L. (2004). The language situation in Botswana. In R. B. Baldauf, Jr., & R. B. Kaplan (Eds.), *Language planning and policy in Africa, Volume 1: Botswana, Malawi, Mozambique and South Africa* (pp. 21–78). Clevedon, UK: Multilingual Matters.

Pennycook, A. (2001). *Critical applied linguistics: A critical introduction.* Mahwah, NJ: Erlbaum.

Pennycook, A., & Makoni, S. (2005). The modern mission: The language effects of Christianity. *Journal of Language, Identity, and Education, 4*(2), 137–157.

Ranger, T. (1995). *Are we not also men? The Samkange family and African politics in Zimbabwe.* Cumbria, UK: James Currey.

Roy-Campbell, Z. M. (2001). *Empowerment through language: The African experience: Tanzania and beyond.* Trenton, NJ/Asmara, Eritrea: Africa World Press.

Ryan, J. (1992). Eroding Innu cultural tradition: Individualization and communality. *Journal of Canadian Studies, 26*(4), 94–111.

Samkange, Reverend T. D. (April 18, 1936). Sindebele or Zulu as a standard language. *Bantu Mirror*, p. 23.

Schroeder, L. (2004). Mother-tongue education in schools in Kenya: Some hidden beneficiaries. *Language Matters, 35*(2), 376–389.

Smith, E. W. (1926). *The Christian mission in Africa: A study based on the proceedings of the International Conference at Le Zoute, Belgium, September 14–21, 1926.* London: International Missionary Council.

Spolsky, B. (2003). Religion as a site of language contact. *Annual Review of Applied Linguistics, 23*, 81–95.

Summers, C. (2002). *Colonial lessons: Africans' education in Southern Rhodesia 1918–1940.* Oxford, UK: James Currey.

Trudell, B. (2005a). Language choice, education and community identity. *International Journal for Academic Development, 25*(3), 237–251.

Trudell, B. (2005b). The power of the local: Education choices and language maintenance among the Bafut, Kom and Nso' communities of northwest Cameroon. Unpublished doctoral dissertation, University of Edinburgh, UK.

Willan, B. (1984). *Sol Plaatje: South African Nationalist, 1876–1932.* Berkeley: University of California Press.

12 Confronting the Empire

Language Teachers as Charitable Guests

Myrrl Byler

The sharp polarization of attitudes and opinions demonstrated by Americans in past presidential elections is not confined to US shores. Americans teaching overseas carry with them political and cultural baggage that dictates how they will interact with individuals and institutions in their host nation. Competing ideas on values, morals, and political ideology are not confined to those who differ in whether they profess religious faith or not, but are also evident among Christian language teachers. Some Christians use English language teaching as a means to evangelize, to promote their conservative religious values and political opinions. However, other Christians oppose the views and actions of the pro-American religious right, focusing instead on building strong cross-cultural understanding and partnerships.

We had only been in conversation for several minutes, but the young university graduate's voice rang with conviction as he told me about the wonders and virtues of the American way of life. The praise for the American dream seemed out of place, since it was coming from someone who had never been to the US or even left his own country. However, he was knowledgeable of American freedoms, of how America was the land of opportunity, and a place where individuals could realize their dreams. He further explained that America's wealth, power, and dominance in the world were a result of America's belief in God.

Not content to praise America, the young graduate commented negatively on his own culture. Not only did he believe radical political change was needed, but his nation's culture and traditions were inherently deficient. Even as I protested and began to point out some of the many positives in his culture, he was quick to counteract with specific examples of what he thought needed to change. When I questioned the value judgments he was making, he declared that since I was also a Christian, I must understand the evil inherent in his own traditions. His culture and traditions needed to change because they had not been blessed by God.

My encounter with this young man is not an isolated occurrence, either for myself or for the North American English teachers with whom I work. While one might want to believe that this attitude might be the result of listening to extremist short-wave radio programs or ambitious Internet surfing, I have found that behind the words and attitude is a Western language teacher—often a teacher who identifies himself or herself as Christian.

There was also an American English teacher behind a story told by a Chinese university student following the 1999 bombing of the Chinese Embassy in Belgrade by the US military. In his comments on the website of the *Ming Pao News*, the student shared what his American teacher said and did on the morning following the bombing incident. The student described how he was curious as to whether his teacher would even come to class, and what he would say if he did. He was not prepared for the teacher's apologetic demeanor, particularly when he began to cry in the classroom. The American teacher apologized for the actions of his government, for the loss of life that the bombing had caused. He gave no excuses or reasons to support the American belief that the bombing was an accident. Instead there was only apology and then a verbal declaration of love for his students.

The university student described the encounter: "We respect and love them [foreign teachers]. We were just friends, with no national boundaries! But today he repeatedly apologized, and our hearts were all pained." The student concluded that "most Americans are trustworthy as friends," and "Sino-American friendship is possible." This young American teacher was also a Christian and part of a church-based program.

As the administrator of a North American church-sponsored program that partners with universities and academic institutions in China, I have experienced and heard numerous stories similar to those above. The worldview of English language teachers who are Christian (CET) is influenced and determined by their individual belief system. How these CET relate to their host environment, to students in the classroom, and how they approach classroom instruction is heavily influenced by their religious views. As demonstrated in the above vignettes, one cannot assume that all CET share the same opinions and will react to events and their environment in the same way. Just as moderate Muslims are frustrated with outsiders who lump them together with violent extremists and thus misunderstand the relationship between their faith and their view of the world, so many Christians are frustrated when it is assumed that their views are identical with Christian fundamentalists.

Church-based agencies may have language teaching personnel with motivations that vary greatly. Some may see language teaching as simply the easiest way to get a visa and carry out covert evangelistic or discipleship activity. There are those who couple their evangelistic zeal with a strong right-wing pro-American political agenda. There are more moderate CET who feel called to evangelize but reject strong American values and do not seek to push their religious, political, or cultural views on others. Some CET feel strongly that evangelism is not their responsibility, but their first and primary duty is to provide quality language instruction. On the far side of the continuum are CET who are accepting and tolerant of other religious faiths, who focus on dialogue and mutual understanding, and do not push the values and political ideology of the American Christian right.

The number of CET continues to grow, particularly in non-North American settings. There is much to criticize regarding the motivations, actions, and rationale of CET as a group. Obviously there are major differences among the various Christian-sending agencies and individual Christian teachers. Divergent opinions and voices divide the Christian community—the purpose here is to better understand where these voices originate and how CET who reject a Christian fundamentalist theology and pro-American values orientation can find their faith making a positive contribution in our world.

America under God

In the past decades many countries have closed their doors to Christian missionaries. Those with a missionary motivation have needed to find other avenues to spread their message. Teaching English and "doing business" have become the most popular ways to get visas to places that do not wish to have a foreign missionary presence. As I rub shoulders with various teacher-sending agencies and university programs, I have heard strong reactions against CET and needed to answer difficult questions about the role of the church agency in which I'm involved. My response has been to attempt an explanation of the motivation and foundational beliefs of CET who have a fundamentalist viewpoint. At the same time I make the case that many CET have a very different perspective, and how their religious faith can be a great asset rather than a detriment.

Many CET leave their homes and go to teach overseas with the conviction that the United States is a rich and powerful nation because it has a unique and historic relationship to God. They believe that America has a special place in the divine order. Jerry Falwell, one of the more influential leaders of the Christian right, states that "the United States is not a perfect nation, but it is without doubt the greatest and most influential nation in the world" (Dobson, 1981, p. 212). The writer of the popular *Left Behind* series, Tim LaHaye, states that without America, "our contemporary world would have completely lost the battle for the mind and would doubtless live in a totalitarian, one-world, humanistic state" (1980, p. 35).

While the political fortunes of the Christian right have ebbed and flowed, the movement continues in its vitality. The image of a movement of Bible-thumping fanatics is not particularly accurate. The Christian right crosses many ethnic lines and represents a cross-section of much of America. As a political bloc, the Christian right was instrumental in electing and re-electing George W. Bush as well as many Republicans in Congress. The Christian right has become more engaged in what is often called the "battle for America" and in the attack on "secular humanism." The Christian right speaks out against abortion, same sex marriages, gun control, removing Christian and biblical symbols and prayer from the public sphere, environmental concerns like global warning, and liberal judges who frustrate attempts at bringing America into line with biblical values (Meyers, 2006, p. xiv).

When CET who subscribe to these views go overseas, even those who do their best to learn about the culture they are entering, will view their host culture and nation through this worldview. Their core beliefs and motivation determine how they answer questions from their students and interact with colleagues, local officials, and others. These beliefs also determine how they view the profession of language teaching. Central to this perspective are their views on evangelism, indigenous Christian faith, the rightness of the American political and economic system, the need for American military power, and a linking of current events to biblical descriptions of the apocalypse.

There are CET who view their profession primarily as a means to an end, particularly in settings where language teaching is one of the only legitimate ways for foreigners to be present in a country. The fact that many Christians hide their real purpose in teaching language so they can evangelize their students has been criticized by others (Edge, 2003, pp. 704–707). This should not come as a surprise. For many Christian language teachers, their primary purpose in life is to respond to the biblical call to bring Christian faith to persons who have not heard the gospel message. This call to evangelism conflicts with laws and expectations in many countries, and may lead to direct disobedience or, more likely, a form of covert presence. Because the higher purpose of evangelism is in conflict with authority, CET may view the government and officials of their host country with suspicion and hostility. As true motives must remain hidden, negative attitudes toward the host country develop, which contrast with perceived American freedoms. These attitudes are communicated to students, particularly those who show an interest in religion.

This lack of respect can also be seen in how non-Christian religions are viewed, or there may be little acceptance of Christian faith already present in the host culture. There is a sense that what has not been delivered directly by or under the control of Western Protestant missionaries may be corrupt or compromised. Teachers may form their own groups of followers in complete isolation from locally led communities of faith. Existing organized Christian communities may be viewed as lacking in fervent spirituality (particularly in historical Orthodox or Roman Catholic churches) or under the control of a government body (communist).

The Christian right's belief that America must remain militarily powerful and confront enemies and evil also causes mistrust overseas. Historically America "saved" the world from Nazism and Japan in the 1940s. American "weakness" led to the abandonment of Vietnam to communism, and during the Cold War years Jerry Falwell lamented the military superiority of the Soviet Union in comparison to the aging and ill-protected American arsenal (Lienesch, 1997, p. 207). American foreign policy failures are viewed as the result of indecision by subversive politicians and leftist academics. Non-proliferation treaties are opposed and those who suggest peaceful solutions to conflict are said to be "misguided or subversive" (p. 209). The role of the United Nations in maintaining peace is criticized. Former President Jimmy Carter lamented that "those of us [Christians] who have advocated for the resolution of international conflict in a peaceful fashion are looked upon as being unpatriotic, branded that way by right-wing religious groups" (McGarvey, 2004, p. 1).

Undoubtedly the greatest enemy of many Americans, particularly of the Christian right, is communism. Communism became the symbol of everything that Americans should act against and avoid. Its tenets of atheism and collectivism identify it as the ultimate enemy. Communism is also seen as being anti-family, and as morally corrupt and devious, never to be trusted. Communism is the system that tramples on human rights—writers like Solzhynetsin found the Christian right to be a very receptive audience. Although with reference to communism much has changed in the past years, I personally have found these attitudes to still be very strong, particularly as I live and work in China. While communism as an ideology has essentially disappeared, the image of "communist officials" as untrustworthy persons to be avoided at all costs has not. There is a core belief that nothing good can come from a nation that has communist leaders—positive change only comes because some may be willing to embrace ideas from the West. Teachers who strongly oppose communism or socialism on religious grounds and preach the gospel of American power and values may influence some individual students but will only perpetuate negative American stereotypes among the general population.

Linked to its aversion to communism is the belief that capitalism is the economic system closest to biblical teachings. Economist George Gilder argues that "socialism is inherently hostile to Christianity and capitalism is simply the essential mode of human life that corresponds to religious truth" (Clapp, 1983, p. 27). Jerry Falwell believes that God is in favor of freedom, property ownership, competition, diligence, work, and acquisition. The justification then for American business practices throughout the world rests on biblical grounds.

That the world is going to end, and for many, the belief that it will end soon, plays a very important role in how many Christians engage the world. It is one reason why many teachers see their ultimate mission to be the salvation of their students, and they will do anything they can to accomplish this goal. Protests of lacking professional qualifications or lacking integrity or using English language teaching for their own ends may carry little weight for those who have the salvation of their students at heart. The popularity of the *Left Behind* series, which also has an appeal among persons who are not conservative Christians, is evidence of the fascination with a millennial interpretation of end times.

Discussions of the apocalypse are often connected to current events in the Middle East. The Christian right has historically been very strong in its support of the nation of Israel. Former Israeli prime minister, Benjamin Netanyahu, remarked that Israel has no better friends than American Christians (Zunes, 2004, p. 2). The effects of how the Christian right views Israel can be felt in other parts of the world. In his book *Jesus in Beijing*, former *Time* magazine Beijing bureau chief David Aikman predicts that the rapid growth of Christianity in China may play a vital role in pushing a future Chinese government to support Israel and an American agenda. He states: "A Christianized China would be unlikely to consent to any resolution of Middle East problems that allows for the elimination of Israel as a Jewish state" (2003, p. 287).

The apocalyptic role of Israel and the importance of America's support for Israel informs how many view predominately Muslim countries. Some of the rhetoric from the Christian right that was directed against communism is now aimed at the Muslim world. Both Jerry Falwell and Franklin Graham were criticized for negative remarks they made regarding Mohammed and Islam after 9/11. The American government's war on terror with its "us versus them" rhetoric is viewed as battle between good and evil. Although the more politically correct avoid a denouncement of all things Muslim, the message that comes across is very one-sided.

While this is only a simplistic overview, I believe that a substantial number of persons who subscribe to this worldview, or some aspects of it, are teaching English in areas like the Middle East, the former Soviet republics, or in countries that have communist governments like China and Vietnam. While they may or may not be professionally well trained, or they may or may not have a good understanding of their host culture, what these teachers believe will in the end determine what kind of teachers they will be. It will determine how they talk about the political system and government leaders, how they respond to the host country's history, and particularly how they interpret for their students the history and current actions of America. Some students will be strongly influenced by the attitude and values of their teachers—a few may become disciples. In some unfortunate cases, as mentioned at the beginning of this chapter, some may reject their own history and culture and uncritically accept what they think is Western or American.

God's Blessing for All

The teacher who apologized to his students for the actions of the American government did not operate from a framework informed by the Christian right. There are many CET who reject this religious extremism and lack of integrity. As an administrator responsible for preparing and supporting those who are teaching overseas, it is my goal to challenge teachers to take an approach that rejects extreme American nationalism and Christian fundamentalism. It is an approach that does not ask teachers to deny or in any way diminish their Christian faith. Rather it encourages teachers to discover how their Christian faith is the basis for cross-cultural understanding, sensitivity, and respect. The emphasis is on integrity (specifically not using language teaching as a means to accomplish a religious agenda), tolerance, reconciliation, and building meaningful relationships.

This approach does not take the rightness of the American way of life as its starting point, but focuses on the larger world. The biblical story of God's entry into the world is in some sense a story of cross-cultural movement. Jesus does not come to earth in triumph, but rather as a baby, born in humble surroundings, heralded and worshipped by simple shepherds. The life of Jesus as described in the Gospels is one of vulnerability—he did not attempt to establish a kingdom built on power, or to overthrow the Roman government that was in power. He spent his short time on earth reaching out to the poor and disadvantaged, criticizing those interested in using religion for their own gain. He reached out to females that society rejected, and showed tolerance for everyone but those who were hypocritical and extremist in their religious beliefs. The gospels provide lasting symbols and examples of how his followers should live, whether in their own culture or as guests in another.

However, Judeo-Christian history has played out very differently from the image given in the gospels, specifically the instructions that Jesus gave in Matthew 5:3–12 on peace making, suffering, humility, sharing, comforting, truthfulness, and not taking revenge. The history of the Christian religion has focused on power, demonstrated by the many wars fought in God's name. Missiologist Calvin Shenk states that, "Perhaps the church's greatest weakness is its failure to be weak" (1997, p. 196). As Westerners and as Christians our tradition has taught us to act decisively and aggressively, pressing our ideas, culture, and language on others. CET face the task of rediscovering and affirming a means of interaction and presence that has integrity and lessens tension and conflict.

Unfortunately there are those who go to live in other parts of the world without a grasp of what others may think or believe about them. My first overseas experience was living in what was then West Berlin in the early 1980s. I was unprepared for the cutting criticism of America that I heard seemingly everywhere. I struggled to provide answers to the many questions about American politics and culture that came my way. For the first time I felt the tension of what it means to be an American living overseas. I quickly learned that if I was going to learn about the new culture, develop friendships, and be an effective teacher, I could not be an apologist for everything American.

The experience in West Berlin contrasted with living in China in the 1980s, at a time when it seemed all Chinese students believed that the US was paradise on earth. While in China I felt very uncomfortable with the uncritical praise of all things American, and I attempted to balance the idealistic image of students. Unfortunately there are CET (and other Westerners) teaching overseas who have little appreciation for the context in which they are living. An understanding of the history of colonial aggression by the West, often understood as the Christian West, can help language teachers avoid perpetuating the myth of American or Western superiority. A recognition of past history and present injustice can lead to humility in and out of the classroom, rather than defensiveness and arrogance.

Of all persons, CET should be aware of the mixed legacy of Christian missions. Retired missionary Ralph Covell remarks: "In 1842 Christian missionaries impatiently assumed that an 'open door' for commerce and diplomacy was also an entrance for the gospel. We are still reaping the results of this tragic action" (1979, p. 77). The Christian message was associated with power, wealth, and privilege, causing many missionaries to come across as arrogant and superior, with little interest in understanding or adapting to the local culture. This view of the mission era continues to haunt modern-day mission endeavors, particularly when the same mistakes are repeated. CET can learn how the mission era impacted their host country and culture, and how they are viewed when they declare themselves to be Christian. In many cases an attempt to justify past mission practices with stories of the many good things that happened only exacerbates the tension.

Respect for other nations and people challenges the belief that God plays favorites when it comes to cultures and nations. While the "God bless America" mantra is often unthinkingly repeated, there are those who are uncomfortable with the idea that God's blessing is somehow reserved only for a small portion of the world's population. A tradition of past mission legacy is the myth that Christians take God and the gospel to other places. This attitude ignores what God is doing in other places, whether it is in Christian churches that are already present, the small groups of Christians who meet, or where there is no established Christian church. God's presence is not dependent on whether Western Christians are present or not.

An awareness of God's universal love can keep Christians from arrogantly assuming that their version of events is the only true one. Where there are Christians worshipping locally, CET can offer support, rather than promoting only the truth that has been brought from afar. An awareness of God's presence encourages tolerance for those who follow a different religion, or differ in their Christian theological outlook. There are CET who focus first on waiting, listening, and learning, rather than aggressively charging ahead. They respect the laws of the host country even where there is official corruption and wrongdoing; they do not sit in judgment or trumpet how much better "their" system is.

As gracious guests, CET can point out injustices in their own society and culture rather than attacking the ills of their host country. Courageous CET can address issues of racism and prejudice in American history as well as the present. Instead of attempting some kind of defense of the abuses of the American military in Iraq, CET can point to groups like the Christian Peacemaker Teams who enter situations of conflict where they may even lose their lives, all in an effort to promote understanding, dialogue, and non-violent ways of solving conflict. By discussing issues of poverty and wealth or environmental degradation in their own country, teachers indirectly challenge their students to consider what is happening in their own region.

CET may mistakenly believe that the religious conversion or salvation of others rests solely on their shoulders. It is this desperation and burden that leads many to view language teaching as simply a means to an end. It is an approach that objectifies persons and approaches all relationships with the goal of conversion. It is an approach that can make a mockery of the language teaching profession.

Each semester I host a group of visiting professors from various Chinese universities in a college community in the US. A few of the persons with whom they come in contact take an aggressive approach in evangelizing. While very curious about Christian faith, a number of the visiting scholars have asked me about the purpose of the more verbal and aggressive persons. The essence of what they want to know is often: "Are they being friendly only because they want me to become a Christian?"

Evangelism, or proselytizing as it is sometimes referred to by critics, is often associated with insensitivity, manipulation, emotionalism, and naïveté. Others associate it with the crusades, arrogance, and triumphalism. Western claims to superiority often become enmeshed with the uniqueness of Jesus. As guests in another culture, Christians may be better received if they acknowledge and are aware of how their attempts to convert others are viewed. Calvin Shenk asserts that, "Words and actions must be sensitive, not aggressive. Warfare vocabulary like strategies, crusades, campaigns, targeting people, fighting or waging warfare for souls—these must be excluded from our thinking and conversation" (1997, p. 206). They only reinforce images that damage the message of peace—words and attitudes that reflect the humility and suffering related in the gospels have more integrity than imagery of soldiers going off to war.

There is nothing more non-Christian than entering relationships only because there is a desire to see the other convert to his or her beliefs. Unethical methods and abuse of authority deny the gospel. However, this does not negate the fact that the Christian gospel is conversionist. Calvin Shenk states that,

> If we deny conversion, we deny the hospitality of God in Jesus Christ by assuming that Christ is only for those who grew up in a Christian environment. But the gospel is not only for some; it is for all.
>
> (p. 209)

Christians need to recognize the tension between the call to share their religious faith and the need to be humble, sensitive, and respectful.

A truly Christ-like presence among language students will not focus on targeting and strategizing for conversion, but rather be concerned with the needs of the students. Unfortunately most language teachers begin their work only a few weeks after entering a country. They do not have or take the time to learn about their new environment. They understand little of how their students have been taught, how they learn, and how they think. Perhaps more critically, those new to teaching cross-culturally may not be able to view their own culture and background critically. They may be blind to how they are viewed by others, and not even think to question why people think or act differently (Lingenfelter & Lingenfelter, 2003, p. 21). Frustration with differences and strangeness leads to enforcing rules and ideas on others, made possible by the dominant position of teaching a language that others need.

A more effective approach focuses on listening and asking questions. It means becoming less Western or American, giving up part of our own identity and values so we can learn to think outside our own contextual boxes. While we cannot stop being American, we can become much more (Lingenfelter & Lingenfelter, 2003, p. 24). Those willing to challenge their own biases can view their own learning strategies critically and accept methods in another culture, which at first may seem misguided or wrong. "Only by understanding the other-culture context can we identify appropriate alternatives for teaching that will have maximum effectiveness for student learning" (p. 31).

When there are crises in the host country, whether political, economic, or social, language teachers have the privilege of living through these experiences with the people around them. Living through the experiences of April, May, and June of 1989 with my Chinese students and colleagues was a difficult but very rich time for me. CET can be present when things go wrong—many times we will be able to do nothing other than be a quiet listening presence. When many teacher-sending organizations or teachers on individual contracts may leave a country when there is a natural disaster, or political unrest, or a health-related crisis like SARS, these provide a wonderful opportunity to be present. While most foreign teachers left China immediately following the June 4, 1989 events there, or organizations kept teachers away during the SARS scare, I found that this was an especially important time to remain in the country and build relationships with persons and institutions. The affirmation from friends and partners was overwhelming.

We can hurt with others when there is failure or disaster; we can rejoice when good things happen to others. Sometimes we may be in a position to apologize, for ourselves, or for the actions of persons and a country that we represent. On occasion our outside perspective may help us point to signs of hope that others do not see.

The image of building bridges between cultures may be passé, but it remains one of the best symbols of the role of CET. At the heart of the gospel is a vision of reconciliation, a mending and healing of that which has been torn apart. This reconciliation is not only between God and humans, but it is also concerned with bringing peace between enemies, between groups of persons and entire cultures.

A new humanity is created when persons from different backgrounds reach across divides and create a relationship. The New Testament vision is one in which God is at work bringing together all of creation. Mediator John Paul Lederach argues that the work of Christians is "about facing divisions and restoring people in their relationships with others and with God. It is about … building bridges and bringing down the dividing walls of hostility between individuals and groups" (1997, p. 166). The focus on reconciliation is reflected in comments by Jimmy Carter who states that there are two principal things that separate the "ultra-right Christian community from the rest of the Christian world: Do we endorse and support peace and support the alleviation of suffering among the poor and the outcast?" (McGarvey, 2004, p. 3).

To borrow terminology from social psychologists, the goal is "recategorization." In simplistic terms this process frames group structures in terms of a larger "we" rather than the conventional "us" versus "them." Peter Hays Gries describes the same encounter that I related in the opening paragraphs, of how a language teacher helped to redefine categories. The Chinese student's conclusion was that "most Americans are trustworthy as friends" and "Sino-American friendship is possible." In the eyes of the student the American teacher and the students have become an "inclusive and good we" (Gries, 2004, p. 149).

This vision is radically different from one that promotes Western values and ideas, which believes that all others must become like "us." The perspective and the agenda are not American, and the United States does not have a special divine role. Rather it is a vision that values relationship building rather than convincing others of the rightness of our views and way of life. It is a vision that begins to address some of the historical injustices and hurts that divide our world. It is a vision that does not pretend to have all the answers, but listens to others, learning and asking questions in a spirit of humility.

Conclusion

At times during the past several decades I have become disillusioned with the negative attitudes, suspect motivations, and lack of integrity of some Christian language teachers I have met. A lack of respect and understanding for another nation and its people, coupled with a messianic view of American or Western culture and religion, breeds intolerance and promotes the "us" versus "them." I have sought ways to avoid becoming enmeshed in group conversations by language teachers that revolve around all that is wrong with the host country, culture, and its people. These conversations lead to paranoia and to the building of a subculture that may attract a few disaffected students. As in the opening example of the young man rejecting his own culture, persons are created who can no longer find a home in their own culture, nor fully become part of another.

I have tried to show that persons going overseas to teach language, whether they are Christian or not, are a reflection of their own society. Some Christian language teachers reflect values and beliefs that are simply a part of mainstream America. The effect of the polarization of America as represented in past presidential elections is not limited only to American shores. The polarization extends to Christians as well—while many pray earnestly for a victory by the Republican Party, other Christians are just as convinced that Democratic Party values are closer to their own. Persons are very dedicated to their beliefs and their way of life—they can be very zealous in pursuing their goals when overseas. It is not an easy matter for them to suddenly change their core beliefs and motivations just because they are language teachers.

I have also attempted to show that a focus on the life of Christ as shown in the gospels provides another option for Christian language teachers. Language teachers can be a force for reconciliation and change, but they must be learners who teach with humility.

References

Aikman, D. (2003). *Jesus in Beijing: How Christianity is transforming China and changing China and changing the global balance of power.* Washington, DC: Regnery Publishing.

Clapp, R. (February 4, 1983). Where capitalism and Christianity meet. *Christianity Today,* pp. 22–27.

Covell, R. (1979). It's time for a fresh look at China mistakes. *Evangelical Missions Quarterly, 15,* 77–84.

Dobson, E. (1981). *The fundamentalist phenomenon: The resurgence of conservative Christianity.* Garden City, NY: Doubleday.

Edge, J. (2003). Imperial troopers and servants of the lord: A vision of TESOL for the 21st century. *TESOL Quarterly, 37*(4), 701–709.

Gries, P. (2004). *China's new nationalism.* Berkeley: University of California Press.

LaHaye, T. (1980). *The battle for the world.* Old Tappan, NJ: Revell Publishing House.

Lederach, J. P. (1997). *The journey toward reconciliation.* Scottsdale, PA: Herald Press.

Lienesch, M. (1997). *Redeeming America: Piety and politics in the new Christian right.* Chapel Hill: University of North Carolina Press.

Lingenfelter, J., & Lingenfelter, S. (2003). *Teaching cross-culturally: An incarnational model for learning and teaching.* Grand Rapids, MI: Baker Book House.

McGarvey, A. (2004). Carter's crusade. *The American Prospect Online, April 5, 2004.* Retrieved September 16, 2008, from www.apomie.com/cartercrusade.htm.

Meyers, R. (2006). *Why the Christian right is wrong.* San Francisco, CA: Jossey-Bass.

Shenk, C. (1997). *Who do you say that I am?* Scottsdale, PA: Herald Press.

Zunes, S. (2004). US Christian right's grip on Middle East policy. *Foreign Policy in Focus.* Retrieved September 16, 2008, from www.atimes.com/atimes/Middle_East/FG08Ak01.html.

13 Christian English Teachers' Presence

Reflecting Constantine or Christ?

James Stabler-Havener

Like other missionaries of the past, Christian English teachers with hidden evangelistic goals (CETHEG) have been accused of being agents of imperial power and morality—in this case, American. In this chapter I will propose that a source of this critique derives from some CETHEG's practice of exploiting the social ethics of Constantine, championed by American Civil Religion, to justify their mission.

If she weren't a spy, Sidney Bristow would've been an English teacher. On the ABC series *Alias*, she leads a dizzying double life. Recruited on a college campus, she spends her "public" life as a bank employee and literature student, a life that quickly unravels. In her "private" life she works for the CIA "behind enemy lines" glamorously saving the world from evil terrorist cells and religious fanatics.

Perhaps some Christian English teachers (CET) also have a fascination with the covert life. Secret strategies, underground connections, anonymous couriers, and, of course, aliases, have a certain mystique. However, CET fill numerous teaching positions around the world and cannot be neatly classified. They may work for a church, or they may work at a business office. They may teach in a Christian setting, another religious setting, or a secular setting. They may teach in a public/private school/university. They may teach in their homeland, or they may teach as a foreign guest. Many view their vocation as English teachers and their Christian identity as overlapping: they would still be an English teacher if they weren't a Christian, and they would still be a Christian if they weren't an English teacher. Nonetheless, one subgroup has received particular attention, Christian English teachers *with hidden evangelistic goals* (CETHEG).

While it is possible for CETHEG to work in most of the situations described above, many end up working in countries/contexts that are closed to traditional missionary evangelists, and a thriving "sending agency" industry has emerged to support CETHEG activity in "the 10/40 window."[1] Most agencies sending CETHEG openly state their Christian identity; what remains concealed is their goal/agenda of evangelism.[2] Plumb (1997, p. 116, italics mine) writes,

> As young people, housewives and businessmen continue to search for *real meaning* in their lives, they often come knocking at the door of an English school. We have the opportunity to first meet their felt need of learning

> English and then to work to gently [sic] meet their *real need* by introducing them to their Creator. Our *goal* as English teachers overseas is not to lead all our students to Christ. *That is our prayer.*

Goals and prayers seem to be synonymous here, and for a significant portion of Christians who are teaching abroad, a deeply felt prayer/goal is the hope of spreading their faith, evangelism (Tennant, 2002). These agencies invest time, money, and personnel to recruit and train Christians who share (or can be convinced of) their conviction that teaching English is a powerful way "to convey what we believe to be spiritually important, and to do it in such a way that our students are empowered to make choices" (Purgason, 1997, p. 60). The prerequisites are relatively simple: a native speaker of English, a Christian faith, a bachelor's degree, and in many cases financial support. For various reasons, including population, financial resources, marketing mechanisms, and religious sentiment, roughly 75% of CETHEG are American.[3]

The American face of CETHEG activity has led some critics to suggest that CETHEG are agents of American imperialism and directly or indirectly advance American foreign policy (Edge, 1996, 1997, 2003, 2004; Pennycook & Coutand-Marin, 2003). The logic is as follows: since most CETHEG are American, and most American CETHEG teaching EFL are evangelical (Tennant, 2002), and since the majority of evangelicals are politically conservative (Green, Smidt, Guth, & Kellstedt, 2004; Wallis, 2005), the CETHEG enterprise implicitly acts as a political instrument of conservative American "soft" diplomacy and hegemony. I propose that a key source of the nationalistic qualities among Christians is to be found in the Constantinian social ethics championed by American Civil Religion and used by some sending agencies and CETHEG to justify their mission.

One Nation Under God

The key assumptions of Constantinian ethical discourse are that (1) "Christian" civil authority is the agent of God's cause/mission, and (2) "civil government is the main bearer of historical movement" (Yoder, 1984, p. 138). The Constantinian establishment of Christianity and Roman Empire dictated that everyone in the empire was Christian ergo the *empire* was Christian. Historically, this required an ethical shift away from the life teachings of Jesus and the practices of early Christian society.

Table 13.1 Common CETHEG characteristics

1. American nationality.
2. Evangelism is understood as persuading others to convert to Christian beliefs.
3. Evangelism is a primary motive for providing ELT services.
4. Effort is made to steer conversations toward "meaning of life" discussions.
5. Records are kept (often by agency) of: seekers, conversions, duplications, etc.
6. Church financial support is encouraged through evangelism stories.
7. Evangelistic goals/motives are hidden from hosts.
8. Code language is employed to maintain secrecy/hidden motives.

Table 13.2 Constantinian juncture

Early Christian Society	*Constantinian Christian Society*
Voluntary, often costly, membership	Mandatory, often nominal, membership
Minority community/sect	Established state religion
Position of civil weakness	Position of Civil Power
"Way" of Jesus as ethical norm	"Duties" of vocation/office as ethical norm
Pacifist	Imperialist

Yoder (1984) notes that in the pre-Constantinian church, membership was voluntary and required a high, often costly commitment to a minority community/sect; in the established Constantinian church, membership was mandatory, and required little other than submission to authority; "henceforth, it would take exceptional conviction *not* to be counted as a Christian" (p. 136, italics mine). In such context, the established church employed a functional dualism to clarify what Christian practices are expected of everyone, and which are reserved for the spiritual elite. Ethical norms were not derived from the teachings of Jesus; rather, they were found in the duties of the office/vocation (p. 136). Hence, what is appropriate for the "Christian" soldier/emperor might not be appropriate for the "Christian" blacksmith, wife, or priest. Priests and rulers were in a convenient position to make those moral/ethical decisions. From this position of power, the direction Christian rulers wanted history to go was the way it might go, and once Christian authorities had perceived "the end of history," right action was what worked to achieve that result. Since Christianity was understood as empire, the outsider (religious or political) was no longer privileged as a test of loving one's enemies; rather, mission was expanding the empire, whatever it takes.

> Before Constantine, one knew as a fact of everyday experience that there was a believing Christian community but one had to "take it on faith" that God was governing history. After Constantine, one had to believe without seeing that there was a community of believers, within the larger nominally Christian mass, but one knew for a fact that God was in control of history … for God's governance of history had become empirically evident in the person of the Christian ruler of the world.… Ethics had to change because one must aim one's behavior at strengthening the regime.
>
> (Yoder, 1984, pp. 136, 137)

Yoder suggests that though history has made several changes to the scale of this pattern, the underlying assumption that God/a Higher Power affirms *this* civil cause still remains in the Christian civic discourse of the West. In the Reformation, one sees the transition from universal Christendom to a more provincial Christian Nation State. In the Enlightenment, there is an institutional separation of church and state, yet the belief remains that society is structured according to the will of God, and the moral identification remains largely unchanged. With the increasing pluralism in contemporary society, that moral identification has shifted from the nation to a narrower region, political party, or a future world. In short, the values affirmed by this specific Empire/Nation/Party are claimed/

accepted/assumed to be the values of Christianity, a neo-Constantinian framework, that is, a "Christian" civil religion.

American Civil Religion

An important distinction should be recognized between believing a nation is protected by a divine power and strengthened by a religious populace and "attribut[ing] transcendental weight to the values, the objectives, the interests of the nation or the ethnic grouping" (Yoder, 1990). The former suggests citizens find comfort and strength through their faith, while the latter uses the language and forms of faith to sanction the nation,[4] hence a "civil religion."

Bellah (1967, 1976) notes how early revolutionary documents and presidential speeches established principles of the American Civil Religion (ACR). A "higher law" rooted in enlightenment philosophy, Puritan theology, and natural religion was used both to justify the colonists' freedom and to stand in historical judgment upon their actions. America's destiny and divinely chosen role in the world were popularly referenced back to biblical Israel. Though references to God were frequent, the founding fathers refrained from using sectarian language (e.g., the inaugural addresses of Washington, Adams, and Jefferson reference God but not Christ), and there is often a pragmatic willingness to compromise in their writings. On one hand virtue is called for in the name of public good, and on the other self-interest is acknowledged as a more realistic source of motivation.

Like other religions, ACR has a credo (life, liberty, and the pursuit of happiness, one nation under God), sacred texts (Declaration of Independence, Bill of Rights), and objects (Flag, Statue of Liberty, Liberty Bell), revered saints (Washington, Lincoln), symbolic rituals (Pledge of Allegiance, National Anthem), and ceremonies (Inauguration, State of the Union), holy spaces (Washington Mall, Arlington Cemetery), and annual festivals (Memorial Day, Independence Day). Historically and presently the majority of Americans identify themselves as Christian (Pew Forum, 2008), and ACR extensively references Christian religious themes. In particular, America is portrayed as a chosen nation imbued with a divine mandate. In the words of George Washington (1789):

> No people can be bound to acknowledge and adore the Invisible Hand which conducts the affairs of man more than those of the United States. Every step by which we have advanced to the character of an independent nation seems to have been distinguished by some token providential agency.
>
> (quoted in Bellah 1967)

Abraham Lincoln (1862) described America as the "last best hope of earth" or in the words of George W. Bush:

> We are led by events and common sense to one conclusion: The survival of liberty in our land increasingly depends on the success of liberty in other lands. [Applause.] The best hope for peace in our world is the expansion of freedom in all the world. [Cheers, applause.] *America's vital interests and our*

> *deepest beliefs are now one.* From the day of our founding, we have proclaimed that every man and woman on this earth has rights and dignity and matchless value because they bear the image of the maker of heaven and earth. [Cheers, applause.] … *Advancing these ideals is the mission that created our nation.* It is the honorable achievement of our fathers. Now it is the urgent requirement of our nation's security and the calling of our time.
>
> (2005, p. 1, italics mine)

Thus, ACR is also a missionary religion, spreading American values and interests while vanquishing evil and injustice as defined by the United States leadership and the powers that be.

American Spirit and English Teaching

American civil religion is vague enough that a broad range of religious and secular traditions can embrace it (perhaps semiconsciously) without overtly contradicting their particular dogmas (Bellah, 1967; Marty, 1976). Nevertheless, these traditions often draw radically different conclusions about the nation's values and vocation. Marty (1976) describes a "priestly" function of civil religion that serves to guide and legitimate government and morality, and a "prophetic" function that confronts the nation in light of its ideals.[5] Wuthnow (1988) notes that priestly ACR typically promotes a belief in God, traditional religious values, capitalist economics, and the metaphysical significance of America's role in the world. The prophetic version typically promotes ecological stewardship, peace and justice, and reducing the gap between poor and wealthy; America's role is important because of the country's resources and the responsibility to serve as an example of liberty and justice. Both functions claim to champion America's most cherished values and ideals; each insists it represents the true "spirit of America."

Wink (1998) argues that every corporate body (e.g., nation, community, team, corporation) comprises more than the sum of its parts; there is a "spirit" of the body as well. Just as the national spirits of America and France are very real and very different, so are the spirits of Google and General Motors, Los Angeles and Dallas, Berkeley and Bob Jones, or the ESL classroom in Atlanta and the EFL classroom in Osaka. These spirits are described as "principalities and powers" in biblical language and are the "soul of the systems" and structures that hold society together. More than merely a corporate culture, Wink (1998) argues these powers have a divine vocation to serve the transforming purposes of God. Those that are fulfilling that vocation are "angelic" and those that have turned away from it can be understood as "demonic." Wink describes how a domination system develops when hosts of demonic powers become integrated around corrupted values. "The Domination System … is characterized by unjust economic relations, oppressive political relations, biased race relations, patriarchal gender relations, hierarchical power relations, and the use of violence to maintain them all" (p. 34).

Wink suggests Christians understand the powers as part of God's creation and therefore good, but broken and in need of restoration. In this sense, people and institutions can be liberated from the domination system and restored to their true vocation. Civil religion, on the other hand, serves to sanctify the spirit of the nation. When the spirit of the nation is angelic this may be relatively benign; however, when the spirit of the nation has been integrated into a domination system, civil religion is certainly demonic.

The character of the American spirit has been debated for some time with limited consensus; however, ACR prioritizes certain attributes of the national spirit and their contributions to American society. These characteristics in turn affect how Americans justify their own actions and priorities. Three values of the American spirit that ACR has historically championed have had a pervasive influence on the ELT endeavors of Christian missionaries: pragmatism, personal freedom, and pride.

Pragmatism

Pragmatism is one of the more rigorous values of the American spirit. ACR often points back to frontier life and the demand for practicality and adaptability in forming the nation. Early heroes such as Ben Franklin personified the utilitarian mindset; the ends justify the means, and the good is that which is useful and profitable for most people most of the time. Pragmatic themes run deep in American politics, morals, and economics (Bellah, 1985). Pragmatism has led to greater efficiency and effectiveness. Americans prize flexibility and thinking "outside the box" in order to get results. The expediency of bending the rules and twisting the truth is tolerated and even welcomed if the consequences are perceived as good/desirable.

Christian-sending agencies and many CET have certainly been possessed by this concept and used it to justify their actions. Several senior executives of a sending agency claimed without any embarrassment that their team would do "whatever it takes" to get more teachers on the mission field. Many agencies and some CET are willing to twist the truth in order to get the results they want. Some will even develop careful strategies of deception and omission to safeguard their endeavors (Yeoman, 2002). These are not malicious efforts; rather, they are

Table 13.3 Values championed by American civil religion

Values	*Basis/support in ACR*	*Contributions to American society*	*Rationalization by CETHEG*
Pragmatism	Practicality Adaptability Utilitarianism	Efficiency Flexibility Expediency	Whatever it takes
Personal freedom	Human dignity Autonomy Individualism	Inalienable Rights Independence Opportunism	Power to choose
Pride	Divine mandate Messianic state Triumphalism	Confidence Egocentrism Violence	Something to offer

a manifestation of utilitarian pragmatism, the belief that the result (in this case evangelizing students) is not only good but also justifies "whatever it takes" to get it done.

Personal Freedom

Personal freedom is one of the most appealing values of the American spirit. ACR frequently references the divine gift of human dignity as the basis for rights and freedoms. From the puritan settlers and republican founders to contemporary times, Americans have struggled to embody a national spirit that values the individual in community (Bellah, 1985; Wilkinson, 1988). To a greater extent than other powers, America affirmed the individual. The freedom to choose a new life, to make one's own choices, to be free of the obligations and definitions that formed such rigid social barriers in the "old world" was (and continues to be) intensely popular. The American Dream that a hard working man could be the master of his own destiny attracted countless immigrants to come and "settle the land." It also instilled an incipient opportunism. Few took the efforts of William Penn to protect the rights of tribal nations already living on the land (Yoder, 1990). As a nation, America freely chose to pursue opportunities for its own growth and wealth at the expense (and in many cases destruction) of indigenous peoples.

The appeal of personal freedom for CET is most clearly evident in the power to choose TESOL as a missional context even if this implies diminishing the value and use of other languages. English has been given great value and dignity, so much so that native speakers have rights and privileges nonnative speakers are denied (McKay, 2002). Agencies and individuals providing ELT services are linguistic power brokers. For many CET serving overseas, fortuitous access to English as Americans has given them remarkable status and opportunities as individuals. There tends to be limited accountability to the host since the majority of CET do not speak the local language, will only be in their positions for a few years (on average less than three),[6] and the demand for native English-speaking teachers so greatly exceeds the supply. This personal freedom can disconnect CET from the world of their hosts. Unlike their local counterparts, most CET have the freedom to leave their teaching position with minimal consequences. Another ELT position can easily be found.

Pride

Pride is one of the boldest values of the American spirit. ACR grants the nation a divine mandate to be the great redemptive force in the world. The spirit of triumphalism was an early facet of the American republic (e.g., principle of "manifest destiny") and reached great heights in the late nineteenth century. American nationalism was mingled with millennialism[7] as America celebrated territorial expansion and a passion for overseas mission (Askew, 1984).[8] America's messianic pretensions have grown with the nation's increasing global dominance. Since the close of the Cold War and the pervasive influence of global capitalism, there has been a revival of triumphal nationalist rhetoric. American powers work with the confidence that they have the blessing of God on their actions. Since America acts with the assumed authority and power of the messianic state, there can be an egocentric indifference to the concerns and interests of other peoples. If these interests become too strident or conflict with the American agenda, the powers that be do not shy away from violence to prove American virtue.

America's ascendancy continued and facilitated the spread of the English language for access to power, wealth, and information, a pattern with roots in British colonialism (Phillipson, 1992; Pennycook 1994, 1998). Technological developments and rapid globalization have heightened the usefulness of the English language for both American and indigenous interests (Canagarajah 1999). Christian agencies have seized upon this as a God-given opportunity with unqualified urgency. Native English speakers have something others want, ELT, but the demand might wane, so action must be taken now. Very few ELT ministries require that the teachers learn the host language, a trend in stark contrast with other missional ministries and missiological insights. The arrogance of this pattern is revealed when teachers mock the spanglish, chinglish, etc., of their students even when they are effectively deaf, dumb, and illiterate in the host language. The condescending message is clear; English speakers have something to offer (be that linguistic or spiritual), and others have something to learn.

Conclusion

Pragmatism, personal freedom, and pride are values of the American spirit, championed by ACR, and have been used to justify CETHEG's enterprises. When CET and agencies are willing to do whatever it takes to gain "creative/limited" access to students, when they exercise their power to choose ELT as a missional context even when it is destructive or isolates them from their hosts, or when they are motivated by the conviction that what they have to offer is more significant than what they have to learn, it is clear that the source and justification of these ministries is not especially Christian. Rather, these values emanate from the American spirit and are validated by American Civil Religion. Through the support of their spiritual and professional communities, CET need to consider whose ethics does their presence reflect: Constantine or Christ?

Notes

1. Some prefer euphemisms such as "creative access" or "limited/restricted access" contexts instead of the term "closed" context. The 10/40 window refers to countries/people/religions within that 10th to 40th latitudes north who are considered the least evangelized.
2. In this chapter, evangelism will refer to verbal proclamation of Christian messages in order to persuade others to convert to Christian beliefs (i.e., to proselytize).
3. Figure taken from five organizations representing almost 400 CET (total 382: US 335, other 47). Ten additional organizations were questioned, but they declined to answer how many of their English teachers were American/other (informal email survey, January 2005).
4. As an example, see Robert Schuller's July 4, 2004 "Hour of Power" telecast "Let

Freedom Ring" (#1796). In this broadcast, Schuller presides over the flag-draped Crystal Cathedral in Southern California and (1) praises the Christian heritage of America, (2) condones and praises American foreign policy in Iraq, and (3) assures the congregants and viewers that God will bless America and leads them in "Battle Hymn of the Republic" as children enter carrying flags and the camera pans across uniformed soldiers in the congregation.

5. Note that there are two prophetic voices. The first, indicated here, is the prophetic voice from *within* the civil religion. The second, which may share objectives with the first, is situated outside the community and uses different standards of critique.
6. The minimum term for most sending agencies is 2–3 years.
7. Millennialism is the belief that once the Christian message has been proclaimed in every tongue, Jesus Christ will return to Earth and reign for 1000 years.
8. Missiologists (e.g., Bosch, 1991; Shenk, 1999) have noted that while many missionaries went overseas with the presumption that Anglo-Saxon culture was superior, encounters with other cultures profoundly reshaped their thinking, reformed missiological discourse, inspired linguistic and anthropological studies, and affected popular attitudes toward other cultures.

References

Askew, T. (1984). *Churches and the American experience.* Grand Rapids, MI: Baker Books.

Bellah, R. (1967). *Civil religion in America.* Retrieved March 15, 2004, from http://hirr.hartsem.edu/bellah/articles_5.htm.

Bellah, R. (1976). *The revolution and the civil religion.* Retrieved January 23, 2005, from www.religion-online.org/showchapter.asp?title=1657&C=1653.

Bellah, R. (Ed.) (1985). *Habits of the heart: Individualism and commitment in American life.* Berkeley: University of California Press.

Bosch, D. J. (1991). *Transforming mission: Paradigm shifts in theology of mission.* Mary Knoll, NY: Orbis.

Bush, G. W. (2005). *President sworn-in to second term.* Retrieved January 25, 2005, from www.whitehouse.gov/news/releases/2005/01/20050120–1.html.

Canagarajah, A. S. (1999). *Resisting linguistic imperialism in English teaching.* New York: Oxford University Press.

Edge, J. (1996). Keeping the faith. *TESOL Matters, 6*(4), 1, 23.

Edge, J. (1997). Julian Edge responds. *TESOL Matters, 6*(6), 6.

Edge, J. (2003). Imperial troopers and servants of the Lord: A vision of TESOL for the 21st century. *TESOL Quarterly, 37*(4), 701–709.

Edge, J. (2004). Of displacive and augmentative discourse, new enemies, and old doubts. *TESOL Quarterly, 38*(4), 717–721.

Green, J. C., Smidt, C. E., Guth, J. L., & Kellstedt, L. A. (2004). *The American religious landscape and the 2004 presidential vote: Increased polarization.* Retrieved March 19, 2005, from www.gallup.com/poll/content/login.aspx?ci=14446.

Lincoln, A. (1862). *Lincoln's second annual message to Congress.* Retrieved January 20, 2006, from www.presidency.ucsb.edu/ws/print.php?pid=29503.

McKay, S. L. (2002). *Teaching English as an international language.* New York: Oxford University Press.

Marty, M. (1976). *A nation of behavers.* Chicago: University of Chicago Press.

Pennycook, A. (1994). *The cultural politics of English as an international language.* New York: Longman.

Pennycook, A. (1998). *English and the discourses of colonialism: The politics of language.* New York: Routledge.

Pennycook, A., & Coutand-Marin, S. (2003). Teaching English as a missionary language (TEML). *Discourse: Studies in the Cultural Politics of Education, 24*(3), 338–353.

Pew Forum (2008). U.S. religious landscape survey. Retrieved June 15, 2008, from http://religions.pewforum.org/pdf/report-religious-landscape-study-full.pdf.

Phillipson, R. (1992). *Linguistic imperialism.* Oxford, UK: Oxford University Press.

Plumb, S. (1997). A key to their hearts. English may develop into an interest in Christ. *Teaching more than English. Using TESL/TEFL on the mission field at home and abroad.* Evanston, IL: Berry Publishing.

Purgason, K. (1997). Christianity in the classroom. Principles and resources for teaching English. *Teaching more than English. Using TESL/TEFL on the mission field at home and abroad.* Evanston, IL: Berry Publishing.

Tennant, A. (2002). The ultimate language lesson. *Christianity Today, 46*(12). Retrieved December 20, 2002, from www.christianitytoday.com/ct/2002/december9/1.32.html.

Wallis, J. (2005). *God's politics. Why the right gets it wrong and left doesn't get it.* New York: HarperCollins Publishers.

Wilkinson, R. (1988). *The pursuit of American character.* New York: Harper and Row.

Wink, W. (1998). *The powers that be: Theology for a new millennium.* New York: Galilee Doubleday.

Wuthnow, R. (1988). *Divided we fall: America's two civil religions.* Retrieved January 23, 2005, from www.religiononline.org/showarticle.asp?title=235.

Yeoman, B. (May/June, 2002). The stealth crusade. Retrieved July 10, 2003, from www.motherjones.com/news/feature/2002/05/stealth.html.

Yoder, J. H. (1984). *The priestly kingdom: Social ethics as gospel.* Notre Dame, IN: University of Notre Dame Press.

Yoder, J. H. (unpublished presentation, 1990). *Religious liberty and the prior loyalty of the people of God.* Retrieved January 30, 2005, from www.nd.edu/~theo/research/jhy_2/writings/churchstate/liber&loyal.htm.

Response

14 A Former "Missionary Kid" Responds

Stephanie Vandrick

This volume on the role of Christian educators in English language teaching (ELT) is very welcome, as the topic has long been a "hidden" one in TESL/TEFL/ELT. (Hereafter, for convenience, I will generally use the term ELT—English Language teaching—as the most inclusive term to refer to this field.) Fortunately, the topic has just recently been increasingly discussed, sometimes in very heated and controversial terms. The book's concern with the role of fundamentalism is particularly relevant in today's world, where religious fundamentalism of all kinds, whether Christian, Muslim, Hindu, or otherwise, has played an increasingly large role on the world stage.

Before I respond to the often very candid chapters in this book, and in particular to those in this Part II, it is only fair that I reveal, as many of the authors have, my own background and stance regarding religion. In this response piece, I draw—as I have in past writing on the topic—not only on my own research, but also on my personal experience, attempting to be as candid as some of these contributors are. I am not a Christian, nor do I practice any other religion. I do care very much about issues of ethics, values, and morality, as most educators do, and I have written about these as they apply to ELT (e.g., Hafernik, Messerschmitt, & Vandrick, 2002; Messerschmitt, Hafernik, & Vandrick, 1997; Vandrick, Hafernik, & Messerschmitt, 1995). I believe that it is very possible to live a moral life without being religious. However, I do have a background in religion, as I was raised in a fairly strict Christian Protestant family. I presume that I was asked to write this response in large part because of my own explorations of my "missionary kid" background in India in the 1950s and 1960s and its connection to my ESL teaching and, by extension, to the field of ELT in general, and my remarks here are informed by that background, as well as by the literature on postcolonialism and English language teaching (e.g., Canagarajah, 1999; Pennycook, 1998; Phillipson, 1992) and the current controversy in TESOL about evangelical Christians teaching English as a foreign language (e.g., Edge, 1996, 2003; Pennycook & Coutand-Marin, 2003; Pennycook & Makoni, 2005; Varghese & Johnston, 2007). These articles provide a powerful exposé of a largely hidden part of the ELT field, one in which some Christian organizations and often untrained individuals use ELT teaching as a pretext (some might call it a ruse) to obtain entry into non-Western countries and do forbidden missionary work there.

As I have reflected on the ways in which I was part of the colonial enterprise, helping the "natives" and presenting them with the "gifts" of our culture as well as our religion, I have wondered if I was doing the same thing in my ESL classes: helping my international students by giving them the "gifts" of English language and Western culture. Yet I cannot—and do not want to—ignore the fact that my missionary parents were extraordinarily kind, good people, and did much good through their medical and educational work. My father, a surgeon as well as a general physician, treated thousands of patients and saved many lives. My mother helped to educate many young people who would otherwise have not had educational opportunities. So I felt, and feel, conflicted about their work as well as my work in my own career as an ESL educator. (See Vandrick, 2002, for a much fuller discussion of the connections between my "missionary kid" background and my career in ESL.)

As I consider the issues addressed in this book, I have a similarly conflicted feeling. I can see that the Christian educators writing here are people of sincerity and goodwill, people who have undoubtedly done good work and contributed much to the lives of their students and to the profession. Yet I feel concerned about any highlighting of religion, any possibility of proselytizing, in the classroom, especially when it involves a power relationship; teachers almost by definition have power over their students, and when they bring to bear their added privilege and authority of (often) representing Western culture, the balance tips even further.

However, it is apparent that the authors contributing to this book do not represent the fundamentalist wing of Christianity. They are thoughtful and even critical in their examination of ways in which some Christian instructors' teaching may be influenced by their religion. They are critical of fellow Christians who obtain EFL teaching positions outside their own countries as a pretext for obtaining visas to other countries and doing missionary work on behalf of Christianity. These authors remind readers not to lump all Christians, even all evangelical Christians, together. But the question remains: what is to be done about those who *do* practice, or support, this subterfuge?

Although various questions to do with the role of Christianity are addressed in this volume, the overriding, critical questions are related to the issues just mentioned: when, if ever, is it acceptable to use deception about one's religion in order to gain access to a country? How does such deception affect students and their communities, and how does it affect the TESOL profession? What can and should be done by ELT professionals, Christian or otherwise, and by ELT organizations, in response to such tactics? What is the role of Christian educators? How can they bring together their goals of being both good Christians and good professional educators? Various authors circle around and around these questions in this volume, providing some tentative suggestions, but no conclusive answers.

Another issue is that the volume focuses almost exclusively on EFL rather than ESL settings. Clearly the issues are starkest in EFL settings, where colonial/postcolonial influences are still factors, but readers might by extension wonder about parallel situations in ESL. What, for example, is the role of Christian educators in teaching immigrants to the United States with different faiths, which

Wong briefly addresses in her chapter? Or even in EFL settings, what is the role of the local teacher—as opposed to a teacher from outside the country—who is Christian, such as a Korean Christian teacher of English in Korea?

Another closely related topic that would have been of interest is that of the faiths of EFL students; this volume focuses only on instructors' faiths. How is the classroom influenced by the religious beliefs and identities of its students (Vandrick, 1997)?

However, no book can cover all related topics, so perhaps it is as well that this book focuses closely on the specific topic of Western Christian EFL educators in non-Western countries. I do hope that the related topics I mention above will be addressed in more detail than they have to date, in other publications and venues in the near future. In any case, although they do not cover all aspects of the title's topic, and although they cannot offer definitive solutions to the problems outlined, the editors of, and contributors to, this volume deserve much credit for providing information about, and engaging with, these important issues regarding Christians teaching English as a second or foreign language.

Now let me turn to the part of the book that I have been asked to respond to, "Ideological and Political Dilemmas." All the authors in this part (like the authors of several other chapters in this volume) agree that many evangelical Christian EFL teachers have entered the field, and gotten jobs in non-Western countries, with hidden agendas; these teachers have been deceitful in using EFL teaching as a subterfuge in gaining access to a country where they would like to do missionary work; furthermore, many of these teachers have only minimal training in teaching EFL. The authors of three of the chapters in this part (Wong, Byler, and Stabler-Havener) particularly struggle with these issues. It is of interest that these three authors are also the ones who explicitly identify as Christians: the co-authors of the fourth chapter (Makoni & Makoni), who have a different, more wide-angled, historical focus, do not specify their religious identifications, or possibly lack thereof. Interestingly, the authors that do not—at least in this chapter—identify as Christians write more sympathetically, in some ways, of missionaries and missionary work than the other three authors write of Christian English teachers who use their teaching situations to proselytize. Perhaps Makoni and Makoni not (at least in this piece) identifying as Christians allows them to step back, take a historical perspective, and see both positive and negative aspects of missionary work, including language teaching and translation.

The three authors who identify as Christians are very concerned about the problems with CETHEG ("Christian English teachers with hidden evangelistic goals"), as Stabler-Havener terms them, and seem both upset with their fellow Christians who engage in these practices and embarrassed to be associated with and perhaps identified with their co-religionists. As Byler puts it, "so many Christians are frustrated when it is assumed that their views are identical with Christian fundamentalists" (p. 121). The three authors each try to identify alternative ways in which they and other Christian educators can reconcile being both good, professional EFL instructors (or teacher educators) and good Christian educators. These three writers are clearly very professional and conscientious themselves, and all three explain ways in which they feel Christian educators can uphold the highest goals of teaching, and language teaching in particular, while simultaneously serving their religion through providing their own teaching and lives as examples.

This stance is very familiar to me, as my parents would describe my father's medical work and my mother's educational work in India as ways to help patients and young students and their families and communities and, through example, to bring people to inquire about and come to understand the principles of Christianity. I see two major differences between the two cases. The first difference is historical; in the 1950s and 1960s, these matters seemed simpler (although as my late father's journals from his Indian years demonstrate, he too sometimes struggled with questions of whether and how his work—as a physician and as a Christian—made a difference); in contrast, the scholars writing for this book have been informed and influenced by postcolonial studies and other postmodern perspectives that make them much more self-conscious about their positions as Christian educators than my parents and their colleagues were about their positions as Christian missionary doctors and teachers. Perhaps this difference accounts for the somewhat apologetic and even almost tormented quality of some of the writing here, as the writers struggle to reconcile their beliefs and to posit and defend honest and appropriate ways to reconcile Christian teachers' religion and their teaching. The second difference is a more substantial one: the missionaries—although many clearly had their faults—were at least honest and open about their desire to convert the people of the countries they were working in; the evangelical Christian EFL teachers written about in this book have often been dishonest about their true reasons for entering other countries, using EFL as a subterfuge for their missionary goals.

In the four chapters in this part, the authors seek to complexify what those in our field think we know, reminding us, for example, that not all Christian educators use deception in obtaining visas, and not all English teaching is imposition. They each try to construct a stance in which Christian educators can do good through their English teaching, while maintaining the highest ethical and professional standards. Because, as discussed above, three authors—Wong, Byler, and Stabler-Havener—identify as Christians and write from that stance, I will discuss their three chapters first, and then will respond to the fourth chapter, authored by Makoni and Makoni.

The first chapter is Mary Shepard Wong's thoughtful contribution, "Deconstructing/Reconstructing the Missionary English Teacher Identity," in which Wong makes a valiant effort at this complexification through a process of renaming and redefining the work of Christian EFL teachers. She delineates the problems alluded to above: some Christian teachers are not qualified and therefore deprive their students of good teaching; some enter countries deceitfully and unlawfully and therefore jeopardize local Christians; some attempt to impose their Christian beliefs on their students. Wong welcomes the recent secular critiques focusing on these points. But she also asserts that discussing Christianity does not necessarily mean imposing one's views of religion.

The main thrust of Wong's chapter is her attempt to find a way to critique deception and imposition, yet assert the possibility for Christian educators to be professional, honest, aboveboard, and effective while not necessarily hiding their beliefs. She explains this possible balance by employing the term "global Christian professional language teacher," which she deconstructs in some detail. She also emphasizes the importance of educators looking at their own identities as "language educators" rather than simply "English teachers," giving a wider scope to their work than the latter term might imply to some. She makes a good point when she reminds us that the Western ideal of strict separation between religion and secular life is not the ideal in many parts of the world; she further argues that there should be space in the EFL classroom for acknowledgment of and discussion of spiritual matters. The terms and concepts Wong puts forward are useful and effective. However, she still does not tackle head on the issues of when she considers it acceptable for an EFL teacher to talk about her/his religious beliefs, and how that discussion should acceptably take place; she is less than specific in responding to this thorny issue. This is understandable, as it is such a difficult question, and perhaps no definite answer exists. Wong's ideal—and that of some other authors in this volume—of a good Christian educator is similar to an ideal of a good educator that many or even most educators would agree with: a person who is professional, knowledgable, well-trained, certified, caring, compassionate, student-centered, open-minded, and respectful. Although I admire the author's effort to recast the work of Christian EFL educators, I am also left with a sense that this effort may be largely wishful thinking when it is applied to the fundamentalist educators who are the problem. In a sense, Wong is "preaching to the converted." She would like the reality to be different, and she advocates change, but I wonder how one dissuades Christian EFL teachers who are so certain that they possess the "truth" that they feel that the means justify the ends: the ends of conversion of those who would otherwise—according to fundamentalist Christian belief—be condemned for eternity.

The predominant point made in Myrrl Byler's "Confronting the Empire: Language Teachers as Charitable Guests" echoes Wong's: not all Christian EFL educators are the same, and not all of them misuse their positions as teachers, but some do. In particular, Byler criticizes Christian fundamentalist teachers who are also of the political right wing and who mix religion and a belief in the United States as the best and most powerful nation. He says that such teachers are close-minded and distrustful of other cultures and countries, including the ones in which they are teaching, and he critiques the idea that God is somehow more present in the United States than elsewhere. Byler's discussion of the connections between fundamentalist Christianity and right-wing politics, as these connections apply in ELT, provides the strongest and most useful contribution made by his chapter.

In looking for an answer to the question of what the role of the Christian ELT instructor should be, Byler takes a position that most TESOL professionals would easily agree with—that teachers should focus on "cross-cultural understanding, sensitivity, and respect" (p. 125)—and then makes connections between this idea and the original Christianity of Jesus and his emphasis on peace and humility, rather than with institutional Christianity's historical focus on seeking power and waging war in God's name. He concludes that the true Christian way for a Christian educator is to focus on the needs of the students.

Although Byler states that using teaching to try to convert people "is an approach that can make a mockery of the language teaching profession" (p. 127), he also attempts to understand and explain the viewpoints and motivations of such fundamentalist teachers. He reports on their beliefs in almost anthropological and, to this reader, frightening detail. Such information is useful for helping non-Christian readers to better understand the thinking of such teachers; after all, as scholars, we need to seek to understand before we form definitive opinions. It is laudable that Byler attempts to understand and not merely condemn. That said, I find nothing in his explanation of these teachers' thinking that mitigates the harm that they do to their students and to the ELT profession.

Like Byler, James Stabler-Havener, in his chapter "Christian English Teachers' Presence: Reflecting Constantine or Christ?" is concerned about the frequent conflation of the Christian religion and American civic beliefs, labeling this connection "American Civil Religion" (ACR). Such conflation encourages some "Christian English teachers with hidden evangelistic goals" (CETHEG) to take advantage of their power as speakers and teachers of English and use it to spread both the Christian religion and "American values and interests" (p. 135). Like Byler, Stabler-Havener offers detailed explanations of the motivations of Christian teachers; his explanations are even more theologically detailed and more explicitly Bible based. Although he is critical of those who have hidden agendas, he seems to be more concerned about the nexus between teaching religion/conversion and teaching ACR. His conclusion emphasizes this distinction, ending with the sentence "CET [Christian English teachers] need to consider whose ethics does their presence reflect: Constantine or Christ?" (p. 138), leaving the reader with the sense that although the religion/ACR convergence is a problem, perhaps the author feels that the teaching of religion would be less of a problem if it were disentangled from the ACR aspect. I strongly agree with the author's very appropriate, in my view, concern about the religion/ACR connection, but I do not think that this concern should allow the other—that of hidden agendas of some Christian ELT teachers—to be overshadowed or downplayed.

The remaining chapter in this part, Sinfree Makoni and Busi Makoni's "English and Education in Anglophone Africa: Historical and Current Realities," does not directly address the issue the other chapters focus on: the issue of evangelical Christian EFL teachers today. Rather it provides very useful historical context for this question. The authors give us a complex and intriguing account of the many economic, political, social, cultural, and religious factors determining the place of English in Africa, in a way that is rarely discussed in ELT venues. I found this chapter refreshing, because the stance was different from what might be expected. First, it is different from the other chapters in this part and, in general, the other chapters in this book, in that it focuses on a historical context in a specific area of the world, and allows that context to speak for itself without too much explicit connecting of that context with the urgent issues the other chapters address. Second, it is different from that of many postcolonial scholars describing some of the same historical material; it does not demonize Western (mostly British) missionaries as so many postcolonial writers have done, but rather gives a nuanced, evidence-packed portrayal of the role of missionaries regarding language use in Africa. While definitely holding missionaries accountable for their share of problems in Africa, the authors point out that in fact it was "mercantile contact and then the conquering colonizing powers" that mainly brought English to Africa, not missionaries (p. 107). They further point out the following: (1) that the real problem we should be concerned with is not the role of English in itself, but the loss of indigenous languages; (2) that we should not underestimate the agency of local peoples and the decisions they made (and make) themselves about wanting and using English for the power it could provide, without wanting to become like the Western colonizers culturally or religiously; (3) that missionary education was often welcomed by locals; (4) that missionaries were often actually allies of local peoples in the resistance to foreign governments' (especially the British government's) destruction of local languages, especially in the schools; (5) that missionaries aided in the conversion of African languages into written forms; and (6) that Christian missionaries no longer have influence, and that the local African Christian churches are very independent and quite pragmatic, using the language(s) that communicate best in any given place. This complex and comprehensive chapter covers many more aspects of these points, with ramifications regarding larger questions of language, politics, and religion in Africa. The authors also note the rather deflating point that nowadays African governments' decisions regarding languages are not much influenced by educators or linguists. (Those of us who live and work in the United States will ruefully recognize this feeling of being marginalized in the setting of government policies about the very area of our expertise.)

I can't leave these chapters without addressing a proposition put forth by Wong and by others in this book: that EFL instructors should learn a second language, preferably the language of the country in which they are teaching. These authors see such language learning as a sign of respect and care to their host countries and the students they teach, as well as, obviously, a way to improve communication with their students and communities. I doubt that anyone would disagree with these points. But it is not clear to me that language learning resolves the issues under discussion here, issues of deceptiveness, lack of training, and proselytizing. And language learning is something that many missionaries have done (with exceptions such as the reprehensible Nathan Price in Barbara Kingsolver's novel *The Poisonwood Bible*); in fact, as Stabler-Havener points out, missionaries have generally been required to learn the languages of the countries where they work, and as Makoni and Makoni remind us, missionaries were often strong advocates for preserving indigenous languages. My own missionary parents, and their colleagues in India, spent hundreds of hours learning Indian languages. I remember them sitting on the veranda of our house for many hours daily with the *munshi* (language teacher). My father, who had a love of languages and a gift for learning them, eventually became fluent in three Indian languages (Telugu, Oriya, and Saora), using them regularly in his medical work, and learned something of several other Indian languages as well. Language learning is definitely a positive thing, but it does not distinguish Christian EFL instructors from missionaries, and it does not address or resolve the problem of untrained, deceptive teachers.

Reading these four chapters, as well as the other chapters in this book, has given me a glimpse into a world that is, as mentioned above, too little discussed in ELT venues. Despite my personal background in the Christian religion, and despite my research and writing on related topics, I have learned something new from each of the chapters. I am certain that most readers of this volume will also find the topics and information eye opening and thought provoking. In addition to the ideas and information presented, the authors give us access to terminology and acronyms that are initially mysterious, such as *tentmaking*, *sending agency*, *missiologist*, *10/40 window*, *CET*, *CETHEG*, and *ACR*. Decoding such terms for readers is one way to bring the wider issues regarding Christian EFL education out of the shadows and into the sunlight.

I admire and find very useful the contributions of all of the authors, and of this volume as a whole. I am left with an urgent sense that the discussions in this book, building on and adding to other current publications on issues of religion and TESOL, provide a good starting point for discussion that must continue. First, Christian educators themselves must make their views known to their co-religionists who misuse the EFL profession by using it for religious proselytizing, and must engage these colleagues in serious discussion. Second, the ELT profession itself, and especially such key organizations as TESOL, have to seriously engage with these issues. As Varghese and Johnston (2007) have pointed out, currently many evangelical Christians have been operating in a sort of hidden separate, parallel ELT universe, with its own schools, organizations, conferences, and materials. Most ELT professionals know nothing of this universe, let alone its large scale. The integrity of the profession is being seriously compromised. All educators in the field of ELT, Christian or otherwise, should be concerned about the issue and educate themselves about it. More attention must be paid; there must be more open discussion. This volume provides a laudable contribution to the debate.

References

Canagarajah, S. (1999). *Resisting linguistic imperialism in English teaching.* New York: Oxford University Press.

Edge, J. (1996). Keeping the faith. *TESOL Matters, 6*(4), 1, 23.

Edge, J. (2003). Imperial troopers and servants of the lord: A vision of TESOL for the 21st century. *TESOL Quarterly, 37*(4), 701–709.

Hafernik, J. J., Messerschmitt, D. S., & Vandrick, S. (2002). *Ethical issues for ESL faculty: Social justice in practice.* Mahwah, NJ: Erlbaum.

Kingsolver, B. (1998). *The poisonwood bible.* New York: HarperCollins.

Messerschmitt, D. S., Hafernik, J. J., & Vandrick, S. (1997). Culture, ethics, scripts, and gifts. *TESOL Journal, 7*(2), 11–14.

Pennycook, A. (1998). *English and the discourses of colonialism.* London: Routledge.

Pennycook, A., & Coutand-Marin, S. (2003). Teaching English as a missionary language (TEML). *Discourse: Studies in the Cultural Politics of Education, 24*(3), 337–353.

Pennycook, A., & Makoni, S. (2005). The modern mission: The language effects of Christianity. *Journal of Language, Identity and Education, 4*(2), 137–155.

Phillipson, R. (1992). *Linguistic imperialism.* Oxford, UK: Oxford University Press.

Vandrick, S. (1997). The role of hidden identities in the postsecondary ESL classroom. *TESOL Quarterly, 31*(1), 153–157.

Vandrick, S. (2002). ESL and the colonial legacy: A teacher faces her "missionary kid" past. In V. Zamel & R. Spack (Eds.), *Enriching ESOL pedagogy* (pp. 411–422). Mahwah, NJ: Erlbaum.

Vandrick, S., Hafernik, J. J., & Messerschmitt, D. S. (1995). Ethics meets culture: Grey areas in the ESL classroom. *CATESOL Journal, 8*(1), 27–40.

Varghese, M., & Johnston, B. (2007). Evangelical Christians and English language teaching. *TESOL Quarterly, 41*(1), 5–31.

Response

15 Caught between Poststructuralist Relativism and Materialism or Liberal and Critical Multiculturalism?

Manka M. Varghese

After reading the chapters in this part, "Ideological and Political Dilemmas," I see a major thread running through them, a thread that I intend to respond to in this chapter, with my own doubts and questions as a professional in English language teaching who has an explicit agenda for social justice.

All the authors in this part of the book ask that CET acknowledge the harmful effects on local communities by those who hold cultural and linguistic imperialistic views. They also fear for the damage that this subgroup of CET may have on other CET who approach teaching English and training future teachers of English differently. That is, by learning from local groups and repudiating the neo-conservative agenda of "seize and conquer." Within this subgroup, Stabler-Havener refers to Christian English teachers with hidden evangelistic goals as CETHEG and repudiates their mission and conduct, as do Wong and Byler. At the same time, in their chapters all three authors also ask readers to see the diversity that exists within CET by expressing that there are many CET who, like them, oppose the hegemonic forces of the past colonial powers and of the United States at present, which has been associated in different ways with evangelical Christianity.

Interestingly, in our empirical study (Varghese & Johnston, 2007), Bill and I were genuine in our approach and intent as researchers outside the community of CET who wanted to understand how and why evangelical Christians chose the profession of English language teaching. We were careful in our article, first, to differentiate between evangelical Christians and other types of Christians and, in analyzing our interview data, what struck us was the diversity of professional identities that these future teachers espoused. In fact, the three teacher identity scenarios that Wong proposes can be actually found embodied in the participants in our study. The participants, such as David in our study, were particularly concerned about being skilled language teachers as well as being culturally sensitive when going abroad to teach English, something that these three authors also worry about and make explicit as essential traits for the ideal CET to have. Although Makoni and Makoni's chapter is different from the other chapters in its genre and focus, they also speak to the diversity within Christian groups by casting doubt on two rigidly held assumptions regarding the spread of English in Africa. The first is the assumption that missionaries coerced local communities into adopting English; in their chapter, as we also partially argued in our article, they articulate that by and large missionaries were actually intent on preserving the local languages although this was mainly to pursue their evangelistic goals. The second is that Christian organizations are the major forces behind the preservation of English as the language of prestige in anglophone Africa. Makoni and Makoni actually claim that it is the parents of children in this part of the world who are actually behind this push and the politicians, in paying heed to them, have passed legislation in support of this. According to them, English is part of these communities, desired by these communities, and is there to stay.

This response provides me with the opportunity to reflect and also make more public some of the dilemmas that both Bill Johnston and I wrestled with, although from slightly different perspectives, when writing our article (Varghese & Johnston, 2007) on evangelical Christians who pursue English language teaching. A major dilemma that we struggled with was how to make co-exist on paper two perspectives we hold dear, perspectives shared also by the authors in this part of the book. One was our desire to highlight our empirical approach and the findings we made, which made salient the diversity of perspectives that were present within our participants. This was for us a central reason for conducting empirical research in this area, to answer genuine questions about these future teachers who identified spiritually with evangelical Christianity. The other perspective that we viewed as critical to represent was our rejection of association between evangelical Christianity and the neo-conservative project of American empire. Writing the chapter required endless drafts as we meticulously attempted to articulate these perspectives side by side. In looking at my past and present work and considering my future research, this multivocality has been important to preserve and express. In my study of bilingual teachers' professional identities (Varghese, 2006, 2008), I used a conceptual framework of cultural production to underscore that what I found in my study was the creative and individual ways different teachers found to enact their identities as bilingual teachers. But the structural constraints and political roles of their professions were also important to convey as essential characteristics of their professional identities (Cahnmann & Varghese, 2006; Varghese & Stritikus, 2005).

While I have found the personal and the political to be important to engage in, I have also recently felt uneasy about whether the emphasis on one lessens the value placed on the other. I have wondered whether my focus on teachers' agency, individuality, and diversity is possibly diluting my attempts at showing the material and structural conditions of their profession. In the same way, I have been concerned that our attempt at solely humanizing evangelical English language teachers might contribute to dampening our critique of the association between fundamentalist Christian groups, English language teachers, and American neo-imperialism. In my recent flirtations with poststructuralist theories and feminist critiques of poststructuralism, I have witnessed that similar concerns have been voiced within the feminist scholarly tradition. Weedon (1999) discusses how feminists working within movements such as Marxism and radical feminism, have criticized the postmodern feminist movement for what they view as their lack of concern for social and material oppression. These feminists ask whether poststructuralist musings have led people to ignore such realities as those of battered women and of women of color experiencing the vicissitudes of racism. At the same time, I have found poststructuralist theories and approaches as extremely helpful in considering the primacy of language in constructing multiple realities as well as in conceptualizing identities as overlapping and shifting, among other contributions. Overall, poststructuralism has pushed many of us engaged in educational research to question what may be viewed as given truths. Davies (2004) writes that a characteristic of poststructural theory is its "troubling of those knowledges that have been taken to be certain and secure" (p. 4). In fact, poststructuralism has been heavily influential in my work in the way I approach a study and the participants in the study. For instance, in our study of evangelical English teachers, what pushed us was to question what we perceived as an essentialization of them as Bible thumpers with solely a proselytizing agenda.

In my response to these chapters, I am expressing my difficulty at being caught between validating the value of poststructuralism in my scholarly work, especially in my work with evangelical English language teachers and my fear of not acknowledging enough the possible material conditions and consequences of these professional roles across the world.

In this response, I also wanted to discuss another thought I had when reading what the authors wrote about how valuable a number of CET view cultural diversity. Byler, in his chapter, went as far as proposing that CET could be advocates who "point out injustices in their own society" and "address issues of racism and prejudice in American history." However, it does seem that a number of the authors lean more toward an espousal of valuing other cultures, which Kubota (2004) refers to as "liberal multiculturalism," which "emphasizes common humanity and natural equality across racial, cultural, class, and gender differences" (p. 32). Another important characteristic of liberal multiculturalism according to Kubota is how it ignores issues of power and privilege that are often associated with whiteness. As expressed earlier in this response, I have experienced a certain discomfort with making most salient in the study, the diversity among evangelical English language teachers, rather than other aspects. Part of this discomfort also comes with that in doing so I may have cast myself as a liberal multiculturalist. A critical multiculturalist might have highlighted the hierarchical relationship that exists not only between teachers and students (and therefore, the greater responsibility these teachers may have held when teaching their students) but also between the United States and many countries. Moreover, the issue of race was left completely out of the piece as well as a number of the chapters in this part of the book. It is undeniable that many CET are white, middle-class individuals (as Byler discussed) and the power of these categories and identities need to be put at the forefront of a discussion of their impact.

As I respond in this manner, I also need to express that one of the reasons I feel caught in between relativism and materialism, liberal multiculturalism and critical multiculturalism, is my fear that adopting this authoritative stance will lessen the force (and genuineness) of our invitation to dialogue. But our emphasis on the necessity of dialogue in the chapter was an aspect of the article that I view as essential. Here, I turn to Hannah Arendt's vision of a public arena of the spirited and courageous expression and exchange of opinion, invoking the Greek polis. This was a coming together of individuals to express their opinions on a particular topic that needed to be debated but it required courage. Arendt argues that it was in such a space that individuals developed ideas that were alien to them once, possible now, and through the process became themselves enlarged as individuals.

Whenever we write scholarly pieces, we always leave out any misgivings and fears of how we represented ourselves and our work. This is especially the case when we tackle what are perceived as controversial topics in our writing. In this response chapter, I wanted to express some of the fears and doubts I had when writing up our study on evangelical Christians teaching English while making connections with the chapters themselves. Once again, this was another move to continue the dialogue and I invite the authors of these chapters as well as others to continue to engage with me.

References

Arendt, H. (1998). *The human condition* (2nd ed.). Chicago: University of Chicago.

Cahnmann, M., & Varghese, M. (2006). Critical advocacy and bilingual education in the United States. *Linguistics and Education, 16*(1), 59–73.

Davies, B. (2004). Introduction: Poststructuralist lines of flight in Australia. *International Journal of Qualitative Studies in Education, 17*(1), 3–9.

Kubota, R. (2004). Critical multiculturalism and second language education. In B. Norton, & K. Toohey (Eds.), *Critical pedagogies and language learning* (pp. 30–52). Cambridge, UK: Cambridge University Press.

Varghese, M. (2006). Bilingual teachers-in-the-making in Urbantown. *Journal of Multilingual and Multicultural Development, 27*(3), 211–224.

Varghese, M. (2008). Using cultural models to unravel how bilingual teachers enact language policies. *Language and Education, 21*(8), 289–306.

Varghese, M., & Johnston, B. (2007). Evangelical Christians and English language teaching. *TESOL Quarterly, 41*(1), 5–31.

Varghese, M., & Stritikus, T. (2005). "*Nadie me dijó* [Nobody told me]": Language policy negotiation and implications for teacher education. *Journal of Teacher Education, 56*(1), 73–87.

Weedon, C. (1999). *Feminism, theory and the politics of difference.* Oxford, Malden, MA: Blackwell.

Response

16 The English Language and the Word of God

Zoltán Dörnyei

I have found the chapters in this part of the book elaborate and thoughtful, and the authors did a very good job outlining the intricacy of an issue that is inherently complex for at least two main reasons: on the one hand, it involves the interface between worldly and spiritual goals, ambitions, and standards, thereby touching upon some of the most fundamental questions of faith and human existence. On the other hand, it also concerns the uncomfortable association of both the Christian faith and the English language with some of the wealthiest and most powerful nations in the world, nations that have left a legacy of colonialism in many countries and whose contemporary reputation as world leaders is far from spotless. Given that the question of language globalization is already a difficult and emotionally loaded one, with English seen by many as the main culprit, and given that this ambitious book adds to this topic the equally divisive question of evangelism and the rapidly growing influence of Christianity worldwide, we should not be surprised that none of the chapters can offer straightforward answers and simple recipes.

So, what can a respondent add to this discussion in a few pages? As I was contemplating this question, my thoughts kept returning to three points that I felt had a special significance in clarifying matters. As such, the following response describes these three points, not because I believe that there is anything particularly new or original in these thoughts, but because they were helpful to me in bringing some clarity to this confusion-ridden area. I hope that others will also find these clarifications useful.

Christians and the Great Commission

Christian believers have been given a task by Jesus Christ, which is usually referred to as the "Great Commission." The most familiar version of this is recorded in the Gospel of Matthew (28:19–20):

> [Jesus said:] All authority in heaven and on earth has been given to me. Therefore go and make disciples of all nations, baptizing them in the name of the Father and of the Son and of the Holy Spirit, and teaching them to obey everything I have commanded you. And surely I am with you always, to the very end of the age.
>
> (NIV)

Therefore, every follower of Christ is, to some extent, a potential missionary, trying to figure out where and how we can best serve the Lord and carry out the Great Commission. This may be seen as a "hidden agenda" in Christian life, except that it is not really hidden because it is stated more than once in some of the best-known verses of the most read book of all times, the Bible. In this sense, this must surely be the most widely publicized hidden agenda in the history of mankind!

Living and Working Abroad

Because the Great Commission mentions "all nations," many Christians feel that they are called to travel to foreign countries to make disciples there. To do so, they need to establish some kind of an "interface" with the host country, a way of entering the society and immersing into it. One option that has been frequently exercised over the past centuries has been to engage in some professional work in the host country, as this can both benefit the particular community and can sometimes also provide the means to support the missionary. As Mary Wong explains in Chapter 9, the most famous missionary of all times, the apostle Paul, started this practice by working as a tentmaker. Teaching English as a foreign language is an obvious "tentmaking" engagement for many native speakers of English, but by no means the only one. My church in Nottingham, for example, has sent out missionaries abroad to be medical workers, carers in an orphanage, teachers of subjects other than English as a foreign language, and even aircraft engineers. These missionaries have all faced the fundamental question of how to be a Christian in the workplace, that is, how to live out our Christian beliefs and exercise our professional competence in a complementary manner. I don't think there is a uniform Christian answer to this question and the chapters in this book present several possible models. Returning to Paul, he said the following about this in his first letter to the Thessalonians (2:8–9):

> We loved you so much that we were delighted to share with you not only the gospel of God but our lives as well, because you had become so dear to us. Surely you remember, brothers, our toil and hardship; we worked night and day in order not to be a burden to anyone while we preached the gospel of God to you.

Did Paul keep his tentmaking business and his public teaching about Christ separate? I cannot find any relevant details about this in the Bible. I suspect that from his point of view, making good tents (because they were of high quality, that I am sure of) and teaching about Jesus were part of the same process, the modeling of Christian life and values. In fact, in his second letter to the Thessalonians (3:8–9) he did specifically write the following:

> we worked night and day, laboring and toiling so that we would not be a burden to any of you. We did this, not because we do not have the right to such help, but in order to make ourselves a model for you to follow.

So, how can we "make tents" in the English language classroom? Don't we wish sometimes that we could receive specific instructions from someone like Paul about concrete questions, such as whether or not to mention Jesus while teaching grammar? Unfortunately, Paul never wrote a "Letter to TESOL" and therefore Christian language teachers need to decide for themselves on the best strategy to follow the Great Commission. I myself really like the advice attributed to St. Francis of Assisi: "Preach the Gospel at all times. Use words if necessary."

The Special Status of English in Evangelism

As is clear from the above, I feel that in many ways teaching English as a foreign language is no different from other "tentmaking" occupations. However, this may be only part of the bigger picture, because I also believe that there is something special about English in contemporary Christianity. Let us, for example, consider one of the most anointed evangelists of the turn of the twenty-first century, Reinhard Bonnke: he is a German missionary to Africa who preaches in English, which is then often translated simultaneously to the local African language. The point about this illustration is that few people would find this practice unusual, even though it involves a twofold language transformation process—someone preaching in his L2, which is then translated into an L3—because the mediating language is English. And if we also consider the international impact of Christian books, journals, and daily devotionals published in English (with many written by nonnative speakers such as Korean pastor David Yonggi Cho), it seems to me indisputable that Global English is becoming the *lingua franca* of Christianity in the twenty-first century.

Why is it significant that Global English is increasingly used to enhance intercultural and interethnic communication in Christian work, just as it is in so many other areas of life? To understand it, let us step back 2000 years and consider evangelism in New Testament times. The intensity of this evangelistic movement was unprecedented and, quite frankly, almost unbelievable: in less than 300 years the radical teachings of a tiny and oppressed sect of a marginal religion in a small and insignificant province of the Roman Empire reached official world religion status with Christianity becoming the official religion of the Roman empire. This was about as likely to happen as, for example, contemporary United States adopting the radical views of a handful of Hungarian extremists as their new constitution. Interestingly, however, this amazing movement was closely linked to the world language of the time, Global Greek. This is so clearly explained by Michael Green in his seminal book *Evangelism in the Early Church*:

> Greece, too, made signal contributions to the spread of Christianity. Perhaps the most important was the Greek language itself. This was now so widely disseminated through the Mediterranean basin that it acted as an almost universal common tongue. Captive Greece captured her conquerors, as Horace complained; and from the second century B.C. when she fell under Roman control, the Greek language rivaled Latin. The conquests of Alexan-

> der had already made Greek the common language of the East more than a century before, and now the West followed suit … Quintilian, the celebrated educationalist of the first century A.D., insisted that a boy should begin by learning Greek, and many of the official Roman inscriptions that century are in Greek. Fifty years earlier Cicero had observed that Greek was read by practically the whole world, while Latin was confined to its own territory. The satirists, Juvenal and Martial, scornfully pointed out that even the womenfolk did their lovemaking in the Greek tongue! It was, therefore, quite natural that Paul the Jew should address the Latins of Rome in Greek, or that Ircnacus, himself a native of Asia Minor, should write in Greek as he conducted his missionary and apologetic work in France in the second century.… The advantages for the Christian mission of having a common language can hardly be overestimated.
>
> (1995, pp. 17–18)

As a Christian, I simply cannot believe that it was sheer coincidence that Jesus came to our world at a time when language globalization had created an ideal situation for the Word of God to reach the civilized world of the time, and in the present age we see a similarly dramatic wave of language globalization: then, Paul the Jew addressed the Latins of Rome in Greek, now Bonnke the German addresses the Africans of Sudan or Nigeria in English. Therefore, I suspect that contemporary language globalization is somehow related to the amazing Christian revival that we see worldwide: people living in the Western world often find it hard to believe that there is an ongoing explosion of the Christian faith in Africa, Latin America, and Asia (see e.g., Aikman, 2006; Hattaway, 2003; Jenkins, 2007), which can only be compared to the events of New Testament times. Then, the Word of God reached the whole of the civilized (i.e., known) world; now it is literally being taken to the "ends of the earth." Interestingly, Green (1995) also adds the following comment about the use of Greek in early Christianity: "Missionaries using it [Greek] would incur none of the odium that English speaking missionaries might find in some of the underdeveloped countries; for Greek, the language of a captive people, could not be associated with imperialism" (p. 18)—this is an important issue that has been discussed in several chapters of this book.

Thus, I do not believe that it is accidental that the portentous spread of English coincides with the contemporary Christian revival.

References

Aikman, D. (2006). *Jesus in Beijing* (2nd ed.). Oxford, UK: Monarch.

Green, M. (1995). *Evangelism in the early church* (updated ed.). Guildford, UK: Eagle.

Hattaway, P. (2003). *Back to Jerusalem: Three Chinese house church leaders share their vision to complete the Great Commission.* Carlisle, UK: Piquant.

Jenkins, P. (2007). *The next Christendom: The coming of global Christianity* (2nd ed.). Oxford, UK: Oxford University Press.

Discussion Questions

Part II: Ideological and Political Dilemmas

1. Discuss your views of the three fictional scenarios of Christian teachers Wong depicts in Table 10.1 (p. 95). Imagine an ideal teacher, one who you strive to be, and describe this teacher in terms of the categories in the table (goal, pedagogy, interactions, correspondence, institution support).
2. Wong uses the term "global Christian professional language teacher." Discuss this identity and what you agree or disagree with. What list of adjectives would you use to describe your identity? Provide three or four adjectives to precede the term "teacher" or "educator," and elaborate on each.
3. How does your identity inform your view of language, learning, students, and your teaching? Which aspects of your identity (spiritual, religious, ethnic, social class, racial, "first" language, linguistic, political, national, gender, sexual, physical, etc.) are most salient to you? Do you feel a teacher's spiritual identity should or should not inform her or his pedagogy any more or any less than other aspects of her or his identity and if so why?
4. In their first paragraph, Makoni and Makoni discuss the problems in using terms that are fluid and inconsistent, and that may be interpreted radically differently by different groups of people at different points in time. They note they use terms out of communicative convenience rather than subscribing to the ideology the term may represent. Which terms in this volume do you feel authors may be "interpreting radically differently" (p. 106)? Which terms need to be more clearly delineated? What "labels" are used by the authors for themselves and each other in the chapters/responses and what does this reveal?
5. Makoni and Makoni provide a historical perspective of the involvement of Christian missions and language use in education in Africa, rendering a more complex and nuanced understanding than what is often portrayed. What were you surprised by in this chapter? They mention it is ironic that today some Christian English teachers in Africa demand "English only" in their classrooms. Why is this ironic and what could CET and missionaries today learn from this?
6. Discuss how Western English teachers might become aware of their modes of teaching and seek out local ways of teaching as suggested by Makoni and Makoni. Discuss how English teachers could be more sensitive to the linguistic ecologies of local languages. Describe strategies that might be used at

the local level to "mitigate the effects" of the use of English over local languages in the schools.

7. Byler notes that political and cultural baggage dictates how we interact in host nations and institutions. Reflect upon a situation in which your political or cultural assumptions and biases were exposed, such as a conversation in which you may have thought or said something that revealed nationalism or a disrespect for a form of government (communist perhaps), economic system (socialist for example), religion, or language, in which you may have been guilty of "preaching the gospel of American power and values" and "making disciples out of your students" (p. 127). Describe that incident and what it revealed. If you cannot provide an example, is it more likely that you have no biases or that you are not aware of them? If the latter, how can you raise your awareness?
8. Byler states, "There is nothing more non-Christian than entering relationships only because there is a desire to see the other convert to his or her beliefs.... [This] approach that can make a mockery of the language teaching profession" (p. 142). Do you agree, and if so, what can mission agencies, teacher education programs, professional organizations, and individuals do to ensure it does not take place?
9. Stabler-Havener makes a connection between CET and American Civil Religion, which values pragmatism, personal freedom, and pride. Do you agree and if so, why is it a concern and what can be done about it?
10. Read the series of questions that Vandrick notes are addressed in this volume and the questions that are not addressed here (p. 142). Choose one question from each group and write your responses and be prepared to discuss them in the following class.
11. Which of Vandrick's points about the four chapters do you agree or disagree with? What does Snow's chapter (this volume) contribute to her question about the connection between a teacher's language learning of his or her students' languages? What do you consider to be the key issues or questions that need to be further explored and researched arising from the nexus of teaching and spirituality?
12. Dörnyei notes that just as the Greek language helped the spread of Christianity in the first few centuries, English is assisting the revival of Christianity in Africa, Latin America, and Asia in this century. He alludes to the legacy of colonialism left from the spread of English and Christianity. What might present-day missionaries learn from their "far from spotless" past in using English and the teaching of English in their work?
13. Varghese makes an observation that the issues of power and privilege that are often associated with whiteness are missing from many of the chapters. How does the power and privilege of whiteness affect CET in terms of their access to teaching positions and influence over students? How can they be made aware of this power and seek to mitigate it? (Also see Morgan's discussion of power in the next part of the book.)

Part III

Pedagogical and Professional Dilemmas

17 The Courage to Teach as a Nonnative English Teacher

The Confession of a Christian Teacher

John Liang

As a nonnative speaker (NNS from here on) teacher in the ELT field, one can face many frustrations and challenges. For instance, Thomas (1999) identified at least four types of challenges regarding NNS teachers' professional credibility—discrimination in the hiring process, invisibility in the professional community, student suspicion of NNS teachers' capability, and lack of self-confidence. These challenges are often disempowering, destroying an NNS teacher's self-confidence, self-efficacy, and even self-worth. Further, as these challenges often deprive NNS teachers of a sense of adequacy, they also deplete NNS teachers of courage to make endeavors to pursue personal and professional growth.

As an NNS teacher, I have encountered many of the challenges mentioned above. In seeking a new identity as an NSS teacher, I came to realize that it takes more than professionalism to teach—it takes courage to teach. Professionalism requires recognition by others, and yet courage does not. It requires conviction. In this chapter, therefore, I will first recount my professional development as an NNS English teacher, and then raise a question for further reflection—what defines a teacher who happens to be an NNS? A review of recent and current literature on NNS teachers' professional development will follow, with an argument that the development of an NNS teacher's professional strengths alone, without a clearly defined sense of direction or conviction, cannot sustain the growth as a language educator, nor does it offer the courage to teach in the face of various challenges against pedagogical credibility. As I further reflect upon my own personal growth as an NNS teacher, I will describe how my religious faith helped reshape my self-perceptions as a language teacher and renew my sense of purpose and direction as an NNS teacher. In particular, I will describe how it has served as an important source of professional strength, a source of reconciliation, and a source of courage for me to teach. Based on these critical reflections, I will argue at the end of this chapter that faith is a relevant and valid construct in ELT; it is not merely a source that sustains one's professional growth as a language educator, it is a source of courage to teach.

Being an NNS Teacher, an Original Sin? Personal Reflections

Toward the end of my college program in English, I became increasingly interested in pursuing language teaching as a career following a number of successful experiences as a tutor. I decided to come to the US for further training in TESOL, dreaming that perhaps I could gather some experience before returning to China. However, I was soon plunged in despair. While my friends' frequent casual derisions about my dream to be an English teacher in the US were discouraging, it was not as debilitating as a "candid" comment made by a supervisor of an ESL program where I worked as a student secretary. He commented that although he would not recognize me as a foreigner in a phone interview because I speak English without a Chinese accent, he would hesitate to hire me in a face-to-face interview because my presence would betray my NNS status. I was shocked and frustrated because not long before I felt greatly encouraged by a group of ESL students who were so pleased with my explanations about grammar that they wished I had been their teacher since their American teacher could not offer explanations like I did, and I felt flattered—and encouraged. But after his comment, I was dejected and decided to no longer apply for a position in his ESL program after graduation.

Gripped with a fear of inadequacy, I decided to proceed to doctoral studies, thinking that further preparation could perhaps strengthen my expertise in defense against any discrimination. Yet, when I was graduating, I once again received a candid comment from one of my professors. Sympathizing with my labored search for a job in vain, she commented, "Honestly, it's very hard for you to find a job because you're a NNS—unless you are established." I was at once dejected and determinedly combative. I realized that I had to prove myself worthy.

Belligerent in spirit, I continued my job search, and eventually secured an opportunity to administrate an ESL program at a state university. While I felt a sense of victory when the director told me that the search committee unanimously voted for me as the only qualified candidate, the fear of inadequacy continued. As a result, I urged myself to prove myself worthy in everything I did. My teaching assignment in a summer bridge writing program served my pride well. In the beginning, my native speaker colleague was worried if I could handle a college writing class where there were native speakers, but he soon changed his mind and expressed his confidence in my training and my ability. Though anxiously self-conscious, I was thankful for his trust and devoted myself completely to the program. On the last day of class, when I walked into the classroom, I found myself speechless and in tears. The blackboard was filled with students' thank-you notes and signatures. One comment particularly caught my attention. "John, thank you for investing your life in us." All of sudden, I realized that in the eyes of my students, I was a teacher in the very first place, the NNS being just an unimportant adjective. On the final exam, half of the students passed the test, 4% slightly higher than my colleague's class, and 20% higher than the average pass rate in the same writing program hosted in the English Department. A prideful thought went through my mind—I'm a better teacher than my native speaker colleague!

With a renewed confidence, I began to be passionate about further development. I began to collaborate with my other ESL colleague in the program, a native speaker teacher. Although I was somewhat self-conscious in the beginning, the urge to grow through collaboration overshadowed my fear. To my surprise, she welcomed the idea of partnership and was eager to collaborate with me. The following years were fruitful, in materials writing, classroom research, conference presentations, and journal publications. Our collaboration, of course, was not without disagreements, i.e., our frequent arguments over different teaching and beliefs. Yet, these differences only strengthened our strengths and eliminated our weaknesses, as we both would attempt to integrate each other's perspectives in our teaching to the benefits of mutual inspiration and growth.

While I appeared to enjoy a renewed sense of security, the fear of inadequacy once again haunted me when I assumed a teacher trainer position at another university years later. This time, I was besieged with two challenges. The first was concerned with the new position: in the past I was an ESL teacher, but now I was a teacher trainer. The second came from my students. In interactions with my students, I sensed a lack of confidence in my credibility as a teacher trainer. My intuition was right. Years later a native speaker student confided to me that she had initially doubted what she could learn from an NNS about teaching English.

In any case, I was plunged into tremendous fear once again. I thought I had tried my best to prove myself worthy—through scholarship and pedagogical expertise. However, in a new teaching environment, all of the confidence I had labored to build up was completely shattered. I could not help inquiring about my own identity as an NNS teacher—what makes me a teacher who happens to be an NNS? Further, by what standards should my pedagogical credibility be defined: by the perceptions of the prospective employer, by those of my students, or by how I am viewed by God as someone unique, different, but equal in his sight? To answer these questions, I now want to proceed to review current literature on NNS teachers' issues.

A Theoretical Consideration of My NNS Teacher Identity

In ELT, the pedagogical credibility of the NNS teacher has been traditionally defined in light of native speaker competence. This "deficiency" model of language teaching basically follows a logic that as nonnative language learners can rarely become native in language ability, nonnative language teachers, who used to be nonnative language learners, can never be competent in language teaching (Cook, 1999).

In challenging this "deficiency" model of language teaching, a number of practitioners and researchers contended that NNS teachers' pedagogical expertise should not be narrowly defined in light of native speaker competence because the concept of nativeness has limited validity for language learning (Davies, 1991), for instance, due to the existence of different varieties of English (Kachru & Nelson, 1996). Furthermore, the "deficiency" model does no good but leaves NNS teachers in a dire sense of inferiority. In her article, for example, Tang (1997) reported a survey she conducted to find out how local English teachers in Hong Kong perceived their language proficiency in comparison to that of their native speaking counterparts. She reported that a high percentage of the NNS teachers believed that native-speaking teachers were superior to them in most of the skill areas, from speaking (100%) to pronunciation (92%) and listening (87%), from vocabulary (79%) to reading (72%). The "deficiency" model of thinking, for NNS teachers, is without a doubt disempowering.

In reaction to the "deficiency" model of language teaching, a group of language educators proposed a "difference" model. They looked into the construct of teaching competence and emphasized the professional strengths of NNS teachers. For instance, Medgyes (1992) argued that fluency in English does not guarantee effective teaching, but teaching competence does. Samimy and Brutt-Griffler (1999) contended that NNS enjoy a considerable number of advantages compared with their native speaker counterparts in the language classroom: they have a strong explicit knowledge of English grammar; are keenly aware of the differences between L1 and L2; are more empathetic to students' learning needs, backgrounds, and difficulties; and represent a source of motivation and a good role model. In his research, Mahboob (2004) added additional attributes that he believes strengthen NNS teachers' professional status: diligence, strong biliteracy skills, ability to answer student questions, and methodology informed by their previous second language learning experience. These arguments came to a consensus that "the untrained or unqualified native speaker is potentially a menace" (Phillipson, 1992, p. 195), whereas the trained, qualified, empathetic NNS teacher can be a blessing—at least potentially.

The "difference" model of pedagogical expertise, in comparison with the "deficiency" model, merits some commendation. It recognizes NNS teachers as an equally valid role model in the language classroom. It emphasizes the need for the language teacher to acknowledge the linguistic and cultural backgrounds of the second language learner. Perhaps, the most valuable contribution of this model is the attainable goal it sets for second language learners—language learners do not have to become native speakers, and they can still be effective and competent language users (Cook, 1999). In short, it strengthens NNS self-perceptions as equally valid contributors in ELT.

However, the "difference" model, in discussing one party's strengths in light of the other party's weaknesses, is not without concerns. Although the researchers above did not intend for a "competitive" model of language teaching, any attempt to emphasize the contrastive differences between native speakers and NNS teachers' pedagogical expertise could result in a misconception of the roles of native speakers and NNS teachers in ELT. Just as revealed in my personal anecdote, subsequent to my initial achievement, I began to feel a sense of competitiveness against my native speaker colleagues. It appeared to be a convenient defense of my vulnerability as an NNS. I was not alone, unfortunately. One time at a local TESOL conference, I was taken aback at a comment by an NNS teacher, "We are better than them! They [referring to native speaker teachers] just don't know how to teach beginning students." I looked at the native speaker teachers among the audience. They looked upset, embarrassed, and disconcerted although they had felt sorry for the various discriminations their NNS counterparts had suffered.

The "difference" model may thus be misleading, though not intentionally. Defining one's strengths in light of someone else's weaknesses does not make one a better teacher. Furthermore, it needs to be noted that the discussion of the NNS teacher's strengths does not mean that native speaker teachers should be displaced. Canagarajah (1999), for instance, maintains that there should be balanced ways of understanding the roles and responsibilities of both parties. He suggests that NNS teachers may have an advantage in teaching students in an EFL setting where the NNS English teacher has the first-hand knowledge of the discourse and conventions of the EFL community, while the native speaker teacher may make greater contributions teaching students in an ESL setting where English is learned for specialized purposes.

Furthermore, the concept of strengths is in fact a relative construct. When NNS teachers are placed in a classroom where students have the same or similar racial, cultural, social, linguistic background, the NNS teacher may be able to be empathetic to the needs of the students. However, when an NNS teacher is assigned to teach a class of students whose cultural backgrounds are different from that of the teacher, the NNS teacher may not be as empathetic as has been claimed. The reality is that they may be as "guilty" as native speaker teachers of lacking empathy, sensitivity, and understanding. This was exactly what happened to me as I began a new career as a teacher trainer. In short, basing one's pedagogical expertise on others' pedagogical weaknesses does not contribute to a valid and solid identity, nor does it provide the ultimate source of courage to teach.

In the literature on teaching expertise, there is yet another model, the "collaboration" model of professional development (see Matsuda & Matsuda, 2001). This model views both native and NNS teachers as having unique roles and responsibilities. Instead of seeing teaching competence as static, it sees pedagogical expertise as a dynamic function that allows for development, integration, and expansion. Therefore, a collaboration model of teacher development may be more appropriate because both the strengths of the native and NNS teacher can be combined to the multiplication of the strengths of both parties (for instance, Liang & Rice, 2006). For example, on the native speaker teacher side, collaboration can help increase the native speaker teachers' experiential understanding of the nature of second language learning and enhance their sensitivity to second language learners' learning needs, whereas on the NNS teacher side, collaboration may help develop NNS teachers' intuitive knowledge of language structure and use and increase their awareness of the target culture. More important, collaboration can help both native and NNS teachers deepen their language teaching awareness and increase their teaching effectiveness.

Indeed, collaborations may produce added strengths through integrative development. Yet, the further development of my professional strengths did not offer me an ultimate sense of security because when I directed my primary attention to the development of my strengths in defense against any further challenges, I had lost the direction of my teaching career. I became disoriented since I suddenly could not understand why I wanted to become a teacher in the first place.

In fact, collaboration may not always be possible for any native speaking or NNS teachers. Many native speaking and NNS teachers, despite the potential benefits of collaboration, are hesitant. In interacting with some of my native speaking friends, I find that they are either not aware that they can benefit from collaboration, or they do not know how to initiate a collaborative partnership with a colleague from a different culture. As for some of the NNS teachers I interacted with, they would desire to collaborate with their native speaker teachers, and yet their fear of inadequacy has kept them from trying. In fact, the idea of collaboration may simply add yet another layer of challenge, another level of fear.

In short, it seems that many of the NNS teacher issues could trace back to an ultimate issue, that is, what NNS teachers perceive themselves to be. As a NNS teacher myself, while self-recognition helped increase my self-confidence, and collaboration helped increase my teaching awareness, neither helped thoroughly remove my fear of inferiority, nor made me feel like a better teacher, nor grant me more courage to teach. Thus, there must be a source of strength that is transcendent and transformative.

Christian Faith: The Redemptive Source for Courage to Teach

As disbelief and disenchantment became a pattern, I realized that I had been so gripped with the fear of inadequacy in my inner life that I had lost connection with the direction and purpose of my teaching life. I realized that for me unless teaching embodies a higher purpose, fighting to be recognized might become the sole purpose of my teaching career. It was at this crisis that I began to turn to my Christian faith for an answer.

On the surface, faith may seem to be irrelevant to teaching as many people nowadays often see it as belonging only in one's private life. However, in my life, faith has turned out to have the redemptive power that has reconciled my inner conflict and restored my courage to teach.

As I turned to the Christian faith, the very first thing I realized was that teaching, for Christian teachers, is more than a job or a career; it is a calling. Van Dyk (2000) indicates that as a calling, teaching is driven by faith commitments, is headed in a certain direction, and is carried out in worshipful service. Within the Christian faith, the teacher's faith is in God, rather than in his or her own powers, expertise, or charisma. Also, teaching is not without a purpose; it is to lead students to the truth and to bring them in awe of the truth, so they can live out the truth in their lives. Furthermore, teaching is a service, a worshipful activity that exalts the glory of God rather than the glory of the self.

For years, being self-conscious of my NNS status, I had long been focusing on establishing my pedagogical and scholarly power to defend myself against any challenges to my NNS status. In so doing, even though my scholarship continued to grow, I never appeared to have achieved a sense of adequacy because seeking recognition appeared to have become the primary focus of my teaching career. This understanding of the religious nature of teaching quickly lifted me up from my bitter, frustrating, and dejected state of thinking and brought me once again face to face with the sense of purpose of my teaching career—my calling as a language teacher.

In fact, ever since I was young, I have always wanted to be a teacher. The influence of traditional Chinese teachings was a major factor. *Wei Ren Shi Biao*, for instance, is one of those teachings, which means that to teach is to model noble character and profound scholarship for students. The teachings of Han Yu (AD 768–824), a Confucian educationalist in the Tang Dynasty, were another source of influence. "To teach is to proclaim the Way, to impart knowledge to students, and to counsel them" Han Yu maintained. This means that the teacher's primary job is leading students to seek truth and truth makes one complete. It also emphasizes the need for the teacher not to simply instruct but also nurture the growth of the whole person.

Now as a Christian believer, I found these traditional Chinese teachings in an amazing parallel to the teachings of the Christian faith. They both hold the belief that teaching is purposeful and direction driven and that to teach is to restore the wholeness of persons in our students. Yet, the Christian faith embodies more than just moral values. It holds that completeness does not reside in the virtues of man but in the virtues of God, the source of all virtues. Therefore, within the Christian faith, teaching is a "redemptive activity" (Graham, 2003), a transformational process that aims to restore the completeness of students' life intellectually, socially, emotionally, physically, and spiritually in Jesus Christ. In short, the awakened sense of direction in me pulled me out of disorientation and helped me refocus on the purpose of my language teaching life.

With a renewed sense of direction and purpose, I began to further understand my role as an NNS teacher, my purpose of development, and my relationship with my native speaking colleagues. Within the Christian faith, just as teaching is a religious calling, teaching is also an office (Van Dyk, 2000). By office, it means a place appointed by God, a place within the community of God's people, and Christian teachers are assigned to teaching office in the Lord's cadre. Since there is office, there are office bearers: some of these office bearers happen to be native speaker teachers, whereas others happen to be NNS teachers. Indeed, there exist differences in teaching competencies between native and NNS teachers as there are differences in teaching competencies within native and NNS teachers respectively. These differences, however, do not negate their equality in the ordination of the office of teaching because both native and NNS teachers are called to teach for the good of their students.

In the Christian faith, one important belief is that people from different backgrounds are all one in Christ Jesus in the justification of righteousness. That is, in salvation, no one is better for being a circumcised Jew, nor is he worse for being an uncircumcised Gentile. In a word, it signifies nothing if a person is a Jew or a Greek. Though equally sinful, they are equally righteous in the Lord Jesus. They thus have equal rights to the same ordinances as well as every spiritual privilege, and share in the same blessings of grace of the Lord. As the privilege of the gospel lies open to all ranks, orders, and walks of life, so should the privilege of serving the common good of second language learners be open to both native and NNS teachers. In the ordinance of language teaching, native and NNS teachers' racial, linguistic, and cultural differences ought not to be seen as deficient, but rather as compensatory to the benefits of both native and NNS teachers.

However, this does not mean that there exists no difference between native and NNS teachers. Truly, in some areas one party is more competent than the other, whereas in other areas one party is less competent than the other. Yet, from the perspective of the Christian faith, the development of competence, or the process, is more valued than competence, the product. In the Bible, there is a parable about a master and three servants. When the master was planning to travel, he gave his first servant five talents of gold, his second servant two talents, and his third one talent. When he returned, the first servant reported that he had invested all five of his talents and he gained five more. The second servant reported that he had invested all two of his talents and he gained two more. From a human perspective, the first servant would be considered as more capable than the second servant, and should therefore receive a greater recognition. However, the master gave the same commendation to these two servants, "Thy good and faithful servants!" When the third servant came up and reported that he did not invest the one talent and instead buried it underground, the master was angry, "Thy wicked and lazy servant!" In reflecting upon this parable, I find that the teaching is in fact applicable to the stewardship and development of our abilities as language educators. It is true that native speaker and NNS teachers are different, and have their own strengths and weaknesses. Yet, the differences that exist between the native and NNS teacher do not make one party less worthy than the other. What makes them worthy instead is their commitment to the development of their talent and gifts that they have been endowed with for the fulfillment of their teaching ministry.

Clearly, one's racial or cultural backgrounds do not validate one's credibility as a teacher; roles and responsibilities in teaching office do. Again, in the assuming of the responsibilities, one's native or NNS status is clearly irrelevant. In the Bible, the scripture gives direction regarding the roles that the teacher needs to play in order to help students shape their well-being. In examining the ministries of the Holy Spirit, Buck (1998) identifies the various roles of the Spirit that are applicable to the roles of the human teacher: create, inspire, illumine, restrain, convict, empower, assure, intercede, encourage, control, strengthen, counsel, help, protect, reveal, teach, declare, guide, comfort, remind, give wisdom, hope, and joy, etc.

Brummelen (1998) also develops a taxonomy of teacher roles. He suggests that teachers can teach as an artist (i.e., teaching creatively and strategically), as a technician (i.e., emphasizing efficient and precise learning), as a facilitator (i.e., providing the right environment and motivation for learning), as a storyteller (i.e., making abstract ideas concrete), and as a craftsperson (i.e., doing systematic reflective teaching). Realizing these teaching functions are not sufficient in fostering the wholeness of persons in students, he then maintains that teachers should also see themselves as an organizer (i.e., cultivating good learner characteristics, creating positive classroom structures and discipline, and managing activities to optimize student learning), as a priest (i.e., interceding for the students, providing counseling to students), and as a guide (i.e., stimulating thought and learning, engaging students in developing discernment through examining conflicting views).

Clearly, if these biblically informed teacher roles represent the constructs of teaching expertise, then the native and NNS status is irrelevant. Rather, these identified teaching functions represent goals that both native and NNS teachers should strive to achieve. They also represent the standards for evaluating the pedagogical competence of native and NNS teachers. For me, the recognition of these faith-informed values for teacher identity formation has been restorative of my courage to teach.

Although native and NNS teachers come from different racial, cultural, and linguistic backgrounds, they are in fact of one community. Exalting one party's strengths over those of the other does not foster the establishment of a community that is bound by love and characterized by grace. Therefore, it is highly important that native and NNS teachers be humble in their professional interaction with one another—and this should permeate their office consciousness. In fact, the Christian faith emphasizes that God's workers be humble in their interaction with one another in ministry. For instance, in his letter to the Philippians, Apostle Paul emphasized that as they were united with Christ, they should be of the same mind, of the same soul, and of one accord; they should not do anything out of selfish ambition or vain pride, but in the spirit of humility see others better than themselves. As applied to language teaching, the scripture here emphasizes the proper attitude native and NNS teachers should hold toward one another: they should be humble before one another rather than claim one's professional credibility over that of the other. For me, this faith-based value has helped reshape my heart for teaching as I interact with my native speaker colleagues.

Conclusion

In this chapter, I have argued that of the three models of language teacher development, the collaboration model has the most potential. Instead of seeing one party as inferior or superior to the other, it views native speaking and NNS teachers as unique, having their own strengths, and capable of making important contributions to the ELT community. Also, the collaboration model has the potential of developing both native speaking and NNS teachers' pedagogical expertise through the integration of their abilities and talents. However, in reflecting upon my professional struggle and growth, I contend that without a clear definition of the purpose and direction of one's teaching life, collaboration misses its purpose, and the development of professional strengths itself does not yield an ultimate sense of security that will sustain an NNS teacher's lifelong development. Through reflecting on teachings from both my Chinese Confucian heritage and my Christian faith, I have found that when a teacher's convictions and courage to teach come from a calling, his or her committed response to the calling will sustain challenges, his or her office consciousness increases, talents are fulfilled, confidence is strengthened, and growth is sustained. As in my case, my Christian faith is not irrelevant to my language teaching career; rather, it restores my conviction and courage to teach—as an NNS English speaking teacher.

References

Brummelen, H. V. (1998). *Walking with God in the classroom* (2nd ed.). Seattle, WA: Alta Vista College Press.

Buck, R. B. (1998). *Spirited-filled teaching: The power of the Holy Spirit in your ministry.* Nashville, TN: Thomas Nelson Publishers.

Canagarajah, A. S. (1999). Interrogating the "native speaker fallacy": Non-linguistic roots, non-pedagogical results. In G. Braine (Ed.), *Non-native educators in English language teaching* (pp. 77–92). Mahwah, NJ: Lawrence Erlbaum.

Cook, V. (1999). Going beyond the native speaker in language teaching. *TESOL Quarterly, 33*(2), 185–210.

Davies, A. (1991). *The native speaker in applied linguistics.* Edinburgh, UK: Edinburgh University Press.

Graham, D. L. (2003). *Teaching redemptively: Bring grace and truth into your classroom.* Colorado Springs, CO: Purposeful Design.

Kachru, B. B., & Nelson, C. L. (1996). World Englishes. In S. L. McKay, & N. H. Hornberger (Eds.), *Sociolinguistics and language teaching* (pp. 71–102). Cambridge, UK: Cambridge University Press.

Liang, J., & Rice, S. (2006). Forging new identities: A journey of collaboration between native and nonnative English-speaking educators. In N. G. Barron, N. Grimm, & S. Gruber (Eds.), *Social change in diverse teaching contexts: Touchy subjects and routine practices.* New York: Peter Lang Publishing.

Mahboob, A. (2004). Native or nonnative: What do students enrolled in an intensive English program think? In L. D. Kamhi-Stein (Ed.), *Learning and teaching from experience: Perspectives on nonnative English-speaking professionals* (pp. 121–147). Ann Arbor: University of Michigan Press.

Matsuda, A., & Matsuda, P. K. (2001). Autonomy and collaboration in teacher education: Journal sharing among native and nonnative English-speaking teachers. *CATESOL Journal, 13*(1), 134.

Medgyes, P. (1992). Native or non-native: Who's worth more? *ELT Journal, 46*(4), 340–349.

Phillipson, R. (1992). *Linguistic imperialism.* Oxford, UK: Oxford University Press.

Samimy, K. K., & Brutt-Griffler, J. (1999). To be a native or non-native speaker perceptions of "non-native" students in a graduate TESOL program. In G. Braine (Ed.), *Non-native educators in English language teaching* (pp. 127–144). Mahwah, NJ: Lawrence Erlbaum.

Tang, C. (1997). On the power and status of nonnative ESL teachers. *TESOL Quarterly, 31*(3), 557–583.

Thomas, J. (1999). Voices from the periphery: Non-native teachers and issues of credibility. In G. Braine (Ed.), *Non-native educators in English language teaching* (pp. 5–14). Mahwah, NJ: Lawrence Erlbaum.

Van Dyk, J. (2000). *The craft of Christian teaching: A classroom journey.* Sioux Center, IA: Dordt Press.

18 English Teachers, Language Learning, and the Issue of Power

Don Snow

English is the quintessential language of power. Its rise as a global language has been driven by power of the rawest kinds—military, economic, political, and cultural—and in today's world command of English offers its users more utility value than any other language.

The question I will examine in this chapter is what responsibilities this reality suggests for English teachers, especially native speakers of English from Inner Circle[1] nations. In particular, I will discuss the responsibility of two distinctive communities of teachers: (1) those in the professional ELT community, as embodied by organizations based in Inner Circle nations such as TESOL (Teachering English to speakers of other languages) and IATEFL (International Association of Teachers of English as a Foreign Language); (2) those who are Christian and perceive their English teaching as a form of Christian mission, whose community is embodied in Western Christian groups that engage in English teaching.

Below I examine ways in which these two communities have been involved in creating and sustaining the dominant position of English, and I suggest that this involvement gives both communities a special responsibility to respond to the dominance of English. I also suggest that, for both communities, uncritical acceptance of the dominant world role of English is incompatible with important strands of their ethical traditions. Finally, I suggest that one response of both communities to the power of English should be increased commitment as individuals and as professional communities to the principle that English teachers, especially those whose first language is English, should also be language learners.

The Historical Legacy

Empire and the Rise of English

The story of how English rose to global prominence is inseparable from that of the British empire. Beginning in the 1600s, Britain amassed a worldwide empire of trade networks and colonies that by the early 1900s made it the world's most powerful nation, directly ruling over approximately one-quarter of the world's land surface, and exerting great influence over much of the rest. In several ways, this led to an expanded world role for English. First, English speakers migrated to other parts of the world where they dominated or replaced indigenous populations and established colonies that eventually grew into independent English speaking nations. Second, in places such as India and Malaya, English was actively promoted to some degree by British colonial governments through schools training local people in English for service in the colonial system. However, British colonial governments often favored educating local people in the vernacular rather than in English (Pennycook, 1998, p. 84), so the impact of this factor was somewhat limited.[2]

A third important factor leading to acquisition of English among non-English speakers was the growth of an international trading network. During its age of empire, Britain tended to use its political, economic, and military muscle to promote liberal trade policies; in fact, as Ferguson points out: "no organization in history has done more to promote the free movement of goods, capital, and labour than the British Empire in the nineteenth and early twentieth centuries" (2002, p. xxi). This created an environment in which English became the language of choice within an expanding global trade network. As Brutt-Griffler (2002, p. 115) notes:

> The more England gained control of the world market—in part a function of the industrial revolution there—the more the international extension of trade and production relations inevitably transmitted English, rather than French, Spanish, Portuguese, Arabic, Chinese, or Turkish.

The worldwide role of English was sustained and strengthened when Britain was replaced in its dominant role by yet another English speaking nation, the United States. In the post-war era of American dominance, the growth of a world market has continued to make English the premier language of trade and commerce. The immense influence of the United States in areas such as technology, scholarship, and entertainment has also contributed to the growing utility value of English.

Christians and the Rise of English

Christian missionaries from English speaking nations were involved from early on in the teaching and promotion of English. On the whole, Christian missionaries did not consciously set out to promote English; in fact, in their religious and educational work they tended to favor use of local vernaculars (Canagarajah, 1999, p. 64).[3] Furthermore, to the extent that missionaries taught English or taught in English, this was often more the result of local demand rather than of a missionary desire to promote English. Consider the case of the 13 Christian colleges established by Western missionaries in China prior to 1949. These colleges initially used Chinese as the medium of instruction, and there was considerable reluctance to either teach in English or even teach English as a subject. However, within a few decades of their founding, all of the Christian colleges were driven by market demand forces to switch to teaching primarily in English. During their early years it was very difficult for the Christian colleges to attract students if they only offered courses taught in Chinese, and such students as the colleges could attract were usually from poor families who could not pay tuition fees. At the same time, growing levels of international trade meant that there were increasing employment opportunities for Chinese students who had a good command of English, and colleges that offered English quickly found that they could not only attract more students but also students who were better qualified and/or able to pay tuition. Thus, by the turn of the century, the Christian colleges all offered English; in fact, "the popularity and reputations of some of the Christian colleges came to depend heavily on their excellent training in English" (Lutz, 1971, p. 71).[4] As this last quotation suggests, the ability of Western missionaries to find an accepted role in local societies depended on their ability and willingness to provide commodities that local people wanted, and English was among the most important of these commodities.

In the postcolonial era, an increase in the number of Christian organizations and missionaries who engage in English teaching has been driven by a similar dynamic. With the end of the colonial era and a corresponding increase in the number of independent nations willing and able to be selective about what kinds of Westerners they allow to live and work on their soil, it became increasingly important for Christian missionaries to offer commodities that would ensure them a welcome, and English has continued to be one of the most important of these. This has led to a growth in the number of missionaries from traditional denominational missions who are employed as English teachers, and has also given rise to large independent para-church mission organizations that specialize in the teaching of English. While one main focus of this mission effort is evangelism, others include social service, education, and promotion of international understanding.[5]

While Christian missionaries generally have not intended to advance the world role of English per se, they have certainly been an important part of the process, and I believe this legacy calls Western Christian English teachers to consider what obligations it leaves them with. Furthermore, Western mission efforts benefit from the dominant global role of English in the sense that it has helped further Western missionary objectives. The association of Western Christian missionaries with the rise of English, however, raises a potential ethical dilemma for Christians in the sense that it can be argued that mission that rides on the dominance of English clashes with the mandate for Christians to carry out mission from a position of servanthood and humility.

Much Christian understanding of mission is based the teachings of Jesus, and he frequently and explicitly emphasized that his followers were to be humble servants of others. For example, Matthew (20:26–7) records the following:

> Whoever wishes to be great among you must be your servant, and whoever wishes to be the first among you must be your slave; just as the Son of Man came not to be served but to serve, and to give his life a ransom for many.

Jesus often underscored such teachings through object lessons, for example, by washing his disciples' feet and then commanding them to do the same for others (John 13:12–17).

A similar mandate is suggested by the very nature of the Incarnation itself, the idea that God willingly accepted humble human status by taking on human form in the person of Jesus Christ. A well-known passage from Philippians (2:5–11) describes the Incarnation as follows:

> Let the same mind be in you that was in Christ Jesus; who, though he was in the form of God, did not regard equality with God as something to be exploited, but emptied himself, taking the form of a slave, being born in human likeness. And being found in human form, he humbled himself and became obedient to the point of death—even death on a cross.

In other words, the medium was the message, and one message of the Incarnation is that in their mission to the world, Christians are called to humble themselves—literally to "empty" themselves of power. Of course, the idea of humility as a virtue is hardly unique to Christians, but the prominent place it holds in Christian thought makes it a particularly difficult challenge for Christians to ignore.

The problem in reconciling such ideas about mission with English teaching is that English is so closely and clearly associated with worldly power. As pointed out above, the spread of English was often based on the power of the gun or the pound/dollar, and much of the appeal of English today lies precisely in the unique range of worldly advantages and opportunities that it promises. I do not believe that the association of English with power makes it inappropriate for Christians to engage in English teaching; in fact, I believe that it is quite possible to teach English in ways that are perfectly compatible with the mandate for servanthood. My concern, rather, lies in the possibility that Christian English teachers may be too uncritical in accepting the advantages offered by the dominance of English, and too comfortable drawing on its power. One problem this may create is that Christian English teachers from Inner Circle countries are seen primarily as ambassadors of the world's most powerful language—and of the countries and cultures with which it is most closely associated. A second problem is that if the practice of Christian English teachers does not seriously and visibly challenge the assumptions implicit in the dominant role of English, the implied message conveyed by their lives may be that the Christian imperative to "empty oneself" of power is only meant for those who live outside Inner Circle countries and don't speak English as their first language.

The ELT Community and the Rise of English

While English teachers—both Christian and non-Christian—have been a part of the spread of English ever since its beginning, the emergence of TEFL as an organized profession is much more recent. The oldest major TEFL organization, the British Council, was established by the British government in the 1930s, and the two most important non-government ELT organizations, TESOL and IATEFL, were set up respectively in the US in 1966 and in the UK in 1967. The appearance of these organizations marks the emergence of ELT as a distinct profession.

While the emergence of these TEFL organizations is relatively recent, today they play a significant role in sustaining and promoting the worldwide role of English. One way they do this is by serving as primary centers of what Canagarajah calls "knowledge construction in ELT" (1999, p. 5). These professional bodies, their conferences, and their publications provide a network through which consensus is built about ELT theories, teacher qualifications, teaching materials, and so forth. They also serve as a marketplace in which materials writers meet publishers, and in which publishers promote their wares. Such networks and organizations give the Inner Circle ELT community disproportionate influence in shaping ELT worldwide, hence a special responsibility when it comes to the issue of how the profession responds to the dominant global role of English.

Another reason why Inner Circle ELT circles have a special responsibility to consider their stance with regard to the global dominance of English is that these circles benefit so directly from it. To put it bluntly, all who work as English teachers, faculty in ESL/EFL teacher training programs, administrative staff in ELT schools, writers and publishers of ELT materials, and even employees of professional organizations like TESOL and IATEFL quite literally owe their livelihoods to the global dominance of English—no other language provides employment to so many people. The degree to which the Inner Circle ELT community benefits from the rise of English leaves it with a special responsibility to consider the implications of this rise. Given the role that the Inner Circle ELT community plays in promoting English and sustaining its position in the world hierarchy, it would be all too easy for observers to assume that the ELT community's view of the world is one in which English not only *is* the dominant language, but also *should be*. The matter of what stance the ELT community takes toward the role of English—and how that stance is conveyed—thus assumes particular importance.

From the perspective of the ELT profession, the ethical dilemma lies in a potential clash between the community's promotion of English and its professed commitment to multilingualism. The dominance of English is an issue of which many in the professional ELT community are well aware, and the community has attempted to address the issue in part by explicitly advocating the values of multilingualism and respect for all languages and cultures. For example, TESOL's *Position Statement on Multilingualism* (2004) states: "Although TESOL's mission is to advance excellence in English language teaching, TESOL values and encourages multilingualism in all learners at every age and level," and expresses the concern that "the importance and value of multilingualism is increasingly underestimated." It also calls on "governments and countries to promote policies that recognize and value the languages in their population—whether they are indigenous, dominant, or foreign."

The problem faced by the ELT community is how to reconcile a professional agenda that primarily focuses on teaching English with promotion of the value of multilingualism. Here my contention is not that these two things are incompatible per se; in fact, I believe that it is quite possible to promote English study in a broader context that encourages respect for and study of all languages. However, we need to remember that the ELT community is sited in a context where the dominance of English makes it normal that non-English speakers are far more likely to learn English than speakers of English are to learn other languages. If this is the pattern that students see among English teachers, the implied message may be that this state of affairs is not only normal but also acceptable or perhaps even desirable, and English teachers' practice will tend to undercut the explicit message of official statements about the value of multilingualism. If this is not the message English teachers wish to convey, it becomes necessary for our practice to challenge the assumption that multilingualism is a value mainly for those whose first language isn't English.

Toward a Response

As a growing number of scholars point out, many people around the world have responded to the growing power of English by learning the language so as to empower themselves in various ways (e.g., Brutt-Griffler, 2002; Canagarajah, 1999), and English teachers can be a part of this process by assisting students in the task of mastering English so as to better take advantage of the opportunities and empowerment it offers.

In responding to the issue of the global power of English, however, I feel it is necessary to do more than use English to empower others, and that this is especially true for English teachers who are native speakers of English from Inner Circle nations. Both as individuals and as a community, Inner Circle English teachers need to challenge the underlying assumptions of the dominant role of English, in particular, the assumption that it is less important for English speakers to learn other languages than for speakers of other languages to learn English. What I wish to suggest is that, within the TESOL profession, we need to make language learning a more prominent feature of our professional culture and identity. Furthermore, I feel commitment to language learning should be built into English teacher training programs; to be specific, I believe that native speakers of English who study to be ESL/EFL teachers should engage in a significant amount of second language study, and achieve at least a high-intermediate level of proficiency in a language other than English. If the goal of English teachers is to help students become bilingual or multilingual language users, English teachers should embody this ideal.

Perhaps here we need to consider whether or not this is really an issue within the TESOL profession. After all, most TESOL professionals are relatively interested in learning other languages, and it is not unusual for TESOL training programs in Inner Circle countries to require native English speakers to study a second language. Furthermore, most TESOL professionals already advocate additive language learning rather than replacement of students' other languages by English. So, is this really a problem?

I contend that it is, and that it manifests itself in a variety of ways. First consider the second language learning requirements for native English speakers in Inner Circle MA TESOL programs. Taking the 185 MA TESOL programs described in the *Directory of Teacher Education Programs in TESOL in the United*

States and Canada, 2002–2004 as a sample,[6] the initial impression is encouraging—106 programs (57% of the total) explicitly require native speakers of English to either study a second language or demonstrate some proficiency in a language other than English. On the other hand, however, 79 programs (43% of the total) explicitly state that they have no second language requirement for students whose first language is English. Furthermore, when we examine the actual nature of the second language requirements for programs that have them, the picture becomes somewhat bleaker. In the *Directory*, most programs are not precise about second language requirements; however, an educated guess is possible based on what we know from those programs that do state requirements explicitly. Of the 20 programs that state their requirements clearly, eight require the equivalent of 1 year of college-level study of the second language, and nine require either 2 years of study or "intermediate proficiency"; only three programs have marginally higher requirements. Based on this evidence, it seems safe to conclude that most programs that have second language requirements only require the equivalent of 1–2 years of college-level study. While this is certainly better than nothing, it does not suggest a very high level of second language mastery. In contrast, all university students in China, regardless of major, are required to engage in at least 2 years of foreign language study (almost always English); this means that the average Chinese physics, art, or even Chinese major generally needs to spend more time studying foreign languages than does a North American student who is training to a professional English language teacher.

Next let us consider introductory TEFL methods textbooks. While such books inevitably devote considerable attention to the issue of language learning, the presumption is that students will do the language learning—and it is rarely argued that teachers should do the same. To be more precise, of 20 widely used introductory textbooks on ESL/EFL teaching, ESL/EFL teacher training, or professional development that I examined, only one devotes an explicitly labeled chapter or section of a chapter to the idea that English teachers should also be language learners.[7] Of course, it could be argued that such books assume that it is important that language teachers also be language learners. However, such books do much to set the tone for teacher training, establishing the norms and expectations of the profession, and if they do not explicitly highlight the idea that language teachers should also be language learners, the idea can easily be overlooked.

Third, if one examines the topics of presentations given at conferences such as the TESOL conference, or the articles which appear in professional journals, one certainly does not come away with the impression that the second/foreign language learning experience of English teachers is a salient part of their identity. By way of illustration, examining the program for one TESOL convention day picked at random (Friday, April 2, 2004), I found that of almost 350 presentations given that day, not a single one was primarily focused on the importance of second language learning in the training of English teachers.

Finally, there is the relatively privileged position that native speakers of English hold within the English-teaching profession. Despite the fact that there are many more nonnative speakers of English than native speakers within the

TESOL profession, native English speakers still tend to have a privileged status with regard to everything ranging from academic influence to preference in hiring (McKay, 2002, p. 42).[8] This tends to suggest that multilingualism—an attribute possessed by all English teachers who have learned English as a second language—is not as highly valued as native speaker status; in contrast, native speaker status is taken as a virtue even if the native speaker lacks significant experience as a language learner and/or significant command of a language other than English.

My point is that while in theory the TESOL profession is favorably disposed to the idea of second language learning for native speaker teachers of English, in practice this is not treated as a very high priority, and questions could be raised about the degree to which multilingualism is genuinely valued as an essential part of ELT training and professional identity in Inner Circle countries.

Here I would re-emphasize my belief that English teachers who are native speakers of English are generally quite sincere in their commitment to the idea of multilingualism as a value, and most would like to have a greater command of other languages than they do. This being the case, why is the issue of second language study for English teachers given relatively little practical emphasis within Inner Circle ELT circles? Why is there a relatively widespread (but quiet) acceptance of the idea that foreign language study need not be a very high priority for English teachers whose first language is English? Much of the answer lies in the fact that since the utility value of other languages is generally not as high as that of English, and learning a new language requires a considerable investment of time and effort, for native speakers of English the benefits of investing significant time in learning other languages are often not perceived as being worthwhile. While ELT professionals would all agree in theory that learning other languages is desirable, when time and energy are in short supply an expenditure of this magnitude needs considerable justification. So we need to ask: how important—really—is study of a second language for English teachers, especially for native speakers of English? Below I will briefly offer several reasons why second language study is in fact important for English teachers, with particular focus on those who are native speakers of English.

Practical Benefits of Learning other Languages

For ELT professionals, one obvious set of benefits of learning additional languages has to do with the many ways second language learning experience enhances one's effectiveness in English teaching. Personal experience with language learning helps teachers gain a better understanding of what the language learning process looks and feels like from the students' perspective. This ability to see and feel things from the learner's perspective is essential for enabling teachers to see how they can best structure a course of study for students—how much new material students can handle at any given time, how much review is necessary, how much encouragement is needed, and so forth.[9] Likewise, personal experience in language learning also gives a teacher a much firmer grasp of various language learning strategies, which can then be passed on to students. Furthermore, Diaz-Rico (2004) argues that, as language acquisition experts,

"English teachers who make sincere attempts to learn the languages of their students and build English on students' prior language expertise will model expert learning" (p. 7). Finally, the experience of achieving some degree of mastery over a foreign language makes real for teachers the idea that it *is* possible to learn a foreign language. While this might seem a strange point to make, we need to remember that many English teachers who are native speakers of English come from a culture in which successful second language learning—at least for speakers of English—is not very common, and it is widely expected that study of a second language in high school or college will not actually lead to a significant and sustained degree of actual proficiency. Without personal experience of success in language learning, it is easy for teachers to be influenced by such expectations rather than being driven by the conviction that students actually can learn the language being taught.

A second way in which language learning benefits English teachers is that learning a second language is an important transformative experience. As Pennycook (1998) argues, in the "discourses of colonialism" that accompanied the expanding power of English speaking nations over the last two centuries, there has been a strong tendency to view the Other—those who are linguistically and culturally different from English speaking Westerners—as strange creatures inhabiting an uncivilized wilderness, and the colonizers' understanding of the Other has often been more manufactured by the imagination of the colonizer than informed by listening to the voices of the Other. While such ethnocentric tendencies are by no means unique to English speaking Westerners, the unusual level of economic, political, military, and cultural power that has driven the expanding influence of English speaking nations also helps ensure that it is relatively easy for English speakers from such nations to go about their lives—even if they live abroad in non-English speaking countries—in a well-padded cocoon where voices from the Other are not often heard.

My point is that a serious effort to learn the Other language tends to pull English speakers out of the cocoon, place them firmly amidst the Others, and enable them to begin listening to the voices of the Others—their original untranslated voices, speaking from their own cultural context. While such an experience is important for all native speaker English teachers, it is especially important for expatriate English teachers teaching in other countries, for the best way to begin understanding the people of the host country and seeing things from local perspectives is to read the books, magazines, and newspapers that the local people read; watch the performances, films, and television programs that local people watch; and talk to the local people—all of them, not merely the few who speak English. This is how members of the TESOL profession can literally and genuinely listen to other voices (to borrow a phrase from the slogan of the 2003 TESOL Convention).

Symbolic Benefits of Learning other Languages

The practical benefits offered to English teachers by second language study are significant in and of themselves. However, we also need to consider the symbolic messages our practice sends to students about what we believe to be true and important. When native speaker English teachers do not learn other languages, this inadvertently but clearly serves as a reminder that the dominant world role of English places English speakers in a position where they are not compelled to learn other languages. This stands in stark contrast to the reality that a great many non-English speakers around the world have little choice but to attempt to master English. It does little good to tell speakers of other languages that their languages are important if they see no concrete evidence that such assurances are based on a genuine appreciation of the value of their languages. In contrast, if native speaker English teachers do learn other languages, the symbolic message sent by this choice is compelling evidence that these teachers genuinely value other languages, and presumably other cultures. As noted above, learning of any additional language, particularly one that differs significantly from one's own, involves substantial cost in terms of time and effort. It is this very cost of the choice to learn a second language that makes it a potent symbol when made by teachers who are native speakers of English—it is compelling evidence that the English teachers who made that choice have a deep-rooted interest in and respect for other languages and cultures. The fact that many English speakers can and do opt out of such study highlights the message sent by those who do make the choice to learn. When the world sees a pattern of TESOL professionals consistently opting to learn additional languages, the profession's advocacy of multilingualism becomes more credible and persuasive. If, on the other hand, the pattern is one of native speakers opting out of study of other languages, there is a real danger that the implied message sent to students is that the dominance of English—and its implied assumption that study of other languages is less valuable to English speakers than to others—is acceptable.

Returning for a moment to the concern raised earlier about the dangers of too close an association between English and power, I would also suggest that making the attempt to learn an additional language is an important practical and symbolic way for English teachers to quite literally step out of the power role in significant and costly ways. As Alan Seaman (1998) notes, "language learning tends to be a humbling experience for the teacher" (p. 38), and also helps redefine the power relationships between teachers and students, placing teachers at least part of the time in situations where students are the experts and teachers are the novices. In symbolic terms, this suggests a balanced relationship in which both parties have something of value to offer. The expectation that English teachers should be language learners as well as teachers is perhaps the most significant way that English teachers can "empty themselves" of power.

Conclusion

Enhanced commitment to language learning among English teachers from Inner Circle nations will probably not make a great impact on the dominant role of English nor the broader picture of power relationships in the world; in fact, it is probably our English teaching work that will do more to empower our students and host communities by giving them access to a wider range of resources. The even more pressing issue for both the larger ELT professional community and the Christian ELT community is probably that of who does and does not have access to the advantages and empowerment English can provide. Sandra McKay (2002) expresses the concern that "in many countries around the world English is being learned only by those who can afford instruction in it" (p. 24) and Janina Brutt-Griffler (2002) reminds us of our responsibility to insist that access to English "no longer be the preserve of the privileged and the powerful" (p. 123).[10]

However, I would suggest that a commitment to the idea that all English teachers should also engage in language learning must be at least part of our response as a professional community to this issue. Without such a commitment, it is less likely that other forms of advocacy we engage in will be taken seriously. If we preach the values of a world in which the role of English is not hegemonic, and in which all languages are valued, we will have more credibility if our public reputation—as individuals and as a profession as a whole—suggests that we live what we preach. Also, as speakers of a powerful language who are concerned with issues of dominance and power, one response should be at times to step out of the power role by becoming learners of other languages, both because of how the experience of learning the other's language transforms us and because of the message that such a choice sends about our vision of what kind of place we think the world should be.

Notes

1. "Inner Circle" nations are those in which English is spoken as the first—and often only—language by the majority of the population, e.g., the United Kingdom and the United States (Kachru, 1992).
2. Phillipson (1992) argues that intentional promotion of English by Britain and the United States has been the primary factor in the spread of English, but his position has been challenged by many; for critiques see Canagarajah, 1999, p. 2; Brutt-Griffler, 2002, pp. viii, 26–27; and McKay, 2002, pp. 21–22.
3. Canagarajah also reminds us that, although it is sometimes assumed that Western missionaries "fully collaborated in the imperialist project," this stereotypical view is not always accurate (1999, p. 64). For book-length discussion of the relationships between Western missionaries and the imperialist project, see Stanley, 2003 and Porter, 2004. See also Makoni and Makoni (this volume).
4. See Makoni and Makoni (this volume) for similar examples in colonial Africa.
5. For my own views on what kinds of agendas Western Christians should pursue through English teaching, see Snow, 2001.
6. Garshick, 2002.
7. The exception was Bailey, Curtis, and Nunan, 2001, which devotes chapter 6 to language learning as a vehicle for pursuing professional development. Here I must confess that even the first edition of my own introductory textbook for EFL teachers, *More Than a Native Speaker* (Snow, 1996) lacks an explicitly labeled section addressed to this topic. This omission has been rectified in the revised edition.
8. There is a growing literature on the challenges faced by nonnative speakers in the English-teaching profession—see Braine, 1999; Braine, 2005; Kamhi-Stein, 2004.
9. Higgins (2003) argues that multilingual English teachers also tend to have more awareness of what is and is not normal in different varieties of English.
10. See Snow, 2001, chapter 6, with regard to the need for Christians to address this issue.

References

Bailey, K., Curtis, A., & Nunan, D. (2001). *Pursuing professional development: The self as source.* Boston: Heinle & Heinle.

Braine, G. (Ed.) (1999). *Non-native educators in English language teaching.* Mahwah, NJ: Lawrence Erlbaum.

Braine, G. (Ed.) (2005). *Teaching English to the world: History, curriculum, and practice.* Mahwah, NJ: Lawrence Erlbaum.

Brutt-Griffler, J. (2002). *World English: A study of its development.* Clevedon, UK: Multilingual Matters.

Canagarajah, A. S. (1999). *Resisting linguistic imperialism in English language teaching.* Oxford, UK: Oxford University Press.

Diaz-Rico, L. (2004). *Teaching English learners: Strategies and methods.* Boston: Pearson Education.

Ferguson, N. (2002). *Empire: The rise and demise of the British imperial world order and the lessons for global power.* New York: Basic Books.

Garshick, E. (Ed.) (2002). *Directory of teacher education programs in TESOL in the United States and Canada, 2002–2004.* Alexandria, VA: TESOL.

Higgins, C. (2003). "Ownership" of English in the outer circle: An alternative to the NS-NNS dichotomy. *TESOL Quarterly, 37*(4), 615–644.

Kachru, B. (1992). Teaching world Englishes. In B. Kachru (Ed.), *The other tongue: English across cultures* (2nd ed.). Urbana: University of Illinois Press.

Kamhi-Stein, L. (2004). *Learning and teaching from experience: Perspectives on nonnative English-speaking professionals.* Ann Arbor: University of Michigan Press.

Lutz, J. (1971). *China and the Christian colleges, 1850–1950.* Ithaca, NY: Cornell University Press.

McKay, S. (2002). *Teaching English as an international language.* Oxford, UK: Oxford University Press.

Pennycook, A. (1998). *English and the discourses of colonialism.* London: Routledge.

Phillipson, R. (1992). *Linguistic imperialism.* Oxford, UK: Oxford University Press.

Porter, A. (2004). *Religion versus empire? British protestant missionaries and overseas expansion, 1700–1914.* Manchester, UK: Manchester University Press.

Seaman, A. (1998). Incarnation or imperialism? The English language teacher as missionary. Unpublished essay submitted for Faith and Learning Requirement, Wheaton College, IL.

Snow, D. (1996). *More than a native speaker: An introduction for volunteers teaching English abroad.* Alexandria, VA: TESOL.

Snow, D. (2001). *English teaching as Christian mission.* Scottdale, PA: Herald Press.

Stanley, B. (Ed.) (2003). *Missions, nationalism, and the end of empire.* Grand Rapids, MI: Eerdmans.

TESOL (2004). *Position Statement on Multilingualism.* Retrieved September 3, 2008, from www.tesol.org/s_tesol/bin.asp?CID=32&DID=2933&DOC=FILE.PDF.

19 Classroom Guidelines for Teachers with Convictions

Kitty B. Purgason

In a class session on professional ethics in an MA TESOL program at a Christian university in southern California, the trainees, who are all evangelical Christians preparing to teach ESL in local adult schools and Intensive English Programs (IEPs) or EFL in international universities and language institutes, are discussing the following scenario:

> Students in your class have expressed dissatisfaction with the current cultural climate of materialism and growing individualism.
>
> - Choose (1) or (2):
>   (1) As a Christian, you share your students' dismay, but feel you can't say more.
>   (2) You feel these students may want to learn more about what the Bible says about materialism; perhaps you can host a group discussion for them.
> - If you choose (2):
>   a. You announce, "I'm hosting an English Bible study on Friday evenings. Since it's in English, you'll get extra credit if you attend."
>   b. You announce in class, "I'm hosting an English Bible study on Friday evenings. All are welcome to come, read, and discuss."
>   c. You announce in class, "I'm starting some extracurricular English activities. I'll be hosting an English Bible study on Friday nights and an English game night on Saturday nights. Feel free to come either night."

Kevin, a novice teacher going to Thailand, is excited about the idea of Bible studies and exclaims, "That's why I'm getting this degree!" Gina states she felt that way before she spent a year in China, but admits "I was too tired for any extracurricular activities with my students." Camden, reflecting on volunteer teaching for a month in Indonesia adds, "As devout Muslims, my students were struggling with how to be people of faith in a newly materialistic world—I think they would have welcomed the opportunity to discuss this." Eric, doing his practicum at a nearby IEP, wonders what the school administration would say if he invited his students to a Bible study.

This scenario portrays the dilemmas Christians face as they try to interpret and follow biblical guidelines. Jesus tells his followers, "Let your light shine before others, that they may see your good deeds and glorify your Father in heaven" (Matthew 5:16, TNIV),[1] and "Be my witnesses ... to the ends of the earth" (Acts 1:8, TNIV). Yet, this might appear to conflict with the professional mandate to follow the policies of the institution and/or government in which one teaches, which usually involve an explicit prohibition against proselytizing and an unspoken responsibility to not only respect but also to protect our students. Because this tension arises from my identity as a Christian, I have tried to resolve it by looking for guidelines in the Bible. At the same time, these guidelines have to fit the world in which my trainees and I teach. My ESL experience was in an IEP in the US, and my EFL experience was in China, Turkey, and Turkmenistan. In each of these locations I was employed by a local institution or US governmental entity, not by a Christian agency, and had to be aware of the communist, secular, or Muslim sensibilities of my employers, colleagues, and students.

Although I am presenting biblical guidelines for Christian teachers, I hope that this chapter will also be relevant to teachers with varying or no religious identity. This is because we all have convictions, be they religious, political, or social. Perhaps ESL/EFL teachers have more or have stronger convictions than the average person. Brown (2007), in his widely used methodology text, assumes that his readers are probably "driven by convictions about what this world should look like, how its people should behave, how its governments should control that behavior, and how its inhabitants should be partners in the stewardship of the planet" (p. 312). In addition, although the guidelines I present are framed in biblical terms, they are congruent with best practices that many in our profession would follow.

Identity and Transparency

One of the biggest complaints about Christian ESL/EFL teachers is that they are not honest about their identities and motivations (e.g., Edge, 2003). It is imperative that I encourage my trainees to be aware of and to negotiate this issue. A key biblical guideline is, "We have renounced secret and shameful ways; we do not use deception" (II Corinthians 4:2, TNIV). From the perspective of students and their advocates who do not wish to be blindsided by anyone's convictions, transparency and openness about our identity and the curriculum we use enables others to know what to expect. From the perspective of Christian teachers who want to talk about their beliefs with students, avoiding a covert approach will help them meet students who are genuinely interested in further conversation.

At the same time, Christians may have legitimate concerns about being prejudged as a certain type of person before being able to prove themselves as teachers. For example, I prefer to call myself a "follower of Jesus" rather than an "adherent of Christianity." Many of my Muslim students assumed that the US is a Christian nation and therefore the North American programs they see on their satellite televisions display Christian behavior, including lack of respect for parents, drinking, extra-marital sex, individualistic decision making and greed. Besides these social behaviors, there are historical events, political stances, and theological positions that people may associate with Christianity that are not necessarily part of my personal identity.

Christians have a model in the person of Jesus as someone who was transparent while still trying to avoid being misunderstood. Sometimes Jesus requests that his followers not tell anyone who he is or what he has done for them (e.g., Matthew 12:16, 16:20; Mark 3:12; Luke 8:56) and other times he is very open about his identity (e.g., John 4:26). In the aggregate he does not try to hide who he is or what he believes: "I have spoken openly to the world ... I said nothing in secret" (John 18:20, TNIV). See Robison this volume.

Context and Students

Even more important than being clear about who I am, is learning who my students are. Getting to know the context, especially prevailing attitudes toward those things I am most passionate about, is crucial. Becoming acquainted with my students and listening respectfully to them lays an important foundation for teacher–student interaction about topics of conviction.

Listening to others is enjoined in several biblical passages from "To answer before listening—that is folly and shame" (Proverbs 18:13, TNIV) to "Everyone should be quick to listen [and] slow to speak" (James 1:19, TNIV). Jesus also models for me how to listen first and be sensitive to who people are. The Gospels show Jesus speaking to crowds and also meeting one-on-one; he has close friends with whom he interacts in depth and he also has single encounters with people he'll likely never see again. His messages range from tender encouragement to challenge. He interacts with men and women, children and adults, rich and poor, the educated and the working class, the ill and the healthy, devoted followers and skeptics, cultural insiders and outsiders. I hope that, inspired by Jesus, I can listen to my students, get to know them, and look beyond my culture and experiential blinders to see their dignity, worth, individuality, needs, goals, and gifts.

In the larger context, teachers must be proactive in finding out what local authorities expect. For example, in one local IEP, a teacher's supervisor was happy to have the teacher invite students to a conversation club at her church. Another teacher found that his supervisor had been troubled by a former employee who scared a student by talking about hell during a field trip—the result was severe limitations on any kind of extracurricular activities between students and teachers at that institution.

In the classroom this may mean seeking out insiders to be cultural informants who can answer questions such as, "What are students with this background likely to be used to? What do they care about? If we talk about religion in class, how might they react?" At the same time, I want to know my students as individuals since, "The conclusions drawn about the students we teach must be open to questioning and critique" (Zamel, 1997, p. 350). So, for example, although I read prior to teaching there that Turkey is 99% Muslim, many of my students were not at all religious.

Power and Empowerment

The more we know the context in which we teach and our students, the more likely it is that we will agree with Johnston (2003) who says that "religious identities that might go unchallenged outside the classroom can find themselves in confrontation within it" (p. 118). The reason for this is the effects of unequal power. Teachers don't always recognize their power and influence over students, simply by virtue of the fact that we are their teachers. Novice teachers, especially young North Americans who value informality and friendship between student and teacher, tend to be less aware of the power inherent in the teacher–student relationship (see Snow, 2006, p. 27). Even in classes where students are challenging and disruptive and the teacher may feel powerless, this is an issue.

Jesus provides a model for Christians who have potential or actual power over others. His human life was that of a child born into poverty, an ethnic minority under a foreign power, a political refugee, a working-class adult, and an itinerant preacher. Paul reminds his readers:

> You must have the same attitude that Christ Jesus had. Though he was God, he did not think of equality of God as something to cling to. Instead he gave up his divine privileges; he took the humble position of a slave, and was born as a human being.
>
> (Philippians 2:5–7, NLT)

I paraphrase this for my trainees: although you may be in a position of power because of your citizenship in a powerful nation, your higher education, your proficiency in English, or your role as a teacher, don't take that for granted or try to hold on to that power; instead, be like Jesus who relinquished power and who came to serve. Most professionals in TESOL serve their students by considering their needs and purposes, but for me as a Christian, it is not just a professional duty to do so, but also a part of my spiritual life.

Humility affects not only my work in general, but also the interaction I have with students. Another biblical guideline that expresses the need to avoid speaking from a stance of power is, "Be prepared to give an answer to everyone who asks you the reason for the hope that you have. But do this with gentleness and respect" (I Peter 3:15, TNIV). Many students come from contexts in which good students are supposed to absorb everything the teacher says and always agree with the teacher (Furey, 1986). When I speak about my personal convictions, how are such students likely to respond? When a student says something about what Muslims believe and I add a comment about what Christians believe, does it come across as respectful, interested, informative, and gentle? Or do I sound shrill, defensive, or pressuring? The impact of what I say may be very different on my students from what I perceive. Recording a class session and asking for feedback on this issue can help us be aware of how we come across, especially when talking about things that matter very much to us and that may be puzzling or threatening to our students.

The issue of power should not only be addressed by teachers becoming aware of their own power, but by teachers empowering students. It is important to encourage students to find ways to use English to express their own voice so class is a place where all students can express themselves, and a place where all opinions are both spoken and heard with respect. I agree that "[i]t is both an ethical and social justice issue to set up a classroom atmosphere of mutual respect and tolerance" (Hafernik, Messerschmitt, & Vandrick, 2002, p. 6). It is in such a context that I feel comfortable communicating who I am in terms of my religious beliefs and values and providing my students with information that will be helpful as they relate to people from other cultures.

Although I feel strongly that it is students who need to be practicing English and therefore I should speak as little as possible, there are occasions when students make comments that I want to respond to, when students ask questions, or when materials call for a comment. For example, on behalf of the whole class, a Chinese student presented me with a card that read: "Merry Christmas! On the night that the angel fell, the infinite stars were twinkling brightly to welcome Santa's arrival." As a teacher, I felt it was important to at least ask them if they knew the difference between Jesus' arrival and Santa's. I could have also gone on to explain the role of the star in Matthew's account of Jesus' birth, and the difference between angels announcing good news and fallen angels, from a completely different biblical story. As appropriate, I want to be able to freely share what I believe as a Christian. The framework of everyone having a voice—a respectful voice—means that students know they are not forced to believe something just because I have said it.

Excellence in Teaching—Curriculum and Choice

A final biblical guideline comes from the instructions that Paul gives believers: "Whatever you do, work at it with all your heart, as working for the Lord, not for human masters ... It is the Lord Christ you are serving" (Colossians 3:23–24, TNIV). Doing all professional tasks is an expression of devotion to God, not simply a good thing to do. Again, many in the field of TESOL approach their work with diligence and excellence; however, as a Christian I have an extra incentive to do a good job. In addition, as Snow (2001) points out, the quality and professionalism of our work is itself a witness to the love of God. I think it is also incumbent on Christians in the profession to encourage more professionalism on the part of Christian volunteers who may not be aware of TESOL or the issues in this volume.

To illustrate what it means to be committed to excellence in teaching, consider the curricular choices that teachers make. The temptation for some Christian teachers is to use the Bible as a textbook or insert a lot of Christian content into the curriculum. Teachers with other convictions face the same temptation. A teacher described by Hafernik et al. (2002) created an art-themed ESL class because of her personal interest—it was fun for a number of students but not all. Topics such as racism, AIDS, the death penalty, and child labor fill the latest ELT textbooks. Osborn (2006) urges foreign language teachers to take up issues of social justice. Yet the college ESL students surveyed by Deckert (1996) reported a preference for writing about practical or informational topics rather than controversial ethical or moral topics, and research done in the 1990s in the Arabian Gulf revealed that university students were reluctant to talk about, among other things, "unpleasant" topics such as poverty or disease (Canning, Barlow, & Floyd, 1999). The standard for professional excellence should be that teachers remember who their students are and what they need. As Hafernik et al. (2002) put it:

> In choosing material, both required textbooks and supplementary materials, foremost is the contractual and ethical obligation of faculty members to comply with the course description, goals, and objective, and to keep in mind that the primary goal of ESL courses is to improve students' English language ability.
>
> (p. 106)

Following this standard does not mean that it is unacceptable to teach a theme-based course or a course with significant content of a certain type in it, including Bible-based ESL. It just means that these classes should not be part of a *required* curriculum and that accurate publicity is important so that students can choose the class for themselves and know what they are getting into before they enroll.

Neither does this standard mean we should reduce our ESL classes to the blandest of content nor try to eliminate controversial content all together. Clearly, language cannot be separated from content. Furthermore, the spiritual dimension of human life is very important to many of our students. Smith and Carvill (2000) draw attention to the imbalance in many language teaching materials. Typical textbooks teach students the language of buying, but not charitable giving, complaining but not necessarily praising, and apologizing, but usually not forgiving. The people students read about are usually drawn from the world of entertainment, not religion (any religion!).

Smith and Carvill suggest that our materials evaluation should include questions such as "How does the text present the humanity of members of the target culture? Do they fear, doubt, suffer, sin, hope, pray, or celebrate as well as work, shop, play, eat, and drink?" (p. 144). Stevick's (1996) *Memory, Meaning, and Method* reminds us that "the deeper the source of a sentence within the student's personality, the most lasting value it has for learning a language" (p. 196). Students who have religious beliefs may not only welcome a class where these beliefs can be discussed, but may also benefit in terms of their language acquisition.

But not all students have religious beliefs. That is why there is another important consideration when it comes to curricular content—choice. Value-laden topics are bound to appear in any ESL/EFL teaching. Even trying to eliminate all references to them conveys a value. The more controversial the topic and the more connected it is to passion and conviction, the more choices we need to give our students. When I include something in my course materials that is related to Christianity, I give students some choices so that they do not feel imposed on. For example, in an activity about love (which I sometimes do around Valentine's Day), I give students several quotations to respond to in their journals. They can choose whether to write about the quote from the Gospel of John in the Bible, Lao Tze, Antoine de St. Exupery, Victor Hugo, or Martin Luther King, Jr.

Conclusion

We do not have to shy away from being teachers with convictions and from letting religion or any other controversial topic come up in the classroom. These issues should come up as a natural part of our humanity. That said, however, there are some steps we can take to make sure that materials or conversation about our convictions do not frustrate, offend, or overpower our students. We should ensure that our curricular content is appropriate for our students' needs and interests—this is just one way we practice excellence overall in our teaching. We should be aware of power inherent in our role as teachers or our materials, practicing and modeling the language of respect so that everyone has a voice in our classes. We should listen, to both our students and ourselves, in order to make the classroom a more hospitable place. We should be transparent about our identity. I believe that these are guidelines that any teacher can embrace, but for my readers who are Christians, let me summarize the biblical principles that underlie them:

1. "We have renounced secret and shameful ways; we do not use deception" (II Corinthians 4:2, TNIV).
2. "Everyone should be quick to listen [and] slow to speak" (James 1:19, TNIV).
3. "Be completely humble and gentle" (Ephesians 4:2, TNIV).
4. "Work … as though you were working for the Lord" (Colossians 3:23, NLT).

Note

1. Quotations of the Bible marked TNIV are from *The Holy Bible, Today's New International Version,* © 2001, 2005 International Bible Society. Those marked NLT are from *The Holy Bible, New Living Translation,* © 1996, Tyndale House.

References

Brown, H. D. (2007). *Teaching by principles* (3rd ed.). New York: Longman.

Canning, C., Barlow, L., & Floyd, J. (1999). Producing culturally sensitive materials for Gulf students. Paper presented at TESOL, New York.

Deckert, G. (1996). Ethical considerations in addressing values in the ESL classroom. Paper presented at TESOL, Chicago. Eric Document Reproduction Service #ED411672.

Edge, J. (2003). Imperial troopers and servants of the Lord: A vision of TESOL for the 21st century. *TESOL Quarterly, 37*(4), 701–709.

Furey, P. (1986). A framework for cross-cultural analysis of teaching methods. In P. Byrd (Ed.), *Teaching across cultures in the university ESL program* (pp. 15–28). Washington, DC: NAFSA.

Hafernik, J., Messerschmitt, D., & Vandrick, S. (2002). *Ethical issues for ESL faculty: Social justice in practice.* Mahwah, NJ: Lawrence Erlbaum.

Johnston, B. (2003). *Values in English language teaching.* Mahwah, NJ: Lawrence Erlbaum.

Osborn, T. (2006). *Teaching world languages for social justice.* Mahwah, NJ: Lawrence Erlbaum.

Smith, D., & Carvill, B. (2000). *The gift of the stranger: Faith, hospitality, and foreign language learning.* Grand Rapids, MI: Eerdmans.

Snow, D. (2001). *English teaching as Christian mission: An applied theology.* Scotdale, PA: Herald Press.

Snow, D. (2006). *More than a native speaker* (2nd ed.). Alexandria, VA: TESOL.

Stevick, E. (1996). *Memory, meaning, and method* (2nd ed.). Boston: Heinle & Heinle.

Zamel, V. (1997). Toward a model of transculturation. *TESOL Quarterly, 31*(2), 341–352.

Response

20 The Pedagogical Dilemmas of Faith in ELT

A Dialogic Response

Brian Morgan

Introductions/Introspections

As I have found writing this chapter, engaging with the personal and professional dilemmas of others invites attention to one's own. In reading these three chapters by John Liang, Kitty Purgason, and Don Snow on Christianity and related pedagogical concerns, I have been made more aware of my own insights and blind spots on this topic. As for the latter, a noticeable gap in my existing publications on language and identity (e.g., Morgan, 1997, 2004, 2007), is any discussion of spirituality or religion as salient components and/or outcomes of language practices and discourses. So, where does this apparent blind spot come from? Upon reflection, I recognize several contributing elements. Certainly, the need to kick-start an academic career requires engaging in the dominant conversations of one's intended community of practice, and in TESOL, the sociolinguistic and cognitive variability that might arise from religiosity has yet to insert itself alongside gendered, racialized, and ethno-linguistic factors as a publishable debating point.

My ambivalence and inattention to spirituality in the context of language and identity research has personal origins as well, in particular, deeply edged memories of growing up Jewish in the small, mid-western Canadian city of Regina, in which being part of a struggling religious minority (now approximately 150 families in a city of 200,000) was often difficult and confusing. I still remember the occasional religious taunts, a few subsequent fights in the school yard, and a general resentment of having to attend Hebrew school and later having a Bar Mitzvah while other kids had the freedom to play. I don't mean to trivialize the notion of freedom here, but what comes to mind is how hard the Jewish community had to work to generate the religious solidarity and group cohesiveness that might sustain itself against the ever-present and often overwhelming pressures to assimilate. It was much later, in 1984, while working as a volunteer laborer at Deganya Bet kibbutz in northern Israel, when I came to appreciate and understand this intensity of activity, the collective obligations it required of community members, and how it seemed to permeate even the smallest performative act of faith in Regina. In terms of identity, being a Jew in Israel was much easier. There was no need to explain or to justify. The architecture of reinforcement was everywhere, allowing for the luxury of choosing to be humble or assertive, innovative, or trangressive in ways unimaginable in my childhood home, where everything around us promoted and underwrote the "normalcy" and "truth" of a Christian world. Coming from Canada to Israel and back, I became more aware of the unacknowledged power that comes with membership in the dominant faith—how members of powerful congregations need not speculate about the adverse consequences of public observance and how even the most narrow, fundamentalist notions may be accorded serious and sustained policy consideration simply because of the religious authority behind it.[1]

Perhaps it is the latent experience of living alongside and against the taken-for-granted power of Christianity that explains the gap in my research literature. Intuitively, for me, faith and spirituality should be kept private and not imported into other worldly domains, nor imposed upon others under the guise of dialogue. I raise these thoughts and recollections as potential insights for pedagogy, especially in regards to how we might—if at all—relate or present our own notions of spirituality to our students, many of whose own social values and religious beliefs may be relatively powerless in the specific national and community settings in which we teach. Even in nominally secular societies, teachers from dominant faiths are unlikely to recognize or understand the complex forms of societal coercion that underpin their openness and well-meaning generosity in the classroom. In short, certainty of faith and certainty in the need to bear its public witness raises serious pedagogical dilemmas in that they intensify the asymmetries of power that erode equitable teacher–student relationships.

Another key point is that the worldly conditions that align with and sustain the taken for granted power of Christianity increasingly extend beyond nation states in which a majority of citizens identify with the faith. As the authors in this collection show, Christianity, in its various forms and activities, has had a complex yet inextricable relationship to the global spread of English. From the civilizing missions of colonialism (Pennycook, 1998) to its current status as, arguably, the default faith of global capitalism, the history of Christian expansion features a wide array of both critics and apologists for social power—of liberation theologists aligned with Marxist revolutionaries and of television evangelists expounding on the earthly rewards of faith from the pulpit as well as the manicured estates financed by their congregations. In common, across these divergent interpretations of gospel, is the motivating force of spiritual certainty, which can easily blind the possessor to the structures of power that underpin his or her worldly activities in the service of faith.

In this regard, Don Snow raises a pertinent point in his chapter: Christ's notion of humility, which he describes as meaning, literally, "to empty oneself of power," is a particular challenge for those who view English teaching as a form of Christian mission. As he observes, "the problem in reconciling such ideas about mission with English teaching is that English is so closely and clearly associated with worldly power." His concern, which I share, "lies in the possibility that Christian English teachers may be too uncritical in accepting the advantages offered by the dominance of English, and too comfortable in drawing on its power."

As a point of clarification, the forms of power to which both Don Snow and I allude are not just those held by designated representatives or realized through the typical instruments of state enforcement such as the judiciary, police, or army. Power here is also very much in the Foucauldian tradition in which power is *productive*—present in the creation of "normalcy" and "truth" through a whole range of everyday acts of meaning-making in schools, communities, and places of worship. Through these everyday acts of normalization (cf. Foucault), a particular faith and its worldly articulations become unmarked and hence less "visible" as a social field—such as ELT—whose potential abuses might require greater vigilance. The key question, then, is how we might ideally and ethically address such concerns in pedagogy without denying our own identity, humanity, or spirituality—if such denial were even consciously possible.

Identifying the Dimensions and Dilemmas of Spirituality in an ELT Curriculum

Addressing pedagogical dilemmas requires us first to consider the ways in which spirituality might infuse an ELT syllabus and those who participate in its contingent realization. Spirituality can be realized in the form of explicit content, as Kitty Purgason's chapter describes in the greatest detail, for example, in her utilization of Bible study for ESL students and as part of a preservice teacher education component. Also in terms of content, Purgason offers a promising Valentine's Day activity in which students choose a quote on the notion of love from one of the following: the Gospel of John, Lao Tzu, Antoine de St. Exupery, Victor Hugo, and Martin Luther King, and write a response to it in their journals. One could imagine these responses, if shared, generating many opportunities for insightful discussion and reflection conducive to both personal and linguistic growth. The element of choice and the openness to non-Christian viewpoints involved in this activity is commendable, as well, and consistent with Purgason's belief that theme-based courses on spirituality "should not be part of a *required* curriculum and it means that accurate publicity is important so that students can choose the class for themselves and know what they are getting into before they enroll" (p. 190). Yet, I would reiterate my earlier point that for numerous reasons and in many settings the presumption of student "choice" may be simplistic, especially *because* of the content involved and the communal symbolism attached to one's participation or absence.

Spirituality can also be implied within a particular method or approach. John Liang, for example, suggests that "from the perspective of the Christian faith, the development of competence, or the process, is more valued than competence, the product" (p. 170). However, product does trump process in Purgason's anecdote in which a Chinese student presented her with a class card that read: "Merry Christmas! On the night that the angel fell, the infinite stars were twinkling brightly to Santa's arrival" (p. 189). Purgason then responded with the following:

> As a teacher, I felt it was important to at least ask them if they knew the difference between Jesus' arrival and Santa's. I could have also gone on to explain the role of the star in Matthew's account of Jesus' birth, and the

> difference between angels announcing good news and fallen angels, from a completely different biblical story.
>
> (p. 189)

It is difficult to recreate what actually transpired at this pedagogical moment. As discourse, the shift in this passage from indicative (i.e., the card's dedication) to subjunctive mood with stative verb ("I felt"), non-referential "it" fronting, embedded hypothetical forms/clauses, and deferral to professional responsibility through role nomination ("As a teacher") and an adverbial hedge ("at least"), all serve to mitigate the personal agency of the author as well as blur the distinction between verbal action and thought. Plus, we do not know what meanings the students made from this response, or how these meanings have been recursively mediated by prior beliefs and accumulated interactions with the teacher. Did the students perceive this response as a "question" or "correction," particularly in the immediate context of the presentation of a class gift? Also, we do not know how many students—or just the writer of the card—genuinely "misunderstood" the religious insignificance of Santa, or how many had made a conscious and deliberate effort—for personal and/or collective reasons—to secularize or appropriate the holiday in a culturally syncretic and/or localized fashion. What we do know is that spirituality can infuse the ELT curriculum in several ways—as explicit content, or as method/approach, or as a moral foundation to challenge the inequities of nonnative speaking teacher discourses, as movingly told in John Liang's narrative. Spirituality, in the service of identity formation is clearly central to all of the contributions in this part of the book. Its most significant and potentially dangerous expression for pedagogy, however, is not in contemplative isolation, but instead in the *interpersonal, inter-subjective* negotiation of teacher–student identities.

That Purgason experienced a dilemma or an element of doubt in the inter-subjective encounter above is indicated by the linguistic choices she has utilized to mitigate and justify her personal (i.e., faith-based) intervention. Again, I would interpret this unplanned moment as inextricably bound up with relations of power in the ELT classroom and one that requires careful thought as to what might be possible ethical guidelines suitable for pedagogy—most specifically, guidelines for how we might relate to those whose own truths fundamentally challenge or disrupt the certainty of our own. The contingent ways we humble ourselves—empty ourselves of power—in these sometimes troubling encounters with our worldly and spiritual "Others" is the focus of the next part of this chapter.

Toward Dialogue and Openness to the "Other"

As Shelley Wong (2006) details in her remarkable book, the philosophical roots of dialogism run through many traditions (e.g., Confucianism, Socratic thought, Marxism), and inform an array of literary, cognitive, educational, and sociopolitical phenomena in the work of Bakhtin, Vygotsky, Mao Zedong, and Paulo Freire. Dialogue can have ultimate ends that are pre-given, or its teleology can be relatively open ended, in both cases inferring particular ontologies and epistemologies, respectively, about the "truth" of reality and our capacity to understand it or participate in its unfolding. These paradigmatic elements may also imply a cosmology, a super-ordinate set of beliefs regarding the origin/creation of our reality and beyond. Dialogue can be intended to problematize power relations, while inadvertently reinforcing them. In this respect, dialogue may purport to be *interactional*, whereby participants allow themselves to be re-formed as a consequence, but in effect remain stubbornly *transactional*, where predetermined values are guardedly exchanged without any intention of change. In this way, ostensible "dialogue" slips into monologue and coercion—an instrument for the teacher to contain the anxiety and threat posed by the student whose values stand as Other to the Self.

Carl Anders Säfström (2003) details the discursive stages by which this coerciveness can emerge in educational settings:

> First, the aim of teaching tends to be primarily focused on developing in students certain conceptual representations of the world. It is understood that through such development the world, so to speak, appears for the student at a higher level of complexity and in a brighter light; it takes them closer to the Truth through which the world becomes transparent and explained. Secondly, not only is the world made transparent, but so too is humanity itself … The so-called secret of humanity is then no longer secret and teaching becomes the name for the effective management of this rationale from which the outcome is already given. The process of teaching is reduced to an instrumental act in relation to a pre-given good and becomes a means to an end, an end already in the possession of the teacher. In this security of knowing the end—what is good, what is truth—the teacher can safely rest.… But this "safety", I would like to argue, is based on a non-human relation in which the subjects involved in the process of teaching are subordinated to the rationality inscribed in knowing the other.
>
> (pp. 21–22)

It is worth contrasting the nondialogical instrumentality described by Säfström with two short passages from Dwayne Huebner's (2005) chapter on Education and Spirituality, and his Christian notion of an ethical relationship to those who first appear as Other:

> When the world no longer appears as "other", no longer seems strange, or has no strangeness, education appears to come to an end. Woe is that day, of course, for the power of knowledge has become prejudice, and the power of influence has become ownership, bringing all "otherness" into a relationship of domination.… The problem is that our controlling tendencies result in the hermetic environment, self or socially constructed, and we fail to recognize, or we forget, our relationship with and indebtedness to the absolute "Other" often manifested through the neighbor and the strange.
>
> (p. 316)

Huebner then describes how a notion of "otherness" underpins educational content:

> Content is, first of all, "other" human beings. Others see the world differently, talk differently, act differently. Therefore they are possibilities for me. They point to a different future for me, another state on my journey. I could be like them. By being different they bring my particular self under criticism. What I am, I do not have to be. What they are, I could be.... Through the presence of the "other" my participation in the transcendent becomes visible—the future is open if I will give up the self that is the current me and become other than I am. As content, other people are sources of criticism and new possibility.
>
> (p. 317)

These contrasting passages, from Säfström and Huebner, are indeed abstract conceptualizations, but what they offer pedagogy can be succinctly summarized. The former can be described as transactional, monological, and coercive—in short, "a pedagogy of closure and a politics, not of debate, but of direction" (Lusted, 1986, p. 10). In contrast, the latter offers a "pedagogy of possibility" (cf. Simon, 1992), one that is fundamentally interactional and dialogical, and oriented toward emergent rather than predetermined forms of knowledge. It does not view the "strangeness" or irreducible difference of the "Other" as a threat to be contained through the power and "expert" knowledge possessed by the teacher. Rather, following Huebner, the strangeness of the Other is a source of self-learning and of new possibilities. The dialogical/interactional approach also suggests that in place of, or alongside Christian notions of "humility" and "witness," we recognize the need for "vulnerability" and "answerability" in the ethical conduct of teacher–student relations.[2] The significance of these two supplementary terms is nicely illustrated by Säfström (2003) and inspired by the moral and ethical writings of the French philosopher Emmanuel Levinas:

> An awakening to humanity requires a question that does not turn toward any pre-given end. Not only does answerability mean that there is no comfort in knowing the meaning of the other, but for teachers this question wrenches them from the safety of even knowledge of themselves ... To respond to the student is to be answerable to the student and defend the rights of the student from a position of [a teacher's] vulnerability. It is the individual uniqueness of the student that exists beyond his/her institutional position *as* student, which teachers meet—and defend—in their answerability and self-questioning.
>
> (p. 28)

To my mind, *vulnerability*, as depicted above, is an essential component of dialogue; *humility*, perhaps less so in that one might be "emptied of power" yet safe from the self-questioning and productive doubt offered by the Other, as Huebner eloquently states. Humility, in this sense, can be merely tactical, a temporary and mortal deferment in the certain knowledge of eternal rewards to come. Whether we see ourselves as transformative intellectuals in the service of social justice or, alternately, as shepherds guiding our scattered flock toward fields of eternal salvation, if the "endgame" is already determined and the spiritual or secular convictions of only one participant—the student—is subject to scrutiny, then the "humility" we might profess is superficial and the so-called "dilemma" of pedagogy is mostly of our own worldly making and self-delusion.

The *interactional/dialogic* versus *transactional/monologic* dichotomy I have sketched out here may be over-simplified. In reality, we may recognize the presence of both tendencies in key events that we remember. Still, these contrasting perspectives offer useful guidelines for pedagogy. I now draw on them as points of reference in my following comments on several of the contributions to this part of the book on the pedagogical dilemmas of spirituality in the ELT classroom.

Selective Readings of a Dialogical/Monological Nature

It would be possible to find examples of both dialogic and monologic text in the chapters offered by Liang, Purgason, and Snow. I will only take up a few and apologize for the selective and biased impression that I leave as a result. The first example is from Don Snow and is noteworthy both for its intrinsic merit and the prominence it has in the overall scope of his chapter. Snow's recommendation is of relevance for both Christian and non-Christian ELT professionals of the "Inner Circle." He proposes that the learning of another language becomes "a prominent feature of our professional culture and identity" and a required component of ELT teacher education (at a high-intermediate level, no less), which would serve to redress, in part, some of the dominant discourses of English in the world. Moreover, this commitment toward bilingualism—especially from those privileged by the power conferred on "native speakers"—would demonstrate a more ethical and empathetic opening to the "other" in the negotiation of teacher–student and native speaker–NNS teacher identities. It would show that respect for multilingualism is more than window dressing, and it would help instill a genuine understanding of the "vulnerable" task at hand.

Another practice-based suggestion with significant dialogic and ethical implications comes from Kitty Purgason. In her section on "power and empowerment," Purgason acknowledges the asymmetries of the teacher–student relationship. In reflecting on the moments in which she expresses her own personal convictions, Purgason is thoughtful in wondering about the reception her religious beliefs might have:

> When a student says something about what Muslims believe and I add a comment about what Christians believe, does it come across as respectful, interested, informative, and gentle? Or do I sound shrill, defensive, or pressuring? The impact of what I say may be very different on my students from what I perceive.
>
> (p. 188)

She then suggests recording such classroom sessions and asking students to provide feedback on how they have perceived or if they have felt threatened by the teacher's comments.

The questions posed reveal care and sensitivity to the "Other." But the pedagogical treatment suggested would have both strengths and weaknesses of note. A strong element exists in the dialogic openness to the possibility that the same Christian message would be "heard" differently and that the worldly power that articulates Christianity with English would be "felt" differently across different sites of practice. Still, it would be this articulated and situated dimension of power around the Christian message that would make it extraordinarily complex and inhibitive for some students to offer an honest response in an ELT classroom. The most significant weakness would arise in the event that Purgason misunderstood silence or the sociable nod of affirmation as genuine openness to the Christian message and an invitation to greater proselytization. The dilemma here is that she might never know beforehand or for certain how such messages are received. Again, ongoing reflection on the notions of vulnerability and answerability to the student as spiritual "Other" would be advisable here.

I now turn to John Liang and the autobiographical journey he shares with us. His story about the redemptive power of faith in his development as a confident and competent NNS teacher reveals, yet again, the monocultural, monolinguistic chauvinism that persists in the ELT profession. Redemption, in the service of professional development, indicates positive developments for pedagogy. However, when redemptive power then becomes the motivation for "worshipful service" or teaching as a "calling" the danger of domination quickly arises, particularly as there would be only one "voice" and one "truth" heard in the mind of the teacher—a profoundly transactional/monological situation. In Liang's own words, "Within the Christian faith, the teacher's faith is in God, rather than in their own powers, or expertise, or charisma, or their ability to win and maintain a good rapport with students." The key pedagogical question arises when rapport breaks down, as it inevitably does, and the teacher must diagnose the source of the problem and seek alternative solutions—simply put from where, and from whom? In such difficult circumstances, I can't help but wonder if such deeply felt faith might become an explanatory crutch that diverts the believer from the needed "vulnerability" and pedagogical exploration required.

Liang's next sentence is also pedagogically significant: "teaching is not without a purpose; it is to lead students to the truth, to bring them in awe of the truth, so they can practice the truth in their lives" (p. 168). The possibility that their might be other "truths" or "Others" who might share in the lead of defining them seems all but impossible in classrooms "guided" by this vision. At the same time, an argument could be made that this critique is somewhat hypocritical in that all of us in the teaching profession—especially those of us promoting ideological and transformative approaches in ELT—work toward imparting various "truths" in the expectation that students will come to accept them as their own. Indeed, this argument is made most vigorously by Brad Baurain (2007) in his article, "Christian Witness and Respect for Persons," which is worth further discussion for the pedagogical issues it raises in common with the chapters in this volume, so I make a few comparisons here.

In contrast to the chapters by Liang, Purgason, and Snow, I find Baurain's article somewhat lacking in the types of interactional/dialogic and "Other-oriented" perspectives that I have discussed above. As text, it is carefully wrought and rhetorically effective in the methods familiar to academic argumentation. Scholarly adversaries such as Pennycook, Edge, and Johnston are selectively cited, repositioned, and subsequently dismissed. Similarly, authoritative metaphors of science (e.g., Christian truths as equivalent to the laws of gravity) are strategically inferred to fortify particular convictions. To be fair, Baurain should not be faulted for taking on a textual persona not unlike those whose published writings against the Christian mission in ELT are objectionable from his perspective. Nonetheless, one of Baurain's (2007) chief arguments that "all teaching is teaching for change" (p. 205) is one that I wish to highlight and critique here, particularly for the classroom consequences it implies.

In Baurain's own words: "The two pedagogical realities I am exploring—that teaching aims at change and that teachers decide at which changes to try to aim their students—are all-encompassing" (p. 207). On the surface, this is a reasonable point to make. As Baurain and other Christian educators in this collection would claim, "why is the 'liberation of the soul' any less legitimate than the 'liberation of society' as part of an ELT curricula?" Before addressing this important point, I want to draw attention to a few textual moves Baurain deploys in support. Note, for example, how religious metaphors are repeatedly used to generalize Christian values upon the profession as a whole; that is, "all teachers *proselytize* in the classroom … they do so with an *evangelistic* fervor or *missionary* zeal" (p. 208, emphases mine). Later, he describes Pennycook as "com[ing] across much like a missionary. He has a gospel, critical pedagogy … [and] a witnessing technique" (p. 213) not unlike Christian educators. Discourse analysis, from a Levinasian perspective, would suggest that this generalized projection of religiosity serves to contain the "strangeness" and "uniqueness" of the Other (i.e., the "secular adversary") within secure, pre-given categories of the Self/Same (cf. Child, Williams, Birch, & Boody, 1995). We might also reiterate Huebner's (2005) perspective and characterize this rhetorical move as "bringing all 'otherness' into a relationship of domination" (p. 316).

What I would define as transactional/monological discourse moves, of course, are being strategically deployed to justify an openly and explicitly evangelical approach to teaching ELT in which bearing witness to the truth of Christ is a legitimate pedagogical activity. But do these moves achieve that end? One of the key concerns for me pertains to the notion of "change." Are *all* "changes" the same, or are they equally "all-encompassing" in the ELT classroom? Moreover, if we argue, in a generalized way, that all teaching is about change, don't we risk creating pedagogical environments in which various forms of indoctrination are more likely to proliferate? This is indeed food for pedagogical thought.

I would argue, and I think Baurain would agree with me, that there are most certainly hierarchies of change—some of higher stakes and consequences than others. Most Christians would claim that there are none as "high" as the eternal salvation of the soul, which is why many Christian teachers see it as a duty to "share" the truth of their faith in their teaching practices. But in contrast to Baurain, I would also argue that most critical pedagogues in ELT do not see their agenda for change on the same level of intensity or equally "all-encompassing"; hence, they are more willing to hedge their bets and negotiate how and what the outcome of change will look like. Simply put, effective action for social justice usually requires coalition building, negotiation, and often compromise. In this respect, the so-called "liberation of society" is not equivalent or commensurable with the "liberation of the soul." Further, if the ultimate form of any given society's "liberation" has been predetermined, then yes, critical theorists who might subscribe to this type of absolutist ideology *are* being hypocritical when critiquing Christian colleagues. Fortunately, critical theory, like spirituality, is a wide umbrella sheltering many divergent and at times conflicting interpretations of "scripture."

Baurain (2007, pp. 211–212) characterizes the secular hedging around the notion of an "absolute truth" as evidence of an impoverished epistemology (i.e., social constructivism) and moral relativism underpinned by postmodern thought. I prefer to characterize this secular relativism as evidence of a realist ontology, not specifically opposed to the notion of "truth" per se, but keenly alert to the material effects that "truths"—both sacred and profane—have on our lives and specifically on our freedoms (cf. Foucault). That is, "absolute truths" in any form are potentially dangerous, especially for those who first appear to us as worldly or spiritual Others. The pedagogical embrace of "possibilities" rather than "certainties" is a more dialogical/interactional stance to take, particularly if we reflect upon the horrific consequences for the human societies in which "absolute truths" have gone unchecked.

In sum, productive doubt and vulnerability are not weaknesses in the paradigms to which we subscribe. To reiterate, they indicate openness to the "other" and answerability to the uniqueness and the strangeness of the "other" and the self-knowledge yet to be acquired in our inter-subjective encounters (cf. Huebner).

Conclusions

As I mentioned in my autobiographical introduction, it is extremely difficult for members of a dominant faith to recognize the worldly power that underpins the normalcy and truth of their spirituality. The worldly prestige of English and its historical articulation with Christianity creates a situation in which it would be almost impossible to safeguard against "coercive relations of power" (cf. Cummins, 2001) emerging through an explicitly faith-based approach to ELT. At the same time, I don't think it is possible or necessarily desirable to hide the values that make us who we are, though in some situations and settings it may be the most responsible contingency. Such dilemmas deserve continuous reflection on the ethical dimensions of teacher–student identity negotiation. Toward this end, I have briefly outlined what are idealized forms of dialogue and openness to our spiritual and worldly others.

While there are substantial differences between the arguments I have made and those put forward by Liang, Purgason, and Snow, there are also areas of common cause that should be briefly mentioned here. I believe we all share a concern with the creeping corporatization of schooling and its dehumanizing emphasis on producing "human capital" for a highly competitive and inequitable global economy. Purgason captures the mood of this concern as she critiques the ways that "typical text books teach students the language of buying, but not charitable giving, complaining but not necessarily praising, and apologizing, but not usually forgiving" (p. 190). Similarly, in a world that increasingly celebrates greed and individuality, it is commendable to find committed professionals who willingly help others for mostly altruistic reasons. So, even if we do not agree on what—if anything—follows our mortality, there are still many positive commonalities from which a genuine, interactional dialogue can develop.

Notes

1. This issue is taken up by Harris (2006), who notes that in spite of overwhelming scientific evidence to the contrary, a majority of Americans believe that the Earth may be only 10,000 years old, a time period that conforms to Judeo-Christian scripture. Similarly, a growing number of American jurisdictions permit the teaching of "intelligent design" as a scientifically valid alternative to evolutionary theory. Both examples indicate the powerful influence of Christian groups on public thought.
2. Much of my thinking here has been stimulated by educators specifically informed by the work of Levinas. In addition to Säfström and Simon, other Levinas-inspired texts I would like to cite in the context of this discussion are Biesta (1999), Child et al. (1995), and Ruiz (2004). My tentative engagement with the moral and ethical dimensions of pedagogy has also been greatly influenced by the work of Bill Johnston (2003), particularly as developed in his wonderful book, *Values in English Language Teaching.*

References

Baurain, B. (2007). Christian witness and respect for persons. *Journal of Language, Identity, and Education, 6*(3), 201–219.

Biesta, G. J. J. (1999). Radical intersubjectivity: Reflections on the "different" foundation of education. *Studies in Philosophy and Education, 18*(4), 203–220.

Child, M., Williams, D. D., Birch, A. J., & Boody, R. M. (1995). Autonomy or heteronomy? Levinas's challenge to modernism and postmodernism. *Educational Theory, 45*(2), 167–189.

Cummins, J. (2001). *Negotiating identities: Education for empowerment in a diverse society* (2nd ed.). Ontario, CA: California Association of Bilingual Education.

Harris, S. (2006). *Letter to a Christian nation.* New York: Alfred A. Knopf.

Huebner, D. (2005). Education and spirituality. In H. S. Shapiro, & D. E. Purpel (Eds.), *Critical social issues in American education: Democracy and meaning in a globalizing world* (pp. 309–324). Mahwah, NJ: Lawrence Erlbaum.

Johnston, B. (2003). *Values in English language teaching.* Mahwah, NJ: Lawrence Erlbaum.

Lusted, D. (1986). Why pedagogy? *Screen, 27*(5), 2–14.

Morgan, B. (1997). Identity and intonation: Linking dynamic processes in an ESL classroom. *TESOL Quarterly, 31*(2), 431–450.

Morgan, B. (2004). Teacher identity as pedagogy: Towards a field-internal conceptualisation in bilingual and second language education. *International Journal of Bilingual Education and Bilingualism, 7*(2/3), 172–188.

Morgan, B. (2007). Poststructuralism and applied linguistics: Complementary approaches to identity and culture in ELT. In C. Davison, & J. Cummins (Eds.), *International handbook of English language teaching* (Vol. 2) (pp. 949–968). Norwell, MA: Springer Publishers.

Pennycook, A. (1998). *English and the discourses of colonialism.* London: Routledge.

Ruiz, P. O. (2004). Moral education as a pedagogy of alterity. *Journal of Moral Education, 33*(3), 271–289.

Säfström, C. A. (2003). Teaching otherwise. *Studies in Philosophy and Education, 22*(1), 19–29.

Simon, R. I. (1992). *Teaching against the grain: Texts for a pedagogy of possibility.* Toronto, Canada: OISE Press.

Wong, S. (2006). *Dialogic approaches to TESOL: Where the ginkgo tree grows.* Mahwah, NJ: Lawrence Erlbaum.

Response

21 Power and Change in ELT

Thoughts from a Fellow Traveler

Dana R. Ferris

I have been both a language teacher and a Christian for quite a while now—approaching 25 years as to the former and over 30 years as to the latter—and for the whole time I have struggled, at times intentionally and at others unconsciously, with what it means to live out my faith in the context of my vocational calling. I certainly do not feel that I have "arrived," either spiritually or professionally, so when asked to contribute a response chapter to this volume, I approached the task with great curiosity and some trepidation. Because most questions of interest for me begin and end in the classroom, I was eager to read the chapters in the "pedagogical dilemmas" part of the book to see what other fellow travelers were thinking about and had learned along the road. Though the chapters by Liang, Snow, and Purgason cover disparate topics, I did notice two related themes emerging: issues of power differentials and the teacher as change agent.

"Power" (or imbalances thereof) is either a subtext or an explicit focus of all the chapters. Liang's personal narrative at least indirectly addresses the power differences between native and nonnative English language teachers and in particular how the nonnative teachers can be made to feel marginalized and less competent than native speakers. He articulates and challenges the smug assumptions held by some native speakers that they are obviously and by definition more qualified to teach English, noting that researchers have found that nonnative teachers have unique strengths:

> They have a strong explicit knowledge of English grammar; are keenly aware of the differences between L1 and L2; are more empathetic to students' learning needs, backgrounds, and difficulties; and represent a source of motivation and a good role model.
>
> (p. 166)

(See Mahboob, 2004; Nemtchinova, 2005; Samimy & Brutt-Griffler, 1999.) Liang describes three possible "models" through which nonnative English teachers can be viewed—the "deficiency" model, the "difference" model, and the "collaborative" model—discussing the impact of these views on his own self-concept and his relationships with other teachers.

As I was reading this chapter, I found myself struggling with a "relevance" question: are the differences between native and nonnative English speaking language teachers really the key issue? Isn't it really about competence and commitment? I was relieved as I read the story of Liang's personal journey to find that he eventually arrived at this same point, saying in fact: "if biblically informed teacher roles represent the constructs of teaching expertise, then the native and nonnative status is irrelevant" (p. 170). This is not to say that questions surrounding the capabilities of NNS (the "deficit" model), the differing knowledge and experience sets teachers bring to the endeavor (the "difference" model), or the ways in which native speaking and NNS teachers can learn from each other (the "collaboration" model) are not real and important. They are very legitimate and have profound impact on the lives of various teachers and their students.

However, for me, these practical issues are not what is most interesting or valuable about Liang's reflections. Liang's chapter raises questions of *identity or self-perception* and of *purpose or calling.* In turn, these issues relate directly to how we as human beings and as Christians see and relate to our colleagues and our students. In the earlier part of his narrative, Liang describes how an unhealthy sense of inferiority due to his NNS status (and several unfortunate native speaker comments that came his way at significant turning points) led him to feel competitive toward others, especially his native speaker counterparts, in an effort to bolster his own sense of worthiness for his chosen profession. As a native speaking teacher, I have not had to struggle with identity or inferiority issues in the ways that Liang has, but I have also grappled with questions of self-worth and competitiveness. My own self-doubt came from a variety of sources, including being in a new field (applied linguistics/TESOL) that was not understood or respected by the power brokers in the linguistics and English departments in which I completed my graduate studies and began my career; and being a young working mother in academia, which was a lot less common 20 years ago than it is today. (As to second issue, I found myself doubly on the fringes—of an evangelical church culture in which mothers who did not stay home with their young children were ostracized, and of a professional culture consisting of men whose wives had raised their children and/or women who had waited until their children were older to begin their careers.)

As a result of these less-than-ideal influences on my evolving professional and personal identity, I found myself acting out in several counterproductive ways. Bitter and resentful toward colleagues who did not understand or sympathize with the challenges I faced in juggling work and family life and who barely knew what TESOL was, let alone respected it as a professional academic discipline, I reacted to others in ways that were defensive and even hostile. In the early years of my career, I spent some sleepless nights stewing over real or imagined injustices and slights. Not only was this extremely detrimental to my emotional and spiritual health, but this attitude hardly put me in the right frame of mind to be "salt and light" (Matthew 5:13–16) or to "value others above" myself (Philippians 2:3).[1]

My next coping strategy was similar to one described by Liang, i.e., to prove myself worthy through the weight of my achievements. To a great extent, I succeeded in reaching this dubious "goal." In fact, I was so productive that the most common question I was asked by people in all arenas of my life was "How do you do it? Do you ever sleep?" However, the personal, physical, emotional, and spiritual costs of this approach have been enormous, and I do not recommend myself as a model for anyone. I now describe myself as a "recovering workaholic," and though I have made progress, missteps and backsliding are frequent.

As Liang aptly points out, Christians should take their identity and sense of self-worth from their relationship with the Living God who has rescued us from ourselves, who accepts us and loves us as we are, and who has adopted us as his beloved children (Romans 8:14–17). Rather than striving to one-up our "competitors" and earn others' approval, we are to, as some have put it, "play for an audience of One." Liang mentions Jesus' Parable of the Talents (Matthew 25:14–30; Luke 19:11–27); in it, the first two servants experienced the thrill of hearing the master say, "Well done, good and faithful servant!" As Christians, our primary goal must be to understand what "earns" *God*'s approval and to seek and value his "Well done!" over the accolades of any human source. It is clear from Jesus' teachings that pleasing God is *all* about relationships, specifically how we treat others. Thus, there is no place for bitterness, resentment, or competitiveness toward our colleagues, whether they are Christians or not, or whether they come from diverse cultural or linguistic backgrounds. As he reflects upon his personal journey, Liang reaches the same conclusion.

In the second chapter, Snow calls upon Christian language teachers to confront the power differential between English and most other world languages and respond with "an increased commitment both as individuals and as professional communities to the idea that English teachers should also be language learners—and particularly to the idea that teachers whose first language is English should learn other languages."

As an American and English native speaker, I have heard the language-learning message from both of my communities (Christian and ELT). As a Christian college student, I remember hearing a talk at an "Urbana Onward" missions conference in which it was strongly stated that "all Christians should learn a foreign language." The argument was that we never know if God might call us to the mission field, and if he does, we need to be prepared. (Even if we had studied a foreign language different from that of the host country, the logic was that the prior experience of having learned a second language would help us in approaching the language of the particular mission field.) I was so inspired by this talk that I actually signed up for a German class the next quarter.

When I entered an MA TESOL program a few years later, I signed up for beginning French, a language I had never studied, along with my graduate coursework. Though foreign language study and/or proficiency was not required by my program at the time (it is now), I independently arrived at the idea that studying a new language at the same time I was learning how to teach English would be good for me, and indeed it was. As Snow suggests, I found the experience "humbling" (I vividly remember my French 1 professor screaming at me in front of the whole class when I made a pronunciation error) and informative as I reflected on the new language itself, on my second language learning process, and on the ways in which my various professors taught the courses. I have used illustrations from those three semesters many times over my years as a teacher-educator.

All that said, I found myself more convinced and motivated by some aspects of Snow's argument than others. Anticipating push-back to his argument, he poses the following hypothetical objection:

> learning a new language requires a considerable investment of time and effort; for native speakers of English the benefits of investing significant time in learning other languages are often not perceived as being worthwhile. While ELT professionals would all agree in theory that learning other languages is desirable, when time and energy are in short supply an expenditure of this magnitude needs considerable justification.[2]
>
> (p. 180)

He then argues that all teachers can benefit (as I did during my MA program) from reflecting upon their own language-learning experiences and how they might relate to present and future teaching. I found this line of thinking convincing up to a point—as I said, I found my own study of French extremely helpful in this regard—but I part ways with Snow when he implies that "investing *significant time* in learning other languages" (p. 180) (emphasis added) is strictly necessary to reap those benefits. While I in no way became proficient in French over those three semesters, as to my primary goal of experiencing a new language while learning to teach others, it was time very well spent. Would I have gathered even more insights about language learning from more study of French? Undoubtedly. Given that I live and work in the United States and am unlikely ever to spend substantial time in a French-speaking country, would the investment required "justify the cost in time and energy"? I am not so certain. Perhaps my time is better spent studying English (which is, after all, the language I teach) and about second language acquisition processes and teaching methods (especially as I can tailor them to the teaching and learning of English).

Snow also argues from both a Christian and professional perspective that second language study is "Other-oriented," that it humbles us, putting us in the position of learner rather than teacher, and that it conveys to our students that we value other languages and especially their language. However, most of his discussion of this point is focused on expatriate Inner Circle teachers who teach in non-Inner Circle countries. This point seems well taken for those professionals; clearly there are practical, pedagogical, and intangible benefits, as Snow describes, of an EFL professional taking the trouble to learn about the language and culture in which s/he is living and working. These benefits seem less obvious to me as a native speaker of English who works with ESL students from a range of linguistic backgrounds in an Inner Circle country.

However, I believe my time and energy as a Christian language educator can be (and is) very well spent on other "power" issues raised by Snow, ones I found intriguing and motivating. First, English language teachers can and should challenge the view held by many in Inner Circle countries "multilingualism is a value mainly for those whose first language isn't English" (p. 178). This assumption plays itself out in two distinct but equally counterproductive ways. The first is that immigrants to English speaking countries should stop using their primary language as soon as possible and especially that their children should not receive primary language and literacy instruction—that maintenance and development of another language is not only unimportant but actually harmful to children's education and assimilation. The second is that, for native English speaking children, second language learning is an extra, a "frill," and certainly far less important than other academic subjects and pursuits.[3] If TESOL professionals in Inner Circle countries truly value multilingualism, they should become advocates both for primary language development for nonnative English speakers and early, substantial second language learning opportunities for native English speakers.

A second point raised by Snow that I found extremely compelling was near the end of his chapter, in which he points out that while the study of English around the world is empowering and opens up a wide range of opportunities for English learners, access to English is not equivalent across different class levels and cultural groups in many countries. Snow suggests that English language professionals, as well as Christians interested in economic and social justice, should become advocates for more widespread English learning opportunities worldwide. Though Snow did not say this, I would extend his argument to Inner Circle countries in which access to English instruction is also limited by an unequal distribution of resources between affluent and impoverished school districts. In short, one important way in which Christian ELT professionals can, as Snow urges, assume responsibility for the power that English has in the world is to help ensure that everyone who wants and needs to learn it has adequate access to high-quality instruction, materials, and facilities. Given limited time and energy resources, our activism with regard to these two issues—valuing multilingualism for all and improving access to English learning—in my view can be much more significant in directly addressing power imbalances than our own intensive study of other languages.

What Liang's chapter and Snow's have in common is that both authors confront us with power differentials (between native and nonnative teachers; between English and other world languages) and argue that Christians in language teaching have a responsibility not simply to acknowledge and meekly acquiesce to "the way things are" but to critically analyze differences and disparities and use our insights and influence to effect change where we can. The other chapter, by Purgason, also addresses power issues but through the more specific lens of the teacher as change agent. In broad strokes, she discusses the issue of whether it is ever appropriate for Christian English language teachers to directly or indirectly share their faith with their students, or whether so doing is an abuse of power and shows disrespect for others.

However, the quarrel that some scholars have with Christian language teachers goes deeper and is more subtle, and in fact extends to the question of "Christian witness" in general, outside of the specific context of language teaching. It is reflective of a pervasive view in larger American/Western society that "proselytization" is at best impolite and at worst morally wrong—though such views about "bearing witness" to one's beliefs in an attempt to persuade others seem to be primarily, perhaps uniquely, aimed at evangelical Christians.

Individuals attempt all the time to persuade others toward accepting their beliefs, whether they be religious, political, social, financial, nutritional, and so forth. I would go a step further with this argument and say that if one does not hold a belief strongly enough to be its passionate advocate, it's not a conviction worthy of much respect. On the contrary, we are told from childhood to "stand up for what we believe in" and to "have the courage of our convictions." People are admired for acting on their beliefs and for defending them, even—or especially—when they are unpopular. For example, why do we hold up individuals such as the baseball player Jackie Robinson, or Rosa Parks, or Martin Luther King, Jr., as heroes and role models in twentieth-century American history and culture? Isn't it *precisely* because they spoke up for and lived out their convictions regarding equality, civil rights, and social justice? It seems apparent and obvious that holding and sharing strong convictions is not only "not wrong," but something to be respected—in most instances.

Curiously, this generally positive view of articulating one's passionately held beliefs does not seem to extend to Christian believers who desire (or feel compelled) to share their faith. There are several possible reasons for this contradiction. First, among major world religions, Jesus Christ stands alone among the founders in claiming that he uniquely is "the way" to God: "I am the way, and the truth and the life. No one comes to the Father except through me" (John 14:6). Statements such as these create a problem for those who prefer to say that "all religions lead to God."[4] Second, in recent American history, religion (in particular Protestant evangelical Christianity) and politics have been intermingled and conflated, arguably to the detriment of both. It is one thing for an individual believer to invite the neighbors to church on Christmas Eve; it is quite another when the leader of the free world claims implicitly that God told him through prayer to attack another country. The institutional use of one's religious beliefs to exert (or abuse) power over others is something that rightly raises suspicion and resentment. Third, over the history of the Christian faith, there have indeed been many sordid incidents of "Christians" using coercion, manipulation, and deceit to spread the gospel. (This is also true of some other world religions.)

Nonetheless, it is not wrong, generally speaking, for Christians to talk about our faith to others. As noted by Baurain (2007), there are at least two distinct reasons why Christians do so. The first is the mandate of Jesus, known as "the Great Commission," to "go and make disciples of all nations … teaching them to obey everything I have commanded you" (Matthew 28:18, 20). Christians, by definition, are disciples (students) of Jesus Christ; among other things, this means we are supposed to follow his example and obey his commands. In short, if Christians do not take Jesus seriously when he calls us "the salt of the earth and the light of the world" (Matthew 5:13–14) and tells us to be his "witnesses" (Acts 1:8), we are failing to obey him and to act like Christians. This, after all, is the definition of a "hypocrite"—one who pretends to be something that they are not. Second, Christians are "compelled by Christ's love" (2 Corinthians 5:14) to share what we have found with others—because we care about them and believe that Christ's message of purpose and transformation and hope has something valuable to offer them. If I were a scientist and discovered a treatment for some rare disease, no one would accuse me of being abusive or unkind if I told others about it and tried to persuade the U.S. Food and Drug Administration to approve it and doctors to prescribe it; on the contrary, it would be morally reprehensible if I kept that discovery to myself. Still, the caveat must be added that while Christians are told to "always be prepared to give an answer ... for the hope that you have," they are also told "*But do this with gentleness and respect,* keeping a clear conscience" (1 Peter 3:15–16, emphasis added). Christians, past and present, have far too frequently fallen short of this standard for communication. That said, those who call themselves Christians are not only entitled to share their beliefs with others but are arguably morally bound to do so.

However, the question of whether Christian language teachers are wrong to share their beliefs with students is far more complex. In my own teaching, I sometimes make comments in class that "out" me as a Christian. For example, in a linguistics class, I might give as one of several examples an interesting use of a word or turn of phrase I heard during a sermon in church, just as an example of how language can be used, but it does communicate to those who are listening that I practice a religious faith. When I teach my classes, I disclose a fair amount of who I am as a person, for instance, the fact that I am married, have children and a dog, attended USC, am a baseball and *Seinfeld* fan, and so forth. Most teachers would find it hard and even unnatural to interact with a group of students over an extended period of time without ever dropping any hints about who they are outside of the classroom. Being a Christian is a part of my story; I am entitled, I think, to tell my own story (but with some limitations, as discussed further below). Further, most people would agree that if being a "Christian teacher" means showing care and concern for students as whole people and treating them with kindness and consideration, there is no problem there, either. In my own one-to-one communication with students (face to face or in email), if a student discloses a personal problem (medical, family, etc.), I will usually say that I will pray for them; this seems consistent with showing care and concern for them.[5]

However, where some people draw the line is on the issue that Purgason raised, that of the "teacher as change agent" (Brown, 2001; Campbell, 2003; Edge, 1996; Johnston, 2003; Pennycook & Coutand-Marin, 2003). As a TESOL professional in recent years, I have observed from a distance the critiques of Christians for attempting to bring about "change" (as to religious beliefs) in their students while simultaneously other scholars urge teachers to view themselves as advocates for change:

> You are an agent for change in a world in desperate need of change; change from competition to cooperation, from powerlessness to empowerment, from conflict to resolution, from prejudice to understanding.... Our professional commitment drives us to help the inhabitants of this planet to communicate with each other, to negotiate the meaning of peace, of goodwill, and of survival on this tender, fragile, globe. We must therefore, with all the professional tools available to us, passionately pursue these ultimate goals.
>
> (Brown, 2001, p. 445)

I have always been uncomfortable with the whole discussion. The only type of "change" I expect or hope to see in my students is a greater mastery of the content or skills covered in a particular course; if their study or work habits also improve as a result of the way I structure my assignments and evaluations, that is an added bonus. I do not see myself as an agent of moral, social, or political change when I teach my courses—*precisely* because if I think that way, I am troubled by the uneasy feeling that I am, in fact, abusing the power I have over them and not respecting them as persons. Further, I am sensitive to the issue raised by Purgason—and illustrated by a quotation she provides from Hafernik, Messerschmitt, and Vandrick (2002)—that course curriculum and materials should be driven by student need and *language-learning* goals, not a personal agenda:

> In choosing material, both required textbooks and supplementary materials, foremost is the contractual and ethical obligation of faculty members to comply with the course description, goals, and objective, and to keep in mind that the primary goal of ESL courses is to improve students' English language ability.
>
> (Hafernik et al., 2002, p. 106)

I believe that it is my job to help students to think and read critically and to express themselves effectively in the target language, not to persuade them to adopt my worldview on *any* issue, whether it be care for the environment, equality for women or homosexuals, war, poverty, oppression, gun control—or my religious faith. As a Christian, I hope that I model Christ-like behavior both in and out of the classroom through excellence, fairness, integrity, humility, kindness, and compassion (values also discussed at some length by Purgason). I would not feel comfortable expounding upon my Christian beliefs or making a gospel presentation in the classroom, and I would probably only discuss my faith with students outside of the class once they were no longer my students. The power differential and the possibility that students might express interest or agreement with my beliefs to curry favor with me are very legitimate concerns that I take quite seriously. On the other hand, exceptions could be made in contexts where the content and goals of the course or program are overtly and explicitly Christian (e.g., in a Christian school or church-based language course).

However, it is not wrong to discuss controversial or current social issues with students; on the contrary, I find that such topics can be engaging to students and provide good opportunities for them to think and develop language skills. Purgason's scenarios from her ethics class at a Christian university remind me that there is a very fine line between open discussion of issues or ideas and manipulation. For example, imagine a language class has taken up the topic of capital punishment, and a student makes the comment that Americans are in favor of it because the US is a Christian country. As the teacher, I would address the several different stereotypes implicit in this statement: (1) all Americans favor capital punishment; (2) all Americans are Christians; and (3) all Christians are in favor of capital punishment (or that the Christian faith prescribes it). However, while it is fair to say that Americans and Christians are divided on the issue and that the Bible has conflicting examples and texts on the issue, I personally would draw the line at saying something like, "As a Christian, I believe that..." In fact, I would draw the line earlier: I would not state my opinion on capital punishment *at all*, and in fact would try hard to point out all sides of the issue so that the students would remain unaware of my personal stand on the question. Why? Am I not a person and do I not have a right to hold and express an opinion? Yes—but when I am the teacher in a classroom, I must be especially careful that my self-expression does not implicitly push students toward agreeing with me in order to gain my approval. Much as American teachers, who tend to value informal relationships and egalitarianism, would like to forget this, in a classroom there are power differentials—we are all *people*, but in that social setting, we are not *equals*.

"Power" is an uncomfortable topic for Christians. After all, Jesus Christ himself both taught and modeled meekness, mercy, humility, and servanthood (e.g., Matthew 5:5, 7; Luke 22:26–27; Philippians 2:2–5), so even *acknowledging* power, much less using or abusing it, feels antithetical to what we are supposed to stand for. Our discomfort notwithstanding, a failure or refusal to grapple with power dynamics in a classroom and their implications for how teachers comport themselves—particularly in this highly sensitive area of sharing our Christian faith—is irresponsible. Though how we talk and act may vary from one context to another, we must always hold in tension our calling as Christ's disciples and our professional role as language teachers, seeking wisdom in the moment, being good listeners, and valuing the needs of others above our own, or, as Purgason tells her Christian trainees:

> Although you may be in a position of power because of your citizenship in a powerful nation, your higher education, your proficiency in English, or your role as a teacher, don't take that for granted or try to hold on to that power; instead, be like Jesus who relinquished power and who came to serve.
>
> (p. 188)

Notes

1. All biblical references are from *Today's New International Version*, 2001/2005, International Bible Society/Zondervan.
2. Earlier in the chapter, Snow had at least implicitly suggested that second language requirements of some TESOL training programs, while "better than nothing," are inadequate, for instance proscribing 1 year of college-level foreign language study or its equivalent, and that such requirements fall short of demonstrating our stated commitment as a profession to multilingualism.
3. In my own hometown of Davis, California, there has been a sizable and thriving dual-immersion program in Spanish and English available in the public schools for over 20 years, and my own two children attended it. Davis is a liberal, progressive, well-educated, and affluent town with excellent public schools. Nonetheless, the Spanish immersion program was controversial for many years after its inception, with critics complaining that the program "took resources away" from what they considered to be the "important" curriculum.
4. It is important to observe that the "problem" should be with Jesus himself—who claimed his uniqueness—rather than his followers. Yet the opposite is usually true—many people when asked have a positive impression of Jesus Christ but a negative view of Christians for their "message of exclusivity!"

5. I have found that most people, even if they do not have a personal faith, will not reject or be offended by an offer of prayer when facing a personal crisis, figuring that it cannot *hurt*, even if they are not convinced it will *help*!

References

Baurain, B. (2007). Christian witness and respect for persons. *Journal of Language, Identity, and Education, 6*(3), 201–219.

Brown, H. D. (2001). *Teaching by principles* (3rd ed.). New York: Longman.

Campbell, E. (2003). *The ethical teacher.* Maidenhead, UK, and Philadelphia, PA: Open University Press (McGraw-Hill).

Edge, J. (1996). Cross-cultural paradoxes in a profession of values. *TESOL Quarterly, 30*(1), 9–30.

Hafernik, J., Messerschmitt, D., & Vandrick, S. (2002). *Ethical issues for ESL faculty: Social justice in practice.* Mahwah, NJ: Lawrence Erlbaum.

Johnston, B. (2003). *Values in English language teaching.* Mahwah, NJ, and London: Lawrence Erlbaum.

Mahboob, A. (2004). Native or nonnative: What do students enrolled in an intensive English program think? In L. D. Kamhi-Stein (Ed.), *Learning and teaching from experience: Perspectives on nonnative English-speaking professionals* (pp. 121–147). Ann Arbor: University of Michigan Press.

Nemtchinova, E. (2005). Host teachers' evaluations of nonnative-English-speaking teacher trainees: A perspective from the classroom. *TESOL Quarterly, 39*(2), 235–262.

Pennycook, A., & Coutand-Marin, S. (2003). Teaching English as a missionary language. *Discourse: Studies in the Cultural Politics of Education, 24*(3), 337–353.

Samimy, K. K., & Brutt-Griffler, J. (1999). To be a native or non-native speaker perceptions of "non-native" students in a graduate TESOL program. In G. Braine (Ed.), *Non-native educators in English language teaching* (pp. 127–144). Mahwah, NJ: Lawrence Erlbaum.

Response

22 Reconsidering Roadside Assistance

The Problem with Christian Approaches to Teaching the English Language

Terry A. Osborn

I am pleased to see such a robust and open dialogue surrounding the elements of Christian language teaching, both within and beyond missionary application. I wish a similar debate would erupt in my own US "foreign" language discipline (see, e.g., Osborn, 2005, 2006; Smith & Osborn, 2006). I must also confess that I'm disappointed as to how we, as language educators, have failed to progress in our understanding of the contexts of language education involving those educated in the United States, both within and beyond the Christian settings. I suspect that, in large part, we scholars are also victims of understanding teaching as a technicist endeavor, one of merely following curricula and engineering outcomes. We are left with little by way of ability to conceptualize moral and ethical dimensions of teaching and, in an attempt to "Christianize" our endeavors, we default to merely adding a spiritual veneer on the seemingly "neutral" act of teaching languages. The better route, I would contend, is to confront the dehumanizing models of teaching within the Western world and interrupt the onslaught of the capitalist and neoliberal forces swallowing up the peoples of the world in a conquest for new markets.

I want to draw on a famous parable taught by Jesus, both because it is so widely known outside of Christian circles, and because I think it serves as a powerful reminder of approaches within those circles. The parable is recorded in Luke 10:30–37 as follows:

> In reply Jesus said: "A man was going down from Jerusalem to Jericho, when he fell into the hands of robbers. They stripped him of his clothes, beat him and went away, leaving him half dead. A priest happened to be going down the same road, and when he saw the man, he passed by on the other side. So too, a Levite, when he came to the place and saw him, passed by on the other side. But a Samaritan, as he traveled, came where the man was; and when he saw him, he took pity on him. He went to him and bandaged his wounds, pouring on oil and wine. Then he put the man on his own donkey, took him to an inn and took care of him. The next day he took out two silver coins[e] and gave them to the innkeeper. 'Look after him,' he said, 'and when I return, I will reimburse you for any extra expense you may have.' Which of these three do you think was a neighbor to the man who fell into the hands of robbers?" The expert in the law

> replied, "The one who had mercy on him." Jesus told him, "Go and do likewise."
>
> (NIV)

It seems that, for the most part, our approaches to teaching English have reduced the obligation of Christian English language teachers to that of roadside assistance.[1] When we encounter an abject victim of the world domination of English, it is our "Christian duty" to have mercy on her/him and to do so in Christian love. Some chapters in this part of the book have expounded that duty to include:

1. performing the tasks of teaching in a manner that reflects Godly excellence;
2. being aware of our privileges and obligations as native speakers in "Inner Circle" English language nations;
3. embracing and understanding the role of the "Office" of language teaching; and
4. avoiding deception as part of an evangelical or teaching approach.

In this response, I will comment on these four, in reverse order, in terms of their limitations, but also wish to revisit the parable of the Good Samaritan in hopes that we can glean a bigger picture of where our scholarship and advocacy could take the Christian scholarly community of language educators. I intend this response as an exhortation to allow the insights of critical theories to push our understanding even further, and exhort the reader not to settle for superficial insights.

Renouncing the use of deception is a necessary, if somewhat obvious position to take. The approach of crafting evangelism through language teaching seems to suggest, however, an understanding of conversion as one based on or influenced by the motives of the evangelist. Further, the overemphasis on an act of convincing a hearer or utilizing logic and reason reflects a view of conversion that would seem to ignore the role of the Holy Spirit in drawing the hearer to Christ.

The conceptualization of language teaching as an office or Godly calling may provide some sense of mission and a romanticized ideal of the language teacher, but it would also seem to provide an important obligation as well: the need to discourage those who want to be language teachers from pursuing the path. Consider James 3:1: "Not many of you should presume to be teachers, my brothers, because you know that we who teach will be judged more strictly" (NIV). Thus, if we build upon a conceptualization of language teaching as Christian office, I would expect that such efforts to dissuade would-be teachers would become a focus of approaches from such a point. Though I recognize the office of teaching within the body of Christ, I do not equate that office per se with the profession of teacher.

Two remaining points need to be addressed: recognizing our own privilege as, by analogy, roadside assistants to the less fortunate, and second, that we should conduct our business with excellence, are certainly appropriate. I would like to point out, however, that these positions assume a significant amount of the context for language teaching as a fait accompli, and they fail to suggest concrete ways in which we can take decisive action to change the status quo.

Returning now to the parable of the Good Samaritan, it is perhaps usual to position the Christian language educator as the Samaritan, a foreigner to that one needing assistance, who acts neighborly to the one whose plight seems abject. But, I would like to offer some additional points to ponder regarding the parable:

1. What if the Samaritan arrives at the scene during the attack? As the robbers rain blows on their victim, what is the obligation of the good neighbor? Should s/he step in to thwart the attack?
2. What if the Samaritan discovers that many who live near or on this road aid and abet the robbers who have victimized many other travelers? Should s/he do something to disrupt the systemic support for such attacks?
3. What if the Samaritan learns that the innkeeper subsequently enslaves the victim after he "recovers?"

The obligation that we as scholars have is to delve deeper into the contexts of language teaching on a global level. We are not merely witnesses to the widespread domination of English, we are parties to the imperialism—not merely by way of our evangelistic outreach, but also through our economic habits, the leaders we elect, and so on. The "attacks" are ongoing, the systems do support them, and the capitalist slavery continues virtually unabated. It may be comfortable to see oneself as being engaged in *roadside assistance*, but it is disingenuous to suggest that we care for the "victim" while we ignore the systems of victimization in which we are active participants in our everyday lives.

The parable of the Good Samaritan is also a helpful analogy, in that we have identified ourselves with the wrong character. We are not the Samaritan, we are the abject victim. We are the ones, in the Western world, who have largely been robbed of humanity and we are the ones who can learn from the so-called "despised" of the world. It is the empty shell of religion, devoid of mercy, that crosses to the other side of the street and offers humans little by way of comfort or direction. To that end, the points Snow makes are right on target:

- organized involvement in promotion of English obligates Western Christian English teachers to consider what obligations this leaves them with (p. 175); and
- Christian English teachers may be too uncritical in accepting the advantages offered by the dominance of English, and too comfortable drawing on its power (p. 176).

Yet, Snow runs the risk of oversimplification of the role played by cultural capital in suggesting that "English teachers can be a part of this process [language learners empowering themselves] by assisting students in the task of mastering English so as to better take advantage of the opportunities and empowerment it offers" (p. 178). On balance, however, Snow moves the discussion clearly ahead and in the right direction—that is, by focusing on the contexts of language education and the obligation of native speakers of English to learn other languages—in stressing that the professional culture of language teachers is most needing change.

In conclusion, the dialogue that Christian scholars have on the subject of pedagogical dilemmas should continue to incorporate insights afforded by critical theories and expand beyond methodological insights, professional obligations, or ethical reflections. We should be looking at sociological and epistemological issues and our obligations as Christians to intervene in the world with mercy—mercy that is manifest in standing against the violence wrought by the forces of capitalism.

Note

1. I do not mean to suggest that this is an appropriate exegesis of the scripture, that is, to reduce the parable to a tale of "roadside assistance for Christ." However, I do contend that some do draw exactly that inspiration from the parable and apply it to their lives.

References

Osborn, T. A. (2005). *Critical reflection and the foreign language classroom* (Rev. ed.). Greenwich, CT: Information Age Publishing.

Osborn, T. A. (2006). *Teaching world languages for social justice: A sourcebook of principles and practices.* Mahwah, NJ: Lawrence Erlbaum.

Smith, D. I., & Osborn, T. A. (Eds.) (2007). *Spirituality, social justice, and language education.* Charlotte, NC: Information Age Publishing.

Discussion Questions

Part III: Pedagogical and Professional Dilemmas

1. Liang is able to draw from both his Christian faith and his Confucian heritage to find a "higher purpose" for teaching. What tenets, stories, or sayings from your cultural heritage or religious faith inform your teaching? Do they complement or conflict with each other and if so, how do you reconcile them?
2. Liang relates that casual comments from native speakers who were friends, colleagues, and former students hurt him deeply, causing him to doubt his teaching ability, which affected his confidence. What can be done to make native speakers more aware of the power structure that renders NNS "invisible?" What can those in positions of power do to become more "vulnerable" as Morgan puts it? How can NNS "markedness" be removed, as they are by definition perceived by how they deviate or are deficient from the "norm" of "nativeness?" How can native speakers be more "open" to what can be learned from NNS? And finally, how can these questions be applied to religious contexts, in which the dominant religion renders others marked and invisible, such as in the US in which Protestant Christian religion is the dominant religion?
3. Snow states: "My concern, rather, lies in the possibility that Christian English teachers may be too uncritical in accepting the advantages offered by the dominance of English, and too comfortable drawing on its power" (p. 176). What are the advantages Snow refers to, and how do CET draw on the power of the dominance of English?
4. Purgason opens her chapter with a scenario (p. 185). In small groups (or for an individual assignment) discuss the scenario. Then write your own scenario in which a teacher's beliefs (religious or other) have great potential to surface in classroom interaction and thus decisions about how to appropriately respond must be made. Discuss how far you as the teacher would go in discussing your religious beliefs in each scenario. See also the scenario on pp. 212–213 that Ferris describes.
5. Context affects the answers to almost any question. Purgason describes how she has taught in predominantly Christian, secular, Muslim, and communist settings and how these contexts change how she approaches the topic of religion. Provide a context in which it would be appropriate for a discussion of students' religious beliefs and one in which it would be inappropriate and discuss why.

6. Purgason provides four biblical principles (p. 191), which she notes could be used by those who are non-Christians. Do you feel these are adequate safeguards in terms of mitigating the power issues described by Morgan? Provide an example with an ELT context that would demonstrate each principle.
7. Do you believe in absolute truth? As Morgan (Chapter 20) states:

   > "absolute truths" in any form are potentially dangerous, especially for those who first appear to us as worldly or spiritual Others. The pedagogical embrace of "possibilities" rather than "certainties" is a more dialogical/interactional stance to take, particularly if we reflect upon the horrific consequences for the human societies in which "absolute truths" have gone unchecked.
   >
   > (p. 202)

   Provide some examples of the "horrific consequences" that have taken place in history as a result of unchecked "absolute truths" and describe your stance on absolute truth.
8. Morgan discusses dialogue, which is the theme of the first two chapters in Part I, and uses the terms *interactional dialogue* to describe participants who allow themselves to be re-formed as a consequence, and *transactional dialogue*, where predetermined values are guardedly exchanged without any intention of change. How does this compare with Johnston's *exploratory* and *conciliatory dialogue* and Edge's *asymmetrical reciprocity*? What do you regard as essential to dialogue, and how do Morgan's insights inform your understanding? To what extent do you agree with Canagarajah's comparison of the models proposed by these authors in Chapter 9?
9. Morgan asks "Are all changes equal?" What is appropriate and inappropriate in terms of changes teachers seek to make in their students? Discuss whether you feel the following changes are appropriate or inappropriate in a specific context that you provide:

   - an understanding of the consequences of global warming and a commitment to reduce waste and abuses of the environment;
   - an awareness of the injustice of domestic violence and a desire to expose and stop it;
   - an understanding of a particular religious faith of the culture being studied in the class and a desire to learn more about it;
   - an awareness of spirituality and a desire to understand how others understand and express their spirituality in their cultures and communities.

10. Morgan states "The key question, then, is how we might ideally and ethically address such concerns in pedagogy without denying our own identity, humanity, or spirituality—if such denial were even consciously possible?" (p. 195). What is key to your identity and how is this addressed in your pedagogy? What dilemmas do you feel as you do (or fail to do) this? Morgan

also states "Such dilemmas deserve continuous reflection on the ethical dimensions of teacher–student identity negotiation" (p. 202). How do you plan to sustain the reflection upon these and other dilemmas?

11. Ferris notes that like Liang, she found a renewed sense of professional identity in her personal spiritual journey. Palmer (2007) would call this integrity of teaching, Gebhard and Oprandy (1999) connecting the personal and professional. Some authors in this volume have discussed the dangers of this. What is your view and how if at all have you sought to do this and mitigate the dangers?
12. Ferris observes that the second issue raised in this part of the book is "teachers as change agents." Although she clarifies that there are exceptions to the following (such as in the case of Christian schools and church-based English programs), she states "The only type of 'change' I expect or hope to see in my students is a greater mastery of the content or skills covered in a particular course" (pp. 211–212) and continues,

    > I believe that it is my job to help students to think and read critically and to express themselves effectively in the target language, not to persuade them to adopt my worldview on *any* issue, whether it be care for the environment, equality for women or homosexuals, war, poverty, oppression, gun control—or my religious faith.
    >
    > (p. 212)

    Do you agree? Relate a classroom experience (as a student or teacher) when you felt that the instructor passed "that very fine line between open discussion of issues and manipulation" (p. 212).
13. Osborn states that Christian English teachers are "parties to imperialism" (p. 217) and not just in "our evangelistic outreach" but also in our economic habits and political actions. List several economic habits and political actions that might indicate that we may in fact be helping imperialistic forces. List those that might apply to anyone, those that are specific to English teachers, and those that apply just to Christian English teachers. Personally, what economic habits and political actions do you engage in (or fail to engage in) that might make you a party to imperialism? Should this be a concern? Why or why not and, if so, what can you do about it?

References

Gebhard, J., & Oprandy, R. (1999). *Language teaching awareness.* New York: Cambridge University Press.

Palmer, P. (2007). *The courage to teach: Exploring the innter landscape of a teacher's life* (10th anniversary ed.). New York: Jossey-Bass.

Part IV

Spiritual and Ethical Dilemmas

23 Spiritual Dimensions in Language Teaching

A Personal Reflection

Ryuko Kubota

As a non-Christian language teacher and teacher educator, having been exposed to Christianity during childhood in Japan, and now as a semi-devoted Buddhist, I have had two experiences, one over 20 years ago and another recently, which made me think about issues of religious faith, ethics, and teaching a second language. In this chapter, I will recount these episodes and explore interconnections among issues in teaching culture, religious faith, power, positionality, and situated ethics. Faith and language teaching pose challenging issues that cannot be resolved in simple terms. Thus, my intent here is to expose the complexity of the issues rather than provide definitive answers to the challenges.

Denial of my Cultural (Spiritual) Identity: Graduate School Experience

It was in the mid 1980s. I was in an MA TESL program in the United States, an international student from Japan in her late twenties. Although I had previously lived in a different part of the United States for nine months as a visiting intern volunteering in public schools, I was still a novice cultural explorer in American society. The MA program consisted of a cohort of students, including both experienced and pre-service teachers and a sizable number of international students. Like many of the domestic and international students in our cohort, I lived in a campus dorm and had to vacate my room during the winter break. A classmate of mine kindly invited me to stay with her at her parents' home for part of the break. She was Caucasian and much younger than I was—as I recall, she came to the MA program straight from her undergraduate education. She was very friendly, caring, and fun to be with. She wanted to teach English in China after graduation. She and I had a good time doing things together for several days during the break.

One day during my stay, she handed me a book and said, "This is a very good book. You should read it." I do not recall the title of the book but it was about Christianity. At night, I began reading it in my bed. Christianity was not something unknown to me. In fact, it had formed part of my childhood experience. The kindergarten (an institution separate from elementary school) I attended in my mid-sized Japanese city was founded by a Canadian Methodist woman missionary in 1904 and run by a Christian church nearby. It was one of the first kindergartens established in Japan and had a good reputation for providing progressive education. Incidentally, my parents who had grown up in two different towns in the same region in the 1930s had each attended a similar kindergarten as well. Their experience might have influenced their decision to provide me with a similar educational experience. While many children in my neighborhood walked to local secular daycare centers (comparable to kindergartens), I commuted by bus to kindergarten every day. Although there were a few religious activities such as a performance of the nativity pageant, there was no instruction in English. After I entered a public secular elementary school, I continued to attend Sunday school at the church for a couple of years. We sang hymns, recited the Lord's Prayer, read the Bible, and listened to the minister speak, all in Japanese. I eventually stopped participating in church activities, as I wanted to socialize more with my friends in my neighborhood. None of my immediate family members, including myself, are baptized, although my mother's younger sister who used to be a teacher at my kindergarten has been baptized and is still involved in church activities.

Given this childhood experience, reading about Christianity was nothing new. However, as I read the first chapter of the book, I was struck by the comment that read something like "Christianity is the only true religion on earth. The faiths promoted by Buddhism, Islam, and other religions are all false." I remember I was quite shocked by this statement because, as an innocent foreigner, I had never encountered such a fundamentalist point of view. At the same time, I felt quite insulted—the message I got was a denial of my cultural identity as something inferior and worthless. I was not a proclaimed Buddhist at that time but the implication upset me. Why did I feel that way? The reason has to do with cultural identities shaped by religious rituals, which have been transformed into everyday cultural experiences.

Multiple religious faiths coexist in Japanese society. Using data from the Keizai Koho Center (1990), Reader, Andreasen, and Stefánsson (1993, p. 33) estimated the following numbers of religious believers out of a total Japanese population of 120,000,000:

Shinto	112,203,000
Buddhism	93,396,000
Christianity	1,422,000
Other religions, incl. new religions	11,412,000
Total	218,433,000

These intriguing figures indicate that many Japanese feel affiliated with more than one religion and that the two major religions they practice are Buddhism and Shinto. While Buddhism is a pan-ethnic religion prevalent in many parts of Asia, Shinto is an indigenous religion of Japan, creating both cultural traditions and political significance and turmoil. For many people, customs that derive from these religions provide cultural rather than purely religious significance, constituting everyday customs, seasonal rituals, and shared cultural knowledge. For instance, my parents held their wedding at a Shinto shrine, my grandparents and their ancestors are buried in a Buddhist temple, and for the New Year's celebration, my parents clean and decorate both their Buddhist and Shinto altars, which are in the same room. This mishmash of religions/traditions/customs goes beyond Buddhism and Shinto—certain aspects of Christianity have also been incorporated into Japanese cultural customs. For instance, the Christmas celebration is observed in illuminated streets and "Christmas cake" made of ice cream. Like many other cultures, Japanese society has turned religious beliefs into cultural traditions, old and new, shaping a significant part of secular life. In other words, traditions stemming from religious rituals are made into a cultural identity for many Japanese. The coexistence of multiple religions and customs is perhaps influenced by the religious tolerance that Buddhism has held up as part of Dharma (Bodhi, 1993). For me, even though I had some Christian experiences in my early life, my identity was significantly influenced by the culture based on Buddhism as well as other spiritualities. Thus, I naturally interpreted the statement in the book as a denial of my cultural identity.

What was more troubling to me was that the caring and kind classmate of mine who was preparing to become a teacher of English overseas believed in this subtractive religious point of view and tried to influence my identity. I also knew that she and a few other classmates in our MA cohort had organized a Bible study group and met regularly, which made me wonder if these friendly classmates too believed that the religions that influenced my cultural background were false and null and that Christianity was the only legitimate religion to be spread all over the world.

Teaching about Culture or Religion? Classroom Teaching Experience

Many years later, I became a teacher of Japanese as a foreign language as well as a second language teacher educator in the United States. Life struggles had led me to join a Buddhist association based in Japan, although my involvement in daily religious practice is minimal. What follows is my teaching experience at a US university where I previously taught. In my advanced Japanese language class, I tried to incorporate various materials that supplement the reading passages in the textbook in order to engage students in cultural learning. For example, students read a passage about the soothing effects of natural sounds including the chirping of crickets (especially *suzumushi* or bell-ringing crickets, which are often bred and sold for their musical qualities). In order to supplement the cultural knowledge that the Japanese appreciate the sound of crickets in autumn and in order to reinforce the recognition of *kanji* (Chinese characters)—such as the one for "cricket (insect)"—in various authentic written contexts, I looked for some websites on *suzumushi.* One interesting website I found was a Zen Buddhist temple where crickets can be heard chirping not just in autumn but throughout the year. Because of this unique feature, the temple has been nicknamed "Suzumushi Temple." I showed the website to the class and asked the students to identify what the website was about by recognizing some of the *kanji* that they had learned. On the same website, there was also a page explaining the connection between the short life of *suzumushi* and the Zen Buddhist philosophy of living with no-mind (cf. Suzuki, 1993) or becoming free from all forms of clinging and bondage. I briefly introduced this connection to the students in addition to the supplementary activities mentioned above. In retrospect, I wonder if I was providing cultural information or instilling religious belief. If the former, taking up this topic is no doubt legitimate, but if the latter, I wonder if some students might have felt uncomfortable being exposed to a religious view different from theirs. However, is it possible to draw an exact parallel between discussing Japanese religious beliefs in teaching Japanese to mostly American students with a Christian cultural background and talking about Christianity in teaching English to non-Christian students from different cultures?

The above two personal experiences made me think about issues of religion, culture, positionality of the teacher and students, the status of language in a power hierarchy, and its impact on discussions of religious faith in the classroom. I will discuss these issues next.

Faith in the Classroom: Issues of Culture and Disclosure

The first anecdote demonstrates a white English native speaker's attempt to impose a fundamentalist Christian faith on a non-white nonnative English speaker without a strong Christian background. When applied to teaching English, this situation can be interpreted as an extremist stance within the "Christian evangelical position" that views teaching English to speakers of other languages as a righteous activity for the purpose of salvation (Pennycook & Coutand-Marin, 2003). This position exhibits blatant superiority of Christianity over other religions—a colonialist view imposed on non-Christians through teaching English to the inferior Other. The conversion mission overtly takes a subtractive approach to replacing the local faith with Christianity. Using English language teaching as a means for such a coercive evangelical mission seems ethically problematic.

Contrary to the Christian evangelical position, the "Christian service position" recognizes some ethical issues involved in the evangelical mission and places more emphasis on serving the poor and disadvantaged, empowering them by teaching English language skills, and promoting peace (Pennycook & Coutand-Marin, 2003; Snow, 2001). This position acknowledges the problem of the ways in which assimilation of the Other into evangelism is delivered coercively and sometimes covertly. Instead, it encourages Christian English teachers (CET) to disclose their Christian faith and openly talk about it in a non-coercive way in class or other occasions when the topic is relevant (Snow, 2001). Thus, for instance, my classmate could have taken an approach to sharing her faith not by handing me the book to read but by sharing her thoughts and experiences with me in a more candid conversation. Despite this more open and non-coercive approach with consideration and respect for non-Christians, the Christian service position still seems to have the evangelical mission as its underlying principle. In other words, behind the warm and fuzzy approach filled with empathy and compassion (Snow, 2001, citing Brown, 1994), there is a strong conviction that Christianity is the only religion that saves and improves humankind on earth. It is still a colonialist view of salvation and enlightenment, which troubles me coming from a different cultural and religious background.

The issue of disclosure mentioned above raises such questions as when and where teachers should talk about faith and what the relationship is between faith and culture, which goes back to my quandary in discussing a Zen Buddhist conception in my Japanese language class. Snow (2001) refers to the tendencies of CET to take advantage of Christian holidays to discuss Christianity and its gospel message as part of a cultural lesson, especially in countries where the proclamation of Christianity or involvement in Christian evangelistic activities is forbidden. As mentioned earlier in the context of Japan, religious practices are often integrated into everyday social and private life, shaping the concrete and tangible aspects of a culture and people's cultural identities. Thus, discussing cultural products and practices often includes some reference to religious influence. While discussing Christianity in this way would be justifiable, Snow (2001) argues that this approach has a pitfall that "may create or reinforce the unfortunate impression that Christianity and Western culture are inherently linked … a major obstacle to the spread of the gospel in many countries" (p. 72). Whatever the rationale for avoiding the equation between Christianity and Western culture is, this non-essentialist and non-reductionist stance applies to many other cultures and religions, constituting an important perspective for language teachers. Nonetheless, the question of whether teachers' discussing their religious faith openly in the classroom is ethically appropriate or whether faith is best discussed indirectly in the framework of culture remains unanswered.

For this question, Snow (2001) advocates disclosing one's faith in public spaces including the classroom and openly acknowledging one's faith in classroom discussions when it is appropriate. This sounds fair enough from the standpoint of promoting religious diversity and equalities among teachers and students. The field of second language education has advocated for equality across various differences and tried to eliminate inequalities that exist among teachers based on such social categories as race, ethnicity, gender, nationality, age, sexual identity, and native speaker status (e.g., Braine, 1999; Kamhi-Stein, 2004; Lin et al., 2004; Nelson, 1999; Simon-Maeda, 2004). In this spirit, a teacher's religious identity, whether it is Christian, Muslim, Hindu, Buddhist, or something else, should be respected and validated. Thus, perhaps talking about Buddhist principles in my class is perfectly legitimate when the circumstance is appropriate.

But what about talking about Shinto in the classroom? Although this faith is slightly different from major religions of the world in that it is based on nature worship and does not have written scriptures or explicit moral codes, my discussions thus far on classroom talk, disclosures of faith, and the religious identities of teachers can apply to Shinto. But Shinto is much more politically controversial than Buddhism—the faith has become an ideology and was exploited during the first half of the last century to support Japanese imperialism, military aggression, and assimilation of the people in East and Southeast Asia into Imperial Japan. Nonetheless, Shinto rituals have been integrated culturally into the everyday life of the Japanese and its uniqueness can provide Japanese language learners from Christian backgrounds with interesting non-Christian perspectives and an opportunity to appreciate cultural and religious diversity in the world. However, Japanese language classes in North America enroll a significant number of students with Chinese and Korean backgrounds whose grandparents or great grandparents were directly affected by Japanese colonialism in first half of the twentieth century. How, then, do we approach discussing this faith? The identities of Japanese language teachers in North America are located in relative positions in the racial, ethnic, cultural, linguistic, and political power hierarchy. This leads to the importance of recognizing unequal relations of power and relative positionalities in teaching, which I will revisit later.

Pedagogy of Faith: Power and Relative Positionalities

The above discussions can lead to a tentative conclusion that discussing religious faith in a language classroom, either directly in appropriate occasions or as part of cultural learning, is legitimate on the ground that there should be religious freedom for teachers as a basic human right and that it promotes diverse perspectives among students. Then, the next question is how to approach it pedagogically. Obviously, preaching the gospel to the students in a secular classroom with an intention of conversion is inappropriate and unethical. Besides the content of instruction, such an approach of knowledge transmission would be incompatible with the current pedagogical trend—it has been resisted by constructivist and critical perspectives of education (e.g., Paulo Freire's critique of "banking"—depositing knowledge into the empty heads of students with no critical reflection). Instead, it would be necessary for teachers to understand and value the social, cultural, and personal backgrounds of the students as well as their prior knowledge, to engage in a dialogue with the students, and to discuss multiple perspectives through critical reflections on knowledge, old or new (cf. Freire, 1973; Moll, 1992). As for the elements of spirituality that can be discussed in the language classroom, one aspect that all religions seems to promote is the domain of dispositions including mutual understanding, love, compassion, empathy, and peace. This, however, seems quite ironic, because many political and military conflicts both past and present have stemmed from clashes of religious doctrines. Nonetheless, this type of discussion can find alliance with peace education promoted in the field of second language teaching (e.g., Gomes de Matos, 1992).

In discussing these values with students, teachers must be aware of the power relations that might position their students and themselves differently in the racial, ethnic, linguistic, and cultural hierarchy. Failure to understand unequal relations of power would merely reinforce the existing power structure. For instance, it can be argued that a major mission of CET, or any other language teachers with certain religious faiths, is to promote love, peace, and mutual understanding among people with diverse backgrounds and that this can be done by developing skills in intercultural communication (Snow, 1991). These skills are obviously necessary for both students and teachers. For teachers, Snow (1991, and this volume) advocates that they learn the local language of the place where they teach. While this is no doubt useful both for the CET's everyday survival and their classroom teaching, CET acquiring the local language increases their cultural capital that is likely already greater than the students', especially if the teachers belong to a privileged racial, ethnic, or linguistic group. This parallels the ambivalent sentiment felt by a Latino teacher in a dual language (two-way bilingual) program in the United States that the dual language program could inadvertently deprive Latino bilingual speakers of the linguistic advantage that they have enjoyed and instead give more power to Anglophone mainstream students through Spanish instruction (Valdés, 1997). Valdés also points out differential expectations for two linguistic groups—language minority and majority—in dual language education:

> For minority children, the acquisition of English is expected. For mainstream children, the acquisition of a non-English language is enthusiastically applauded. Children are aware of these differences. The reporter who writes a story on a dual-language immersion program and concentrates on how well a mainstream child speaks Spanish while ignoring how well a Spanish-speaking child is learning English sends a very powerful message. (p. 417)

When we apply this case to the situation of CET abroad, the CET's ability to use the local language would be highly praised, giving him/her a heroic status in the local community and making it easier not only to spread the gospel but also to manipulate the local people intentionally or unintentionally. Such a situation stems from unequal relations of power that already exist between whites and people of color, Western culture and non-Western culture, English and other languages, and native speakers of English and nonnative speakers of English. Many CET who go abroad to teach English already bring with them a bagful of privileges, and thus fluency in the local language would further inflate the bag. It is necessary to acknowledge that people are not placed on an equal playing field in the first place. Failing to recognize this reality would only endorse social practices and structures constructed by difference blindness (Kubota, 2004; Larson & Ovando, 2001). This of course does not lead to a conclusion that CET should not learn the local language. Rather, I suggest that teachers develop a critical awareness of the racial, linguistic, and cultural power relations that position people at different levels in the hierarchy and engage in a reflexive practice of using one's power in counter-hegemonic ways.

This leads to my quandary of bringing up cultural/religious issues in a Japanese language class that enrolls students with different racial, ethnic, and cultural backgrounds, including European American, African American, Asian American, and Asian students. Obviously, as a Japanese native, I want students from non-Asian backgrounds to understand perspectives that are different from Christian or Western traditions. At the same time, my social identity has a different status in the power hierarchy vis-à-vis Asian students, which requires a different stance or perspective with regard to the role of Shinto and such historical events as the atomic bombing in Hiroshima and Nagasaki. In a way, my relative identity is similar to what Vandrick (2002) experienced as a missionary kid in postcolonial India. Teachers should acknowledge that their day-to-day practices both reflect and construct their positional or relational identities, which "have to do with how one identifies one's position relative to others" (Holland, Lachicotte, Skinner, & Cain, 1998, p. 127). This also corresponds to the view that one's personal attributes are not the sole determinant of social practice—rather, social practice is the product of the interrelationship between the unequal distribution of various forms of power, resources, or capital, and a structured social space, or field, which organizes such distribution (Bourdieu, 1991; Swartz, 1997). In short, I must acknowledge the fact that my objectified cultural identity is constituted as both a victim and a perpetrator, depending on where I am placed in a specific social space and in the global relations of power and how much capital I have in the specific space.

Conclusion and Unresolved Questions

Based on my personal experiences, I have scrutinized the legitimacy of teaching religious faith in language classrooms and explored some issues of power and relative positionality as a language teacher. My experiences indicate that issues of religious faith and language teaching are not limited to what CET face in their practice. As I was writing this, I learned that a Korean Buddhist nun opened a temple in our area in the US south and invites children from Korea every year for a few weeks to a summer camp to provide them with an immersion experience of American life including learning English. While this seems to be an atypical example of missionary activity compared to the prevalence of Christian evangelists outside of the United States, it provides an interesting set of questions. How does teaching/learning English relate to the promotion of Buddhism in the United States or other English speaking countries? How is the popularity of learning English and living in America exploited in spreading not only Christian but also non-Christian evangelical mission? What positionality does a Korean nun develop in promoting Buddhism in the US south? Would the same set of issues regarding power and privilege that are faced by CET apply to such a missionary activity?

These issues speak to the relativity of ethics according to the location that one's status occupies in the power structure, a location that is not always fixed but has the potential to be transformed. This requires second language professionals to reflect on their own practice within situated ethics rather than based on an illusive notion of universal morality (Corson, 1997; Pennycook, 2001). For instance, rather than assuming that every student has the same sociocultural and historical background and, even worse, shares similar assumptions with the instructor, it is necessary to acknowledge that the positionalities of students in the classroom in relation to race, ethnicity, gender, class, age, and any other social categories might vary and that they would be different from the teacher's. Thus, in approaching various topics in the classroom, including religious faith, teachers need to critically reflect on the social, cultural, political, and historical factors that shape their and students' views and identities and to engage in a dialogue that both respects and interrogates multiple standpoints.

To apply situated ethics to my own experience with my classmate in the MA program, her acknowledgment of the coexistence of multiple faiths as part of my cultural identity, or simply her awareness of the impact of religious traditions on one's cultural identity, would have been necessary in order to prevent the emotional blow caused by the perceived denial of cultural identity. In fact, the reason I remember this incident so clearly was because it was quite shocking and psychologically painful.

In the globalized world where many perspectives, faiths, and beliefs interact in dynamic ways, it seems worthwhile for CET to explore and affirm an additive, rather than subtractive, religious perspective. This stance is comparable to the notion of additive bilingualism advocated for teaching culturally and linguistically diverse students (Cummins, 2000) or pluralization of English for speakers of underprivileged varieties of English (Canagarajah, 1999) but it goes beyond simple pluralism. By additive religious perspective, I mean maintaining one's religious faith while affirming and critically understanding multiple views and practices that shape people's social and cultural identities, a view that transcends mere religious tolerance or sensitivity. As such, the additive perspective is different from the apolitical "multiplicity of perspectives" position, as seen in a liberal approach to multicultural education, which cannot escape the acceptance of all views, including racist or any other hostile ones, as equally valid (Nieto, 1995). The additive approach encourages CET to affirm religious and cultural backgrounds of their students, while reflecting critically how teaching English is related to Anglo Christian hegemony and how political and military conflicts around the world might be implicated in religious, cultural, and racial arrogance among the self or the other. In engaging in such critical reflection and situated ethics, teachers need to acknowledge relational identities and positionalities as I have discussed.

The idea of additive religious perspectives I am promoting here is partly influenced by the religious tolerance of Buddhism, which is part of my cultural identity. On the one hand, I feel I can legitimately promote this idea from the relatively marginalized space I occupy in the power structure. On the other hand, by promoting this, I wonder if I am imposing my own cultural and religious view onto various groups of people. Am I suggesting a kind of universal principle that may not go hand in hand with situated ethics?

References

Bodhi, B. (1993). Tolerance and diversity. Buddhist Publication Society. Retrieved September 16, 2008, from www.vipassana.com/resources/bodhi/tolerance_and_diversity.php.

Bourdieu, P. (1991). *Language and symbolic power*, trans. G. Raymond and M. Adamson. Cambridge, MA: Harvard University Press.

Braine, G. (Ed.) (1999). *Non-native educators in English language teaching.* Mahwah, NJ: Lawrence Erlbaum.

Brown, D. (1994). *Teaching by principles: An interactive approach to language pedagogy.* Englewood Cliffs, NJ: Prentice-Hall Regents.

Canagarajah, S. (1999). *Resisting linguistic imperialism in English teaching.* Oxford, UK: Oxford University Press.

Corson, D. (1997). Critical realism: An emancipatory philosophy for applied linguistics? *Applied Linguistics, 18*(2), 166–188.

Cummins, J. (2000). *Language, power and pedagogy: Bilingual children in the crossfire.* Clevedon, UK: Multilingual Matters.

Freire, P. (1973). *Education for critical consciousness.* New York: Seabury.

Gomes de Matos, F. (1992). Peace through TESOL: A practical approach. *TESOL Matters, 2*(2), 14.

Holland, D., Lachicotte, Jr., W., Skinner, D., & Cain, C. (1998). *Identity and agency in cultural worlds.* Cambridge, MA: Harvard University Press.

Kamhi-Stein, L. D. (Ed.) (2004). *Learning and teaching from experience: Perspectives on nonnative English-speaking professionals.* Ann Arbor: University of Michigan Press.

Kubota, R. (2004). Critical multiculturalism and second language education. In B. Norton, & K. Toohey (Eds.), *Critical pedagogies and language learning* (pp. 30–52). Cambridge, UK: Cambridge University Press.

Larson, C. L., & Ovando, C. J. (2001). *The color of bureaucracy: The politics of equity in multicultural school communities.* Belmont, CA: Wadsworth/Thomson Learning.

Lin, A., Grant, R., Kubota, R., Motha, S., Sachs, G. T., Vandrick, S., & Wong, S. (2004). Women faculty of color in TESOL: Theorizing our lived experiences. *TESOL Quarterly, 38*(3), 487–504.

Moll, L. C. (1992). Funds of knowledge for teaching: Using a qualitative approach to connect homes and classrooms. *Theory into Practice, 31*(2), 132–141.

Nelson, C. (1999). Sexual identities in ESL: Queer theory and classroom inquiry. *TESOL Quarterly, 33*(3), 371–391.

Nieto, S. (1995). From brown heroes and holidays to assimilationist agendas: Reconsidering the critiques of multicultural education. In C. E. Sleeter, & P. L. McLaren (Eds.), *Multicultural education, critical pedagogy, and the politics of difference* (pp. 191–220). Albany: State University of New York Press.

Pennycook, A. (2001). *Critical applied linguistics: A critical introduction.* Mahwah, NJ: Lawrence Erlbaum.

Pennycook, A., & Coutand-Marin, S. (2003). Teaching English as a missionary language. *Discourse: Studies in the Cultural Politics of Education, 24*(3), 337–353.

Reader, I., Andreasen, E., & Stefánsson, F. (1993). *Japanese religions: Past and present.* Honolulu: University of Hawaii Press.

Simon-Maeda, A. (2004). The complex construction of professional identities: Female EFL educators in Japan speak out. *TESOL Quarterly, 38*(3), 405–436.

Snow, D. (2001). *English teaching as Christian mission.* Scottdale, PA: Herald Press.

Suzuki, D. T. (1993). *The Zen doctrine of no-mind: The significance of the sutra of Hui-neng (Wei-lang).* York Beach, ME: Samuel Weiser.

Swartz, D. (1997). *Culture and power: The sociology of Pierre Bourdieu.* Chicago: University of Chicago Press.

Valdés, G. (1997). Dual-language immersion programs: A cautionary note concerning the education of language-minority students. *Harvard Educational Review, 67*(3), 391–426.

Vandrick, S. (2002). ESL and the colonial legacy: A teacher faces her "missionary kid" past. In V. Zamel, & R. Spack (Eds.), *Enriching ESOL pedagogy* (pp. 411–422). Mahwah, NJ: Lawrence Erlbaum.

24 Spiritual Lessons Learned from a Language Teacher

Christopher A. Bradley

The exploration of possible links between spirituality and second language pedagogy has been little discussed in Applied Linguistics circles. I hope in this chapter to provide a rationale for such an endeavor. To this end, I shall first attempt to distinguish between the terms "spirituality" and "religion." After referring the reader to a few of the studies related to spirituality in the fields of medicine, psychology, mainstream education, and ELT, I'll examine data from my case study of Julie,[1] who until recently taught English in Japan. I conclude this chapter with thoughts on how a spirituality based upon compassion, such as that held by my interviewee, can help language educators gain fresh perspectives on teaching, learning, as well as cultural and linguistic imperialism.

Defining Spirituality and Religion

In the spirit of sages who compassionately but resolutely oppose coercive means of persuasion (e.g., Hanh, 1998), let me begin this part of the chapter by stating categorically my conviction that research into possible links between spirituality and ELT must never be used as a pretext for proselytizing. I contend, though, that the word "spirituality" need not automatically conjure up images of oppressive fundamentalism. Glazer (1999) summed up a consequence of the strong reluctance of some Americans to examine links between spirituality and education thus: "Out of this fear of imposition, however, a great tragedy has taken place in our public schools: the wholesale abandonment of the inner world" (p. 2).

To further dispel notions that spirituality is inevitably linked with religious extremism, I think it important from the outset to distinguish between spirituality and religion. In my own research and writing, I have adopted the following definition of spirituality: "the eternal human yearning to be connected with something larger than our own egos" (Palmer, 2003, p. 377). Hence, according to Palmer, following a prescriptive faith or even believing in a divine being need not necessarily be prerequisites to spirituality. Elucidating a view of religion differing widely from the aforementioned definition of spirituality, Campbell (1991) averred that religion "begins with a sense of wonder and awe and the attempt to tell stories that will connect us to God. Then it becomes a set of theological works in which everything is reduced to a code, to a creed" (pp. 173–174).

I have, however, tried to give Julie and my other dissertation participants the autonomy to define "spirituality" and "religion" as they so choose, particularly given that in the minds of most people surveyed by Hill and his colleagues (2000) these concepts overlap somewhat.

Spirituality, Medicine, and the Social Sciences

Given the restrictions on word length for this chapter, a thorough literature review that is warranted by this topic is impossible. Below is a summary of a few of the more salient studies from a number of disciplines.

In a particularly revealing experiment, participants in experimental groups consisting of Tibetan Buddhist monks trained in meditative techniques exhibited low levels of anxiety, as well as immune systems that were far stronger than the norm. By contrast, control group participants who had received little or no training in meditation did not experience these physiological and psychological benefits (Begley, 2007).

As to mainstream education and spirituality, some scholars have, through the lens of transformative learning theory, analyzed their data on how North American teachers of adults, as well as tertiary educators, perceive that their spiritual beliefs relate directly to their teaching (e.g., Cranton & Carusetta, 2004; Tisdell & Tolliver, 2003). The founder of this framework has argued that learning becomes transformative when students' deeply held assumptions are challenged and changed through a process of critical reflection and dialogue (Mezirow, 2000).

As to articles on spirituality and ELT, these have been confined mainly to the raging debate on possible connections between Christian missionary activities in English teaching and imperialism (e.g., Edge 2003; Pennycook & Makoni, 2005; Purgason, 2004; Varghese & Johnston, 2007). Other than work by the latter two authors, who explored the views on missionary work and imperialism of 10 Christian evangelical L2 teachers in an MA (TESL) program, the articles addressing this controversy have primarily been based upon literature reviews rather than on empirical research. To my knowledge, no published data-based research exists on the spiritual beliefs and classroom practices of L2 educators adhering to a variety of belief systems. This chapter represents a fledgling attempt on my part to begin addressing this yawning gap in the literature. In so doing, I offer, through the conceptual lens of transformative learning theory, a preliminary analysis of data from the following case study.

Learning from Julie: A Case Study

Methodology and Research Questions

I asked Julie to recount her life story because, other than longitudinal ethnographies, the analysis of participants' life narratives has been one of the most effective ways for specialists in transformative learning to evaluate the changes taking place in people over long periods of time (Taylor, 2000). At the time that I conducted my interviews with Julie, she resided and taught in a city almost

700 kilometers from my home. Thus, due to the prohibitive cost that would have entailed any observations of Julie's classrooms, I have determined that for the preliminary analysis of data outlined in this chapter, it is sufficient to let the interview data stand alone.

It should be noted, too, that efforts to generalize the findings of a case study to a larger population often deny the intrinsic richness and complexity of a given case (Stake, 2005). Rather, my more modest hope for readers of this chapter is that if I describe selected interview data in a sufficiently rich fashion (Davis, 1995), some educators will be able to transfer relevant findings of this case study to their own personal and pedagogical contexts (Lincoln & Guba, 1985).

The two research questions that have thus far emerged from my case study data are as follows:

1. What were the major turning points in the participant's spiritual journey?
2. How did the participant perceive that her core beliefs, which have evolved from these turning points, intersect with her pedagogical practices?

I endeavored to rigorously code Julie's interview data according to emergent themes stemming from the above research questions (Miles & Huberman, 1994). I shall now summarize my preliminary interpretation of this taxonomy.

Findings and Implications: Introduction to Julie

Julie, an EFL educator who lived in Japan for over two decades before embarking in 2008 on a different phase in her life and career in another nation, began teaching in Japan shortly after graduating from an American university. After working at a private language institute, a middle school, and a senior high school, she obtained a Master's degree in language teaching, which enabled her to secure full-time employment at the tertiary level. She then completed a doctoral program in second language education. A lesbian who is open about her sexual orientation, Julie was active in various movements in Japan promoting human rights and progressive social change.

Spirituality and Compassion

Space limitations for this chapter preclude a more thorough explanation of my findings of the first research question related to the turning points in Julie's spiritual life, particularly those of her early years. Suffice it to say that while attending her family's mainstream Protestant church as a child and teenager, she felt that neither she nor most of the members of her church had any profound, life-changing experiences with the divine. By contrast, although she deplored the exclusivist views held by some members of more conservative American churches, she nonetheless admired the genuine joy she felt emanated from many of these same individuals.

After coming to Japan from the USA in her late twenties to teach English, Julie explored a number of non-Christian spiritual traditions, but was disenchanted with the sexism and homophobia that she felt were prevalent in many of them. She eventually embraced a particular discipline of yoga in which she felt fully accepted both as a woman and as a lesbian. While embarking on this spiritual path, Julie underwent *shaktipat*, an awakening of spiritual energy, and a transformation of her outlook on life. Julie described the profound manner in which *shaktipat* affected her:

JULIE: I was falling in *love*, you know that state when you're newly infatuated ... You look at somebody sitting on the train, and you think, "Ah ... they're so cute looking" and "Oh, this guy is so beautiful."

Addressing Christian language teachers in particular, Smith and Carvill (2000), have, by encouraging educators to practice hospitality and empathetic intercultural understanding, outlined practical ways that L2 educators can cultivate compassion. Compassion is said to be a universal value amongst followers of many faiths and philosophies (Armstrong, 2001). By focusing on compassion as the overarching ethic of missionary work, Smith and Carvill have sought to challenge the more traditional view of some that missionaries should maintain as their primary foci the conversion of souls and the promotion of imperialistic agendas. Hence, perhaps language educators of all creeds could consider learning from the advice proffered by Smith and Carvill, as well as from the compassion practiced by Julie.

Spirituality and Classroom Pedagogy

Julie described her spiritual discipline thus:

JULIE: What yoga *is* ... the word means "union" right, so it's related to the word "yoke" where you yoke two oxen together ... the purpose of yoga is to experience yourself as connected to everything ... as not different from outside forces, as not different from other people, as not different from God.[2]

Regarding the second research question of this study that concerns how spiritual beliefs impact upon teaching, Julie also told of the joy she felt in connecting students with each other. For instance, if she knew that two students in a given class that she taught were interested in the same genre of music, she encouraged them to get to know each other better.

Palmer (1999) wrote of the conviction shared by many of his readers that the best teachers "connect themselves to their students, their subjects to each other, and everyone to the subject being studied" (p. 27). Julie's attempts to foster ties amongst her learners appeared to be a direct expression of her adherence to yoga which, as Julie noted, is a philosophy founded upon connection. Language teachers could perhaps learn from Julie by endeavoring to promote a relaxed and cooperative atmosphere amongst their learners and by interesting them in meaningful materials related to global issues and values education. The judicious use of such materials can transport language learners beyond the four walls of an otherwise staid language classroom by raising their awareness about social justice and human rights (Brown, 2007).

Spirituality and Outward Appearances

Julie recounted a fascinating narrative regarding the oft-told maxim that first appearances can be deceiving. At a weekend retreat she attended with other adherents of her particular discipline of yoga, Julie and the other participants were asked to take a walk in the woods and to reflect upon what they observed. During this saunter, Julie came across the incongruous sight of snails that appeared to be perched one or more meters up in trees. Doing a double take at this unusual scene, she checked again, and saw that the snails were indeed there.

The aforementioned incident reminded Julie of her doctoral research in which she interviewed some Japanese high school students who asserted that they were bored during their mainstream English courses. Many of these informants also claimed that they neither spoke English nor volunteered to answer questions. She held, however, that as with the surprising location of the snails at her retreat, Julie's study participants astonished her. That is to say, despite their apparent lack of motivation in their high school English classes, her interviewees were boldly seeking out non-Japanese interlocutors in many different contexts and spending extra money to take lessons at privately run conversation schools, where they would chat in an uninhibited manner. Therefore, Julie tried not to make dismissive assumptions about her own college-level learners, for she felt that such speculations would be based upon shallow generalizations and stereotypes about Japanese university students. In the same way, perhaps Julie's experiences can encourage language educators not to judge their learners' motivation based solely upon their outward comportment, but instead to view them as complex individuals who bring unique needs and desires to the classroom.

Discussion

As we have seen, Julie's beliefs about language teaching are informed by a sense of personal transformation, compassion, the forging of connections, as well as her desire to refrain from making judgments based upon outward appearances. My main purpose in this chapter has been to begin to suggest to language teachers in general the impact that spirituality can have upon language pedagogy. Since this volume includes discussions of possible relationships between imperialism and missionary endeavors in ELT, I now devote a small amount of space to delineating how some of Julie's words and actions might serve as guideposts to Christian English language teachers, particularly those who view themselves as having a sense of mission.

Some specialists in Applied Linguistics have pointed out a number of explicit historical connections between colonialist projects and certain missionary undertakings related to ELT (e.g., Edge, 2003; Pennycook & Makoni, 2005). Although they acknowledge the disturbing nature of various imperialist missionary projects described by the above-mentioned writers, Varghese and Johnston (2007) have also criticized as essentialist some aspects of this scholarship. Based upon their interviews of 10 Christian language teacher trainees, the authors painted complex and detailed portraits of the inner conflicts of their participants, who were considering the pros and cons of using ELT as a tool for missionary work. The multifaceted feelings of their participants prompted Varghese and Johnston to call for more dialogue and less stereotyping among all parties in the long-running debate in TESOL circles vis-à-vis possible links between L2 missionary work and imperialism.

It is my sincere hope that the words and actions of Julie underscored in this chapter can provide a catalyst for the furthering of such a dialogue. In this vein, I believe that Julie, by her apparent rejection of all forms of prejudice, as well as through her compassion, may be an exemplar of transformative learning (Mezirow, 2000). That is to say, because of her lifelong spiritual transformation and her pronounced love of humanity, she could potentially inspire many Christian L2 missionary educators to reject the imperialist ideology of some ELT missionary enterprises delineated by various scholars (e.g., Pennycook & Makoni, 2005). Such educators could perhaps embrace a more inclusive, compassionate view of the word "missionary," such as that outlined by Smith and Carvill (2000) and explicated earlier in this chapter.

In sum, whether or not we as language educators consider ourselves to be spiritual beings, it could plausibly be argued that when we are able to cultivate compassion in our classrooms, as well as the connections amongst learners, educators, and materials that Palmer (1999) has described, language teachers and students alike will reap the benefits.

Notes

1. In order to protect the anonymity of my participant, I have employed a pseudonym and, when necessary, disguised other details of her life narrative. To this end, too, I have done my utmost in the preparation of this chapter to adhere to all *TESOL Quarterly* informed consent guidelines for qualitative research (2008). After carefully reading earlier drafts of this chapter, Julie suggested changes to my occasionally inaccurate interpretations of her interview data, which fulfilled to my satisfaction ethical guidelines related to member-checking (Lincoln & Guba, 1985). Moreover, I hasten to point out here that Julie is one of 10 participants in a larger multiple case study that is part of my ongoing doctoral dissertation.
2. I have employed the following transcription conventions: *italics* mark an emphasis (e.g., raised voice pitch, quality, and/or volume); dots (...) between utterances indicate a pause in speaking. For example, each dot represents a one-second pause, so three dots would represent a three-second pause.

References

Armstrong, K. (2001). *The battle for God.* New York: Ballantine Books.

Begley, S. (2007). *Train your mind, change your brain: How a new science reveals our extraordinary power to transform ourselves.* New York: Ballantine.

Brown, H. D. (2007). *Teaching by principles: An interactive approach to language pedagogy* (3rd ed.). White Plains, NY: Pearson Education.

Campbell, J. (1991). *The power of myth.* New York: Anchor Books.

Cranton, P., & Carusetta, E. (2004). Developing authenticity as a transformative process. *Journal of Transformative Education, 2*(4), 276–293.

Davis, K. A. (1995). Qualitative theory and methods in applied linguistics research. *TESOL Quarterly, 29*(3), 427–453.

Edge, J. (2003). Imperial troopers and servants of the Lord: A vision of TESOL for the 21st century. *TESOL Quarterly, 37*(4), 701–709.

Glazer, S. (1999). Introduction. In S. Glazer (Ed.), *The heart of learning: Spirituality in education* (pp. 1–14). New York: Jeremy P. Tarcher/Putnam.

Hanh, T. N. (with Eppsteiner, F.) (1998). *Interbeing: Fourteen principles for engaged Buddhism* (3rd ed.). Berkeley, CA: Parallax.

Hill, P. C., Pargament, K. I., Wood, R. W., McCullough, M. E., Swyers, J. P., Larson, D. B., et al. (2000). Conceptualizing religion and spirituality: Points of communality, points of departure. *Journal for the Theory of Social Behavior, 30*(1), 51–77.

Lincoln, Y., & Guba, E. (1985). *Naturalistic inquiry.* Beverly Hills, CA: Sage.

Mezirow, J. (2000). Learning to think like an adult: Core concepts of transformation theory. In J. Mezirow, & Associates (Eds.), *Learning as transformation: Critical perspectives on a theory in progress* (pp. 3–34). San Francisco, CA: Jossey-Bass.

Miles, M. B., & Huberman, A. M. (1994). *Qualitative data analysis: An expanded sourcebook* (2nd ed.). Thousand Oaks, CA: Sage.

Palmer, P. (1999). The grace of great things: Reclaiming the sacred in knowing, teaching, and learning. In S. Glazer (Ed.), *The heart of learning: Spirituality in education* (pp. 15–32). New York: Jeremy P. Tarcher/Putnam.

Palmer, P. (2003). Teaching with heart and soul: Reflections on spirituality in teacher education. *Journal of Teacher Education, 54*(5), 376–385.

Pennycook, A., & Makoni, S. (2005). The modern mission: The language effects of Christianity. *Journal of Language, Identity, and Education, 4*(2), 137–155.

Purgason, K. (2004). A clearer picture of the "Servants of the Lord." *TESOL Quarterly, 38*(4), 711–713.

Smith, D., & Carvill, B. (2000). *The gift of the stranger: Faith, hospitality, and foreign language learning.* Grand Rapids, MI: Eerdmans.

Stake, R. (2005). Qualitative case studies. In N. Denzin, & Y. Lincoln (Eds.), *The Sage Handbook of Qualitative Research* (3rd ed., pp. 443–466). Thousand Oaks, CA: Sage.

Taylor, E. W. (2000). Analyzing research on transformative learning theory. In J. Mezirow, & Associates (Eds.), *Learning as transformation: Critical perspectives on a theory in progress* (pp. 285–328). San Francisco, CA: Jossey-Bass.

TESOL (2008). *Informed consent policy statement and release.* Alexandria, VA: TESOL. Retrieved September 11, 2008, from www.tesol.org/s_tesol/sec_document.asp?CID=476&DID=1014.

Tisdell, E., & Tolliver, D. (2003). Claiming a sacred face: The role of spirituality and cultural identity in adult higher education. *Journal of Transformative Education, 1*(4), 368–392.

Varghese, M., & Johnston, B. (2007). Evangelical Christians and English language teaching. *TESOL Quarterly, 41*(1), 5–31.

25 The Spiritual Ecology of Second Language Pedagogy

David I. Smith

Current moves away from the discourse of method and toward ecological perspectives on learning invite consideration of how belief and spirituality affect the ecology of the language classroom. The shift also suggests that faith and spirituality could affect pedagogy, and not merely aims or motivations. This chapter explores these implications, considering in particular how Christian belief and spirituality can influence thinking about second language pedagogy.

Autobiographical Reflections

In my first school my classroom was next door to the classroom where Religious Education—compulsory in British schools—was taught. Teenage students would periodically march directly from Religion to French or German, or vice versa. Religious Education was valued, and taught by talented colleagues. I began to wonder about my students' overall learning experience. Next door they grappled with God, salvation, life, death, abortion, euthanasia, pluralism, and purpose. In my room they repeated set phrases and learned how to order food, change money, and talk inconsequentially about the weekend. Even allowing for differing purposes in different curriculum areas and students' limited facility in the new language, the contrast seemed sharp. If my colleagues were succeeding, must my class not seem shallow and trivial? If my classes were successful, were learners inferring that spiritual questions are irrelevant to other cultures and speakers of other languages?

There were signs that there was more afoot than my own overworked imagination. During a French class a 12-year-old student raised a hand. I expected a query concerning French usage. Instead she startled me by asking how the Bible could be true given what they had been taught in history class. Suspecting a diversionary tactic designed to postpone labor, I sidestepped the question, only to be hit with a follow-up: "Sir, are you afraid of dying?" Her friend joined the conversation: "We are, we talk about it all the time." Such experiences suggested another way of framing the question that was bothering me: how should I teach students who did not leave their spirits at the door and turn into the well-behaved information-processing brains familiar from SLA research, but instead brought their personal complexity into my teaching space?

My own Christian faith probably affected my receptivity to such incidents, encouraging me to reflect on them and influencing my responses. My beliefs led me to think that students' spirituality was an important and all too often stymied part of their personhood, and an important element of the target culture. I felt that the thinly disguised consumerism of communicative textbooks was ultimately too unsatisfying to motivate deeply. I believed that spiritual matters were not adequately dealt with by relegating them to private preference as if they were of little more consequence than a liking for strawberries (a matter more likely to be labored in textbooks than any spiritual question). I began to attend to ethical dimensions of the communicative interactions taking place in my language classes, exploring the boundaries between role play and untruthfulness (Smith, 1997, 2007). I introduced biographical narrative in early stages of language learning—not the vapid mini-narratives of shopping and parties that my teaching materials already provided, but stories of people who hoped, wept, suffered, chose, believed, died (Smith & Dobson, 1999; Smith & Osborn, 2007). I wanted students to encounter target language speakers as real human beings (a value-laden, tendentious concept if ever there was one). In all of this, my Christian beliefs functioned neither as a source of private special revelation about language learning, nor as a linear determinant of divinely sanctioned teaching practices, but as a frame and orientation, a source of hunches about what might most honor the personhood of my learners and thereby enhance their learning, and what strategies might best fit my own developing sense of self as a teacher.

I offer these autobiographical reflections to foreground a simple point: spiritual convictions are more existentially relevant to both learners and teachers than much modern theorizing has assumed. Learners come to class not only with language aptitude, affective filters, language acquisition devices, and the like, but also as Christians, Muslims, Agnostics, Atheists, etc., or representing more hybrid spiritual constructions. I now teach at an American college. Recent surveys of American college students suggest that over half see finding their purpose in life as an important reason for entering higher education, more than a third say that integrating spirituality into their life is essential or very important, and around a quarter expect that their experiences during their college or university education will strengthen their religious convictions (*Chronicle of Higher Education*, August 26, 2005, Vol. LII, No. 1). For both teachers and learners, such identity factors are likely to influence attitudes and behaviors in classroom settings. I experienced this in my own classroom from when I began teaching, yet I soon found that such factors had been given scant attention in professional literature on language education.

Here I will focus on one neglected aspect of this broad area of concern. Where the role of religion in language education has been discussed, the focus has (understandably) tended to be on the relationship between language education and religious communication, such as the use of ESL for evangelistic purposes or the use of the Bible in ESL. Such discussion is necessary, but limited. Here I am more interested in the connection between belief and pedagogical vision, a connection that may be active whether or not identifiably religious discourse is present in the act of teaching or learning. In other words, does faith affect only the *ends* to which language teaching is turned or the choice to include religious *language* in the classroom, or might it also affect the shaping of language *pedagogy*? This still leaves various issues in play (curriculum materials, classroom relationships, institutional constraints, etc.). My main focus here will be on the design of classroom language learning activities.

The Shrinking World of "Approach"

It is instructive to chart the fate of Edward Anthony's influential characterization of pedagogy (Anthony, 1963). Anthony was originally attempting to define "method" more closely, a concept now in disrepair (Brumfit, 1991; Kumaravadivelu, 1994, 2003; Larsen-Freeman, 1991). What matters for now is his notion of "approach." In Anthony's terminology, "techniques" are discrete actions—a classroom visitor sees mostly techniques as the teacher arranges chairs, asks a question, writes on a chalkboard. Techniques are not random, but patterned. A constellation of techniques is what Anthony termed "method" and others rebaptized "design" (Richards & Rodgers, 1982). This pattern in turn depends on assumptions and beliefs; it seeks to realize a certain vision. Anthony (1963, pp. 63–64) referred to "assumptions dealing with the nature of language and the nature of language teaching and learning," and termed them an "approach."

Anthony (1963, p. 64) describes an approach as a "point of view, a philosophy, an article of faith—something which one believes but cannot necessarily prove." This suggests broad avenues for exploration—an apparently open-ended range of unproven beliefs. In later discussions, however, the contents of an "approach" became rhetorically restricted to specifically *theoretical* assumptions (with a persistent tendency to conflate "belief" and "theory"), and even more specifically to theories in linguistics and psycholinguistics (Anthony & Norris, 1969; Byrnes, 1991; Richards & Rodgers, 1986; Strain, 1986). In retrospect, this seems a remarkably narrow interpretation of the role that "philosophies" or "articles of faith" play in language pedagogy. It is, however, entirely consonant with the impulses toward technical control, suspicion of non-positivist discourses, and top-down application of scientifically sanctioned theory associated with method talk (Pennycook, 1989).

In the more pluralist atmosphere of life after method, ecological metaphors are advanced as alternatives to the technical metaphors of the method era (Kramsch, 2003; Larsen-Freeman, 1997; Leather & van Dam, 2003; Tudor, 2003). The metaphor of the classroom as an ecology focuses on how multiple factors interact to create and sustain a particular local equilibrium. Any metaphor is prey to the winds of ideology; ecological metaphors can be pressed into the service of a new reductionism (Pennycook, 2004), seeking to treat language learning naturalistically as reducible to biological processes (Fettes, 2002; Lemke, 2002). Other accounts, however, suggest more expansive possibilities—a move from closed-system analyses to examining learners' interactions with all facets of their environment on the basis of "minimal a priori assumptions about what can be ignored" (Van Dam, 2002, p. 237). This suggests that ecological metaphors need not be pushed in reductive directions, but could encourage attention to a wider range of contextual factors, including power, identity, and spirituality.

The idea that everything might be relevant can be too unfocused to be helpful; before exploring examples, therefore, I will sketch some areas of inquiry that might prove fruitful. In doing so, I want to point to some broader possibilities than those typically canvassed in debates defending (Purgason, 2004; Snow, 2001; Stevick, 1996/1997) or attacking (Edge, 1996; Griffith, 2004; Pennycook & Coutand-Marin, 2003; Pennycook & Makoni, 2005; Phillipson & Skutnabb-Kangas, 1996) the relationship between language teaching and Christian mission. Important as that topic is, it can foster a narrow focus on questions of conversion that obscures other necessary discussions about how faith and spirituality interact with teaching practices, suggesting that as long as the gospel is preached or not preached, language pedagogy itself can proceed with business as usual. There is more than this at stake.

Hall (2002) suggests four contexts of inquiry in research into language and culture—sociocultural structures, institutional contexts, communicative practices, and individual experiences. These domains offer a helpful basic framework for thinking about where the role of religious belief and spiritual conviction in language learning might be investigated.

Sociocultural structures include "large-scale, society-wide worldviews" that "encompass beliefs, values and attitudes towards social phenomena such as group identities … and intergroup relations … personhood and freedom" (Hall, 2002, pp. 175–176). Here there is no room to imagine that only linguistic theory is pertinent. The question raised here is how basic spiritual orientations and frameworks (Taylor, 1989) and the way life is experienced and approached in their light might affect approaches to language education. As Pannenberg notes (1984, p. 16), "a particular type of piety involves not only a specific theological focus and corresponding life-styles but also a particular conception of the human world, the world of human experience." Some published work (Kemp, 1994; Mendelsohn, 1999; Smith, 2000, 2002; Smith & Carvill, 2000; Snow, 2001; Stevick, 1990) has examined how such theologically rooted conceptions might influence language teaching approaches; more is needed.

Hall's examples of *institutional contexts* include churches and special-interest groups; faith-based schools and universities should be added. Given the widespread existence of religious institutional contexts for language learning, this is a second obvious area of inquiry regarding possible relationships between Christian belief and the practice of language education. There has been some discussion of the interaction (positive and negative) between religious institutional contexts and language education (Baquedano-López, 2003; Farr, 2000; Foster, 1997; Pritchard & Loulidi, 1994; Warschauer, 1998), but the literature is very limited.

Hall's fourth domain (I will return to the third) focuses on *individual experience*, and how individuals construe and negotiate with their contexts, particularly in relation to the formation of personal identity. Recent interest in identity in relation to language learning (Norton, 1997, 2000; Vandrick, 1997) is pertinent here. Faith and spirituality are so deeply connected with questions of identity for such an overwhelming proportion of the human race (and continue to be so, causing rethinking of once-confident theories of progressive secularization (Berger, 1999)) that excluding them is myopic. Again, some existing literature deals with religious aspects of the identity of language teachers and learners (Bradley, 2005; Foster, 1997; Johnson, 2003; Platt, 2005; Scovel, 1999; Varghese & Johnston, 2007), but it is sparse.

I have reviewed this literature in more detail elsewhere (Smith & Osborn, 2007); here I focus on Hall's third domain, "communicative activities and language socialization practices" (2002, p. 174). *Interpersonal language practices* might seem less open to questions of faith and spirituality. However, in Hall's model the four domains are interconnected; communicative practices are to be understood in relationship to sociocultural, institutional, and individual factors—the aim is to "identify, describe, interpret and ultimately explain the locally situated meanings" of such practices (p. 188). This returns us to questions that opened this chapter: how might Christian (or other) beliefs influence classroom communicative practices? I will briefly explore an example, focusing on the teacher's pedagogical choices (which, of course, underdetermine learner interpretations and appropriations).

Humility and Self-Assertion

Consider two teachers teaching the use of adjectives. The first draws from Moskowitz's (1978) humanistic pedagogy. In one activity, each student must imagine giving a public speech. The stranger chairing the event wants the speaker to draft a complimentary self-description for the purpose of introduction. Students are told that "they don't have to be modest but should point out all of the terrific things about themselves and be honest" (Moskowitz, 1978, p. 82). The prepared introductions are brought to class, exchanged, and read aloud.

The second teacher uses *Charis Deutsch* (Baker et al., 1998), a resource for intermediate German classes. In one activity, students are given various adjectives that describe personal character. They are asked to circle words that others have used to describe them, draw a rectangle round those they would use to describe themselves, and draw a triangle round aspirational qualities. The sorted vocabulary is then inserted into a provided framework that enables students to construct and share a poem about their identity. Finally, having also worked with a simple narrative of Dietrich Bonhoeffer's life, they read his prison poem *Who am I?* In the poem, Bonhoeffer records others' positive assessments of his spiritual state, then his own contrasting perceptions of his yearning, sick, exhausted, lonely self. He wrestles with the contrast—am I a hypocrite?—and finally leaves the question of who he really is in God's hands.

The two activities have superficial resemblances—both seek to engage the learner's sense of self and encourage reflection on values and character qualities. Their ethos, however, differs radically. Moskowitz wants learners to realize that "we all know what we need and what is right for us. We just have to tune into ourselves to find the answers. We are our own gurus" (1978, p. 188). Her approach consistently has learners talking about themselves, explicitly excludes expression of negative feelings, and rejects self-denial (pp. 2, 25). The activity described is aptly titled "Me power." Emotional transparency, sensitivity, and self-exploration are the cardinal virtues fostered, framed by a basic affirmation of inner goodness and self-sufficiency and a firm belief that the answers to questions of identity lie within the individual self.

The second example came from a Christian curriculum project concerned with spiritual and moral development across the curriculum. The Bonhoeffer poem is explicitly suspicious of the public praise that the "Me power" exercise courts, and also of over-reliance on gazing into one's own self as the path to truth. Both suspicions are rooted in Christian traditions that emphasize humility and the deceitfulness of the human heart, and value frank confession as a step toward healing. The activities encourage students to reflect on discrepancies between present character and character ideals, and encourages a more sober form of self-examination. Though there is a focus on selfhood, students do not merely talk about themselves, but encounter a voice from the target culture. In the design of this activity, the biblical theme of love of neighbor and hospitality to the stranger played a role in motivating both the attempt to hear the voice of a real cultural other and the use of narrative highlighting the other as partaking of suffering, courage, and spiritual concern (Smith & Carvill, 2000). An underlying aim is to challenge students to face spiritual issues as articulated by target culture voices. The single sentence of God-talk at the end of Bonhoeffer's poem openly signals its religious background, but to focus on that would miss the broader issue; that line could be omitted without effacing the clash of values between the two learning activities, the one promoting unconditional self-affirmation and self-reliance, the other promoting humility and caution concerning praise from others. Teacher identity and institutional context may condition a choice for the one or the other (or for a further option).

This underlying contrast also surfaces in theoretical discussions. Consider, for instance, this claim:

> you are proficient in a language to the extent that you possess it, make it your own, bend it to your will, assert yourself through it rather than simply submit to the dictates of its form ... Real proficiency is when you are able to take possession of the language, turn it to your advantage, and make it real for you. This is what mastery means.
>
> (Widdowson, 1994, p. 384)

Kramsch has articulated a similar approach, arguing that learners must seize the power of discourse, *possess* the new language, and impose their own meanings. This leads to conflict between voices present in the classroom, a conflict that is to be encouraged, for "[t]his struggle is the educational enterprise per se" (Kramsch, 1993, p. 239). Both accounts suggest a form of aggressive self-assertion as a normative basis for learning, and are thus far from value neutral in relation to spiritual convictions about selfhood.

It is, I believe, true that learners must make the new language their own in the sense of progressing beyond mechanical repetition of predigested fragments, and that inequalities of power are intimately intertwined with discourse, so that resistance may be the needed stance. The question is whether the language of autonomous self-assertion is the normative frame within which to approach these matters. Consider some alternative ways of developing the point. What would change if "real proficiency" were, for instance, formulated in terms of a playful, appreciative enjoyment of linguistic resources and possibilities (Cook, 2000)? Or in terms of the ability to turn language to the purpose of serving, encouraging, or consoling others? Or in terms of the ability to form strong relationships with others through its medium (Reyes, 2002)? Regarding any of these as simply instances of asserting oneself, bending language to one's will or turning it possessively to one's advantage seems tendentious at best. Moreover, emphasizing any of these alternatives hardly entails a denial that power and justice are important and relevant concerns; it merely suggests a refusal to consider struggle for dominance as the normative frame.

From a set of claims about what "real" language proficiency means emerges a set of questions about matters as relevant to our basic ways of seeing the world as whether we might best characterize successful learning as aggressive and autonomous self-assertion, as the exercise of humility, as playful appreciation, or as the ability to do good to others or to build compassionate relationships. These characterizations in turn inform choices with regard to "interpersonal language practices." My own identity as a Christian language teacher has at least two effects in relation to approaching these tensions. On the one hand, it leads me to be unsurprised by the observation that we most commonly turn out to be using language in service of the power of the self, even (or perhaps especially) when we think we are being noble and altruistic; something like this is what Christian theology has always said about humans. On the other hand, it inclines me to see this as something to be struggled against, to affirm the graced possibility of humility, service, healing, and joy, and to look for pedagogical ways of incarnating hope. This entails skepticism toward accounts that make self-affirmation or individual success the main aim of education or that make struggle for dominance an ontologically necessary feature of language. Faith, in other words, is relevant to weighing theories and pedagogical prescriptions in an ideologically plural field of practice such as education; holding faith in Christ (or Allah, or Reason, or the Self) makes certain options seem truer and thus more worth pursuing.

Concluding Considerations

In closing I would like to suggest some implications for further discussion of the relationship between Christianity in particular (or religion and spirituality more generally) and the practices of language educators. First, none of the above implies a straight, deductive line from Christian spirituality to a single set of teaching techniques. The alternatives are not method sanitized from non-scientific beliefs versus worldview-based pedagogical determinism. Faith commitments will always be in interaction with other components of an educational approach; the challenge is to trace the role of faith and spirituality in the complex ecology of the language classroom, with its unpredictable interactions between multiple factors (Larsen-Freeman, 1997, 2002).

Second, Christian faith itself is pluriform. Worldviews grow and interact with others through history and are subject to variations as they are refracted through the experiences and capacities of individuals and groups in particular eras and social settings. Christian belief may in particular times and places become closely intertwined with particular political, pedagogical, or cultural positions, but the connection may be ultimately contingent. Western monolingualism has, for instance, been historically linked with Western interpretations of the Babel story as presenting multilingualism as a curse (Phillipson & Skutnabb-Kangas, 1996); however, these interpretations are themselves subject to Christian theological critique (Smith, 1996), and cannot be taken (as they commonly are) as monolithically representative of biblical theology. The same tradition (even the same text) can be a source of resources that point toward hospitality to the stranger and celebration of linguistic and cultural difference (Smith & Carvill, 2000; Smith, 2009). The very association of Christianity with the West is rapidly becoming anachronistic; some 60% of the world's Christians now inhabit Africa, Asia, and Latin America, while Christian adherence has waned sharply in Europe and the West has shifted to exporting secular ideologies. The view that Christianity should be understood as a Western religion is contested by both Western and non-Western scholars (Bediako, 1995; Jenkins, 2002; Sanneh, 2003; Sanneh & Carpenter, 2005; Walls, 2002) who protest the condescension implicit in viewing burgeoning indigenous, non-Western Christian movements as merely Western colonial residue or syncretism. Christianity must be treated as a complex entity.

Third, inserting the individual Christian into the picture complicates matters further. Beliefs and attitudes not unique to Christianity (such as a concern for honesty) may in specific instances be motivated by Christian commitment and influence pedagogical decision making (Smith, 1997). Moreover, Christians are as vulnerable as anyone to the formative effects of their contexts, and as prone as anyone to thinking and behaving in ways that are not consonant with what might normatively represent their commitments. Thus neither proponents nor opponents should assume too quickly that empirical connections uncovered between Christian belief and language pedagogy are essential ones with permanent force, or that all Christians think alike. Equally, we should not assume that more limited, contingent connections are without power to affect teaching and learning. For the Christian teacher this entails both humility and engagement; humility enough not to assume that our grasp of the implications of our faith is automatically correct or normative, and engagement in seeking creatively and fallibly to design pedagogy that is faithful to the nature of learners, language, and the world that both inhabit as illuminated by faith.

Fourth, while the suspicion that openly including faith in discussion of pedagogy invites indoctrinatory practice has merit in some contexts, the overall reality is again more complex. Religious faith may itself undergird avoidance of unethical indoctrination due, for instance, to a commitment to do to others what one would have them do to oneself. Wider educational discussions of the relationship between faith and indoctrination need to be consulted here (see e.g., Thiessen, 1993). Moreover, the problem can be inverted—students who come to class with spiritual commitments may find them ignored, trivialized, or undermined by pedagogical materials and approaches and teacher rhetoric; secular approaches may just as easily indoctrinate as religious ones (Haydon, 1994). Given the relative secularization of the West and the massive resurgence of religion (prominently including Christianity) in the wider world, necessary discussions of how to safeguard the personal integrity of the non-Christian student subjected to teaching informed by Christian values are only part of the picture. Students also seek out Christian learning environments because they feel that the values informing secular learning environments are incongruous with their own sense of self and desires for personal growth. In the classroom, as in the guild, enforcement of secularity can be hegemonic. Since classrooms are seldom entirely homogeneous with regard to the values and aspirations of learners, the challenges surrounding commitment to pedagogical visions rooted in views of human well-being not shared by students face all teachers, not merely religious ones.

Such challenges are unavoidable since any consistent pedagogy will embody particular visions of human flourishing. As Jerome Bruner puts it:

> Any choice of pedagogical practice implies a conception of the learner and may, in time, be adopted by him or her as the appropriate way of thinking about the learning process. For a choice of pedagogy inevitably communicates a conception of the learning process and the learner. Pedagogy is never innocent. It is a medium that carries its own message.
>
> (1996, p. 63)

Bill Johnston (2003) has more recently echoed essentially the same point:

> Language teaching, like all other teaching, is fundamentally moral, that is, value-laden, in at least three crucial ways. First, teaching is rooted in relation ... and relation, in turn—the nature of our interactions with our fellow humans, is essentially moral in character ... Second, all teaching aims to change people; any attempt to change another person has to be done with the assumption, usually implicit, that the change will be for the better. Third, although "science" ... can give us some pointers, in the overwhelming majority of cases, it cannot tell us exactly how to run our class. Thus the decisions we make as teachers ... have to be based on what we believe is right and good.
>
> (2003, p. 5)

This suggests that pertinent goals may be honesty, transparency, self-awareness, resistance to the abuse of power, and commitment to ethical relationships with students, rather than the attempt to teach from nowhere or enforce secularity. It also suggests that to understand language teaching (and our own behaviors as teachers) we must devote far more attention than positivist applied linguistics has given to questions of basic worldview and how they affect the classroom, not just through explicit mention of doctrine, but also through value-laden process. Language pedagogy is shot through with contestable assumptions concerning the truth about learners and their flourishing. Differences in belief will not be removed or resolved by theoretical exclusion, critical thrust, or professional fiat.

Focusing discussion of Christianity and language teaching around the question of conversion risks impoverishing the discussion (I say this despite continued gratitude for the processes that led to my own conversion). For Christians to see evangelism as the sole point at which their faith relates to language teaching is to frame the connection as extrinsic to pedagogy, and all too easily accommodates an uncritical and utilitarian relationship to the various pedagogical prescriptions, whether behaviorist, humanist, critical, or liberal, that come along. This makes neither for a strong Christian contribution to language education, nor for a Christian life of wholeness and integrity. The desire of Christians to share their faith, a desire that seems to me to be part of the internal logic of that faith itself, does (like the desire of critical theorists, positivists, liberals, humanists, etc., to persuade others that the world would be better if everyone believed their accounts) raise issues of power, integrity, and contested truth claims that must be debated in a plural context. My concern here, however, has been to point out that there is much more to investigate in terms of the relationship of faith to pedagogical practice.

Scottish educator Alex Rodger (1996, p. 48) suggests that:

> our spirit ... relates to the basic orientation or disposition of our life: the way we are in the world, in terms of those things to which we are sensitive; of which we are aware; by which we are attracted; which we value; by which we can be moved to act; which shape and guide our lives.

Any adequate exploration of the ecology of language education needs to take into account the role of such orientations and dispositions in shaping pedagogical approaches and learner responses. At present, such exploration is not well developed; there is plenty of scope for further inquiry.

References

Anthony, E. M. (1963). Approach, method and technique. *English Language Teaching, 17*(2), 63–67.

Anthony, E. M., & Norris, W. E. (1969). Method in language teaching. ERIC focus reports on the teaching of foreign languages 8. New York: Modern Language Association of America.

Baker, D., Dobson, S., Gillingham, H., Heywood, K., Smith, D., & Worth, C. (1998). Charis deutsch: Einheiten 6–10. Nottingham, UK: The Stapleford Centre.

Baquedano-López, A. P. (2003). Language socialization in children's religious education: The discursive and affective construction of identity. In J. Leather, & J. van Dam (Eds.), *Ecology of language acquisition* (pp. 107–122). Dordrecht, Netherlands: Kluwer.

Bediako, K. (1995). *Christianity in Africa: The renewal of a non-western religion.* Edinburgh, UK: University of Edinburgh Press.

Berger, P. L. (1999). *The desecularization of the world: Resurgent religion and world politics.* Washington, DC/Grand Rapids, MI: Ethics and Public Policy Center/Eerdmans.

Bradley, C. A. (2005). Spirituality and L2 pedagogy: Toward a research agenda. *Journal of Engaged Pedagogy, 4*(1), 26–38.

Brumfit, C. (1991). Problems in defining instructional methodologies. In K. de Bot, R. P. Ginsberg, & C. Kramsch (Eds.), *Foreign language research in cross-cultural perspective* (pp. 133–144). Amsterdam, Netherlands/Philadelphia, PA: John Benjamins.

Bruner, J. (1996). *The culture of education.* Cambridge, MA/London: Harvard University Press.

Byrnes, H. (1991). In search of a sense of place: The state of the art in language teaching methodology. In J. E. Alatis (Ed.), *Georgetown university round table on languages and linguistics 1991* (pp. 355–367). Washington, DC: Georgetown University Press.

Cook, G. (2000). *Language play, language learning*. Oxford, UK: Oxford University Press.

Edge, J. (1996). Cross-cultural paradoxes in a profession of values. *TESOL Quarterly, 30*(1), 9–30.

Farr, M. (2000). Literacy and religion: Reading, writing and gender among Mexican women in Chicago. In J. K. Peyton, P. Griffin, W. Wolfram, & R. Fasold (Eds.), *Language in action: New studies of language in society: Essays in honor of Roger W. Shuy* (pp. 139–154). Cresskill, NJ: Hampton Press.

Fettes, M. (2002). Critical realism, ecological psychology and imagined communities: Foundations for a naturalist theory of language acquisition. In J. Leather, & J. van Dam (Eds.), *Ecology of language acquisition* (pp. 31–48). Dordrecht, Netherlands: Kluwer.

Foster, M. (1997). What I learned in Catholic school. In C. P. Casanave, & S. R. Schecter (Eds.), *On becoming a language educator: Personal essays on professional development* (pp. 19–27). Mahwah, NJ: Lawrence Erlbaum.

Griffith, T. (2004). Unless a grain of wheat.... *TESOL Quarterly, 38*(4), 714–716.

Hall, J. K. (2002). *Teaching and researching language and culture*. London: Longman.

Haydon, G. (1994). Conceptions of the secular in society, polity and schools. *Journal of Philosophy of Education, 28*(1), 65–75.

Jenkins, P. (2002). *The next Christendom: The coming of global Christianity*. New York: Oxford University Press.

Johnson, K. A. (2003). "Every experience is a moving force": Identity and growth through mentoring. *Teaching and Teacher Education, 19*(8), 787–800.

Johnston, B. (2003). *Values in English language teaching*. Mahwah, NJ: Lawrence Erlbaum.

Kemp, J. B. (1994). Arousing the sixth emphasis within humanism in English language teaching. *ELT Journal, 48*(3), 243–252.

Kramsch, C. (1993). *Context and culture in language teaching*. Oxford, UK: Oxford University Press.

Kramsch, C. (Ed.) (2003). *Language acquisition and language socialization: Ecological perspectives*. New York: Continuum.

Kumaravadivelu, B. (1994). The postmethod condition: (E)merging strategies for second/foreign language teaching. *TESOL Quarterly, 28*(1), 27–48.

Kumaravadivelu, B. (2003). *Beyond methods: Macrostrategies for language teaching*. New Haven, CT: Yale University Press.

Larsen-Freeman, D. (1991). Research on language teaching methodologies: A review of the past and an agenda for the future. In K. de Bot, R. P. Ginsberg, & C. Kramsch (Eds.), *Foreign language research in cross-cultural perspective* (pp. 119–132). Amsterdam, Netherlands/Philadelphia, PA: John Benjamins.

Larsen-Freeman, D. (1997). Chaos/complexity science and second language acquisition. *Applied Linguistics, 18*(2), 141–165.

Larsen-Freeman, D. (2002). Language acquisition and language use from a chaos/complexity theory perspective. In C. Kramsch (Ed.), *Language acquisition and language socialization: Ecological perspectives* (pp. 33–46). New York: Continuum.

Leather, J., & van Dam, J. (Eds.) (2003). *The ecology of language acquisition*. Dordrecht, Netherlands: Kluwer.

Lemke, J. L. (2002). Language development and identity: Multiple timescales in the social ecology of learning. In C. Kramsch (Ed.), *Language acquisition and language socialization: Ecological perspectives* (pp. 68–87). New York: Continuum.

Mendelsohn, D. J. (1999). Janusz Korczak. Untunnelling our vision: Lessons from a great educator. In D. J. Mendelsohn (Ed.), *Expanding our vision: Insights for language educators* (pp. 173–186). Toronto, Canada: Oxford University Press.

Moskowitz, G. (1978). *Caring and sharing in the foreign language class: A sourcebook on humanistic techniques.* Cambridge, MA: Newbury House.

Norton, B. (1997). Language, identity and the ownership of English. *TESOL Quarterly, 31*(3), 409–429.

Norton, B. (2000). *Identity and language learning: Gender, ethnicity and educational change*. Essex, UK: Longman.

Pannenberg, W. (1984). *Christian spirituality and sacramental community.* London: Darton, Longman and Todd.

Pennycook, A. (1989). The concept of method, interested knowledge, and the politics of language teaching. *TESOL Quarterly, 23*(4), 589–618.

Pennycook, A. (2004). Language policy and the ecological turn. *Language Policy, 3*(3), 213–239.

Pennycook, A., & Coutand-Marin, S. (2003). Teaching English as a missionary language (TEML). *Discourse: Studies in the Cultural Politics of Education, 24*(3), 337–353.

Pennycook, A., & Makoni, S. (2005). The modern mission: The language effects of Christianity. *Journal of Language, Identity, and Education, 4*(2), 137–155.

Phillipson, R., & Skutnabb-Kangas, T. (1996). English only worldwide or language ecology? *TESOL Quarterly, 30*(2), 429–452.

Platt, E. (2005). "Uh uh no hapana": Intersubjectivity, meaning and the self. In J. K. Hall, G. Vitanova, & L. Marchenkova (Eds.), *Dialogue with Bakhtin on second and foreign language learning: New perspectives* (pp. 119–147). Mahwah, NJ: Lawrence Erlbaum.

Pritchard, R. M. O., & Loulidi, R. (1994). Some attitudinal aspects of foreign language learning in Northern Ireland: Focus on gender and religious affiliation. *British Journal of Educational Studies, 42*(4), 388–401.

Purgason, K. B. (2004). A clearer picture of the "Servants of the Lord." *TESOL Quarterly, 38*(4), 711–713.

Reyes, X. A. (2002). Authentic "migratory" experiences for language learners: Macrocontextualization as critical pedagogy. In T. A. Osborn (Ed.), *The future of foreign language education in the United States* (pp. 167–178). Westport, CT: Bergin & Garvey.

Richards, J. C., & Rodgers, T. S. (1982). Method: Approach, design and procedure. *TESOL Quarterly, 16*(2), 153–168.

Richards, J. C., & Rodgers, T. S. (1986). *Approaches and methods in language teaching: A description and analysis.* Cambridge, UK: Cambridge University Press.

Rodger, A. (1996). Human spirituality: Towards an educational rationale. In R. Best (Ed.), *Education, spirituality and the whole child* (pp. 45–63). London: Cassell.

Sanneh, L. (2003). *Whose religion is Christianity? The gospel beyond the West.* Grand Rapids, MI: Eerdmans.

Sanneh, L., & Carpenter, J. (Eds.) (2005). *The changing face of Christianity: Africa, the West and the world.* Oxford, UK: Oxford University Press.

Scovel, T. (1999). Myra Scovel: A woman of spirit. In D. J. Mendelsohn (Ed.), *Expanding our vision: Insights for language teachers* (pp. 75–92). Toronto, Canada: Oxford University Press.

Smith, D. I. (1996). What hope after Babel? Diversity and community in Gen 11:1–9, Exod 1:1–14, Zeph 3:1–13 and Acts 2:1–13. *Horizons in Biblical Theology, 18*(2), 169–191.

Smith, D. I. (1997). Communication and integrity: Moral development and modern languages. *Language Learning Journal, 15*, 31–38.

Smith, D. I. (2000). Faith and method in foreign language pedagogy. *Journal of Christianity and Foreign Languages, 1*(1), 7–25.

Smith, D. I. (2002). Incarnation, education and the boundaries of metaphor. *Journal of Christian Education, 45*(1), 7–18.

Smith, D. I. (2007). Moral agency, spirituality and the language classroom. In D. I. Smith, & T. A. Osborn (Eds.), *Spirituality, social justice and language learning*. Greenwich, CT: Information Age Publishing.

Smith, D. I. (2009). *Learning from the stranger: Christian faith and cultural difference*. Grand Rapids, MI: Eerdmans.

Smith, D. I., & Carvill, B. (2000). *The gift of the stranger: Faith, hospitality and foreign language learning*. Grand Rapids, MI: Eerdmans.

Smith, D. I., & Dobson, S. (1999). Modern languages. In S. Bigger, & E. Brown (Eds.), *Spiritual, moral, social and cultural education: Exploring values in the curriculum* (pp. 98–108). London: David Fulton.

Smith, D. I., & Osborn, T. A. (Eds.) (2007). *Spirituality, social justice and language learning*. Greenwich, CT: Information Age Publishing.

Snow, D. (2001). *English teaching as Christian mission*. Scottdale, PA: Herald Press.

Stevick, E. W. (1990). *Humanism in language teaching: A critical perspective*. Oxford, UK: Oxford University Press.

Stevick, E. W. (1996/1997). Keeping the faith. *TESOL Matters, 6*(6), 6.

Strain, J. E. (1986). Method: Design-procedure versus method-technique. *System, 14*(3), 287–294.

Taylor, C. (1989). *Sources of the self: The making of the modern identity*. Cambridge, MA: Harvard University Press.

Thiessen, E. J. (1993). *Teaching for commitment: Liberal education, indoctrination, and Christian nurture*. Montreal, Canada: McGill-Queen's University Press.

Tudor, I. (2003). Learning to live with complexity: Towards an ecological perspective on language teaching. *System, 31*(1), 1–12.

Van Dam, J. (2002). Ritual, face, and play in a first English lesson: Bootstrapping a classroom culture. In C. Kramsch (Ed.), *Language acquisition and language socialization: Ecological perspectives* (pp. 237–265). New York: Continuum.

Vandrick, S. (1997). The role of hidden identities in the postsecondary ESL classroom. *TESOL Quarterly, 31*(1), 153–157.

Varghese, M. M., & Johnston, B. (2007). Evangelical Christians and English language teaching. *TESOL Quarterly, 41*(1), 5–31.

Walls, A. (2002). *The cross-cultural process in Christian history*. New York: Orbis.

Warschauer, M. (1998). Online learning in a sociocultural context. *Anthropology and Education Quarterly, 29*(1), 68–88.

Widdowson, H. G. (1994). The ownership of English. *TESOL Quarterly, 28*(2), 377–389.

26 Truth in Teaching English[1]

Richard E. Robison

The growing presence of evangelistically motivated Christian English teachers across the globe has raised concern within the TESOL profession (Edge, 1996, 2003; Pennycook & Coutand-Marin, 2003). In particular, undertaking English teaching as a platform for evangelism has been labeled deceptive and manipulative. Christians do well to listen and reflect on the questions posed by their professional colleagues, with the aim of conducting their activities in a manner that is at once above reproach and consistent with their faith.

What follows in this chapter is a reflection on some of the issues that have been raised, with a focus on the ethical obligations of Christian English teachers in relation to truthfulness. First, I articulate four ethical dilemmas that confront Christian teachers with respect to truthfulness, and, next, review some of the philosophical, theological, and biblical material pertinent to the nature and practice of truthfulness. Finally, I revisit the dilemmas and suggest responses.

Ethical Dilemmas

The first dilemma is this: at what point does one become untruthful in representing oneself as an English teacher, or the curriculum as promoting English proficiency? What minimum qualifications and practices are required? When is an "English class" not really an English class? Clearly, the obligation to truthfulness requires that the quality and content of instruction be accurately represented; that is, the curriculum and class activities should fulfill the learning outcomes represented for the classes offered. But what of an evangelistic organization that offers English conversation classes and makes no claims other than that they are an opportunity to practice conversation with proficient speakers? Does "English conversation class" imply certain restrictions as to the content of the conversations?

Perhaps at the heart of this first dilemma is the issue of motivation. Does representing oneself as an English teacher require only certain minimum educational and experiential qualifications, or does it also imply a restricted set of purposes and no others? In the event that teachers are fully qualified professionally and the classes fulfill the curricular objectives, what if their motivation is evangelism? Edge (1996) voices the opinion that "teachers whose greater aim in getting involved in TESOL is to bring more people closer to Jesus" are "taking on educational responsibilities under false pretenses" (p. 23). Pennycook and Coutand-Marin (2003) likewise suggest that evangelistically motivated teachers are "using ELT as a cover for their activity" (p. 345). Snow (2001) also points out that integrity becomes an issue when a gap develops between a stated ELT agenda and a second evangelistic agenda.

Whereas the first dilemma concerns the accuracy of representation, the second relates to the extent of disclosure, specifically of underlying motivations and activities inside and outside the classroom. If teachers have competently fulfilled their professional obligations, proving themselves above reproach in that regard, does truthfulness also require that they reveal to all stakeholders their ultimate motivation, particularly if their primary incentive is to introduce their students to Christianity? And if they weave Christian concepts into the lessons—for example, in reading materials or conversation topics—is this an unethical exercise of power? Does truthfulness require full, prior disclosure of religious content? Finally, to the extent that an obligation to transparency exists, does it pertain just to potential students and their immediate families, or also to educational institutions and government agencies?

The conviction of many within the TESOL profession is that complete transparency is a moral duty.

> If such transparency is to be ruled out for tactical reasons, and the argument is that the end (saving souls) justifies the means (deception and manipulation), then I am simply bewildered, and finally repelled, by the morality of the stance being taken.
>
> (Edge, 2003, p. 705)

Concealment of motives or activities, however, is not necessarily a matter of "deception and manipulation." In some cases, it might be required to protect the work, or even the lives, of Christian teachers, and perhaps of their students as well, especially in regions hostile to Christianity. The question then becomes whether such concealment exhibits moral failure or justifiable prudence. A parallel case would be the issues facing underground churches (or synagogues or mosques) in countries that restrict religious freedom. Should such gatherings be publicly transparent about their practices and face persecution? Does their practice of secrecy and concealment suggest cowardly self-protection? Or is it rather a matter of prudent shepherding?

On the other hand, one must consider the right of "consumers" to know the possible side consequences of services offered. Edge (2003) points out that transparency "enables learners and, where appropriate, their parents, to make informed judgments about the conditions under which English lessons are on offer" (p. 705). But since every teacher brings personal philosophies and viewpoints to the classroom that might influence students, the same demand for transparency could equally be made of any teaching situation. The issue then becomes whether all stakeholders have a right to know the personal philosophies and subtexts that teachers bring to the classroom, and a right to withdraw students from classes taught by undesirable teachers, even in a public school system.

The third dilemma pertains to truthfulness about potentially conflicting identities. What obligations does honesty place on Christian English teachers toward their professional colleagues? If one self-identifies as an English teacher, must one conform to a well-defined code of values and behavior, to a TESOL ethos? In essence, this dilemma concerns whether a conflict of interest exists between Christian vocation and professional identification with TESOL. To put it baldly, can one be both an evangelical Christian and an English teacher? If a teacher's driving motivation is to be a witness to Christ, does this devalue the ELT profession?

Truthfulness toward the profession is problematized by fundamental differences in presuppositions between evangelical Christians and others in the profession. Some constituencies consider evangelism of any sort as antithetical to the multicultural ethos of TESOL, holding that respect for other cultural systems includes deference toward students' religious beliefs and a strict avoidance of even the appearance of imposing one's own values on others. Edge (1996) asserts that "it is surely demanded of us ... that as language teachers we restrict the purpose of our teaching to facilitating the life purposes of our students" (p. 23).

One response to this dilemma might be that this is a conundrum that confronts Christians in any profession, as their primary identity is in being followers of Christ. The point can be made, however, that because teachers carry greater moral authority than do members of other professions, their driving motivations must be subject to greater scrutiny. Another approach is to point out that from a Christian perspective, any profession, English teaching in particular, should be seen as service to God in its own right, and never as a means to another end (Snow, 2001). However, evangelical teachers who take such a stance retain the hope that the excellence of their teaching and of their conduct might influence students and stakeholders to become followers of Christ. The question then becomes whether maintaining such a hope causes Christian teachers to be "disingenuous," or even untruthful, as Pennycook and Coutand-Marin (2003) suggest.

This final dilemma addresses truthfulness about the practice of ELT itself, and confronts not just evangelical Christian teachers but any ELT practitioner. Many evangelical Christians have seized upon the escalating international demand for English not only as an open door for evangelism, but also as an opportunity to meet genuine human needs and thus to demonstrate compassionate Christian service. But is this valid? Are we truthful in portraying ELT as inherently humanitarian service in light of global realities? Does ELT in fact meet genuine needs in all contexts, or might it at least in certain contexts be causing more harm than good?

Pennycook and Coutand-Marin (2003) argue that the worldwide demand for English is in itself problematic. They question whether ELT can justifiably be portrayed as service, particularly to the disadvantaged, in a world where "access to and knowledge of English has become one of the major distributors of social, cultural and economic capital" (p. 347). They imply that rather than helping the disadvantaged, ELT reinforces global inequalities.

Another aspect of this dilemma is how ELT impacts the health of indigenous languages. Pennycook and Coutand-Marin indicate that the global demand for

English tends toward an agenda of cultural and linguistic assimilation and deprivation. Honest English teachers must certainly interrogate how their teaching might be contributing to this agenda. That is, how might they be abetting the extinction of indigenous languages and the diminution of language diversity?

One last element of this dilemma has to do with the impact of international teachers on local economies. Particularly those English teachers from (Kachru's) "Inner Circle countries" (primarily North America and Great Britain) who go abroad to teach English must inquire how their presence might negatively impact the employment of qualified local teachers, and whether such negative effects might outweigh any economic advantages gained by their students.

The Ethics of Truthfulness

Before attempting a tentative response to these dilemmas, it is important to establish a philosophical framework for viewing matters of truthfulness. First, a distinction must be made between truthfulness, or truth telling, and transparency. The former has to do with the accuracy of one's representations; the latter with the extent of one's disclosures. The antithesis of truthfulness, of course, is lying and deception; the converse of transparency is concealment—which, though it can support deception, must not be confused with it. Second, by way of preliminaries, it must be admitted that essentially just one side of a dialogue is presented here. An attempt is made below to articulate a Christian perspective on truthfulness and transparency, which will then inform the ensuing response to the dilemmas articulated above. Since this perspective is substantially informed by the Christian scriptures, judicious reference to said scriptures will be made in what follows.

In addressing issues of truthfulness, an axiom of the Christian faith is that truth originates in God and is revealed in the person of Jesus Christ. The claim here is not that Christians have a corner on the truth, nor does it necessarily imply an a priori moral absolutism. Rather, honest Christians acknowledge that their own understanding is limited and that ethical questions must be open for dialogue. However, they hold that fundamental to truthfulness is the acknowledgment that God exists and that Jesus Christ is his Son. Distinguishing between truth in the practical sphere and truth in a higher, more essential spiritual sphere, Rahner (1971) reasons that God is the foundation of all truth, and that truthfulness in its most basic form is submission to the ultimate essence of truth, who is God. Barth (1961) analyzes human falsehood as fundamentally a spiritual rather than a moral problem. He asserts that "man" in his natural state is a liar, and that the essence of lying is self-assertion in place of submission to God. Bonhoeffer (1965) likewise finds the essential character of "the lie" to be:

> the denial of God as he has evidenced himself to the world.... Consequently the lie is the denial, the negation and the conscious and deliberate destruction of the reality which is created by God and which consists in God, no matter whether this purpose is achieved by speech or by silence.
>
> (p. 369)

Gill (1984) attributes to Thielicke this same approach to biblical teaching on truthfulness and falsehood. He summarizes the view thus:

> A lie is … an intentional denial or contradiction of the truth and reality of Jesus Christ in a given situation. It is Jesus Christ to whom truth is owed and by whom truth is measured, not independent, abstract facts in themselves. (p. 640)

Related to this truthfulness on a theological plane, Rahner (1971) posits a second form of truthfulness as truthfulness with oneself. The opposite of self-deception, this consists in acknowledging and accepting oneself as one is. Such truthfulness requires great courage and is possible only by means of the supernatural liberation that comes from God.

Truthfulness in its usual sense contrasts with lying, and consists in honesty and reliability. Moral philosophers over the centuries have deliberated over the precise limits of morally reprehensible lies. Aristotle (Molinski, 1968) and Augustine (Deferrari, 1952) distinguished between deliberate and unconscious falsehoods, labeling both lies but attributing moral consequences only to the former. Augustine added that a true statement made in the belief that it was false was also a formal lie and morally reprehensible. He considered any lie to be immoral, but acknowledged gradations in seriousness. Officious lies, told for benevolent purposes, are least reprehensible; malicious lies are most heinous; and jocose lies, such as practical jokes, mediate between the extremes. Aquinas (1947) refined this classification into an eightfold hierarchy. Following Augustine, Luther held that officious lies are permissible and condemned only lies that "caused unjustifiable damage [to others]" (Molinski, 1968, p. 316).

Building on a contemporary theory of lying that focused on its social character, Grotius narrowed the definition of lying to reflect the concept of "the right to the truth." Rather than including all deliberately false statements, he defined lies as "speech violating the actual and continuing right of the person addressed … to make up one's mind freely, without the hindrance of false information" (Molinski, 1968, p. 316). Similarly, Bonhoeffer (1965) rejected the idea that any consciously false statement is a lie and hence a moral offense. He asserted that a lie is only that that deceives others to their detriment. More generally, it is any speech—or even deliberate silence—that disrupts the reality of relationships, even if factually correct. Bonhoeffer also reasoned that the realization of truthfulness differed according to the situation, the subject matter, and the relationship of the interlocutors. The relationship between parent and child, for example, is asymmetric in terms of obligations to truthfulness.

Other ethical philosophers have argued that any deliberately false statement is problematic. Kant (1993) asserted that the phrase "a right to the truth" is meaningless. He reasoned that truth is not a possession that can be given or withheld; the only right that a person has with respect to truth is the right to be truthful in all statements, which is also a strict duty. Any false statement made for whatever reason, no matter how beneficent, not only damages one's own trustworthiness, but also damages society in general. Bok (1978) likewise classifies all consciously false statements as lies, including social niceties and inflated reference letters. She agrees that lies damage the integrity of the liar and the shared trust essential to human society. She concedes, however, that some lies may be practical necessities and attempts to apply an evaluative metric in terms of their consequences, noting that in evaluating a particular form of deception, one must examine the effect of its cumulative practice, not just an individual instance.

While the exact boundaries of what constitutes lying remain open to debate, there is general agreement that lying is destructive to the liar, to interpersonal relationships, and to the wider human community. A faith perspective must add that lying alienates the liar from God, who is truth. Rahner (1971) discerns the root cause for all lying in fear and a corresponding need for self-protection. In contrast, people of faith, who trust in God's grace for protection, have no need to defend themselves and have been freed to speak truthfully at all times.

The Bible is replete with prohibitions against lying. While the Eighth Commandment proscribes only false statements that bring harm to others, other passages condemn lying unequivocally. The Apostle Paul exhorts his readers to "put off falsehood"; and the Apostle Peter, to rid themselves of all deceit and hypocrisy. The fate of Ananias and Sapphira in the New Testament church and the doom of liars in the final judgment suggest that lies are a mortal offense against God.

However, other passages suggest that lying may be permissible under particular circumstances. Abraham's deceptions about his relationship to Sarah, Jacob and Rebekah's deception of Isaac, and David's apparent lie to Ahimelech all appear to have been perpetrated with impunity, and appear to be examples of what theologians have labeled "officious" lies. While one must guard against an argument from silence, subsequent pronouncements of blessing on these individuals suggests that God overlooked whatever moral offense their deceptions entailed. More salient are the cases of the Hebrew midwives and Rahab, who gave aid to God's people by means of their deceptions. The midwives were commended and rewarded for their fear of God, and Rahab for her faith and works. Although it is common to make a distinction between the faith of these women and their deception, attributing the commendations only to the former, it is difficult to discern how their faith could have been manifested apart from their deceptions.

Complementary to the matter of truth telling is the practice of transparency. To what extent does truthfulness preclude concealment? Kant (1993), who proscribed falsehoods of any sort, said only that "every man [*sic*] has ... the strictest duty to be truthful in statements that are unavoidable" (p. 66). He thus allowed the possibility of concealment through avoidance. Aquinas (1947) argued that truthfulness is a moral virtue because it entails a mean between excess and deficiency: "The mean is to tell the truth, when one ought, and as one ought. Excess consists in making known one's own affairs out of season, and deficiency in hiding them when one ought to make them known" (p. 1661).

Rahner (1971) likewise observes that truthfulness does not mean revealing the whole of one's thoughts and motives. He applies the principle of charity, asserting that "truth must be either stated or withheld as the circumstances demand" (p. 247). Bonhoeffer (1965), although he includes deliberate silence as a possible form of lying, equally affirms that truthfulness does not equal "disclosure of everything." He takes God's provisions of clothing for Adam and Eve as symbolic of "the truth that since the Fall, there has been a need also for concealment and secrecy" (p. 372). He also points out that the cynic who claims ultimate truthfulness through full exposure in fact fails to attain the truth.

From the perspective of a philosophical ethicist, Bok (1982) states that a degree of concealment accompanies all that humans do or say, and indicates through thought experiments that universal transparency is neither desirable nor practicable in human society as it exists. Secrecy, or personal control over information flowing out from oneself, is essential to psychological wholeness. Complete transparency is a symptom of psychosis (Bok, 1982). One can in fact find almost universal agreement that no moral obligation exists to make all one's affairs known to everyone. Complete transparency is impractical, undesirable, unhealthy, unwise, and even unethical.

Nevertheless, scriptural passages describing the practices of Jesus and the Apostle Paul suggest an ethic of transparency. Jesus, at his trial before the high priest, characterized his ministry as open for public inspection. He had "spoken openly to the world" and "said nothing in secret." His teaching to "let your light shine before men" suggests a similar kind of transparency. Paul wrote that he did not employ trickery or mask ulterior motives; he renounced secret ways and refrained from using deception.

Other passages, however, appear to advise guardedness and suggest that secrecy is sometimes justified. Jesus would not entrust himself to those who believed in his name because "he knew what was in a man." When his brothers urged him to show himself more publicly, he told them that he was not going up to the Feast of Tabernacles yet and then went in secret after they had left. He advised his followers not to throw their pearls to pigs, lest they "trample them under their feet, and then turn and tear you to pieces." Similarly, when he sent out the Twelve, he warned them to be "shrewd as snakes." In explaining his use of parables, he appeared to model a practice of obscuring his meaning to certain audiences, in place of being fully transparent. The Apostle Paul alluded to being caught up into heaven and hearing things that he was constrained to keep concealed. Finally, when the prophet Samuel went to Bethlehem to anoint David as king, he stated only that he had come to offer a sacrifice and concealed his primary purpose; and in so doing he was following the direct counsel of God.

Application

I conclude with a sketch of possible responses to the dilemmas posed earlier. A fundamental assumption underlying all that follows is that any response must be context dependent. The demands of truthfulness and transparency must depend on the particular requirements, restrictions, and risks of any given teaching situation.

To begin, there is no question that teachers should have sufficient qualifications to perform the services offered and should diligently labor to accomplish the learning outcomes advertised. Course objectives must never be trumped by evangelism in the classroom. On these points, all persons of integrity can agree. Two questions remain, however. First, what constitutes sufficient qualification? Second, to what degree is underlying motivation essential to the job description?

Concerning the first, the obligation to truthfulness would seem to be met if teachers and their organizations clearly and accurately represent the qualifications of the teachers and the expected course outcomes. The ideal qualifications to teach, however, remain open to discussion and depend on the requirements of varying instructional contexts. It is possible that an advanced degree in second language education might not be essential preparation for all teaching situations. For some highly restricted assignments, a two-week orientation to TESOL might suffice. Alongside academic training such qualifications as a genuine concern for student learning, strong communication skills, and experience acquiring a second language are also critical.

As for motivation figuring into the matter of professional qualification, such a stipulation appears unrealistic. If someone takes up teaching duties because she desires to see people come closer to Jesus, how is she essentially different from someone who takes the job simply to earn a living? Or what of teachers whose prime motivation is to advance their careers, or seek the limelight, or gain personal satisfaction? By the metric articulated earlier, one must hold that such teachers are "taking on educational responsibilities under false pretenses" (Edge, 1996, p. 23) and "using ELT as a cover" (Pennycook & Coutand-Marin, 2003, p. 345). But what teacher has ever entered a classroom with no other motivation than to help students fulfill their own self-defined life purposes?

Concerning the second dilemma, an "ethics of disclosure" (Pennycook & Coutand-Marin, 2003) needs to be balanced by an ethics of concealment. In fact, no proponent of full transparency could affirm complete public disclosure of every personal motive and every planned activity. As Aquinas indicated, it can be just as unethical to disclose that which should remain concealed as to conceal that which should be disclosed. The question remains: who has a right to know what? The answer is highly context dependent and requires ethical judgment.

That said, certain general principles can be articulated. First, apart from special circumstances, evangelical Christians have no reason to hide their identity or their beliefs, or their potential influence on students. Likewise, they have scriptural precedent to be completely transparent about their motivations and about any religious content in their classes or extra-curricular activities to which students are invited. If deliberate silence can be considered lying, then Grotius' definition may apply here. In concealing their underlying objectives or any religious content of classes offered, evangelical Christian teachers could be "violating the actual and continuing right of [students and other stakeholders] to make up [their] mind[s] freely" about the desirability of classes offered.

On the other hand, specific circumstances may justify concealment. Honesty and integrity require only that one be truthful in all statements, not that one tell all. In the case of the prophet Samuel visiting Bethlehem, his primary purpose was disclosed to David and his immediate family, but it remained concealed from the government, specifically King Saul, who might have had Samuel executed had he known. Certain circumstances may parallel this narrative, where complete disclosure could endanger either teacher or students. Government and institutional agencies have statutory rights to certain information, but those rights are limited.

The third dilemma concerned truthfulness about identities. Does the ELT profession embrace a set of values that conflict with the evangelical Christian agenda? Does the presence of evangelicals in TESOL somehow devalue the profession? On the one hand, there is much common ground. At the core of orthodox Christian theology is a respect for the diversity of cultures. What is more, the genuine Christian mission is not to impose Christian values on others but rather to make them available in the marketplace of ideas (Stevick, 1996; 1997).

At the same time, a Christian's professional and faith identities cannot be divorced; a Christian's vocation is to Christ, who commissioned his followers collectively to make disciples and who stated as fact that they are his witnesses. Rahner (1971) identifies the essence of public truthfulness on the part of Christian laity as publicly bearing witness to the Christian faith. To be a Christian is to believe that the greatest good achievable is to know God through Jesus Christ; and Christian teachers who are genuinely concerned for their students lack integrity if they do not desire that they also come to know God.

This value-laden nature of the Christian identity makes Christian teachers both in harmony with the rest of the TESOL profession and at the same time alien. The harmony emerges in the fact that any teacher brings a distinct set of values into the classroom. Johnston (2003) has sought to bring to light the influence of values on teaching:

> On the one hand ... we teachers of ESL and EFL profess a respect for alternative cultural values and undertake not to impose our own values on others. On the other hand ... we hold certain of our own cultural values so dear that we want them to guide our work.
>
> (p. 65)

He further acknowledges that "all teaching aims to change people ... with the assumption ... that the change will be for the better" (p. 23). However, the definition of "better" must depend on the teacher's values.

In a sense, all teachers are constrained by the corollary of the observer's paradox: a teacher's mere presence in the classroom unavoidably influences the students. Students often "learn" more from who teachers are and how they teach than from what they teach. The teacher's belief system—whether Christian, Muslim, Buddhist, Jewish, Atheist, etc.—may influence students as much as the content of the lessons.

Still, Christians have a worldview that makes them in some sense outsiders within the secular world. The Bible identifies them as "aliens and strangers on earth" who are citizens of a "heavenly" kingdom. This suggests that Christians by their essence cannot be fully at home in their countries of birth. In this same sense, Christians are perhaps strangers within the TESOL profession. This suggests that dialogue among TESOL constituencies, though not impossible, must remain inherently problematic.

Concerning the final dilemma, truthfulness about the practice of ELT, it is incumbent on Christians to engage the hard ethical questions, to question the worldwide demand for English, and to interrogate the practice of ELT. In keeping with their core beliefs, Christians trust in a God who is gracious and compassionate, who forgives sin, redeems lives, and sets people free. One product of that Christian emancipation is the freedom to exercise humility and to confess faults. On the one hand, Christian teachers should diligently pursue doing good as best as they can perceive what that good is. And in discerning what is good, they can join with other TESOL professionals, despite differences in presuppositions, in critically evaluating professional practices. At the same time, exercising humility means acknowledging that even on their best days they may not actually be accomplishing as much good as they think and may even be causing harm unawares. It is by such a humble acknowledgment, along with the aforementioned interrogation, that one can at least begin to be truthful about the practice of ELT.

Note

1 A version of this chapter appeared in the Newsletter of the Christian Educators in TESOL Caucus, 2006, Volume 10, Number 3.

References

Aquinas, T. (1947). *Summa theologica, 2.2,* ques. 109, 110. Literally translated by the Fathers of the English Dominican Province. New York: Benziger Bros.

Barth, K. (1961). The falsehood and condemnation of man. In G. W. Bromily (Trans.), *Church dogmatics* (Vol. 4, Pt. 3.1, pp. 368–478). Edinburgh, UK: T. & T. Clark.

Bok, S. (1978). *Lying: Moral choice in public and private life.* New York: Pantheon.

Bok, S. (1982). *Secrets: On the ethics of concealment and revelation.* New York: Pantheon.

Bonhoeffer, D. (1965). What is meant by "telling the truth." In E. Bethge (Ed.), *Ethics* (pp. 363–372). New York: Macmillan.

Deferrari, R. J. (Ed.) (1952). *Saint Augustine: Treatises on various subjects.* New York: Fathers of The Church.

Edge, J. (1996). Keeping the faith. *TESOL Matters, 6*(4), 1, 23.

Edge, J. (2003). Imperial troopers and servants of the Lord: A vision of TESOL for the 21st century. *TESOL Quarterly, 37*(4), 701–708.

Gill, D. W. (1984). Lie, lying. In W. A. Elwell (Ed.), *Evangelical dictionary of theology* (pp. 639–640). Grand Rapids, MI: Baker Book House.

Johnston, B. (2003). *Values in English language teaching.* Mahwah, NJ: Lawrence Erlbaum.

Kant, I. (1993). On a supposed right to lie because of philanthropic concerns. In J. W. Ellington (Trans.), *Grounding for the metaphysics of morals* (pp. 63–67). Indianapolis, IN: Hackett.

Molinski, W. (1968). Truthfulness. In K. Rahner (Ed.), *Sacramentum mundi: An encyclopedia of theology* (Vol. 6, pp. 313–318). New York: Herder and Herder.

Pennycook, A., & Coutand-Marin, S. (2003). Teaching English as a missionary language. *Discourse: Studies in the Cultural Politics of Education, 24*(3), 337–353.

Rahner, K. (1971). On truthfulness. *Theological investigations VII: Further theology of the spiritual life 1.* Translated by D. Bourke. New York: Seabury.

Snow, D. B. (2001). *English teaching as Christian mission: An applied theology.* Scottsdale, PA: Herald Press.

Stevick, E. (1996/1997). Letter. *TESOL Matters, 6*(6), 6.

Response

27 Imperatives, Dilemmas, and Conundrums in Spiritual Dimensions of ELT[1]

H. Douglas Brown

In recent years the language teaching profession has witnessed a number of articles, chapters, books, and presentations on the moral, spiritual, and critical nature of language pedagogy. We language teachers and teacher educators are reminded that we are all driven by personal convictions—whether religious or philosophical—about what this world should look like, how its people should behave, how its governments should control that behavior, and how its inhabitants should be partners in the stewardship of the planet. We are exhorted to "embody in our teaching a vision of a better and more humane life" (Giroux and McLaren, 1989, p. xiii). Or, as Pennycook stated it, "the crucial issue here is to turn classrooms into places where the accepted canons of knowledge can be challenged and questioned" (1994, p. 298; see also Pennycook, 1999; Edge, 2003).

Questions about moral and religious imperatives of teachers have been raised for a number of decades. In the 1960s, Postman and Weingartner (1969) shook some educational foundations with their bestseller, *Teaching as a Subversive Activity*. In their stinging critique of the American educational establishment, they challenged teachers to enable their students to create change in social, economic, and political systems, to cut through burgeoning bureaucracies (which, they noted, are repositories of conventional assumptions and standard practices), and to release us from the stranglehold of the communications media, which was (and is still) creating its own version of censorship. While the charge to teachers to stimulate critical thinking among our learners is undoubtedly universally embraced, Postman and Weingartner's notion of teachers as "subversive" covert agents raises more than some eyebrows. And then Richard Robison notes in his chapter that the "ethics of truthfulness" for English language teachers poses further moral dilemmas today.

David Smith reminds us in his chapter that in the same decade of the 1960s, Edward Anthony (1963, p. 64) referred to an "approach" to language teaching as "a point of view, a philosophy, an article of faith." In the 1970s, the early seeds of Communicative Language Teaching (CLT) were sown (Savignon, 1972), with its assumptions about the roles of learners and teacher, power and authority in the classroom, and the value of student opinion, voice, and identity. Ryuko Kubota's chapter aptly demonstrates cross-cultural dilemmas in practicing CLT. Our ostensibly harmless references to the "gospel according to CLT," may have more than a grain of truth in them.

In the 1970s, I was introduced to Community Language Learning (CLL), and attended a weekend seminar taught by the founding father (literally!) of CLL's precursor, "Counseling-Learning," Fr. Charles Curran. In some ways the seminar was more like church summer camp than a seminar! Among the parade of methods in our "methodical" history in language teaching, CLL is perhaps the most overtly religious in its themes of redemption, salvation, and service.

So, lest you be tempted to think that concern with spiritual dimensions of language teaching is a brand new topic, perhaps these and other reminders can persuade you otherwise. On the other hand, what *is* new to the debates and discussions is the *open* dialogue—represented in these four chapters—on dilemmas, conundrums, and, I hope, imperatives that are rooted in a person's inner sanctum of beliefs about morality, relationship, and divinity. In our quite recent global sensitization to religious fundamentalism and fervor (a byproduct of media attention to the 9/11 incidents, terrorism, holy wars, and an unfortunate widespread misperception of Islam), the ELT profession is now facing the hard questions of religious identity, proselytizing, coercion, truthfulness, and other moral dilemmas in the classroom.

Some Cautionary Observations

In my reading of the four chapters in this part of the book, I was impressed with the honesty and scholarly critique represented in all four sets of comments. While the personal perspectives of all four authors were either overtly stated or implicitly indicated, all were fair in viewing numerous sides of issues surrounding spirituality in ELT. Their serious, scholarly commentary is in the tradition of others who have made cautionary observations on similar issues.

The literature on critical language pedagogy brings with it the reminder that our learners of the English language must be free to be themselves, to think for themselves, to behave intellectually without coercion from a powerful elite (Clarke, 1990, 2003), to cherish their beliefs and traditions and cultures without the threat of forced change (Edge, 1996). However, as Kubota appropriately comments, for all of CLT's laudable goals of empowerment and liberation, the dynamics of power permeate the fabric of classroom life (also noted by Auerbach, 1995). And with Robison's list of ethical dilemmas, is it possible that a teacher could possess a covert religious agenda beneath an overt pedagogical agenda? (See also Phillipson, 1992, p. 27.)

What has come to be known as "liberation education," among other terms (see Clarke, 1990, 2003; Freire, 1970), takes on new dimensions when infused with potential spiritual or religious (note Bradley's important distinction between the two) motives. Are CLT-inspired approaches like "whole language education," "learner-centered teaching," or "cooperative learning" universally accepted by all cultures and all educational traditions (see Holliday, 1994)? I liked Smith's quote from renowned educator Jerome Bruner, "Pedagogy is never innocent." In an article titled "Towards less humanist English teaching," Gadd (1998, p. 225) cautioned *against* viewing ourselves as a "nurturer of souls," because this "inappropriate and oppressive role … does not encourage or permit the students' intellectual and cognitive development."

The counterpoint to this rallying of teachers to change a world mired in oppression and/or ignorance is epitomized, as I see it, in a linguistic (and religious?) imperialism referred to by Bradley. (For further reading, see Phillipson, 1992; Skutnabb-Kangas & Phillipson, 1994.) All four authors in this part of the book demonstrate acute awareness and concern over issues of imperialistic motives that may lie behind ELT professionals' zeal for their chosen vocation.

Is there a middle ground? In their own way, each of the four chapters here offer some enlightenment on such a question. In so doing, they follow a number of articles and books that address the dilemmas (Clarke, 2003; Edge, 2003; Johnston, 2003; Snow, 2001). Can English language teachers facilitate the formation of classroom communities of learners who critically examine moral, ethical, political, and religious issues surrounding them, and do so sensitively, without pushing a personal subversive agenda? I would like to suggest three guidelines, along with some examples for engaging in critical pedagogy while respecting the values and beliefs of our students.

Guidelines for Dealing with Controversial Issues in the Classroom

When we focus on critical pedagogy, what first comes to mind is a number of so-called "hot topics" that we can address in our classrooms. Topics like non-violence, human rights, gender equality, racial/ethnic discrimination, sexual orientation, environmental action, religious fundamentalism, and political activism are controversial, sensitive to students' value systems, and demand critical thinking. Here are some guidelines for dealing with such topics:

1. Teachers are responsible for giving students opportunities to learn about important social/moral/ethical issues and to analyze all sides of an issue. A language class is an ideal locus for offering information on topics of significance to students. The objectives of a curriculum are not limited to linguistic factors alone, but also include developing the art of critical thinking. Complex issues (say, religious fundamentalism or homosexuality) can become the focus of intrinsically motivating content-based language learning.
2. Teachers are responsible for creating an atmosphere of respect for each other's opinions, beliefs, and ethnic/cultural diversity. The classroom becomes a model of the world as a context for tolerance and for the appreciation of diversity. Discourse structures such as "I see your point, but..." are explicitly taught and used in classroom discussions and debates. Students learn how to disagree without imposing one's own belief or opinions on others. In all this, it is important that the teacher's personal opinions or beliefs remain sensitively covert, lest a student feel coerced into thinking something because the teacher thinks that way.
3. Teachers are responsible for maintaining a threshold of morality and ethics in the classroom climate. Occasionally a teacher needs to exercise some discipline when students show disrespect or hatred based on, say, race, religion,

ethnicity, or gender. Teachers should ascertain that "universal" moral principles (love, equality, tolerance, freedom) are manifested in the classroom. This guideline is, in effect, a paradox because it presupposes certain values to be beyond reproach. Such a presupposition violates the very principle of respect captured in the guideline (2) above. Nevertheless, this is where one's pedagogy becomes "critical" in that the teacher's vision of "a better and more humane life" is usually predicated on such basic values.

Examples From Around the World

Consider the following examples of classroom activities from around the world. Do they abide by the above guidelines? Can your classroom recreate any of them?

In Brazil, a curriculum for children takes them on an adventure trip searching for "magic glasses" that, they discover, will enable them to see the world as it could be if everyone respected it. The program teaches appreciation for Native Indians of Brazil, their culture, stories, and music; it teaches gender roles, animal rights, and environmental stewardship (Maria Rita Vieira).

In Japan, a classroom research project called "Dreams and Dream Makers" had students choose a person who "worked to make the world a more peaceful place" (Donna McInnis).

In Singapore, an activity called "stamping out insults," focused on why people insult others and helped students to learn and use kind, affirming words as they disagreed with one another (George Jacobs).

From China, a teacher had students study oppression and suppression of free speech in the former Soviet Union, calling for critical analysis of the roots and remedies of such denial of freedom. Without espousing any particular point of view himself, and under the guise of offering criticism of another country's practices, students were led to comprehend alternative points of view (anonymous by request).

In Armenia, a teacher had students share their grandparents' experiences during the 1915 Armenian "genocide" when more than 1.5 million Armenians were killed in Turkey. Nearly every student had family members who had been killed. Discussions focused on how ethnic groups could overcome such catastrophes and learn to live together as cooperative, peaceful neighbors (Nick Dimmitt).

A teacher in Israel told of a unit in which students had to create an ethical marketing and advertising campaign for a product. Cases of Colgate widening the mouth of toothpaste tubes and of Revlon making the glass on nail polish bottles a little thicker led students to debate ethical business issues (Stuart Carroll).

In Egypt, a culture where equal opportunities and rights of women are abridged, a teacher used an activity in a class with both men and women in it that culminated in the students collaboratively writing up a "bill of rights" for women in Egypt (Mona Grant Nashed).

In the USA, following the September 11, 2001 terrorist attacks, a student asked the teacher what "Middle East" meant; when the teacher defined the term, the student responded with, "Oh, you mean 'terrorists.'" The teacher used the next 10 minutes to sensitively guide students through a discussion of stereotypes and the misinformation that they often convey.

Moral Dilemmas and Moral Imperatives

The process of engaging in a critically pedagogical approach in which we teachers take up the challenge of being agents for change brings with it some moral dilemmas. How far should we push our own personal beliefs and agendas in our zeal for realizing visions of a better world and for creating critically thinking future leaders among our students? At least six moral dilemmas present themselves, but each dilemma carries with it what I claim is a moral imperative. Consider the following dilemmas, and their corollaries in the form of imperatives, that call us to action as socially responsible teachers:

Moral Dilemma #1:
Our widely accepted communicative approach to language teaching (CLT), which aims to empower and value students, may itself reflect a cultural bias that is not universally embraced.
Moral Imperative:
Respect the diversity of cultural patterns and expectations among our students, while utilizing the best methodological approaches available to accomplish course goals and objectives.

Moral Dilemma #2:
Our altruistic "agendas" for bringing English to the world at large have the potential of legitimizing an unequal division of power and resources.
Moral Imperative:
Help students to claim their own power and resources, and to bridge the gaps that separate countries, political structures, religions, and values through a unifying language, but to do all we can to celebrate indigenous heritage languages and cultures.

Moral Dilemma #3:
Our language—English—is itself so imbued with metaphor, covert messages, and other pragmatic conventions that we can hardly teach this language without teaching a set of values.
Moral Imperative:
Without judgment on students' native languages or cultures, help them to understand and produce the sociolinguistic and pragmatic conventions of English, in full awareness of the cultural (and covert) messages inherent in any language.

Moral Dilemma #4:
In our curricular materials, our choices of topics and issues present us with opportunities to stimulate critical thinking but also to offend and polarize students.
Moral Imperative:
Sensitively, with due attention to the potential for students to be offended and polarized, approach critical, relevant, and informative issues in appropriate pedagogical contexts with as balanced a perspective as possible.

Moral Dilemma #5:
Our discussions, debates, group work activities, essays, and other classroom techniques offer opportunities for us to be agents for change, but does our zeal for realizing our own vision of a better world stand in the way of truly equal, balanced treatment of all sides of controversial issues?
Moral Imperative:
Guided by a clear vision of your own mission as a teacher, promote critical thinking on complex issues, remain as neutral as possible in the process, but be fully aware that you are promoting a set of values in your classroom, even if somewhat covertly.

Moral Dilemma #6:
Large-scale standardized tests are widely embraced by a budget-conscious establishment, but are they all free of cultural and socioeconomic bias?
Moral Imperative:
Carry out research to improve the authenticity and predictive validity of standardized testing, lobby for funding for more performance-based assessment, and in our classroom assessments, model principles of authenticity, biased-for-best performance, and beneficial washback to students.

I think all these dilemmas are commonly experienced among teachers around the world. However, if we are too daunted by the dilemmas and we shrink from our responsibility as change agents, surely we will have lost the opportunity to act on the imperatives that can drive us as teachers.

I believe all four authors in this part of the book are encouraging English teachers to engage in sensitive critical pedagogy in their classrooms. We are all united in our desire to stir students to a higher consciousness of their own role as agents of change, while respecting their diversity of beliefs and attitudes. The little differences here and there that we teachers make can add up to fulfilling visions of a better and more humane world.

Note

1. Selected segments of this chapter appeared in Brown, H. D. (2004). Some practical thoughts about student-sensitive critical pedagogy. *The Language Teacher, 28*(7), 23–27.

References

Anthony, E. (1963). Approach, method, and technique. *English Language Teaching, 17*(2), 63–67.

Auerbach, E. (1995). The politics of the ESL classroom: Issues of power in pedagogical choice. In J. W. Tollefson (Ed.), *Power and inequality in language education* (pp. 9–33). Cambridge, UK: Cambridge University Press.

Clarke, M. (2003). *A place to stand: Essays for educators in troubled times.* Ann Arbor: University of Michigan Press.

Clarke, M. A. (1990). Some cautionary observations on liberation education. *Language Arts, 67*(4), 388–398.

Edge, J. (1996). Cross-cultural paradoxes in a profession of values. *TESOL Quarterly, 30*(1), 9–30.

Edge, J. (2003). Imperial troopers and servants of the Lord: A vision of TESOL for the 21st century. *TESOL Quarterly, 37*(4), 701–709.

Freire, P. (1970). *Pedagogy of the oppressed.* New York: Seabury Press.

Gadd, N. (1998). Point and counterpoint: Towards less humanistic English teaching. *English Language Teaching Journal, 52*(3), 223–234. (Reply by Jane Arnold, and reply to the reply by Gadd.)

Giroux, H. A., & McLaren, P. L. (1989). *Critical pedagogy, the state, and cultural struggle.* Albany: State University of New York Press.

Holliday, A. (1994). *Appropriate methodology and social context.* Cambridge, UK: Cambridge University Press.

Johnston, B. (2003). *Values in English language teaching.* Mahwah, NJ: Lawrence Erlbaum.

Pennycook, A. (1994). *The cultural politics of English as an international language.* Harlow, UK: Longman.

Pennycook, A. (1999). Critical approaches to TESOL. *TESOL Quarterly, 33*(3), 329–348.

Phillipson, R. (1992). *Linguistic imperialism.* Oxford, UK: Oxford University Press.

Postman, N., & Weingartner, C. (1969). *Teaching as a subversive activity.* New York: Dell Publishing Company.

Savignon, S. (1972). *Communicative competence: An experiment in foreign language teaching.* Philadelphia, PA: Centre for Curriculum Development.

Skutnabb-Kangas, T., & Phillipson, R. (Eds.) (1994). *Linguistic human rights: Overcoming linguistic determination.* Berlin, Germany: Mouton de Gruyter.

Snow, D. (2001). *English teaching as Christian mission.* Scottdale, PA: Herald Press.

28 Additive Perspective on Religion or Growing Hearts with Wisdom

Ahmar Mahboob

Growing up bilingually in a multicultural city, it never occurred to me that religion and language were tied up in any fashion. To me, English was a language in which I watched cartoons and found out about snow and Santa Claus. It was the language in which I found out when Holi and Diwali were being celebrated. And, it was the language in which I learnt about Ramadan and wrote essays on how we celebrated Eid. Language, for me, was areligious. It was a way of expressing and communicating and did not inherently carry any religious ideology.

It was during my early days in the United States—in a small mid-western campus town—when I first noticed how English was seen as a Judeo-Christian language. During my early days on campus, the first few people who befriended me asked me if I wanted to go to church with them. Being new to the country, and quite lonely, I was happy to make friends. My conversations with these friends opened a new world for me. As I became more aware of their ulterior motives, however, I noticed how their religiosity was not a personal matter, but was about trying to "save" others. I did not feel that I needed to be saved from anything, but I did not want to offend these nice people. My conversations with them have been very insightful and opened American cultural and religious vistas that I didn't know existed. In discussing their views, I noticed that in some ways their absolute belief in Jesus, their attempts to convert others, and their willingness to go to any lengths to make others see the world from their "true" understanding were similar to the evangelical Muslim clerics and political parties in Pakistan. Both were trying to "save" others based on their own "true" positions. The difference was more in the mannerism in which they tried to impose their opinions than in the goal: where my new Christian friends were more subtle and indirect in their approach, my old Muslim friends I had left behind tended to be more direct and imposing.

Through my exchanges with my new friends I gathered that they believed that the English language represented a Judeo-Christian ethos and that by teaching people English, they can attract them to Christianity. They passionately argued that the reason that America was such a great nation was that Americans believed in Jesus and that the world would be a better place if other people could see how Jesus loved them and could be their savior. For these people, English (and teaching of English) was not simply a language (or teaching of a language), but it was a language that best carried the word of God; and teaching English was a way of spreading this message. It was at about the same time that I encountered the Sapir-Whorf hypothesis and became aware of discourses that engaged with the idea that language determines thought. It was through a combination of my conversations with my friends and my readings on linguistic determinism (and criticisms of it) that I realized how, for these friends, language encoded their cultural and religious beliefs and therefore it was important for them to teach English so that they could bring these people the love of Jesus Christ. In addition to Christianity, they accepted linguistic determinism and believed that language encodes and creates thought, and therefore to teach a concept as important as religion, one must become familiar with the language that best encodes it—for them, this was the English language. As I thought about these beliefs and read postcolonial literature and research, I found it hard not to think of a link between teaching as a means to proselytize, the current American wars for democracy, and the American belief in their "manifest destiny."

The purpose of sharing my early experiences in the United States and my interactions with my Christian friends is to share the position that I have developed over time and take with me as I read the chapters in this part of the book. My reading, understanding, and response to these chapters are shaped by these experiences and beliefs.

In reading the four chapters in this part of the book, I empathized with some of the authors' experiences, agreed with some of the opinions, and disagreed with other arguments. I use the words experiences, opinions, and observations here being cognizant that with matters of personal beliefs and positions, one cannot have any evidence, but only arguments, opinions, and experiences. In this chapter, I will briefly discuss some of the key issues raised in the chapters and, if relevant, will relate them to some of my personal and professional experiences.

Kubota (Chapter 23) begins by sharing her early experience in the United States and tells us about a book that she was given about Christianity that promoted a position that all religions other than Christianity were wrong. Although I have not been placed in such a situation, I have read Christian books that maintain this position. I therefore see how Kubota finds these books to be subtractive in the view of religion—which marks one religion as better than others. In contrast to this experience, she shares her own Japanese language class where, when the language content requires it, she shares Shinto and Buddhist belief systems and approaches with her students using an additive approach to religion. For Kubota, an additive approach to religion encourages "maintaining one's religious faith while affirming and critically understanding multiple views and practices that shape people's social and cultural identities, a view that transcends mere religious tolerance or sensitivity" (p. 233). Kubota's discussion of additive and subtractive approaches to religion is one of the most important contributions to the chapters in this part of the book; and, in fact, serves as a lens to look at the other chapters in the volume.

In one of her examples, Kubota shares how she allows students to explore religious philosophies when these connect to specific linguistic elements (in this instance *suzumushi* and the Zen Buddhist philosophy of living with no-mind). She points out that while this may be interpreted by some as "instilling religious belief," it is not meant in such a way. Her purpose is to help students understand Japanese culture by looking at their traditions and beliefs and she does this when the context of language requires it. Kubota's discussion of the need for raising religious and cultural issues in class that are encoded in language is the closest that we come to in terms of a discussion of linguistic determinism in this series of chapters. I find this lack of a discussion of linguistic determinism in these chapters a huge gap. As I hinted earlier, the way that linguistics as a discipline has evolved in the West and the core theories that inform it have shaped how we see language and its relationship to other human belief systems. Thus, an absence of examination of these relationships in chapters that seek to explore the association between language teaching and spirituality is a loss. Perhaps, this relationship between religion/spirituality, linguistic theory, and the application and impact of linguistics in language teaching and learning can be examined in detail in a future study.

Another issue raised in Kubota's chapter that I can empathize with is the exploitation of unequal power relations that are sometimes used by Christian educators to influence students. She argues that CET (Christian English teachers) who speak local languages are held in high esteem and this makes it "easier not only to spread the gospel but also to manipulate the local people intentionally or unintentionally" (p. 231). She further argues that "such a position stems from unequal relations of power that already exist between whites and people of color, Western culture and non-Western culture, English and other languages, and native speakers of English and nonnative speakers of English" (p. 231). Among other things, my support of this position stems from my research on NNS (non-native English speakers) in which I observe that nonnative teachers at times see their native speaker colleagues to be their ideals and from my research on race and native-speakerism that shows how a native speaker is assumed to be a white Anglo male Christian. (The NNS theme will be discussed later.)

Bradley (Chapter 24) focuses on transformative learning. Based on Mezirow's (2000) work, he defines learning to be transformative when one challenges and changes deeply held views and assumptions through dialogue and self-reflection. Transformative learning is couched in research on spirituality and education where spirituality is understood as being different from religion. Religion is seen as a set of theological codes, while spiritualism is not necessarily connected to a prescriptive faith. Bradley builds his understanding of spirituality mostly on Palmer's (2003) work that sees spirituality as "the eternal human yearning to connect with something that is greater than our own egos" (p. 377). Differentiating between religion and spirituality is an important contribution to the volume and it would perhaps benefit some of the other chapters here to be explicit about how they use these words.

One of the strengths of Bradley's chapter is that his examples show transformative learning as part of life-long learning and not just a part of classroom-based learning. Furthermore, he illustrates that transformative learning cannot be forced, but is something that is achieved through reflection and critical engagement with core issues. As such, his work fits in well within an additive perspective of religion in which others' perspectives are valued and affirmed.

A strength of transformative learning is that it can help us understand how and why people change their positions. It is not as much about a person becoming more or less religious or spiritual, but rather about the process of change. This aspect has been little explored in ELT contexts and deserves more attention.

In sharp contrast to Kubota and Bradley, Robison (Chapter 26) attempts to justify what Edge (2003) has termed "stealth evangelism." Robison grounds his reasoning in the Christian belief that "truth originates in God and is revealed in the person of Jesus Christ" (p. 258). He argues that as long as this "truth" is upheld, other truths or lies are relative and may be placed on a scale based on whether or not they cause "unjustifiable" damage to others. Robison builds his arguments by showing that truth and lies, openness and concealment are all relative terms and need to be seen in terms of the absolute truth—which is Jesus Christ. In many ways, Robison's chapter reminds me of my early days in the United States that I have shared before. He, like my evangelical friends at college, believes that there is only one "truth" and that we all need to share it in order to be saved. This strong belief in an absolutist position invokes a subtractive perspective on religion where Christianity is seen to be the absolute truth and people of other religions are seen as being in a need to be saved.

Robison justifies his approach to religion and the use of ELT to proselytize by referring to scripture and sharing stories that show how lying and concealment are condoned in specific instances. I find this reasoning and use of scripture to be an example of circular thinking: there is one truth only, others must be shown this truth so that they too may be saved, it is ok to conceal and lie to others in order to achieve this goal, the lies used to convert others are not really "lies" because there is only one truth … It becomes hard, if not impossible, to respond to an argument that becomes circular in this way. I will therefore leave it to the readers of this part of the book to take up their own positions here. I will instead take up another issue presented in Robison's chapter that I find very problematic.

In my work with the NNEST (nonnative English speakers in TESOL) caucus, one of my goals has been to encourage professionalization and training in TESOL and Applied Linguistics. The argument is that it is not sufficient to speak a language proficiently nor merely to have the best intentions, but to become an English teacher one must have adequate theoretical and procedural knowledge as well. A de-emphasis on training results in native speakers being hired as English language teachers based on being native speakers only—no other qualification is required. It also creates a situation where nonnative speakers with strong credentials are denied jobs because of their nonnative status. This leads to professional discrimination that I find unethical—and my Christian friends tell me that discriminatory practices based on one's mother tongue are unethical to them as well. Given this context, I find it alarming that Robison states that:

> It is possible that an advanced degree in second language education might not be essential preparation for all teaching situations. For some highly restricted assignments, a two-week orientation to TESOL might suffice. Alongside academic training such qualifications as a genuine concern for

> student learning, strong communication skills, and experience acquiring a second language are also critical.
>
> (p. 262)

The following job advertisement for native speaking Christian teachers found online is an example of how some Christian schools discriminate against NNES and de-emphasize training:

> WANTED: Teachers who want to make an eternal impact: Full Time Job Description: All Nations Christian Academy (ANCA) (Grades K-9) Native English Speaking Preschool/Elementary/Middle School Teachers wanted. Do you want to make an eternal impact for Christ's kingdom? Do you want to make your life count? Do you want to take part in a dynamic school ministry of training the next generation of Korean missionaries and discipling servant leaders to be shining beacons of light in this world? Here's your chance to make a significant and lasting impact in our next Joshua generation's lives as we disciple and teach our future global servant leaders.
>
> 1. About our school and the ministry: Our school's mission is to train up young people, especially Korean missionary kids (MKs), in the way they should go according to God's Word. We also have an after school English academy (grades 1–9) which reaches out to the community that we serve with the gospel of Jesus. We seek to provide the best well-rounded Christian education and to disciple students to become fully devoted followers of Christ and to equip them to be "radical world changers." We believe that teachers are disciplers as well as teachers. We come alongside the Christian parents to assist them in providing the necessary discipleship for each student. We offer Preschool/Kindergarten through 4th grade in the International School, which uses mainly curriculum from Christian publishers such as ABeka, Bob Jones, and other reputable educational providers. The classes are taught mainly in English. We believe in close, personal, individual interaction and relationship building discipleship, so classes are small. Our team has worked hard to create a unique learning environment which differentiates ANCA from other schools. We don't just impart knowledge, but we impart a Godly life. We don't just grow the heads of the students with knowledge, but grow the hearts with wisdom.
> 2. Qualifications—Believe in Jesus as Lord and Savior and have a personal relationship with Him everyday—Have a mission/discipleship mind—Hold at least a Bachelor's degree or equivalent.—DON'T need a teacher's certificate or other ESL certificates, but preferably have professional classroom teaching experience. (Early-childhood Development or a Kindergarten teaching license is favored)—A native speaker of American English—Retired people are welcome

Among other things, a reader will note how the ad conforms to the belief that specialized training in TESOL is not necessary in order to "grow the hearts with wisdom." The key qualifications for the job are (1) being a believer in Jesus as Lord and Savior, and (2) being a native speaker of American English. Not only is TESL certification not required, the need to have one is discounted by an explicit statement that emphasizes that candidates "DON'T need" a certificate (emphasis in original). As the past-Chair of the NNEST caucus and an active member of this community, I find such job advertisements and the justification behind these to be inappropriate and discrediting to the professional expertise and respect that we promote and deserve.

Smith (Chapter 25) considers how Christian beliefs may impact pedagogical practices. This is a fresh perspective on religion-based discourses in TESOL that focus primarily on the motivation and purpose of Christian educators. Smith shares two sets of hypothetical teaching situations and argues that there is a difference in the ethos of the Christian and secular practices. In one set of examples, he points out that while the aim of the secular practices is to encourage "self-affirmation and self-reliance," the Christian perspective presents "humility and caution concerning praise from others" (p. 247). It is not in the analysis of the particular activities that he presents, but in the selection of the activities that I find a problem. At best, the classes compared have only "some superficial resemblances." The model descriptions are discussed theoretically and not actually observed in practice—which may yield different results. Furthermore, self-knowledge and humility are not opposites—one can be aware of their abilities and be humble at the same time. Having said this, I think that Smith's contribution here is to help direct the debate into looking at the relationship between religious beliefs and practices.

Research on teachers' beliefs and their relationship to pedagogical practices has a long history in ELT research. I wonder how Smith and others will distinguish between teachers' beliefs about language learning/teaching in general and their religious and/or spiritual beliefs. Although tempting, it would be hard to make a case that all beliefs spring from a person's religious/spiritual beliefs. For example, teachers show great variation in their belief (and practice) of using L1 (or another shared language) in teaching English as an additional language. They also take different positions in their understanding and beliefs about the role of imitation in language learning, the role of motivation in language development, and how and when learner errors should be corrected in teaching contexts. Teachers' beliefs on these issues impact classroom practices, but it would be hard to argue that these beliefs are tied in with their spiritual/religious perspectives. These beliefs do, however, relate to and change with teachers' professional training and experience.

On the other hand, it could be argued that some other teacher beliefs may be linked to their spiritual/religious beliefs. For example, teachers' presentation of the self in the class and their relationship with the students may be linked to cultural beliefs (which include religious positionings). However, in this case, it would be hard to argue if these links (if they do exist) are based on any specific religion, or to a pan-religious ethos. Focusing on the example from Smith's chapter, he points out that Christian curriculum is "concerned with spiritual and moral development ... both emphases are rooted in Christian spiritual tradition that emphasize humility and the deceitfulness of the human heart" (p. 247). The two qualities raised here, to me, are not just Christian values, but pan-religious. Below, I'll share some relevant quotations from world religions on humility:

> *Confucianism*
> The life of the moral man is plain, and yet not unattractive; it is simple, and yet full of grace; it is easy, and yet methodical. He knows that accomplishment of great things consists in doing little things well. He knows that great effects are produced by small causes. He knows the evidence and reality of what cannot be perceived by the senses. Thus he is enabled to enter into the world of ideas and morals.
>
> (Doctrine of the Mean 33)

> *Hinduism*
> Be humble, be harmless, Have no pretension, Be upright, forbearing; Serve your teacher in true obedience, Keeping the mind and body in cleanness, Tranquil, steadfast, master of ego, Standing apart from the things of the senses, Free from self; Aware of the weakness in mortal nature.
>
> (Bhagavad Gita 13.7–8)

> *Islam*
> Successful indeed are the believers Who are humble in their prayers, and who shun vain conversation, and who are payers of the poor-due, and who guard their modesty.
>
> (Qur'an 23.1–5)

> *Jainism*
> Subdue pride by modesty, overcome hypocrisy by simplicity, and dissolve greed by contentment.
>
> (Samanasuttam 136)

> *Judaism*
> Be of an exceedingly humble spirit, for the end of man is the worm.
>
> (Mishnah, Abot 4.4)

The references from some of the major religions of the world illustrate that humility is not just a Christian value, but pan-religious. Thus, to claim that a particular activity that embraces and encourages humility is Christian in its perspective is to take away the relationship of that particular principle to other religions and spiritual belief systems. Marketing of pan-religious beliefs as being the domain of one religion, whether it is Christianity, Islam, Judaism, or any other religion is equally subtractive. In the given example, the focal element of humility, if it is to be taught in a language class at all, can be couched in pan-religious discourses creating an open and accommodating view of the world and various religions. A pan-religious discussion of spirituality will fit in well with discourses on peace education and perspectives on ELT for social responsibility. Such a broader discussion of humility and an encouragement to look at the spiritual dimensions of human societies will be productive and educate people so that they do not fall victims to political ambitions (both global and local) that exploit religion for their own purposes. This suggests that while Smith's undertaking to explore the relationship between religion and pedagogical beliefs and practices is a step in the right direction, it can be improved by taking a pan-religious and spiritual perspective rather than to be tied down to a particular religion.

In summarizing my reading of the chapters in this part of the book, I note that the primary question that the chapters respond to is: what role should religion and/or spirituality have in ELT, if any? The chapters look at this question by focusing on four questions: (1) what are subtractive and additive perspectives on religion, (2) what contributions can an understanding of spirituality make to ELT, (3) what are some of the Christian arguments for using ELT to proselytize, and (4) how do personal beliefs relate to pedagogical practices? As I see it, the arguments presented in these chapters are a good starting point for an in-depth discussion and analysis of these questions and I hope that the readers will engage in their own research and understanding of these questions.

Reference

Eastern Mennonite University's Career Services. Retrieved April, 27, 2007, from www.emu.edu/careers/jobs/fulljoblisting.php?id=4089.

Edge, J. (2003). Imperial troopers and servants of the Lord: A vision of TESOL for the 21st century. *TESOL Quarterly, 37*(4), 701–708.

Mezirow, J. (2000). Learning to think like an adult: Core concepts of transformation theory. In J. Mezirow, & Associates (Eds.), *Learning as transformation: Critical perspectives on a theory in progress* (pp. 3–34). San Francisco, CA: Jossey-Bass.

Palmer, P. (2003). Teaching with heart and soul: Reflections on spirituality in teacher education. *Journal of Teacher Education, 54*(5), 376–385.

Response

29 A Question of Priorities

Andy Curtis

In the first part of this response chapter, I briefly review and highlight some of the main points from three recent, best-selling books, all of which happen to be highly critical of religion in general and of notions of God in particular. I then use the words of those three authors to help me comprehend and respond to the words of the four writers of the chapters in this part of the book. Although the writings are considered to some extent individually, there is a good deal of deliberate and natural overlap.

Some Current Contested Thinking

A search of Amazon.com in August 2007 showed that they currently have listed well over 400,000 books with the word "God" in the title. Using "religion" as the search keyword, nearly 600,000 titles were found. Interestingly, with "Christianity" as the search keyword, fewer than 300,000 titles were found, though this is still a very large number of volumes, compared to the search for "Islam," with approximately 79,000 titles, or "Judaism," with approximately 69,000 titles listed. This is partly a function of the different languages in which books on different religions are written, but it is also interesting to note that in this section three of books in English all take a decidedly negative perspective, as the titles clearly indicate: *The God Delusion* (2006) by Richard Dawkins, *God: The Failed Hypothesis. How Science Shows that God Does Not Exist* (2007) by Victor Stenger, and *God is Not Great: How Religion Poisons Everything* (2007) by Christopher Hitchens.

Another striking aspect of these books is their popularity. For example, Dawkins' *God Delusion* was ranked Number 2 on the Amazon.com bestsellers list in November 2006 and it reached Number 4 in the *New York Times* Nonfiction Best Seller list in December 2006. Why are books that are so obviously anti-God and anti-religion so popular? Perhaps the current and increasing popularity of such titles may indicate a growing discontent with established notions of God and religion that are being more openly questioned and challenged.

The first chapter of Dawkins' *The God Delusion* (2006) is entitled "A Deeply Religious Non-Believer" (pp. 31–51), which is taken from Albert Einstein's description of himself as "a deeply religious nonbeliever" for whom "the idea of a personal God is quite alien … and seems even naïve" (p. 36). In that chapter, Dawkins describes how a boy lying in the grass suddenly felt the "micro-forest of the turf ... swell and become one with the universe, and with the rapt mind of the boy contemplating it. He interpreted the experience in religious terms and it led him eventually to the priesthood" (p. 31). This boy eventually became an Anglican priest and the chaplain at Dawkins' school. According to Dawkins: "It is thanks to decent liberal clergymen like him that nobody could ever claim that I had religion forced down my throat" (p. 31). This last point may be especially relevant to the chapters in this book and in this part of the book, as one of the central spiritual dilemmas in English language teaching is how to be sure that we are not doing the same thing, i.e., not forcing our own religion down the throats, to be digested from there into the hearts and minds, of our students.

It may be that some English language teachers with strong religious convictions do this without the explicit intent to do so. In this case, those teachers need to develop their self-awareness, through critical and conscious self-reflection, to a point where their level of self-awareness at least matches the strength of their faith, as without this matching, such teachers may find themselves—or may be found by others—to be demonstrating behaviors that go against their own statement of beliefs that it is wrong for teachers to do this. However, this is, of course, not the case for teachers who specifically set out to persuade their students to adopt a particular religion or belief system through their teaching of English.

It is interesting to see that Dawkins makes a number of references to language in his opening chapter. First when he is critical of "those physicists who occasionally slip into the language of religious metaphor" (p. 40), and second when he concludes the first part of that chapter with the following distinction: "The metaphorical or pantheistic God of the physicists is light years away from the interventionist, miracle-wreaking, thought-reading, sin-punishing, prayer-answering God of the Bible, of priests, mullahs and rabbis, and of ordinary language" (p. 41). It is not clear what Dawkins means by "ordinary language" but his recurring references to language are an indicator of the power of language and therefore the power English language teachers can have over their students.

In Stenger's more recent *God: The Failed Hypothesis* (2007), he claims that "the overwhelming majority of prominent American scientists have concluded that God does not exist" (pp. 21–22). Stenger is a keen advocate of logic, but there appear to be a number of logical oversights in his premise, based on questions that arise from his exclusion of four major groups: what about non-Americans, non-scientists, non-American scientists and Americans who are not scientists? Assuming there are more non-Americans in the world than Americans and assuming that there are more non-scientists in the world than scientists, the claim made by Stenger, even if true, represents the conclusion of a relatively small minority. However, Stenger goes on to cite the "lack-of-evidence" argument put forward by the philosopher Theodore Drange, a Professor of Philosophy at West Virginia University, whose work focuses on the philosophy of religion, the philosophy of language, and theories of knowledge.

Stenger contests St. Paul's statement in Romans 1:20, that "Ever since the creation of the world, his invisible nature, namely his eternal power and deity, have been clearly perceived in the things that have been" (p. 22). He also draws on the work of the philosophers Karl Popper and Rudolph Carnap and their notion of the importance of Falsification, which Stenger summarizes as stating that "when a hypothesis is falsifiable by a direct empirical test, and that test fails, then the hypothesis can be safely discarded" (p. 26). "Falsifiability" is also known as refutability or testability, the latter being an important concept in language teaching, in relation to language testing, and which relates to questions of truthfulness and true scores in terms of reliability and validity.

Christopher Hitchens' *God is Not Great* starts, as Dawkins' book does, with a childhood story of an early and formative experience, in this case, related to Hitchens' teacher, Mrs. Watts, when he was nine years old, attending a school in the south of England. According to Hitchens, Mrs. Watts instructed him "in lessons about nature, and also about scripture" (p. 1). After an entertaining account of Mrs. Watts, Hitchens describes an epiphany, like that experienced by Dawkins' school chaplain-to-be, but in Hitchens' case brought about by Mrs. Watts telling the children that evidence of God being "powerful and generous" was that He "had made all the trees and grass to be green, which is exactly the color most restful to our eyes" (p. 2). Then, after a brief characterization of his headmaster as "a bit of a sadist and a closeted homosexual" (pp. 3–4), Hitchens presents us with what he refers to as the "four irreducible objections to religious faith":

> that it wholly misrepresents the origins of man and the cosmos, that because of this original error it manages to combine the maximum of servility with the maximum of solipsism, that it is both the result and the cause of dangerous sexual repression, and that it is ultimately grounded on wish-thinking.
>
> (p. 4)

To these four objections, Hitchens adds "the more vulgar and obvious fact that religion is used by those in temporal charge to invest themselves with authority" (p. 4). Although in Hitchens' book, that last phrase is in parentheses, it is perhaps one of the most relevant and potentially damaging of any of the lines from these three books in relation to this book, as "those in temporal charge" and those who "invest themselves with authority" could be taken as completely negative but completely accurate phrases to describe teachers. This may be especially applicable to some English language teachers in certain contexts, for example, if they are working with newly arrived immigrants in an English-dominant country, for whom such teachers may be primary and significant authority figures who hold the key to knowledge about the new culture that can only be accessed through the target language.

Juxtaposing the Three Best Sellers with This Collection

As Ryuko Kubota writes in the introduction to her personal reflections: "Faith and language teaching pose challenging issues that cannot be resolved in simple terms" and wisely decides to "expose the complexity of the issues rather than provide definitive answers to the challenges" (p. 225). It is interesting to note that in this part of her chapter, Kubota states that she "eventually stopped participating in church activities," as this seems to be a common experience among many people, including English teachers. This raises not only the question of why some of us stop going to church, but whether or not some English language teachers attempt, accidentally or deliberately, to turn their classrooms into churches and their students into a congregation. This, in turn, relates directly to Hitchens' parenthetical point above.

Also in her introduction, Kubota describes how upset she was when she was given a book which claimed that Christianity was the one "true" religion and that all the others were "false" in relation to "cultural identities shaped by religious rituals, which have been transformed into everyday cultural experiences" (p. 226). This may also be relevant to Hitchens' same point, as English language classrooms are also governed by rituals, such as roll call, and in both spaces, the church and the classroom, the cultural experiences and identities of our students are at the core of the language teaching and learning that occurs within that space.

Later in her chapter, Kubota identifies within her experiences "a colonialist view of salvation and enlightenment" (p. 229) that is important in relation to language teaching and cultural imperialism, as identified by Canagarajah (1999) and others, as this may relate to the view held by some that English is in some way of inherently greater value than the other languages of the world, with the questionable justification that the world needs a lingua franca for doing business in the global marketplace. This may also relate to the debate about native and nonnative speakers of English who are teachers of English, as the latter are still sometimes seen as inferior to the former, in the same way that languages other than English are sometimes seen as inferior to English, and in the same way that some see certain religions as inferior or superior to others.

As Kubota correctly points out "the question of whether teachers discussing their religious faith openly in the classroom is ethically appropriate or whether faith is best discussed indirectly in the framework of culture remains unanswered" (p. 229). This raises the central issue of "appropriateness," as there are occasions in which it may be appropriate to openly discuss aspects of Christianity in the classroom, such as at Christmas time, if that particular celebration is allowed in that particular country. Another key point raised is Kubota's discussion of "additive" versus "subtractive" beliefs systems, which may be addressed at least in part by having a multifaith approach to the classroom, in which if aspects of one religion are taught then aspects of other religions must also be taught, thus avoiding the exclusivity that some religious groups claim.

Kubota cites Snow (2001) stating:

> it can be argued that a major mission of CET, or any other language teachers with certain religious faiths, is to promote love, peace, and mutual understanding among people with diverse backgrounds and that this can be done by developing skills in intercultural communication.
>
> (p. 230)

This is true, as Snow argues, but it is also true that all of these things, i.e., love, peace, mutual understanding, and intercultural communicative competence, can be taught and learned without any reference to any religion. This raises the question of necessity, as opposed to appropriateness: how necessary is it to include references to religious belief systems in the English language classroom? The answer might be that it is entirely unnecessary, in which case why would teachers be doing something that is not necessary, which could lead to the discomforting conclusion that teachers who are engaged in unnecessary activities in their classroom are primarily there to promote a specific agenda, which may be being promoted at the cost of the teaching and learning that is supposed to be taking place.

Kubota concludes her chapter by returning to her additive versus subtractive analogy:

> The additive approach encourages CET to affirm religious and cultural backgrounds of their students, while reflecting critically how teaching English is related to Anglo Christian hegemony and how political and military conflicts around the world might be implicated in religious, cultural, and racial arrogance among the self or the other.
>
> (p. 233)

This is, again, good advice from Kubota, but a very tall order for anyone to complete successfully. Given the tremendous challenges of doing all of those things, and doing them well, this raises the possibility that it might be better to keep our religious beliefs out of the classroom altogether if we are not able to do all those things as well as teach English.

Christopher Bradley's chapter, on the spiritual lessons he has learned as a language teacher, focuses on the important differences between "spirituality" and "religion," which is central to the notion of spiritual dilemmas in the English language (or any language) classroom, as the first challenge is to establish the nature of the dilemma, assuming one exists, and if so whether or not the dilemma is spiritual or religious. The online version of the *Cambridge Advanced Learner's Dictionary* (*CALD*) defines "spiritual" as "related to deep feelings and beliefs, especially religious beliefs," and for "religious" it gives the following definition, "having a strong belief in god or gods." As is often the case with languages, perhaps especially English, it is that last, little letter that makes all the difference. Apart from the use of the lower case "g," it is the final plural marking "s" that is most important. Bradley makes much use of Parker Palmer's work, including his 2003 article in the *Journal of Teacher Education*, in which Palmer defines spirituality as "the eternal human yearning to connect with something that is greater than our own egos" (p. 377).

Bradley makes his position clear when he states categorically his "conviction that research into possible links between spirituality and ELT must never be used as a pretext for proselytizing" (p. 235). This comment of Bradley's relates to the point made above regarding the importance of balancing strength of religious belief with self-awareness of how our beliefs are influencing our behaviors. These are key points at which our religious beliefs and teaching behavior intersect and influence each other in ways that can be difficult to identify and almost impossible to quantify, but which nonetheless can have a profound impact on the students in our classrooms.

Although the central part of Bradley's chapter is based on one hour of interviews with one individual, so it cannot make any claims to be representative of anyone except those two people, he makes many important points. For example, he identifies four aspects of his interviewee's spirituality, which he refers to as "a sense of personal transformation, compassion, the forging of connections, and the need to refrain from making judgments based on outward appearances" (p. 239). Again, while all of these may also be central aspects of learner-centered, humanistic language teaching, it is possible to experience, to promote, and to create all of these aspects in the classroom without a particular spiritual or religious belief system. In a number of different ways, Bradley's chapter brings us back to the moral and ethical aspects of our spiritual dilemmas as English language teaching professionals and again underscores the importance of not only articulating our position to ourselves, as part of raising our own self-awareness through internal dialogue, but also the importance of us articulating our position to others, including our students and colleagues, if those beliefs are significantly influencing what we do, how we do it, and why we do it in our English language teaching lives.

In spite of David Smith's dismissal of "vapid mini-narratives," his chapter starts in the same way as Dawkins' and Hitchens' books do, i.e., with a story from early schooldays, though in Smith's case it is his first teaching position that he is recalling. This recurring pattern of starting with early recollections shows the lasting impact of early experiences, which English language teachers would do well to bear in mind, whatever their spiritual or religious belief system, as newly arrived immigrants in an English-dominant country may remember their first English teacher and/or their first English lessons with the same kind of long-lasting memory that Smith, Dawkins, and Hitchens all illustrate.

Unlike Christopher Bradley, Smith does not seem to make the same distinction between "spirituality" and "religion" and appears to consider them to be somewhat synonymous, for example, when he writes about "the relationship between Christianity in particular (or religion and spirituality more generally) to the practices of language educators" (p. 248). This may be one of the concerns of language educators such as Edge (2003, 2004), Pennycook and Coutand-Marin (2003), and others, as the lack of such a distinction may raise a number of questions and lead to a number of dilemmas, as discussed above. However, Smith does make some important points, for example, when he highlights what he refers to as "a simple point," the point being that "spiritual beliefs, convictions and orientations are often more important and existentially relevant to both learners and teachers than much modern theorizing has assumed" (p. 243). Although this is not really a simple point at all, it is an important one, which raises the issue of relevancy and appears to assume an equal relevance for students and teachers, although it seems unlikely that both parties would share the same concern for "spiritual beliefs, convictions and orientations" unless both the teacher and the students were explicitly focused on this as part of their language teaching and learning.

Smith also poses some important questions, for example: "Does faith affect only the *ends* to which language teaching is turned or the choice to include religious *language* in the classroom, or might it also affect the shaping of language *pedagogy*?" (p. 243). Apart from being a convoluted series of questions combined and rolled into one, the question may also reveal a series of assumptions that may not necessarily be true. For example, unraveling the question and asking it without the same assumptions, it could be phrased as: Should faith affect the ends to which language teaching is turned? Should faith be the basis for the choice to include religious themes or language in the classroom? Should it also affect the ways in which the language learning process itself becomes structured?

Smith revisits this question later in his chapter, by asking: "How might Christian (or other) beliefs influence classroom communicative practices?" (p. 246). Again, it is the apparent assumptions underlying the question that might be questioned. Again, changing "how might" to "should" makes far fewer assumptions about the rightness—and righteousness—of the approach, which in turn may allow for a more plural perspective, related to Kubota's additive versus subtractive analogy. Smith emphasizes the importance of "emotional transparency, sensitivity, and self-exploration," (p. 246) which he describes as "the cardinal virtues," and though this may be true, at least for Smith, as has been discussed above, it is possible to be all these things, i.e., emotionally transparent, sensitive, and committed to self-exploration, and more, without an explicit, codified, religious belief system.

The fourth chapter in this part of the book is by Richard Robison and focuses on "truth in teaching English." Robison explores the ethics of "evangelistically motivated Christian English teachers" (p. 255). The *CALD* defines an "evangelist" as "a person who tries to persuade people to become Christians, often by traveling around and organizing religious meetings." It is important to note that the definition of "an evangelist" is not "a person who tries to persuade people to become spiritual" or as "a person who tries to persuade people to become religious." This brings us back to the question that has been raised a number of times in this response chapter: why focus on one particular religion to the exclusion of others?

A missionary is defined by *CALD* as "a person who has been sent to a foreign country to teach their religion." The possessive aspect of this definition is important as, according to *CALD*, missionaries are not sent to teach English, or spirituality, or religion, but quite specifically *their* religion. This brings us back to Kubota's concerns about subtractive versus additive approaches to religion and how subtraction must, by definition, leave less. A missionary by definition moves across one or more cultures, but there is also, within the notion, the inherent sense of at least the awareness of other cultures and cultural perspectives, including belief systems. Beyond basic awareness, there is tolerance, and beyond that comes acceptance through understanding. It is, then, very difficult to see how an evangelical, missionary approach to ELT can allow for such cross-cultural interaction, in any setting, but perhaps especially in the English language classroom, where the teacher is often in a position of power and therefore able to preach whilst they teach, to what may be a captive audience.

In his conclusion, Robison describes "humility" as "a product of Christian emancipation" (p. 264). The unacceptable and incomprehensible implication that were it not for Christianity, there would be no humility in the world illustrates more clearly than any of the other chapters responded to in this chapter the importance of either adopting a multifaith approach to religion in the international English language classroom, assuming it has any place there at all to begin with, or of seriously considering leaving it well away from the classroom, as a private and personal aspect of ourselves that remains that way.

References

Cambridge Advanced Learner's Dictionary. Retrieved August 1, 2007, from dictionary.cambridge.org.

Canagarajah, A. S. (1999). *Resisting linguistic imperialism in English teaching*. Oxford, UK: Oxford University Press.

Dawkins, R. (2006). *The God delusion*. New York: HarperCollins.

Edge, J. (2003). Imperial troopers and servants of the Lord: A vision of TESOL for the 21st century. *TESOL Quarterly, 37*(4), 701–709.

Edge, J. (2004). The author replies: Of displacive and augmentative discourse, new enemies, and old doubts. *TESOL Quarterly, 38*(4), 717–722.

Hitchens, C. (2007). *God is not great: How religion poisons everything*. New York: Hachette Book Group.

Palmer, P. (2003). Teaching with heart and soul: Reflections on spirituality in teacher education. *Journal of Teacher Education, 54*(5), 376–385.

Pennycook, A., & Coutand-Marin, S. (2003). Teaching English as a missionary language (TEML). *Discourse: Studies in the Cultural Politics of Education, 24*(3), 337–353.

Stenger, V. (2007). *God: The failed hypothesis. How science shows that God does not exist.* Amherst, NY: Prometheus Books.

Discussion Questions

Part IV: Spiritual and Ethical Dilemmas

1. Describe an encounter in a classroom in which students asked questions or made comments that touched on the spiritual or related to religion. How did you (or the instructor) respond? Discuss how the response might change in light of the issues of power that Kubota raises. Discuss how the response might change in light of issues of spirituality that Smith describes.
2. Snow states that when Western teachers learn their students' languages it demonstrates respect for their culture and is a way of humbling oneself; however, Kubota notes that learning students' languages can add to a Western teacher's capital, and CET who do so receive "heroic status" (p. 231). Which position do you agree with? What is in your "bag of privileges?" List as many as you can. Discuss how teachers can develop a critical awareness to power differentials and as Kubota suggests, "develop a critical awareness of the racial, linguistic, and cultural power relations that position people at different levels in the hierarchy" (p. 231).
3. Kubota suggests that teachers "affirm an additive, rather than subtractive, religious perspective ... comparable to the notion of additive bilingualism advocated for teaching culturally and linguistically diverse students" (p. 233). She notes that this perspective is influenced by the religious tolerance of Buddhism, and thus she may be imposing her own religious views on others by suggesting this approach. Do you feel she is doing so, or does her awareness and critical understanding mitigate the imposition and demonstrate what she is suggesting?
4. Bradley makes an important distinction between spirituality and religion. How do you define the two and, based on your definition, can a claim be made that one has a more legitimate place in the classroom than the other?
5. Respond to Smith's four implications for further discussion (pp. 248–251) and state your beliefs on each one and on the place of spirituality in the classroom.
6. Smith appeals to CET for the discussion and inquiry of spirituality and language teaching to move beyond the issue of Christian mission and ELT. He contends that the many ways that religious belief and spiritual conviction interact and influence language learning and teaching are ripe for investigation and have heretofore been ignored. Morgan (this volume) refers to this as a "blind spot" in ELT. Discuss how an inquiry into spirituality and lan-

guage teaching might be conducted and what questions might be explored. What research questions would you investigate within this area of inquiry? Describe the data you would collect and the methods of data collection and analysis.

7. Describe a scenario in a specific ELT context that involves issues of students' or teachers' religious beliefs in which, as Robison indicated, it would be just as unethical to disclose that which should remain concealed as to conceal that which should be disclosed (p. 262). What are the ethical questions that arise in making your decision?
8. Kubota, Bradley, and Mahboob suggest a pan-religions approach to teaching English so that teachers can acknowledge students' and teachers' spirituality yet not impose one particular religion over another. Discuss your reaction to this approach and if it addresses the dilemmas raised about spirituality and religion in ELT.
9. Brown provides six moral dilemmas and imperatives and lists three guidelines for dealing with controversial topics. Discuss each one noting which you find the most helpful and why.
10. Mahboob presents an advertisement for a native speaking Christian English teacher that he found online. List the assumptions that underpin this advertisement and discuss what you would do if you had received this in an email or found it online. Discuss TESOL's Position Statement Against Discrimination of Nonnative Speakers. What responsibility do we have in light of this? Retrieved September 22, 2008 from www.tesol.org/s_tesol/bin.asp?CID=32&DID=5889&DOC=FILE.PDF.
11. Mahboob concludes his chapter with four questions (p. 279). Choose one question and discuss it as a small group finding evidence from chapters to support your positions.
12. Curtis discusses several assumptions he finds within questions raised by the authors in this part of the book and believes much can be revealed "by questioning the questions." What questions have authors raised in this volume that you would like to question? What assumptions do you find and how would you rephrase the questions?
13. Curtis states that, "teachers need to develop their self-awareness through critical and conscious self-reflection to a point where their level of self-awareness at least matches the strength of their faith" (p. 281). How might teachers become more self-aware of ways in which they influence their students? If the word "faith" were replaced by another term or the phrase "belief in [fill in the blank]," which is more salient for you than "faith," what would that be?
14. Respond to Stevick's poem that ends this volume (p. 297) and to his probing question, "How is language teaching relevant to the vertical dimension of spiritual sensibilities that many stakeholders bring to the language classroom?" (p. 296).

30 Conclusion

Christian and Critical English Language Educators in Dialogue: Imagining Possibilities

Mary Shepard Wong and Suresh Canagarajah

We refrain from providing a summary conclusion as the threads of discussion in this book are too diverse and seem poised to take surprising new directions. As we mentioned in the Introduction, we would like to encourage our contributors and readers to develop these threads in fresh avenues in time to come. However, we would like to take a leap of imagination (or faith?) and consider the type of changes in scholarly activity, pedagogical practice, and professional relationships this dialogue should lead to.

We would like to see more balanced research on the role of missionaries in language teaching and education in the colonial period. The understandable backlash against the colonial experience has delayed a sound and objective appraisal of the role of missions in colonized communities. Whereas we have very sophisticated and subtle studies of English language and cultural contact during the colonial period by scholars in World Englishes (for language) and postcolonial and subaltern studies (for culture), religion has received short shrift.

We would like to see more classroom research on ways in which teachers and students negotiate their beliefs in teaching and learning. Empirical research hasn't kept pace with the amount of theoretical discussions on the role of spirituality in language learning. It would be even better if the research is collaborative or modeled after participant action research. This way, teachers can be sensitive to the belief system many students come from. It is difficult for an atheistic scholar to give voice to the concerns and aspirations of students and communities that are spiritual, or vice versa, however heroic the effort by the researchers concerned. We know the difficulties and complexities in representation, even in objective research, in the context of postmodernism and identity politics.

We would like to see more philosophical discourse on how to share our values and challenge each other in the age of pluralism. How can we learn from intercultural contact in precolonial times? Are there models that we can refurbish for our purposes? What are the models developing in scholarly communities outside TESOL as scholars attempt to speak to each other across national, cultural, and religious borderlines in present-day universities?

We would like to see space for values and beliefs in teacher development programs. While we are slowly breaking away from a positivistic focus on methods and skills, "soft" areas like morality, beliefs, and imagination haven't received adequate attention. We would like to see course work and research proposals on these topics further exploring the role of spirituality and faith in the professional identity formation of teachers.

We would like to see a TESOL convention, AERA or AAAL annual meeting treat moral and spiritual values as the theme for the whole conference. Even lesser efforts, such as organizing panels and accepting presentations on teachers' experiences dealing with morality and spirituality in their pedagogical practice, would be helpful. We would like to see a forum in which scholars come together to engage with one another face to face to further explore these issues in an open dialogue.

We would like to see Christian English teachers who have come to new and deeper understandings of issues of power and integrity actively communicate with their mission organizations and churches, helping them to: adopt a holistic view of witness (combine sensitivity to social and personal well-being of people along with a concern for their spiritual well-being); engage with the social and political realities of the countries they serve in along with a critical engagement of the political policies of their own countries; recruit only those teachers who have the appropriate training, experience, and academic qualifications for the assignments they are given; provide means for continued professionalization of their teachers; discontinue any policies or advertising that discriminate against NNEST, diminishes the value of professionalization, or is insensitive to the host people and nation; monitor teachers to ensure they are not abusing their power and using the classroom to proselytize; and take measures to be more transparent about their organization's identity and mission.

We would like to see this dialogue extend to other faith traditions to move beyond the focus on Christianity and to explore how other ideologies, faiths, and religions influence teaching and learning, and the identities of teachers and students. We would like teachers to develop more robust ways of understanding how their worldview and religious beliefs influence their pedagogy. We would like to see teachers challenge that which they find to be inappropriate in this intersection of the spiritual and professional and to strengthen that which they find brings wholeness to their teaching and their lives.

On the personal level, we would like to see more of our members in our professional community feeling comfortable about discussing and representing their values and belief systems in their teaching and scholarly life. The culture of political correctness that silences people's innermost values is not healthy for education or for our professional development. Our employers and institutions have to create the needed space to be more open about our diverse identities.

For all this to happen, much depends on the way scholars with values conduct themselves. We need to practice the models of discourse articulated in this book—i.e., exploratory dialogue, nonjudgmental discourse, transformative dialogue, or transactional dialogue—which would enable us to be honest about our values, understanding of the positions of others, engaged in civil conversation, and committed to help each other in our mutual spiritual and professional journeys.

Afterword

The Dilemma

Earl Stevick with Carolyn Kristjánsson

At the time of my birth, my father was supporting his small family as a Professór of Learned and/or Impracticable Studies (e.g., philosophy, psychology, New Testament Greek) at various small denominational colleges in the Midwest. With the coming of the Great Depression, however, the college where he was teaching collapsed and he had to support us, mostly from the meager pay that he received for pastoring a few small and impecunious churches in the vicinity.

As for me, I grew up as best I could. I was a preacher's kid and small for my age, with no known non-academic talents I can remember. I had no skill in music, athletics, or business. For example, when I tried to start a delivery route for *Liberty* magazine, the only people who subscribed were a few nice ladies from one of my father's churches. Any exceptions were dependent on my ability with language—an illustration being the straight "A"s that I got in four years of Latin. In the non-foreign language area of education, the curriculum at the time consisted largely of verbalizations about biology or history or English or whatever, with the exam questions often in an objective format. This enabled me to earn a very nice four-year scholarship at a prestigious university, where I majored in government. It also put me in over my head, I'm afraid. I did manage to stay on the dean's list, but only by taking a foreign language every semester. The unanimous word from my parents and my dean was that no one had ever escaped poverty by having majored in foreign languages.

As I look back to the pre-job miasma of my early years, it occurs to me that I was looking for some combination of five things in a profession:

- a degree of economic self-sufficiency;
- opportunities for witness;
- a measure of intrinsic enjoyment;
- a chance to be not permanently the lowest on the totem pole;
- a credible, interesting answer to the question of the ages: "What do you do for a living?"

Just before graduation, an apparently chance encounter in a stairwell got me signed up to teach English for a Christian organization in Warsaw. In this role I expected to be working alongside other Christians attending to the spiritual as well as the linguistic needs of ordinary people. The dropping of the Iron Curtain killed that plan, but as part of the preparation for it I'd had an intensive two-week exposure to teaching English as a foreign language. That was how the way opened for my career in TESOL. With the help of the GI Bill and a working wife, in 1949 I found myself in a secular MA TEFL program studying about how to meet linguistic needs, but with mention of the spiritual side either missing or even frowned on. Another apparently chance encounter, this one in an elevator, led me into training short-term missionaries in the learning and teaching of languages. That work put me in touch with Eugene A. Nida of the American Bible Society, who was later helpful in arranging a teaching fellowship at Cornell, where I got a doctoral degree in linguistics.

After graduate school, I took a full-time job in a Christian college. That was much closer to what I had been hoping for, but within a few years the language program collapsed, and I was back in the secular professional world, where any mention of Christian faith was—or at least seemed—awkward at best and possibly illegal or dangerous or both. My motivations and my methods were pretty much cut adrift from each other, and remained so until the 1970s. This disconnect was demonstrated in part by the first four books I wrote for teachers (Stevick, 1957, 1963, 1971, 1976). In these publications my thoughts were purely professional, with no conscious attention to matters of faith.

However, the reactions to *Memory, Meaning and Method* (1976) changed that. Three unconventional approaches that I described in the 1976 book came to be called "humanistic" (apparently in the sense that all of them tried to explore and exploit human potential more fully than previous approaches had done) and I came to be known as an exponent of "humanism" in language teaching. That didn't bother me. The words "humanism" and "humanistic" carried a wide range of meanings and emotional associations that were sometimes overlapping and sometimes contradictory. What did bother me was that in another sense, "humanistic" in philosophy is the position that there is no "god" of any consequence, and that we humans are entirely responsible for our own salvation, mainly through the use of reason. Anyone who thinks otherwise is regarded as a dangerous saboteur of the scientific quest for a better world. Some critics of the three unconventional approaches seemed to use words like "theological" as epithets to discredit those approaches. Religion was now portrayed not as a saboteur of right thinking, but as a feeble-minded cousin.

I began to include elements in my writing that reflected my Christian outlook, not the least of which was a chapter on Dostoyevsky's Grand Inquisitor (Stevick, 1980) and my reinterpretation of Curran's theory (Stevick, 1990). In *Humanism in Language Teaching* (1990), I tried to deal in a non-polemic tone with the concerns noted above, pointing out that the supposedly objective stance adopted by some critics both of "humanistic" methods and of religious faith, is itself dependent on unprovable articles of "faith" in a more generic sense. In subsequent published work I continued to include touches indicative of my faith-informed orientation (listed in the index under "outlook" in the 1996 and 1998 books). When the proofs of my last book went off to the editor, I began to write and assemble the *Afterwords*,[1] an open-ended collection of chapters for teachers interested in the faith aspect of language teaching from one point of view or another.

Dwight Eisenhower is reported to have said that "Everybody should have some strong faith, no matter in what." In this spirit, teachers who have mutually contradictory reactions toward a new approach or toward affectively oriented teacher education programs, or whatever, can simply say:

> Well, what's true for you is not the same as what's true for me. Our convictions about what is or is not 'true' are products of our genetic makeup plus our experiences, and are 'true' or 'not true' only in relation to those factors. So let's not defend or insist upon our individual convictions, and let's not try to change each other's views. Let us rather listen carefully and respectfully *to* each other's views, in the hope that from this dialogue will arise a new body of shared truths.

Briefly, "What you believe makes no difference, but believe something, and let's talk about it."

As a matter of fact, Eisenhower's aphorism should work fairly well on matters of low or medium urgency. But for most or all of us, there are certain matters that are of such high urgency that we feel we simply cannot afford to let the wrong side win. In regard to matters at this level, it commonly happens that people in each position would like to see people from the other position limited in their power and in their range of functioning. The urge to protect ourselves and society from the wrong kind of influences may express itself through limitations on access to the communications media, or through destroying credibility by means of slander and innuendo, and so on.

A language course (like any other sustained and organized activity) can have effects that are deeper than just the learning or teaching of a language. Here is where the teacher and his/her *ideas* are important. Consider this:

- *If* ideas don't affect what happens in life (though I think they do), then there's no reason to worry about truth.
- *And if* there is no truth, *or if* truth is purely relative, then there's no reason to try to maintain and propagate one position, or to reject another position and try to keep it from affecting our own lives and the lives of others.
- *But if* there is truth that's not just relative, then there's good reason to search it out, and to put it into practice.
- *And if* I think I've found some of that truth, I (or you, or anyone) may—and indeed should—try to make it widely available to others.
- *And if, moreover*, I think my knowledge of the truth is certain, then I could possibly conclude that there's no reason to be civil in my expression of it, or to be moderate in my efforts to limit the influence of error. I think it was Reinhold Niebuhr who spoke of "the natural cruelty of the self-righteous."
- *But even if* it's possible for humans to find pieces of non-relative truth, I recognize my own fallibility in identifying truth, and in preserving it, and in stating it. I do believe there is non-relative truth, but I'm wary of any person including myself who is absolutely sure that his or her understanding of absolute truth is the absolutely correct one. Recognition of my own fallibility should

> incline me (or you, or anyone) to be civil about presenting a bit of truth, and in pressuring others to adopt it. This is appropriate diffidence. But at the same time, if I (or you, or anyone) believes that there is truth, and that the search for truth is worthwhile, and that we have found a bit of it, then we need not and should not remain silent. This is a basis for honest confidence.

Of course, "having" a bit of truth or even "having" + "communicating" doesn't necessarily equal "imposing" or even "trying to impose." On the other hand, "wanting to communicate" + "political power" often has become "wanting to impose." Of this we must be wary. On my first trip overseas, I was an enthusiastic part of a movement to eradicate the bad, benighted, old method Grammar-Translation, and replace it with the shiny new one, Audiolingualism, and I had no patience with representatives of the old. At present, Audiolingualism has long been denounced as bad, benighted, and old. For some time, proclamations about the virtues of its successor, Communicative Language Teaching, have rippled from centers in the West to circles beyond. Now we are beginning to hear voices from these parts of the world introducing perspectives that should well give those in the West cause to reflect.

This brings us back to the basis for action—the basis on which we do certain things and react in certain ways under certain circumstances. Bases for present and future action can be seen to include a*warenesses* and *beliefs.*

- *Awarenesses* come from experiences. Experiences come from exploring. Exploring means choosing a (metaphorical) spot, then going to that spot, and finally noticing how things look from there. If a series of exploratory acts are planned and carried out by a particular mind, then the awarenesses that they lead to may become experience for that mind. Awareness does not consist of words even though people often try to use words to summarize their awarenesses. Awarenesses involve the whole person and are realized in relatively rich and complex networks in the brain.
- *Beliefs* consist of words. Some beliefs come from hearing other people's words about their explorations, and about the conclusions they have drawn from them. But beliefs may also come from hearing not other people's explorations, but their beliefs, and then trying to fit the beliefs together so as to produce the basis for one's own future actions. A single set of beliefs may be held by many people at the same time. In fact, such sharing of a large set of beliefs (about what has happened in the past, what can happen in the future, what should happen among people, how to find out the contents of a cylinder, the best thing to do when coming down with a cold, and so forth) is a widely accepted purpose of formal education. But in this kind of education, most of the responsibility is carried by the "teacher." As a result, the "learners" never have occasion to form the most important awareness, which is the awareness of awareness.

An awareness is something that seldom gets challenged. It seems to me there are at least two reasons why this is so. First, an awareness arises directly out of one's own experience. Second, it doesn't consist of words. A belief, by contrast, is easier to challenge because it is—or can more readily be—expressed in words, and ideas that have been expressed in language can very quickly compete with each other and sometimes annihilate each other. Whenever Jill expresses a belief that Jack does not share, Jack becomes tense or wanders out of the yard and into the street—the classic fight or flight response to a threat on any level.

Why then bother with beliefs? Again, it seems to me there are two reasons. First, beliefs require less work, less self-discipline than the corresponding awarenesses would. We don't have to actually walk in a belief-based path in order to consider it our own; we need only buy (into) it, or accept it when offered, or even just draw a map of it. There is a trade-off though. Not being based on experience, a belief-based map is unreliable and may fail to provide needed information in any but the easiest of terrain. Second, beliefs can cover questions of any size, including questions that are so broad that to assemble all the experiences needed for the awareness that these questions call for would go beyond human capacity and human life span. Beliefs, then, are less costly than awarenesses, they may be mutually contradictory, they are more flexible, and they come in all sizes. Holders of beliefs tend to try to transmit their beliefs to other people. They do so for one or more reasons such as:

- They think their belief will be helpful or salutary to others.
- The assent of other people is reassuring, especially to anyone who has any half-suppressed doubts about the particular belief.
- Agreement on beliefs will make relationships and cooperation easier in the future.
- Some beliefs are such that they lead to unequal power relationships between certain groups of believers.

As I understand it, our actions are shaped by our values and our values are derived, more than we usually think, from our awarenesses, and less than we usually think from our beliefs. If our teaching is an enactment of the values we hold dear then our students and others around us will meet those values as parts of their experiences, and eventually these will become parts of their awareness. If we fail to do that, if we are overly or prematurely concerned about bringing others to an acceptance of our doctrines, whether these be about language teaching, life purposes, or anything else, we are working in the area of "beliefs," something reminiscent of passing paper money instead of gold, silver, or copper coinage.

At a time of reignited spiritual interests and global religious vitality, it is highly likely that we will encounter both colleagues and students whose spiritual awarenesses and beliefs differ from our own. Years ago I suggested that relevance in language learning connects something on the horizontal dimension of external experience with something on the vertical dimension of appreciation of self (Stevick, 1980). How is language teaching relevant to the vertical dimension of spiritual sensibilities that many stakeholders bring to the language classroom? Can we as educators afford to be relevant in this way? Or should we rather ask:

can we afford *not* to be relevant? How relevant can we afford to be? Does relevance for one stakeholder mean imposition or irrelevance for another when it comes to depth of a spiritual nature? Questions such as these inhabit the dialogue of this volume. It is a volume that provides a unique forum for the voices of language educators from a range of backgrounds and religious and spiritual positions. It is timely and valuable!

As we consider these contributions I urge each of us to remember that confidence without diffidence can result in chaos or autocracy. On the other hand, diffidence without confidence can result in stagnation, or worse, produce subservience to whoever lacks appropriate diffidence. Honest confidence and appropriate diffidence—the dilemma is in how to balance them. But balance them we must!

The impatient gate, that swings both in and out,
Whose work is lost when no one passes through;
The faithful fence, that marks off false from true—
No time for hanging back, no room for doubt—
Exist, not in the world, but in the mind.
Yet God forgive if what is there for me
I either hide, or try to press on thee,
To shout thee deaf, or leave thee lost and blind.
This dreadful choice sets sister against brother,
Either to injure, or to fail each other.

Note

1. Available at: www.celea.net.

References

Stevick, E. W. (1957). *Helping people learn English.* Nashville, TN: Abingdon Press.
Stevick, E. W. (1963). *A workbook in language teaching.* Nashville, TN: Abingdon Press.
Stevick, E. W. (1971). *Adapting and writing language lessons,* Washington, DC: Superintendent of Documents, cit. in MMM p. xi (preface).
Stevick, E. (1976). *Memory, meaning and method.* Rowley, MA: Newbury House.
Stevick, E. (1980). *Teaching languages: A way and ways.* Rowley, MA: Newbury House.
Stevick, E. W. (1990). *Humanism in language teaching.* Oxford, UK: Oxford University Press.
Stevick, E. W. (1996). *Memory, meaning and method: A view of language teaching.* Boston: Heinle & Heinle.
Stevick, E. W. (1998). *Working with teaching methods: What's at stake?* Boston: Heinle & Heinle.

Subject index

Author Index